The Approach of Armageddon?

An Islamic Perspective

A chronicle of scientific breakthroughs and world events that occur during the last days, as foretold by Prophet Muhammad ﷺ

Shaykh Muhammad Hisham Kabbani

Islamic Supreme Council of America

Published and Distributed by:

Islamic Supreme Council of America (ISCA)
1400 Sixteenth Street NW, #B112
Washington, DC 20036 USA
Tel: (202) 939-3400
Fax: (202) 939-3410
Email: staff@islamicsupremecouncil.org
Web: www.islamicsupremecouncil.org

Printed in Canada

Publishing Office:

17195 Silver Parkway, #201
Fenton, MI 48430 USA
Tel: (888) 278-6624
Fax: (810) 815-0518

Second Edition, September 2003
Library of Congress Control Number: 2003107762
ISBN: 1-930409-20-6

On the Internet, please visit www.islamicsupremecouncil.org
for more titles in Islamic spirituality and traditional scholarship.

بِسْمِ اللهِ الرَّحْمٰنِ الرَّحِيمِ

﴿إِنَّهُ لَقَوْلُ رَسُولٍ كَرِيمٍ ذِي قُوَّةٍ عِندَ ذِي الْعَرْشِ مَكِينٍ مُطَاعٍ ثَمَّ أَمِينٍ﴾

In the name of God, the Compassionate, the Merciful

Verily this is the word of a most honourable Messenger,
Endued with Power,
with rank before the Lord of the Throne,
With authority there, (and) faithful to his trust.

(Holy Qur'ān, at-Takwīr 81:19-21)

DEDICATION

I humbly dedicate this book to my beloved master Shaykh Muhammad Nāẓim 'Adil al-Qubrusī al-Haqqānī an-Naqshbandī, world leader of the Naqshbandī-Haqqānī Sufi Order and to all those who love the Prophet and his family.

Shaykh Muhammad Hisham Kabbani
12 Rabi' al-Awwal 1424
11 May 2003

CONTENTS

PUBLISHER'S NOTES

References from the Qur'ān and the hadith (Prophetic traditions) are preceded as a rule by the original Arabic, followed by the English translation, italicized and offset. References from the Qur'ān are highlighted by a calligraphic font and centered thus:

a mercy for all creation. (al-Anbiyā' 21:107)

with the *Sūrah*/Chapter name, number and verse parenthetically-cited. References from hadith are attributed to their transmitter in footnotes: i.e. *Bukhārī, Muslim, Āhmad,* etc. Quotes from other sources are offset and referenced as well.

NOTE: We have taken great pains to insure correctness of Qur'ān and hadith source texts, but success is only by Allāh ﷻ. If the reader detects any errors in the Arabic sources we request you notify us as soon as possible by mail, email or phone at our Publishing Office, so the correction can be made in successive versions of the book.

Dates of events are characterized as "AH/– CE," which infers "after Hijra (migration)" on which the Islamic calendar is based, and "Christian Era," respectively.

Muslims traditionally offer praise upon speaking, hearing or reading God's proper name in Arabic *Allāh,* and the numerous other Islamic Names of God. Muslims also offer salutation and/or invoke blessings upon speaking, hearing or reading the names of Prophet Muhammad, other prophets, Prophet Muhammad's family, his companions, and the saints. We have applied the following international standards, using Arabic calligraphy and lettering:

ﷻ   *subhānahu wa ta'alā* (Glory be He, the Most High) following the name Allāh.

ﷺ   *sall-Allāhu 'alayhi wa sallam* (God's blessings and greetings of peace be upon him) following the names of the Prophet.

عليه السلام   *'alayhi as-salām* (peace be upon him) following the names of other prophets, angels, and Khidr.

عليها السلام   *'alayhā as-salām* (peace be upon her) following the name of Mary, Mother of Jesus.

﷽ *radī-Allāhu 'anh* (may God be pleased with him/her) following the name of a male or female companion of the Prophet.

ق *qaddas-Allāhu sirrah* (may God sanctify his secret) following the name of a saint.

FOREWORD

THE STATION OF THE ELECT OF GOD

A l-Hasan ibn al-Mansūr ق said:

The identity of God's elect servant becomes extinguished in the Divine Presence. No one bears such a person nor does that person put up with [standards of behavior] others [tolerate]. Still, the elect one among God's servants is like unto the earth; it accepts every type of refuse and yet nothing issues from it but sweetness. Both the good and the sinner walk over and step on the servant of God. And the vilest of creation are they who pretend to be the elect of God when in fact they are stingy.

Ash-Shiblī ق said, "the elect servant of God is cut off from creatures and connected to the Truth."[1] Ibn 'Ajība ق relates that it has been said, "Whoever owns states whose character indicates proximity to God is insupportable. The mountains carry him not." Such is the aspect of whoever realizes the station of extinction. Al-Hasan ibn al-Mansūr wrote of the one who became extinguished (fānī) in the love of Allāh 🕮, maqām al-fanā[2]:

People find it difficult to tolerate the one who has lost any sense of self and who stands in awe stunned before God's Absolute Existence. Whoever reaches that station (maqām) and would in any way divulge its secret, will act differently from the commonality of humankind.

For that reason, the Friends of God (awlīyāullāh) who reach that maqām hide themselves. The story in the Holy Qur'ān about al-Khidr 🕮 illustrates this truth. He did things people do not usually do; things that even the Prophet Moses 🕮 found difficult to accept. Allāh instructs us by means of that example, to learn, not because Moses 🕮 is lower in station, for after all he is one of the five greatest Prophets. No one attains the level of the prophets and the Prophet's Companions (Sahāba). By informing us of Moses' 🕮 relation to Khidr 🕮, the Qur'ān wishes to give us the example of one brought near to Allāh, one of His saints. Such individuals are just as the hadith qudsī describes

---

[1] From *The Commentary of the Hikam of Ibn Ata'illah as-Sakandarī* by Ibn 'Ajība. (*'Ikāz al-himmam fī sharhi al-hikam li Āhmad bin Muhammad bin 'Ajībā al-Hasanī*, p. 4.)
[2] *maqām*—what the servant realizes in his station in terms of *adab*, spiritually-perfected manners, and what is communicated... [al-Qushayrī]

them, "My saints are under My domes; no one knows them except Me." Allāh Himself hides saints, since they are exceedingly precious to Him. Another hadith illustrates this, "Whoever comes against a Friend of Mine I declare war on him."[3]

In the midst of people, God's Friends say and do things that others do not accept. That is the meaning of Ibn 'Ajība's words, "No one bears such a person." For the same reason, when the Prophet Sayyidinā Muhammad ﷺ came forth, his people rejected him. All prophets were rejected by their people. Since that is the case of the prophets what then can be expected for *awlīyā*? It is natural that they will be rejected completely by common people, because *awlīyā'* are ordinary human beings upon whom Allāh ﷻ has bestowed heavenly power.

Today's *'ulama* (religious scholars) say there no longer remain any *awlīyā'*. This is not true. Rather, these people have become blind so that they cannot see them. Why have they become blind? Because *awlīyā'* have hidden themselves, especially in the present era. They know that no one will accept them and the power granted them by the Lord. If they display anything of what they have been empowered with, people come against them.

Thus the highest level of *walī*, is one who acts like normal people and does not appear different from them in aspect or behavior. Thus one of God's friends (*awlīyā'*) behaves like others to the extent that people say about him, "He is like us. What is different?" What they don't know about him is that he has been tested by *awlīyā'*, by the Prophet ﷺ, and finally by Allāh the Exalted. He passed his tests and was given his spiritual trusts (*amānāt*).

Ibn 'Ajība ق continues: *Wa lā yaqbalu āhad*—"nor does that person put up with [standards of behavior] others tolerate." This means he watches as they go astray, calling them to return to the Path, but they do not listen. After a while, the saint leaves them. Bayāzīd al-Bistāmī ق, one of the greatest saints of Islam, was constantly worshipping Allāh ﷻ, ascending in closeness, until he could even hear the angels. He arrived at a station where he sought the Divine Presence saying, "O my Lord! Open for me the gate to Your Divine Presence." He heard a voice in his heart saying, "O Bayāzīd! If you want to enter My Presence, you must become people's refuse pile." Hence, al-Hasan ibn Mansūr ق says here, "The elect servants of God are like the earth. They accept every type of refuse to be cast upon them and yet nothing issues from them but sweetness. Both the good and the sinner walk upon it."

The "earth" is characterized by strength. Whatever Allāh Wills the earth accepts. It has no will of its own. In this respect *awlīyāullāh* resemble the earth: "every vile and ugly thing is cast upon it," and it accepts. The Arabic word

---

[3] Even the rigorous Ibn Taymīyya verified this hadith.

used, *qabīh* does not means just "vile" or "ugly" but rather, "rank" and "putrid" suggesting the worst refuse thrown on the earth. Yet, after he accepts it, the verse continues, "nothing comes from him except goodness."

The Friend of God (*walī*) does not treat you the same way you treat him. Rather he returns good for evil. It is related that Bayāzīd ق tested the *'ulama*, with extreme ecstatic utterances, until at last they elected to stone him. This was due to their lack of understanding the station from which he was speaking. Bayāzīd ق was not someone inclined to commit heresy, for even Ibn Taymīyyā praises his piety. But his intention was to test them, for they in fact had tried to test him.

Finally, when they had stoned Bayāzīd ق and left him for dead, his inert body was thrown in a garbage dump. Actually, he was still alive, but very weak. Eventually after lying injured in the dump seven days, he revived slightly and was able to move. He began searching about for something to eat. He found a bone, with a bit of fetid meat on it, probably thrown out one week before. When he took it a dog appeared growling and spoke to him, saying, "This is my territory, and this my food. You cannot touch it." Thus did Allāh reveal to him the understanding of animal speech.

Bayāzīd ق relates, "I was beseeching God and saying, 'Ya Allāh! O my Lord! What I have sought I sought only for the sake of Thy love. I willed for them to kill me but Thou quickened me and caused me to live. And once I regained my life I wished them to put me to death yet again; and that then Thou wouldst quicken me once more, and they would stone me yet another time. And again wouldst Thou revive me, over and over, because each time they stone me I would pray for them that Thou, My God, wouldst forgive them of their sins. So whatever Thou hast granted me of rewards for prayer and spiritual struggle, do Thou, O Lord, cause them to share in that same reward with me." This shows how much the Saint (*walī*) will love God's servants when he enters into His love.

Today many Muslim scholars say, "There are no more *awlīyā'*." In reality, they exist, but since only a few will understand their states, they are hidden. Another saying of today's scholars is, "Every *mu'min* (believer) is a *walī*." If that is the case, Allāh would not differentiate between *mu'min* and *walī*.

In any case, who can truly say he is a believer (*mu'min*)? Do these scholars not recall Allāh's saying:

قَالَتِ الأَعْرَابُ آمَنَّا قُل لَّمْ تُؤْمِنُوا وَلَكِن قُولُوا أَسْلَمْنَا وَلَمَّا يَدْخُلِ الإِيمَانُ فِي قُلُوبِكُمْ وَإِن تُطِيعُوا اللَّهَ وَرَسُولَهُ لاَ يَلِتْكُم مِّنْ أَعْمَالِكُمْ شَيْئًا إِنَّ اللَّهَ غَفُورٌ رَّحِيمٌ

The Arabs say, "We believe." Say, "Ye have no Faith; but ye (only) say, 'We
have submitted our wills to Allah,' For not yet has Faith entered your
hearts. But if ye obey Allah and His Messenger, He will not belittle aught
of your deeds: for Allah is Oft-Forgiving, Most Merciful." (al-Hujurāt 49:14)

Who can grant one the certification that *īmān* (faith) has entered his
heart? Such certification is not given from one Muslim to another; it is given
from Allāh 🕌 to the believer.

Wherever they find themselves, *awlīyā'* build places of prayer, *zawīyas*,
khāniqas or *ribāts* (gathering places for spiritual training and practice). Once
raised, people come from far and wide to visit them and they receive all in their
meetings. They do not say, "We will not meet this one or that one." Today
people say, "These individuals are enemies. We cannot meet them. These
people cursed us, we cannot meet them." But the Prophet 🕌 came to all
humankind—enemy or not.

وَمَا أَرْسَلْنَاكَ إِلَّا كَافَّةً لِّلنَّاسِ بَشِيرًا وَنَذِيرًا وَلَكِنَّ أَكْثَرَ النَّاسِ لَا يَعْلَمُونَ

We have not sent thee but as a universal (Messenger) to men, giving them
glad tidings, and warning them (against sin), but most men understand
not. (Sabā' 34:28)

If an enemy came to him 🕌 he was obliged to open his door. As *awlīyāullāh*,
are inheritors of the Prophet's states and character, their doors must always be
open. Else what is the benefit of *wilāyat* (sainthood)? Allāh bestowed *wilāyat*
upon them in order to hear people out, to deal with them and to bring them to
Islam. When you close your door and say, "I don't work with those people,"
you have isolated yourself and become a barrier to the Way. You have to work
with people of any faith, any religion, and any group to convey them to *Haqq*
(Truth). That is why Grand Shaykh ق met with everyone, and we seek to follow
in his footsteps. You cannot close the door saying, "You are not a member."
Now everything is based on membership—for money. They tell you, "Pay fifty
dollars and become a member." Nothing is done purely for Allāh's sake any
longer.

"Both good people and the ugliest of sinners walk over and step on the
elect servant of God." That means he will carry burdens—he is everyone's
garbage disposal. And in return, he offers prayers for people in order to turn
their hearts round to God. The elect servants of God try to do their best for
people although people do their worst for them. That is why the good and the
bad step on them and walk all over them.

Ibn 'Ajība ق said, "And the vilest ones are they who pretend that they are
an elect servant of God while failing in generosity." An elect servant of God
does not fail in generosity. He is not stingy. A servant of God is always

generous with the gifts his Lord has granted him or her, by not withholding it. Allāh ﷻ is the Most Generous of the generous (*Akram al-akramīn*).

Similarly, the Prophet ﷺ is described by Allāh ﷻ as:

بِالْمُؤْمِنِينَ رَؤُوفٌ رَّحِيمٌ

to the Believers is he most kind and merciful. (at-Tawba 9:128)

and

وَمَا أَرْسَلْنَاكَ إِلَّا رَحْمَةً لِّلْعَالَمِينَ

We sent thee not, but as a Mercy for all creatures. (al-Anbīyā 21: 107)

This verse means that Prophet Muhammad ﷺ will ask Allāh's forgiveness on everyone's behalf. In short, a servant of God cannot be stingy. The worst person is someone who pretends to be an elect servant of God and is stingy. Not stingy with his money, but stingy in carrying the difficulties of people and holding back from himself, whatever Allāh gave him of *hasanāt* (rewards), as gifts to them.

Worse yet, are those of God's servants on whom he has bestowed the gifts of knowledge of the religion and its inner meanings and who withhold this knowledge from those who are capable of receiving it. These are the *'ulamā'* that tell lies about Allāh and pronounce permitted what He has prohibited. Of these, we have many examples today. They say for example, that Allāh wills people to lay down their lives in support of the corrupt or, serve false causes or to propagate wrong doctrine. These servants are the spiritually stingy. Such persons never succeed and on the Day of Judgment they will be reckoned among the losers. They are like a tree covered with beautiful blossoms in spring, but which is infertile and fails to yield fruits in autumn.

To be perfectly clear, the true authorized servant of Allāh carries the sins of those who are under his authority by asking Allāh's forgiveness for those under him and by requesting Allāh bestow whatever he received of rewards on them from whatever levels Allāh has raised him to. That is for whoever comes to visit him.

The Prophet ﷺ said:

Allāh has angels roaming the roads seeking the people of His Remembrance (*dhikr*), and when they find a group of people reciting *dhikr*, they call each other and encompass them in layers until the first heaven …. And someone not from them, but who came only for a certain issue, sits with them. Allāh said, "no regrets will come to whoever sits with them—*lā yashqā jalīsahum*."[4]

That means that anyone coming for only a few minutes, even if he is not one of them, will be rewarded for being with them. Anyone who comes to the *walī*, the *walī* will give to him from what Allāh ﷻ and the Prophet ﷺ gave him. That is what it means—the opposite of stingy. It means giving what Allāh adorned him with in the way of mercy. It means taking on and carrying the difficulties and problems of people who came to see him.

Now Ash-Shiblī ق goes on to say, "The elect servant of God is disconnected from creation and connected to the Truth, *al-Haqq*." He continues, *"Munqaṭi' 'an il-khalq,"* meaning "his heart is cut off from people and connected with the Divine." At the most literal level, it means he severs himself from creatures and connects himself spiritually with Allāh's Love. But at a deeper level it also means that he rejects all that is false and loves all that is true. The servant of God does not involve himself in issues that do not concern him or in what people do and say contrary to the Truth. He is connected with Truth. He likes everything about Truth and dislikes whatever is false. When he disconnects himself from falsehood, he veils it, as if he is not seeing it, even while being perfectly aware of it. At the same time, he does not backbite and draw attention to the falsehood and wrongdoing perpetrated by people.

He connects himself to Truth and disconnects himself from falsehood. He does this in order to balance their falsehood by bringing Truth to the other side of the balance. Otherwise, if falsehood goes unchecked, it will cause disaster both in the Ummah and in the world. Thus the *awliyā'* are like mountains in the Ummah; they balance everything, as the mountains keep the earth in balance:

$$\text{وَالْجِبَالَ أَوْتَادًا}$$

And the mountains as pegs? (an-Nabā' 78:7)

If falsehood were to increase unchecked there would no longer be any balance in the world and it would turn upside down. Thus, the *awliyā'* bring everything into balance. For this reason Allāh said:

$$\text{أَلَّا تَطْغَوْا فِي الْمِيزَانِ وَأَقِيمُوا الْوَزْنَ بِالْقِسْطِ وَلَا تُخْسِرُوا الْمِيزَانَ}$$

In order that ye may not transgress (due) balance. So establish weight with justice and fall not short in the balance. (ar-Rahmān 55:8-9)

These verses mean, "Make everything balanced in the scale." If the *awliyā'* do not balance falsehood by means of worship, if they do not balance what the

---

[4] *Sahīh Bukhārī* and *Sahīh Muslim*.

workers of iniquity perpetrate in the way of falsehood with truth, this *dunyā* (world, material life) would have disappeared long ago.

Among the Signs of Last Days, 'Abd Allāh bin 'Amr Ibn al-'Ās ❧ related that the Prophet ﷺ said:

> Allāh will not take knowledge from the hearts of the scholars but he takes the scholars (they die). There will be no more scholars to take their place so people will take extremely ignorant leaders. They will be asked questions and will give *fatwas* (legal rulings) without knowledge. They are misguided and they misguide others.[5]

The pious servants (*sālihīn*) have been balancing everything from the time of the Prophet ﷺ. Indeed, throughout all ages, they are balancing falsehood with truth. But now that balance they have brought to the world is reaching its end so that there is no longer a balance. Indeed, the lack of a sense of proportion has become the dominant characteristic of our epoch. That is why today one sees so much killing. And while everyone speaks of peace, peace, peace, in fact everywhere people are dying. May Allāh keep us under the wings of His pious servants whom He has endowed with knowledge and entrusted with the guidance of the community of Muhammad and balance our deeds to be in a good way.

The Prophet of Allāh ﷺ said:

> After me come caliphs, and after the caliphs come princes, and after princes there will be kings and after the kings, there will be tyrants. And after the tyrants a man from My House will fill the earth with justice, and after him is al-Qahtānī. By the One who sent me with the Truth! Not a word less.[6]

We see that the caliphs are spoken of in this hadith are "the Rightly-Guided Ones": Abū Bakr, 'Umar, 'Uthman and 'Alī, may Allāh the Exalted be pleased with them all. The princes are the Umayyad Caliphs of Damascus and the Abbasid Caliphs of Baghdad. As for the kings, they are the Ottoman Sultans of Istanbul. Following the kings, according to the hadith, are tyrants, and that is what is commonly seen today.

Awliyā are not looking to the future, mentioned in such hadith, as far away. Rather they are communicating to those who would learn from them, that these hadith are signposts for mankind on the road to the Hereafter. If we act

---

[5] *Bukhārī* 1:33, "Kitāb al-'ilm." *Muslim* #157, "Kitāb al-'ilm":
Inna Allāha la yaqbidu al-'ilma intiz'ān yantazi'uhu min al-'ibad wa lākin yaqbid ul-'ilma bi qabd il-'ulama hatta idha lam yabqa 'aliman itakhada an-nāsu ru'usan juhālan fa su'ilu fa aftaw bi ghayri 'ilmin fa dallu wa adallu.
[6] Na'īm bin Hammād in "Fitan" from 'Abd ar-Rahmān bin Qays bin Jābir al-Sadafī. *Kanz al-'ummāl*, hadith #38704.

as the blind, ignoring what is apparent in the signs of the times, then of what benefit is such luminous guidance? The duty of the *awliyā*, as inheritors of the Prophets, is to remind, give glad tidings (*bushrā*) and to warn.

Let us heed then, the clear guidance that the Prophet ﷺ has brought us, and prepare for times of tribulation. Following these trials, we hope to be present in a Golden Age of Prophetic civilization, the like of which the world has never witnessed.

Shaykh Muhammad Nāzim 'Adil al-Qubrusī al-Haqqānī an-Naqshbandī
12 Rabi' al-Awwal 1424
11 May 2003
Lefke, Cyprus

ABOUT THE AUTHOR

Shaykh Muhammad Hisham Kabbani is a world-renowned author and religious scholar. He has devoted his life to the promotion of traditional Islamic principles, such as peace, tolerance, and opposing extremism in all its forms. The shaykh is a member of a respected family of traditional Islamic scholars, which includes the former head of the Association of Muslim Scholars of Lebanon and the present Grand Mufti[7] of Lebanon.

In the U.S., Shaykh Kabbani serves as Chairman, Islamic Supreme Council of America; Founder, Naqshbandi Sufi Order of America; Chairman, As-Sunnah Foundation of America; Chairman, Kamilat Muslim Women's Organization; and, Founder and President, *The Muslim Magazine.*

Shaykh Kabbani is highly trained, both as a Western scientist and as a classical Islamic scholar. He received a bachelor's degree in chemistry and studied medicine. In addition, he also holds a degree in Islamic Divine Law, and under the tutelage of Shaykh 'Abd Allāh Dāghestānī license to teach, guide and counsel religious students in Islamic spirituality from Shaykh Muhammad Nāzim 'Adil al-Qubrusī al-Haqqānī an-Naqshbandī, the world leader of the Naqshbandi-Haqqani Sufi Order.

His books include: *Remembrance of God Liturgy of the Sufi Naqshbandi Masters* (1994); *The Naqshbandi Sufi Way* (1995); *Angels Unveiled* (1996); *Encyclopedia of Islamic Doctrine* (7 vols. 1998); *Encyclopedia of Muhammad's Women Companions and the Traditions They Related* (1998, with Dr. Laleh Bakhtiar); and *Classical Islam and the Naqshbandi Sufi Order* (projected November 2003).

In his long-term efforts to promote better understanding of classical Islam, Shaykh Kabbani has hosted two international conferences in the United States, both of which drew scholars from throughout the Muslim world. As a resounding voice for traditional Islam, his counsel is sought by journalists, academics and government leaders.

---

[7] The highest Islamic religious authority in the country.

INTRODUCTION

THE PROPHET'S ﷺ MIRACULOUS KNOWLEDGE

From the Ocean of *Shari'ah*

Praise be to Allāh ﷻ Who made the pure *Shari'ah* an ocean from which all oceans of knowledge and rivers of divine lights gush forth. Praise be to Him Who let these rivers of gnosis flow to His creation, quenching the dry barren ground of the hearts both near and far. Praise be to Him who chose Prophets from the best of His creation: from Adam ﷺ to Noah ﷺ, Abraham ﷺ, Moses ﷺ, Jesus ﷺ and ending with Muhammad ﷺ who disclosed the divine message with all its particulars, in exquisite detail, from beginning to end.

Praise be to Allāh ﷻ Who made His Prophets the hope of humanity. They are the sources of light and the energy of creation. They are the beacons for every seeker, the oases in every desert, the waves in every ocean, the springs of every river and the crystals in every diamond. They are the dew from heaven on every leaf, they are the stars, the suns and the moons in every firmament. They are the messengers known by all traditions.

It is very well-established that God created Prophets to carry out His orders and transmit His divine message to human beings, pertaining both to this life and life in the world to come. They exemplify the qualities of perfection, obedience and dedication. They carry boundless miraculous powers through which they can reach anyone by means of the knowledge that they have spread. They use their divine knowledge to help and to heal; to serve and to console; to love and to be loved; and to prepare humanity for the day that they will meet their Lord with what they have done in this life.

From an Islamic perspective the knowledge, brought by the Seal of the Messengers Prophet Muhammad ﷺ, illumines the physical and spiritual life for every time and place for us. Just as water takes its form from the cup into which one pours it, so do these divine lights coursing through our souls and bodies take the crystalline form of our heart's discernment of what is required of us in this life. For these requirements begin with the day we are born to the day that we die, through our time in the grave and up to the Day of Judgment, where people will be gathered in their locations in Paradise. The knowledge that the Prophet Muhammad ﷺ brought is like a rainbow adorning the sky. From it our minds and hearts may take whatever they need to understand all the events of our inner lives. Thus, through this knowledge we have the capacity to comprehend our past, present and future as well as the past, present and future of the world in which we live.

The Divinely-revealed Law (*Shari'ah*) brought by the Prophet Muhammad ﷺ encompasses all levels of religion, from the five pillars of Islam to the six pillars of faith (*iman*) to the state of moral excellence (*ihsan*). Thus, the *Shari'ah* spreads out like a huge expansive tree, whose broad leafy branches represent the practical applications (*furu'*) of the divine principles (*usul*) represented by the roots. From this divine guidance we may learn to accommodate not only our behavior to the *Shari'ah*, but also our beliefs to the Last Day and its corresponding Signs. For our beliefs generate actions pleasing to God.

As Allāh said in the Holy Qur'ān:

وَالشَّمْسِ وَضُحَاهَا(1) وَالْقَمَرِ إِذَا تَلاهَا(2) وَالنَّهَارِ إِذَا جَلاهَا(3) وَاللَّيْلِ إِذَا يَغْشَاهَا(4) وَالسَّمَاءِ وَمَا بَنَاهَا(5) وَالْأَرْضِ وَمَا طَحَاهَا(6) وَنَفْسٍ وَمَا سَوَّاهَا(7) فَأَلْهَمَهَا فُجُورَهَا وَتَقْوَاهَا(8) قَدْ أَفْلَحَ مَن زَكَّاهَا(9) وَقَدْ خَابَ مَن دَسَّاهَا(10) كَذَّبَتْ ثَمُودُ بِطَغْوَاهَا(11)

By the sun and His glorious splendor, and by the moon as it follows it, by the day as it shows up the sun's glory, by the night as it conceals it; by the firmament and its wonderful structure. By the earth and its wide expanse. By the soul and the proportion and order given to it and its inspiration as to its wrong and its right. Truly he succeeds who purifies it. And he fails that corrupts it. (ash-Shams 91:1-10)

إِذَا السَّمَاءُ انفَطَرَتْ(1) وَإِذَا الْكَوَاكِبُ انتَثَرَتْ(2) وَإِذَا الْبِحَارُ فُجِّرَتْ(3) وَإِذَا الْقُبُورُ بُعْثِرَتْ(4) عَلِمَتْ نَفْسٌ مَّا قَدَّمَتْ وَأَخَّرَتْ(5)

When the sky is cleft asunder and when the stars are scattered and when the oceans are suffered to burst forth. And when the Graves are turned upside down; (Then) shall each soul know what it hath sent forward and (what it hath) kept back. (al-Infitār, 82:1-5)

In these verses, Allāh ﷻ bestowed on every soul He created guidance to discern right from wrong. He inspires each one to know what benefits and harms it, what ails it and cures it. He causes each soul to anticipate its lying down in death and its rising again in eternal life. It becomes incumbent, therefore, on all Muslims and non-Muslims alike to walk the path to Allāh and furnish themselves with every provision ordained by Him, with worship, with study and learning so that they may recognize the wonders He has worked for the children of Adam as recounted in the Holy Qur'ān and explained by the Prophet ﷺ in hadith. Through revelation, the Prophet ﷺ was able to give indications of the future through scientific developments as well as to describe the conditions that would prevail in the world towards the Last Day as signs of its imminence. By means of these miraculous revelations, not only do people in our time have the opportunity to take precautions for the future; they are also granted to see an aspect of the greatness of the Holy Qur'ān and hadith.

In the first volume of this book, the reader will find out what Islam has told us about this last chapter in the world's history according to the Book of Allāh and the pure Sunnah of His Prophet Muhammad ﷺ.

Allāh ﷻ said in the Holy Qur'an:

$$
\text{وَيَعْلَمُ مَا فِي الْبَرِّ وَالْبَحْرِ وَمَا تَسْقُطُ مِن وَرَقَةٍ إِلَّا يَعْلَمُهَا وَلَا حَبَّةٍ فِي ظُلُمَاتِ الْأَرْضِ وَلَا رَطْبٍ وَلَا يَابِسٍ إِلَّا فِي كِتَابٍ مُّبِينٍ}
$$

He knoweth whatever there is on the earth and in the sea. Not a leaf doth fall but with His knowledge: there is not a grain in the darkness (or depths) of the earth, nor anything fresh or dry (green or withered), but is (inscribed) in a record clear (to those who can read). (al-An'am 6:59)

The prophecies contained in these verses and traditions belong to a category of knowledge unknowable to humankind except through revelation. For that reason, only the Prophet Muhammad ﷺ was able to bestow this order of knowledge. In this way, he functioned as an intermediary between heaven and earth bringing the Qur'ān. In a miraculous fashion he still functions in this role for us today by continuing to mediate between God and human beings and bringing us knowledge of the events and signs of the Last Days through hadith.

These prophecies were revealed to him that he might deliver the message with which Allāh entrusted him, the Last Testament and final installment of the Divine Message to the children of Adam. That is why the Prophet, our Master Muhammad ﷺ is far more knowledgable than any other prophet or human being and has been adorned with numerous beautiful attributes, such as, "The Messenger from the Divine Presence," "Noble in God's sight," "Empowered by God with a power rendering him capable of pure obedience," "Well-regarded and firmly established in the Divine Presence," "The one who is obeyed in the earthly world" and "The Trustworthy one in receiving, observing and delivering the revelation."

In this book we will explore and examine some of the Divine revelations that were sent down to the Prophet Muhammad ﷺ in the light of the discoveries of modern science, current events and events yet to come. By examining these precious sources, it hopefully will be made plain that the miraculous knowledge the Prophet ﷺ brought could have only come through Divine revelation. May the lucid clarity of Muhammad's ﷺ prescience strengthen our faith in him, his message and in the nearness of that final hour which he told us is upon us even now.

It is hoped that while perusing the following chapters, readers will behold the fulfillment of the Prophet Muhammad's ﷺ words as they unfold in today's events. At the same time, they are urged to call to mind that this course of history was charted in detail fourteen hundred years ago but now unfolds before us in the glaring light of our present time. With this realization, the hope is that they will feel pressed to anticipate the hereafter in their present lives by living each moment as if it is their last. For only in this way can they be counted as truly striving to gain the rich rewards and endless mercies of which the Prophet ﷺ was so eager to remind us with his every living breath.

لَقَدْ جَاءَكُمْ رَسُولٌ مِّنْ أَنفُسِكُمْ عَزِيزٌ عَلَيْهِ مَا عَنِتُّمْ حَرِيصٌ عَلَيْكُم بِالْمُؤْمِنِينَ رَؤُوفٌ رَّحِيمٌ

Now hath come unto you an Messenger from amongst yourselves: it grieves him that ye should perish: ardently anxious is he over you: to the Believers is he most kind and merciful. (at-Tawbah 9:128)

We have compiled a selection from the nearly one thousand hadith which touch on subjects concerning the end of the world. They are culled from a variety of sources, from the canonical collections of Imams Bukhārī, Muslim, Tirmidhī, Abū Dāwūd, and many others. It should not escape us that the descriptions of the locations and events are not related in support of any particular region or nation. It is hoped that the reader will readily recognize the non-partisan character of the Prophet's ﷺ utterances. They side not with any party, nation, land, or civilization. Rather, they relate with precision what Allāh revealed to him, describing in detail the portentous events that are to greet us in the near future and which even now overshadow our every waking hour. In short, the motive is simply to transmit the words of the Prophet ﷺ just as he spoke them, as transmitted in the commonly accepted books of hadith. To this end, they are presented in their original Arabic in their entirety for the sake of authenticity. These verses and hadith reflect the tribulations and calamities taking place in various parts of the world today and which will eventually end in the wars, deaths and tragedies foretold in the Prophet's ﷺ miraculous predictions.

Hadith are Revelation from Allāh to the Prophet ﷺ

The Qur'ān is Holy. It consists of the Inviolable Words of Allāh ﷻ. It is for all times and all peoples. The Prophet ﷺ whose title is "The Messenger of God," was inspired and divinely guided in every word and every action. Allāh ﷻ said in the Holy Qur'ān:

وَالنَّجْمِ إِذَا هَوَى مَا ضَلَّ صَاحِبُكُمْ وَمَا غَوَى وَمَا يَنطِقُ عَنِ الْهَوَى إِنْ هُوَ إِلَّا وَحْيٌ يُوحَى

(I swear) by the star when it sets, your companion is neither astray nor is deceived; Nor does he say (aught) of (his own) desire. It is naught but revelation that is revealed (to him). (al-Najm 53:1-4)

Allāh ﷻ swears by the setting star that His Prophet ﷺ does not stray in the least from what Allāh ﷻ commands him. Nor does the Prophet ﷺ speak from his own whims or desires, whether good or bad. Every utterance, every movement, every breath of the Prophet ﷺ was, in fact, revelation from Allāh ﷻ and consequently of utmost value in the quest to understand and follow the Qur'ān and the religion of Islam.

> The Companion, Jābir ibn Abd Allāh ؓ said, "Allāh's Messenger ﷺ was among us while the Qur'ān was being revealed to him and he knew its explanation. Whatever he put into practice, we put into practice."[8]

حدثنا عبد الله حدثني أبي حدثنا هاشم بن القاسم قال حدثنا مبارك عن الحسن عن سعيد بن هاشم بن عامر قال أتيت عائشة فقلت: يا أم المؤمنين أخبريني بخلق رسول الله صلى الله عليه وسلم قالت: كان خلقه القرآن...

When asked about the Prophet's ﷺ character, (his wife and leading juris-consult of the time), 'A'isha ؓ said, "His ﷺ character was the Qur'ān."[9]

The hadiths demonstrate how to implement the principles set out in the Qur'ān, from the most rudimentary acts of worship to the most sublime. For example, Allāh ﷻ commands multiple times in the Qur'ān:

وَأَقِيمُوا الصَّلَاةَ وَآتُوا الزَّكَاةَ

Establish prayers (salat) and pay the poor-due (zakat).
(2:43, 2:83, 2:110, 4:77, 24:56, 73:20)[10]

---

[8] Narrated from Muhammad al-Bāqir as part of a long hadith by *Muslim, Abū Dāwūd*, and *Āhmad*.
[9] Āhmad in his *Musnad* #23460.
[10] Text of the other verses:

We clearly understand from this that both prayer and the poor-due are required of us. However, to find the necessary details to complete the prayer, i.e. the manner and timing of the prayer and upon whom it is obligatory, etc., we must turn to the hadiths. Similarly, a practicable description of the poor-due, its amount, upon whom it is obligatory and to whom it may be given, etc., is found only in the hadiths, and this is the case with all other obligations.

In summary, the hadiths of the Prophet ﷺ are necessary to understand the Qur'ān. For every single event in his lifetime, Allāh ﷻ revealed to the Prophet's heart what to say and what to do. The Qur'ān and the hadiths both derive from revelation and are inseparable sources for understanding and implementing the divine message of Islam.[11]

As Qur'ān is the Last Testament and Allāh's final revelation to humanity, so the Prophet Muhammad ﷺ is the last messenger and with him lies the completion of the Divine Message. Allāh ﷻ said in the Holy Qur'ān:

وَأَقِيمُوا الصَّلَاةَ وَآتُوا الزَّكَاةَ وَارْكَعُوا مَعَ الرَّاكِعِينَ

Establish worship, pay the poor-due, and bow your heads with those who bow (in worship). (al-Baqara 2:43)

وَأَقِيمُوا الصَّلَاةَ وَآتُوا الزَّكَاةَ ثُمَّ تَوَلَّيْتُمْ إِلَّا قَلِيلًا مِنكُمْ وَأَنتُم مُّعْرِضُونَ

and establish worship and pay the poor-due. Then, after that, ye slid back, save a few of you, being averse. (al-Baqara 2:83)

وَأَقِيمُوا الصَّلَاةَ وَآتُوا الزَّكَاةَ وَمَا تُقَدِّمُوا لِأَنفُسِكُم مِّنْ خَيْرٍ تَجِدُوهُ عِندَ

Establish worship, and pay the poor-due; and whatever of good ye send before (you) for your souls, ye will find it with Allah. (al-Baqara 2:110)

أَلَمْ تَرَ إِلَى الَّذِينَ قِيلَ لَهُمْ كُفُّوا أَيْدِيَكُمْ وَأَقِيمُوا الصَّلَاةَ وَآتُوا الزَّكَاةَ

Have you not seen those to whom it was said: Withhold your hands, and keep up prayer and pay the poor-rate; (an-Nisā' 4:77)

وَأَقِيمُوا الصَّلَاةَ وَآتُوا الزَّكَاةَ وَأَطِيعُوا الرَّسُولَ لَعَلَّكُمْ تُرْحَمُونَ

Establish worship and pay the poor-due and obey the messenger, that haply ye may find mercy. (an-Nūr 24:56)

وَأَقِيمُوا الصَّلَاةَ وَآتُوا الزَّكَاةَ وَأَقْرِضُوا اللَّهَ قَرْضًا حَسَنًا

So recite of it that which is easy (for you), and establish worship and pay the poor-due, and (so) lend unto Allah a goodly loan. (al-Muzzamil 73:20)

[11] The Prophet said:

Verily this Qur'ān is difficult and felt as a burden to anyone that hates it, but it is made easy to anyone that follows it. Verily my sayings are difficult and felt as a burden to anyone that hates them, but they are made easy to anyone that follows them. Whoever hears my saying and preserves it, putting it into practice, shall come forth together with the Qur'ān on the Day of Resurrection. Whoever dismisses my sayings dismisses the Qur'ān, and whoever dismisses the Qur'ān has lost this world and the next.

Narrated from al-Hakam ibn 'Umayr al-Thumalī by Khatīb in *al-Jāmi'li Akhlāq al-Rāwī* (1983 ed. 2:189), Qurtubī in his *Tafsīr* (18:17), Abū Nu'aym, Abū al-Shaykh, and Daylamī.

مَّا كَانَ مُحَمَّدٌ أَبَا أَحَدٍ مِن رِّجَالِكُمْ وَلَكِن رَّسُولَ اللَّهِ وَخَاتَمَ النَّبِيِّينَ وَكَانَ اللَّهُ بِكُلِّ شَيْءٍ عَلِيمًا

Muhammad is not the father of any of your men, but (he is) the Messenger of Allāh, and the Seal of the Prophets... (al-Ahzāb 33:40)

Contained in the Qur'ān and hadiths is all the knowledge needed for success in this world and the next, both for his generation and all future generations until the Judgment Day. Not the least among this knowledge are the signs and events that relate to the community of the Last Days.

عن حذيفة قال: قام فينا رسول الله صلى الله عليه وسلم مقاما . ما ترك شيئا يكون في مقامه ذلك إلى قيام الساعة، إلا حدث به . حفظه من حفظه ونسيه من نسيه . قد علمه أصحابي هؤلاء . وإنه ليكون منه الشيء قد نسيته فأراه فأذكره . كما يذكر الرجل وجه الرجل إذا غاب عنه . ثم إذا رآه عرفه

Hudhayfa ⚘ reported:

> Allāh's Messenger ﷺ stood before us one day, and he did not leave anything unsaid (that he had to say) at that very spot which would happen (in the shape of turmoil) up to the Last Hour. Those who had to remember them preserved them in their minds and those who could not remember them forgot them. My friends knew them and there are certain things which slip out of my mind, but I recapitulate them when anyone makes a mention of them just as a person is lost from one's mind but is recalled to him on seeing his face.[12]

༺✾࿇✾༻

---

[12] *Sunan Abū Dāwūd*, "Kitāb al-Fitan." *Sahīh Muslim*, "Kitāb al-Fitan."

Proximity of the Final Hour

Fourteen hundred years ago Allāh ﷻ mentioned in the Holy Qur'ān:

اقْتَرَبَتِ السَّاعَةُ وَانْشَقَّ الْقَمَرُ

The Hour (of Judgment) is nigh and the moon is cleft asunder.

(al-Qamar 54:1)

The moon was split in the Prophet's time as a sign to the pagan Makkans who demanded a miracle to prove his prophecy. In *Sūrat al-Qamar* ("The Moon"), Allāh is not only bearing witness to this miracle but He is also showing that this portent is very close to the Last Hour. As Muhammad ﷺ is the Last Prophet, his Community will be the last community to exist on earth, and after their time will come the Judgment Day.

حِدَّثَنِي عبد الله بن محمد هو الجعفي: حدثنا وهب بن جرير: حدثنا شعبة، عن قتادة وأبي

التَّيَّاح، عن أنس، عن النبي صلى الله عليه وسلم قال: بعثت أنا والساعة كهاتين (أخرجه مسلم في

الفتن وأشراط الساعة، باب: قرب الساعة)

The Prophet ﷺ said, "I was sent so close to the Judgment Day like these two fingers next to each other."[13]

While the exact time of the Judgment Day is known only to Allāh ﷻ there are signs mentioned in the Qur'ān and hadith by which to know of its approach.

In another *Sūrah*, Allāh ﷻ gives an oath:

وَالْعَصْرِ

I swear by the Time. (al-ʿAsr 103:1)

ʿAsr carries many meanings: one of which is time in general, or a specific period of time, or the *ʿAsr* (afternoon) canonical prayer. Another meaning of *ʿAsr* is *ʿAsr an-Nubūwwa* or the Era of the Prophecy of Muhammad[14] ﷺ which began with Muhammad ﷺ first receiving revelation through Archangel Gabriel and continues until Judgment Day. Allāh is swearing by *al-ʿAsr* showing the importance of keeping one's time occupied with good deeds, the importance of observing the *ʿAsr* prayer, and the significance of the Time of Prophet Muhammad's Community. An indication of the actual lifespan of the Community is found in the Prophet's hadith:

---

[13] *Sahīh Bukhārī*, (8:510) "Kitāb al-Tafsīr." *Sūrat an-Nāziʿāt.*
[14] Haqqī, Isma'il. *Tafsīr rūh al-bayān.*

إِن إِسْتَقَامَتْ أُمَّتِي فَلَها يَوْم و إِنْ لَمْ تَسْتَقِمْ فَلَها نِصْفُ يَوْم (روح البيان)

When my Community keeps on the right, it is going to enjoy
an age of one day, and when it does not keep on the right, it
will have an age of half a day.[15]

Allāh 🕮 said in the Holy Qur'ān:

وَإِنَّ يَوْماً عِنْدَ رَبِّكَ كَأَلْفِ سَنَةٍ مِّمَّا تَعُدُّونَ

And one day according to Allah's estimation is 1,000 years according to
yours. (al-Hajj 22:47)

Thus the Islamic community of the right way would flourish for one
thousand years and the community in decline would last for another five
hundred years.

For the first millennium of Islamic civilization, the Muslims were favored
by Allāh 🕮 with an advancement unparalled before or after. Muslims were at
the forefront of not only religious development but also were the world's
leading researchers, physicians, chemists, astronomers, botanists, philosophers,
and architects. Muslims were the shining lights that illuminated Europe and
touched off the Renaissance. After its first millenium a gradual yet definite
decline began within the Ummah which has continued until our present time.
As the Muslims have wandered away from the way of the Prophet 🕮 and
Allāh's heavenly message of Islam, the divine blessings and support have
similarly diminished. Miraculously, the Prophet 🕮 predicted that this process
would take one thousand years and it came to pass.[16] The second prediction in
this hadith is that the Ummah will continue further for five hundred more
years in decline.

Thus, according to this understanding of this hadith Allāh 🕮 has granted
the Ummah a lifespan of fifteen hundred years, and Allāh knows best, and
today we have already arrived to the year 1424 *Hijrī* (2003 CE). This prediction
of a fifteen hundred year lifespan is also in keeping with the recent appearance
of the Signs of the Last Days. These signs have not appeared in their totality
until lately. Even a cursory examination of these signs shows their present-day
fulfillment as foretold by Prophet Muhammad 🕮 over fourteen hundred years

---

[15] Hadith mentioned in *Rūh al-Bayān*, *Tafsīr* of *Sūrat al-'Asr*. *"In istaqāmat ummatī falahā yawm
wa in lam tastaqim falahā nisfa yawm."*
In another version the Prophet 🕮 said, "If my Community keeps on the right, it is going to enjoy
an age of one day, and if it becomes corrupt, it will have an age of half a day."
Al-Munawī cites it in *Fayd al-Qadīr* from Shaykh Muhyī al-Dīn Ibn 'Arabī.
[16] The 1000th year of the Islamic Hijrī calendar was marked by the rule of Ottoman sultan Murād
III 1546–95 (ruled 1574–95), son and successor of Selim II. He was dominated by his family,
and although his generals were successful against Persia, his reign marked the beginning of
the decay of the Ottoman Empire and the Islamic caliphate as a whole.

ago. These detailed predictions are milestones by which to locate ourselves on the eschatological timeline.

One clear example of such prescience are the following two hadiths, in which the Prophet foretold the different forms of leadership the Muslim Ummah would experience as time passed, ending with a prediction about its final destiny.

حدثنا سليمان بن داود الطيالسي حدثني داود بن إبراهيم الواسطي حدثني حبيب بن سالم عن النعمان بن بشير قال

كنا قعودا في المسجد مع رسول الله صلى الله عليه وسلم وكان بشير رجلا يكف حديثه فجاء أبو ثعلبة الخشني فقال يا بشير بن سعد أتحفظ حديث رسول الله صلى الله عليه وسلم في الأمراء فقال حذيفة أنا أحفظ خطبته فجلس أبو ثعلبة فقال حذيفة قال رسول الله صلى الله عليه وسلم تكون النبوة فيكم ما شاء الله أن تكون ثم يرفعها إذا شاء أن يرفعها ثم تكون خلافة على منهاج النبوة فتكون ما شاء الله أن تكون ثم يرفعها إذا شاء الله أن يرفعها ثم تكون ملكا عاضا فيكون ما شاء الله أن يكون ثم يرفعها إذا شاء أن يرفعها ثم تكون ملكا جبرية فتكون ما شاء الله أن تكون ثم يرفعها إذا شاء أن يرفعها ثم تكون خلافة على منهاج النبوة ثم سكت (مسند أحمد)

Hudhayfa ⬥ related that the Prophet Muhammad ﷺ said:

> Prophecy will be in your midst as long as God wills it to remain there. Then it will be removed when God wills it to be removed. Then there will be *Khilāfa* (divinely-ordained rule) on the pattern of prophecy and so it will remain as long as God wills. Then there will come kingship (*mulkun 'ad*) and so it will remain as long as God wills. Then it will be removed when God wills. Then there will come tyranny (*mulkun jabri*) and so it will remain as long as God wills it to do so. Then it will be removed when God wills. Then there will come *Khilāfa* on the pattern of prophecy.

Then he kept silent. [17]

يكون بعدي خلفاء، وبعد الخلفاء الأمراء، وبعد الأمراء الملوك، وبعد الملوك الجبابرة، وبعد الجبابرة رجل من أهل بيتي يملأ الأرض عدلا، ومن بعده القحطاني، والذي بعثني بالحق! ما هو دونه. (نعيم بن حماد في الفتن عن عبد الرحمن بن قيس بن جابر الصدفي)

The Prophet of Allāh ﷺ said:

> After me come caliphs, and after the caliphs come princes, and after princes there will be kings and after the kings, there

---

[17] *Musnad* of Imām Āhmad ibn Hanbal, 4.273.

will be tyrants. And after the tyrants a man from My House will fill the earth with justice, and after him is al-Qahtānī. By the One who sent me with the Truth! Not a word less.[18]

Commenting on this hadith, Mawlana Shaykh Nāzim al-Haqqani identifies the caliphs spoken of in these two hadiths as "the Rightly-Guided Ones"—*ar-rāshidūn*: Abū Bakr, 'Umar, 'Uthman and 'Alī, may Allāh be pleased with them all. The princes are the Ummayad Caliphs of Damascus and the Abbasid Caliphs of Baghdad. As for the kings, they are the Ottoman Sultans of Istanbul. Following the kings, according to the second hadith, are tyrants, and that is what is commonly seen today. Finally, what for us is a prediction: the appearance of a man from the family of the Prophet ﷺ who will rule with justice.

And Allāh knows best for He did not reveal the Unseen to anyone. Allāh said:

$$يَسْأَلُونَكَ عَنِ السَّاعَةِ أَيَّانَ مُرْسَاهَا قُلْ إِنَّمَا عِلْمُهَا عِندَ رَبِّي لاَ يُجَلِّيهَا لِوَقْتِهَا إِلاَّ هُوَ ثَقُلَتْ فِي السَّمَاوَاتِ وَالأَرْضِ لاَ تَأْتِيكُمْ إِلاَّ بَغْتَةً$$

They ask thee about the (final) Hour, when will be its appointed time? Say: "The knowledge thereof is with my Lord (alone): none but He can reveal as to when it will occur. Heavily will it weigh on the heavens and the earth. It will only come to you suddenly." (al-Arāf 7:187)

From this it is clear that no one knows the exact day or hour of the Judgment. However we can understand from the signs which the Prophet brought that we are approaching the end of time, though no one can predict a certain date for it. As human beings, there always exists the possibility of error. Only the prophets are infallible (*ma'sūm*). What we are attempting here is not to predict the timing of the Last Day precisely, but to analyze the signs given to us by the Prophet Muhammad ﷺ in expectation of that final day.

$$يَسْأَلُونَكَ عَنِ السَّاعَةِ أَيَّانَ مُرْسَاهَا(42) فِيمَ أَنتَ مِن ذِكْرَاهَا(43) إِلَى رَبِّكَ مُنتَهَاهَا(44) إِنَّمَا أَنتَ مُنذِرُ مَن يَخْشَاهَا(45)$$

They ask you about the Hour, "When will be its appointed time?" Wherein are you (concerned) with the declaration thereof? With your Lord is the limit fixed thereof. Thou art but a warner for such as fear it.

(an-Nāzi'at 79: 42-46)

Those who believe in the Last Day, live in fear of its coming upon them

---

[18] Na'īm bin Hammād in "Fitan" from 'Abd ar-Rahmān bin Qays bin Jābir al-Sadafī, *Kanz al-'ummāl,* hadith #38704.

suddenly, when they are unprepared. It is such promptings as the above verses, which urge us to vigilance of its appearance and it is for that this book was written, for the Prophet ﷺ was constantly urging his Companions to keep conscious of the Last Day before them.

حدثنا عبدان أخبرنا أبي عن شعبة عن عمرو بن مرة عن سالم بن أبي الجعد عن أنس بن مالك أن رجلا سأل النبي صلى الله عليه وسلم متى الساعة يا رسول الله قال ما أعددت لها قال ما أعددت لها من كثير صلاة ولا صوم ولا صدقة ولكني أحب الله ورسوله قال أنت مع من أحببت

Narrated Anas bin Mālik:

> A man asked the Prophet ﷺ, "When will the Hour be established O Allāh's Apostle?" The Prophet ﷺ said, "What have you prepared for it?" The man said, "I haven't prepared for it much of prayers or fast or alms, but I love Allāh and His Apostle." The Prophet ﷺ said, "You will be with those whom you love."[19]

In this hadith a Bedouin asked when the Hour would occur. Instead of providing a timeline, the Prophet ﷺ said, "What have you prepared for it?" It is thus an essential aspect of faith to keep the Day of Judgment in one's view, not as something that is far off, but as something imminent—something that could occur at any time. These signs are but indicators that the Judgment Day is near, when Allāh ﷻ will judge all of humanity. As Allāh ﷻ said:

يَسْأَلُكَ النَّاسُ عَنِ السَّاعَةِ قُلْ إِنَّمَا عِلْمُهَا عِندَ اللَّهِ وَمَا يُدْرِيكَ لَعَلَّ السَّاعَةَ تَكُونُ قَرِيبًا

Men ask thee of the Hour. Say: The knowledge of it is with Allāh only. What can convey (the knowledge) unto thee? It may be that the Hour is nigh. (al-Aḥzāb 33:63)

❧❦❧

---

[19] *Saḥīḥ Bukhārī.*

ISLAM AND MODERN SCIENCE

SCIENTIFIC REALITIES IN DIVINE REVELATION

Secrets of Qur'ān and Hadith Uncovered in the Modern Era

Not only did the Prophet ﷺ precisely describe the events and conditions of the Last Days, but he also demonstrated a remarkable awareness of scientific discoveries unknown until the contemporary scientific era.

حدثنا سعيد بن عفير حدثنا الليث حدثني عقيل عن ابن شهاب أخبرني سعيد بن المسيب أن أبا هريرة قال سمعت رسول الله صلى الله عليه وسلم يقول بعث بجوامع الكلم...

The Prophet ﷺ said, "I was sent with the pithiest expressions with the vastest meanings..."[20]

Examining the hadiths of the Prophet ﷺ today, many of these vast meanings are now being grasped by both Muslims and non-Muslims. It is not desirable for science to determine one's faith because Muslims believe in whatever is in the Qur'ān and hadiths regardless of what scientists say. However, today's researchers are discovering many realities previously unknown to them, but which were alluded to by Prophet Muhammad ﷺ and mentioned in the Holy Qur'ān and the hadiths fourteen hundred years ago.

These things were not elucidated by the Prophet ﷺ to the people of his time for two reasons. Firstly, they were not able to understand these discoveries. Secondly, the Prophet did not explain the meaning of these verses of the Qur'ān or these hadiths so they would exist as independent proofs for later days when scientists would discover them for themselves and verify their reality. They were left for future generations to appreciate the greatness of Prophet Muhammad ﷺ and the miraculous knowledge Allāh ﷺ gave him in the Qur'ān and hadith. When non-Muslim researchers make a "discovery" using today's advanced scientific knowledge and technology, it is a compelling testimonial to the Qur'ān and hadith, which mentioned them centuries before it was possible to know of such things.

If Muslims discovered these things, one might speculate they were merely trying to bolster their own faith. Yet it is non-Muslims who are independently corroborating these facts, verifying realities which were mentioned by the

---

[20] Narrated from Abū Hurayra in *Sahīh Bukhārī*.

Prophet ﷺ fourteen hundred years ago. In this way Allāh ﷻ is guiding non-Muslims, through their own research, to realize that the Prophet ﷺ spoke the truth when he mentioned these things, and hopefully to infer that he also spoke the truth in conveying the message of Islam, Allāh's religion. Many things have been discovered and some things are still in process of unfolding. The Prophet ﷺ knew of discoveries on earth and beyond the earth, in space.

سَنُرِيهِمْ آيَاتِنَا فِي الآفَاقِ وَفِي أَنْفُسِهِمْ حَتَّى يَتَبَيَّنَ لَهُمْ أَنَّهُ الْحَقُّ أَوَلَمْ يَكْفِ بِرَبِّكَ أَنَّهُ عَلَى كُلِّ شَيْءٍ شَهِيدٌ

We will soon show them Our signs in the Universe and in themselves, until it will become manifest to them that it is the truth.... (Fussilat 41:53)

The verse does not say, "We **are** showing them," but "*We will show them Our signs in the horizons,*" i.e. the skies and space. Signs are not juristic rulings or legal verdicts based on historical precedents. Signs are the uncovering of realities. Allāh ﷻ said, "I will show them in the atmosphere." A discovery on earth may have somehow been discovered before. However, it is impossible for someone fourteen hundred years ago to have known the discoveries made possible by space exploration. Islamic scholars who read this verse in the past were wondering what kind of signs Allāh ﷻ was going to show in the horizons. The Prophet ﷺ did not explain some aspects of the Qur'ān and hadith, but left them to be discovered later. That is why, up to today, there are many things that scientists are discovering in Qur'ān which were not understood, even recently.

The Prophet ﷺ gave each of the Companions something specific. For this reason the compilers of the Prophet's hadith, such as Imām Bukhārī, had to collect from everywhere, because no Companion knew everything, but everyone knew something. This shows that knowledge can only be given to those who can understand it, whatever the container of their heart can carry.

As Allāh ﷻ said:

لاَ يُكَلِّفُ اللهُ نَفْسًا إِلاَّ وُسْعَهَا

Allah does not impose upon any soul a burden greater than it can bear...

(al-Baqara 2:286)

Allāh ﷻ does not burden anyone beyond his capacity. The Prophet ﷺ knew the capacity of each person and gave to him or her accordingly.

Abū Hurayra ﷺ is a well-known Companion of the Prophet ﷺ who narrated over four thousand hadiths.

حدثنا إسماعيل قال: حدثني أخي، عن ابن أبي ذئب، عن سعيد المقبري، عن أبي هريرة قال
حفظت من رسول الله صلى الله عليه وسلم وعاءين: فأما أحدهما فبثته، وأما الآخر فلو بثته
قطع هذا البلعوم(صحيح البخاري في كتاب العلم)

Abū Hurayra ❀ said:

> I memorized from the Prophet ﷺ two bodies of knowledge.
> One of them I propagated to everyone, and as for the other
> one, if I spread it my throat would be cut.[21]

This is an indication that some scholars understand this knowledge as a gift from the Prophet ﷺ which was given to Abū Hurayra ❀ by Allāh—as if it had been poured into his heart. He said this not in our time, but during his life, when he was among the Companions of the Prophet ﷺ. He did not disclose one body of knowledge that the Prophet ﷺ gave to him because for some people their understanding was not sufficient to appreciate or comprehend it.

What was it that Abū Hurayra ❀ did not reveal? Many things that are in the Qur'ān are not understood even today. Even today's scholars say that there are many secrets in the Qur'ān, and that is an aspect of its miraculous knowledge (*i'jāz al-Qur'ān*). Those are secrets that were not even explained to the Companions, for they were not in a position to understand them.

نضّر الله عبدا سمع مقالتي فوعاها و حفظها و بلغها فربّ حامل فقه غير فقيه و ربّ حامل فقه إلى
من هو أفقه منه ثلاث لا يغل عليهن قلب مسلم إخلاص العمل لله منا صحبة أئمة المسلمين و لزوم
الجماعة فإن الدعوة تحيط من ورائهم

The Prophet ﷺ said:

> May Allāh brighten the face of that of His servants who hears
> my words, remembers them, guards them, and hands them
> on. Many a transmitter of knowledge does not himself
> understand it, and many may transmit knowledge to others
> who are more versed in it than they...[22]

Here the Prophet ﷺ foretold that the transmitters of hadith might not understand the import of a particular statement he uttered, but in order that later generations, more able to grasp their significance, would hear them

---

[21] *Sahīh Bukhārī*, (1:121):
   Hafiztu min rasūlillāhi wi'a'ayn fa amma ahaduhumā fa bathathtuhu lil-khalq wa amma al-ākhar law bathathtuhu quti'a hadha al-bal'ūm.
   In another version reads, "*sabba fī qalbī rasūlullāh*"—"The Prophet poured into my heart..."
[22] Narrated from Zayd ibn Thābit by *Tirmidhī* (hasan), Abū Dāwūd, Ibn Mājah, Ahmad, al-Dārimī, and al-Shafi'ī in his *Risāla* (#1102). Al-Tirmidhī's version does not mention the last sentence. On the variant wordings of this important hadith see Shaykh 'Abd al-Fattāh Abū Ghudda's *al-Rasūl al-Mu'allim* (p. 55-56).

correctly, urged the transmitters of hadith to take utmost care in preserving their original wording.

The miraculous knowledge taught by the Prophet ﷺ comes to us today from two sources, the Holy Qur'ān and the hadith. Today, scientists are finding an amazing congruence between what is in Qur'ān and hadith and what science is discovering from the wonders of Allāh's creation. These discoveries cover a wide scientific spectrum, and reveal the divinely inspired levels of knowledge of the Prophet Muhammad ﷺ fourteen hundred years ago.

The astounding detailed foreknowledge of these realities could not have been independently discovered without the benefit of modern technology nor could they be happenstance or a lucky guess. Quite simply, the predictions made by Prophet Muhammad ﷺ are of unprecedented accuracy, detail, and content that did not come before him or after. These demonstrate the divine knowledge that the Prophet ﷺ brought that could only be known through revelation from Allāh ﷻ.

With the benefit of modern science people of today are in a unique position to appreciate the incredible and miraculous knowledge found in the message of Islam brought by Prophet Muhammad ﷺ in the Holy Qur'ān and hadiths. Before delving into the hadiths regarding the signs of the Last Days, a few verses of the Holy Qur'ān and their significance in light of recent scientific discoveries, will be examined. These verses illustrate the miraculous knowledge with which Allāh ﷻ favored the Prophet ﷺ, and are a compelling testimony to why everyone, both Muslim and non-Muslim, must examine the message of Prophet Muhammad ﷺ in its entirety and especially what he predicted was to come in the future.

As the Qur'ān gives astounding examples of the divine knowledge given to Prophet Muhammad ﷺ, so too are the Prophetic hadiths on the Last Days similarly miraculous in both their scientific insights as well as their precise description of the world today. The signs of the Last Days mentioned by the Prophet ﷺ eloquently demonstrate that the hadiths as well as the Qur'ān are a divine revelation from Allāh ﷻ to the Prophet Muhammad ﷺ. All of the foregoing is a mere drop in the oceans of divine knowledge given to the Prophet ﷺ, about whom Allāh ﷻ declared:

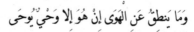

*Nor does he say (aught) of (his own) desire. It is naught but revelation that
is revealed (to him). (an-Najm 53:3-4)*

In the following lectures we will describe five of the scientific discoveries whose existence was already established fourteen hundred years ago in the Holy Qur'ān.

Iron

In the Holy Qur'ān Allāh said:

وَأَنْزَلْنَا الْحَدِيدَ فِيهِ بَأْسٌ شَدِيدٌ وَمَنَافِعُ لِلنَّاسِ

And We sent down Iron, wherein is mighty power, as well as many benefits for mankind... (al-Hadīd 57:25)

Islamic scholars in the past, and even recently, explained *anzalnā* (We caused to descend, revealed) as *khalaqnā* (We created). They knew iron was mined out of the depths of the earth, and could not conceive that iron descended or was brought down from above the earth.

Scientists have uncovered that iron is found not only on earth but in the sun, in many types of stars, and throughout the universe. Moreover, the Muslim scholars learned that it is not possible for even a single atom of iron to be created on earth or even with the extremes of energy inside the earth. To produce one atom of iron (*hadīd*) requires energy greater than that of the sun. According to the theory of nucleosynthesis, the only place in the universe that is sufficiently hot to produce iron is in a supermassive star which then explodes, spreading the iron throughout the universe.[23] This confirms that iron

---

[23] Donald Clayton says:

Today's astrophysicists believe based on observational evidence that the universe is primarily composed of hydrogen and helium. They hypothesize that Big Bang from which the universe was originally created, produced mainly hydrogen and helium with very tiny amounts of lighter elements and with no significant production of carbon, nitrogen, oxygen, iron, magnesium, silicon and other elements heavier than iron. They hypothesize that the thermonuclear furnace in the core of very hot stars are the "foundries" where these elements were "synthesized" long after the Big Bang took place.

In a process known as nucleosynthesis, the most common type of stars, known as main-sequence stars, generate energy by converting hydrogen into helium through thermonuclear fusion. As stars use up their hydrogen fuel, they evolve off the main-sequence into what are known as giant or supergiant stars, whose energy given off may exceed one hundred times its original luminosity. During these stages stars will begin to "burn" helium or other even heavier elements as the core of the star reaches higher and higher temperatures and densities. How far this process proceeds depends on the initial mass of the star. The lowest mass stars will never go past burning hydrogen while the highest mass stars can produce elements all the way up to iron in their cores.

In the more massive stars as Hydrogen is converted into helium and is used up, the pressure inside the star decreases allowing the core to collapse and heat up more. At some point, instead of fusing hydrogen into helium, the temperature will reach the point where helium begins to fuse into Carbon. The core will go through several such stages in which the product of thermonuclear fusion at one stage becomes the fuel for the next stage, with each succesive product being a heavier element in a series of evolutionary steps, depending on its mass, beginning with helium, then carbon, oxygen, silicon, and last being Iron.

was not created here on earth, but, as Allāh ﷻ said, *descended* or *was sent down* to the earth from above.[24] It was impossible for someone living fourteen hundred years ago to know that iron did not come from the earth but descended into the earth from space. This is an example of the miraculous knowledge with which Allāh ﷻ favored the Prophet Muhammad ﷺ in the Holy Qur'ān and the hadith.

There is the *i'jāz al-'ilmi* (astonishing or miraculous knowledge) and there is *i'jāz al-raqami* (or *i'jāz al-'adadi*) the astonishing numerology in the Qur'ān. In the Qur'ān there are many instances of the numbers pointing to something that is later discovered by science.

The atomic number (number of protons in the nucleus) of iron is 26.

With each change in fuel, there is an increase in core temperature and simultaneously the outer layers of the star heat up and begin to expand creating what are known as giant or supergiant stars. The most massive of these stars have an onion-skin structure -- an iron core surrounded by layers of the different elements which were "products" of previous stages, with the heaviest burning at the core to produce the star's energy output.

A start in the red giant stage will have expanded to about 40 times its normal radius, reaching 30 million km. and a temperature of 400 million degrees K.

The fusion of lighter elements produces a star's energy. However, once Iron becomes the fuel at the star's core, it no longer produces energy—instead it uses up energy. When this takes place, and this only occurs in extremely massive stars, at some point the star's core will collapse inward causing a massive explosion known as a supernova, in which all the outer layers are blasted into space at gigantic speeds. In the process, all kinds of nuclear reactions take place, synthesizing elements as high in the periodic table as plutonium or higher. It is this process which is believed by astrophysicists to have "seeded" the star clouds within galaxies with heavier elements—elements which at some point may condense during the formation of planets such as the earth, and from which life finally emerges.

After the supernova event, what remains of the original star is a tiny core, perhaps 100 km. in radius but burning at an incredible 100 billion degrees K. and spinning at 2000 rpm. Such stars are known as neutron stars, for the protons and electrons have joined together under the tremendous gravitational field to become neutrons.

For even more massive stars, the result is more extraordinary. Gravitational forces are so strong that the star collapses inward forever, and becomes a point, with an infinite density. These are known as black holes. Not even light can escape the gravitational field of a black hole.

The Origin of Elements and Life of a Star, Clayton, Donald, Clayton University, 1999

[24]

...the numbers of naturally occurring atoms of the metals between atomic weights 45 and 65... are dominated, like a mountain, by four abundant isotopes of iron. This is the sort of abundance data that the theory of nucleosynthesis must consider. The scientific method has achieved a great triumph here, from the first argument half a century ago that iron is the natural product of the evolution of the stellar core, to the recent proof by detected gamma rays from supernovae that the iron isotopes were ejected as isotopes of radioactive nickel and cobalt, and in just the ratios found within a common hammer!... The calcium in our bones, the iron in our hemoglobin, all, all but the initial hydrogen and helium, are thermonuclear debris from exploding stars.

The Origin of Elements and Life of a Star, Clayton, Donald, Clayton University, 1999

There are four naturally occurring stable isotopes of iron with atomic weights of 54, 56, 57, and 58 (see Table 1). The isotope iron 56 is the most abundant form of iron on earth.[25] The 57th *Sūrah* of the Qur'ān is named after iron, *Sūrat al-Hadīd* and iron 57 is possibly the most abundant isotopic form of iron in the universe.[26] In this *Sūrah* the word iron appears in the 25th verse. All of the chapters of the Qur'ān (except one) begin with the *basmala*[27] and it is considered by many scholars to be a verse. Counting the *basmala* as a verse brings us to the word iron (*hadīd*) in the 26th verse which is the same as the atomic number of iron, the number of protons. The *Sūrah* itself contains 29 verses, but with the *basmala* the total is 30, the number of neutrons in iron.

Isotope of Iron	Atomic mass (ma/u)	Natural abundance (atom %)
54Fe	53.9396127 (15)	5.845 (35)
56Fe	55.9349393 (16)	91.754 (36)
57Fe	56.9353958 (16)	2.119 (10)
58Fe	57.9332773 (16)	0.282 (4)

Table 1 Abundance of Iron Isotopes on Earth

Some non-Muslim scientists were surprised at this uncanny correlation. Some scientists who heard of this Qur'ānic revelation regarding *hadīd* have even become Muslims. It was unthinkable that someone fourteen hundred years ago could have known that iron came not from the earth, but descended into the earth from the skies, and also known the exact number of protons (before protons were even discovered), and known the atomic weight of the most plentiful naturally occurring form of iron, and use these numbers as coordinates to precisely locate the major reference to iron in Qur'ān (57:25) in the chapter of Iron, *Hadīd*.

Before he passed away the Prophet ﷺ called the Companions and instructed them as to where each verse and *Sūrah* would go, putting *Sūrat al-Hadīd* number 57. Although iron 56 is the most common form of iron found on earth, the Prophet ﷺ nevertheless chose *Sūrah* 57 to be the chapter of Iron in the Qur'ān. Iron 57 is the most abundant form of iron in space, and the Prophet ﷺ is demonstrating to scientists of today and to all people that the guidance which he followed exceeds the limits of any ordinary knowledge possible on this earth. This is the Holy Qur'ān, Allāh's revelation to all humanity through His beloved Prophet Muhammad ﷺ, and this is only one

---

[25] Commission on Atomic Weights and Isotopic Abundances report for the International Union of Pure and Applied Chemistry in Isotopic Compositions of the Elements 1989, Pure and Applied Chemistry, 1998, 70, 217. [Copyright 1998 IUPAC]

[26] 57 is the weight of the most Abundant stable isotope (variant nucleus) of iron seen in the solar neighborhood, according to measurements made by Charge, Element, Isotope Analysis System (CELIAS) on the SOHO spacecraft. It may be that in the entire universe, this is in fact the dominant isotope.
The Origin of the Elements and the Life of a Star, Clayton, Donald, Clayton University, 1999]

[27] *Bismillāh ir-Rahmān ir-Rahīm* in the Name of God, the Most-Merciful, the Mercy-Giving.

example of its miraculous nature and the Prophet's ﷺ perfect transmissiom of his Lord's message.

Oceans Meet but do not Mix

In these verses Allāh ﷻ is giving a compelling sign of His Power by constructing that which is unimaginable in the realm of human experience.

مَرَجَ الْبَحْرَيْنِ يَلْتَقِيَانِ بَيْنَهُمَا بَرْزَخٌ لَّا يَبْغِيَانِ فَبِأَيِّ آلَاءِ رَبِّكُمَا تُكَذِّبَانِ

He has let free the two seas to flow, meeting together. Between them is a barrier which they do not transgress. So which of the favors of your Lord will you deny? (ar-Rahmān 55:19-21)

These verses refer to two bodies of salt water which meet, but do not *transgress*, or mix together. The two bodies of water have between them a barrier (*barzakh*, isthmus). A cup of salt water and a cup of sugar water will mix together when poured into a container. Two cups of salt water will mix together very easily when combined as they contain the same solute. Yet this verse of the Qur'ān says that the two bodies of salt water do not mix.

The Prophet ﷺ is describing a barrier, like the border of a country, which neither body of water can encroach upon or transgress. One would expect a huge body of water like the Atlantic Ocean to overrun the much smaller Mediterranean Sea, yet researchers have found that their waters do not mix.[28] The waters of one body of water do not mix with the other, nor do the fish of the Atlantic cross into the Mediterranean and vice versa. If a fish from one body of water is put into the other, it will become ill. The water of each does not cross the invisible border between them, rather when they come to the barrier they descend and go back, not crossing. No doubt there are rare cases of fish crossing between the two oceans, but not generally—just as diplomats of different nations cross each other's borders, but not the common citizens.

As we noted above, Allāh ﷻ has declared that He will make His signs manifest:

---

[28] Richard Davis states:
    Occasionally, water becomes very heavy due to its high salinity. An example of this is the Mediterranean Sea. The water flowing outward through the Gibraltar Sill has greater salinity than the adjacent water of the Atlantic Ocean, and because it is heavier, it sinks. This Mediterranean flow can be tracked as a tongue of high salinity water most of the way across the Atlantic Ocean. This means that the incoming flow of sea water from the Mediterranean Sea does not admix or combine with the sea water of the Atlantic Ocean. The incoming flow does not loose its identity after traveling a short distance. Surprisingly, the flow from the Mediterranean Sea keeps on traveling 'most of the way across the Atlantic Ocean.' Since the area of the Atlantic Ocean is about 31,831,000 square miles, it is a very vast distance covered by this flow. ...this high density water is like a protruding 'tongue' surrounded by the low density water.
Principles of Oceanography, Davis, Richard A., Jr. and Don Mills, [Ontario, Addison-Wesley Publishing,1972], p. 92-93.

سَنُرِيهِمْ آيَاتِنَا فِي الْآفَاقِ وَفِي أَنفُسِهِمْ حَتَّى يَتَبَيَّنَ لَهُمْ أَنَّهُ الْحَقُّ

We will soon show them Our signs in the Universe and in themselves, until it will become manifest to them that it is the truth.... (Fussilat 41:53)

Allāh ﷻ says He will show them His signs *in themselves*, meaning here on earth.

In another verse, Allāh ﷻ mentions the barrier between a body of salt water and a body of fresh water. In addition to the barrier (*barzakh*) mentioned above, Allāh describes something akin to a quarantine area.[29]

وَهُوَ الَّذِي مَرَجَ الْبَحْرَيْنِ هَذَا عَذْبٌ فُرَاتٌ وَهَذَا مِلْحٌ أُجَاجٌ وَجَعَلَ بَيْنَهُمَا بَرْزَخًا وَحِجْرًا مَّحْجُورًا

And it is He Who has let free the two seas to flow: One palatable and sweet, and the other salty and bitter. And He has made a barrier between them and an area forbidden (to pass) and isolated.

(al-Furqān 25:53)

Fresh water is found in smaller bodies of water such as rivers or lakes, while the large oceans and seas are all salty. Although the enormous salty oceans could easily overrun the sweet freshwater rivers, for some reason they cannot encroach on the rivers and the two waters do not pass the barrier between them. The salt water fish do not go into the fresh water river and the same is true for the fresh water fish; neither can survive in the environment of the other as was mentioned also for the two bodies of salt water. The case of salmon and steel-head trout, which are conceived and born in fresh water and then spend most of their life in the oceans only to return to their place of birth to mate and die, are exceptions whose rarity and uniqueness only go to prove the rule.

In *Sūrat al-Furqān*, Allāh ﷻ mentions that in addition to the barrier (*barzakh*, also mentioned in *Sūrat ar-Rahmān*), there is a *hijran mahjūrā* which means a completely separated area, partitioned off and inaccessible. *Hijran mahjūrā* is an affirmation of absolute isolation such as in a quarantine. Quarantines are needed to separate and protect people from dangerous elements such as infection or violence. There is also a quarantine area for the fish between the fresh and salt waters. At the point where the fresh water river or waterfall meets the sea water, the fresh water moves down. At that point there is a distinct area which is neither fresh water nor salt water and is off

---

[29] Allāh described this area as *hijran mahjūrā*. The *al-Mawrid* Arabic-English Dictionary defines *hijr* as: forbidden, prohibited, banned. *Mahjūrā* is: restrained, constrained, held (back), limited, confined, restricted, isolated, secluded.

limits to both. It descends in a cylindrical fashion and has its own specific species of fish which can survive in it. Neither the fresh water fish nor the salt water fish can survive in this quarantine area. It is a mixture of fresh and salty water and sustains only its own variety of fish. The fish in this quarantine area also are unable to cross into either the fresh water or the salt water, or else they will perish. Fourteen hundred years ago the Holy Prophet 攤 alluded to these phenomena which were only discovered and understood centuries later by modern scientists.

The mighty ocean is keeping its limits in not overtaking the smaller fresh waters. In comparison to humans the ocean is much greater and more powerful, yet it is humble not overstepping the boundaries set for it by its Lord. Allāh is showing that even if someone is powerful or huge, he still should show respect for all and not show arrogance, ferocity, or aggression. Humans cannot drink salt water, although many other creatures can. Thus Allāh indicates to us not to be harsh and bitter like salt water, but to be sweet and tolerant. Allāh is showing that humans must strive for pleasantness and sweetness in their lives and in their deeds. Allāh wants sweet good actions from humans, He does not want transgression into bitter evil deeds.

Qur'ān's Description of the Rounded Earth

Many years before Copernicus (d. 1543 CE) and Galileo (d. 1642 CE) the Qur'ānic phraseology points to a profound understanding of the physical world. For example, the Qur'ān uses several similar expressions to show that the earth is spread out in a continuous rolling expansion.

وَالْأَرْضَ فَرَشْنَاهَا فَنِعْمَ الْمَاهِدُونَ

And We have rolled out the (spacious) earth: How excellently We do roll out![30] (adh-Dhāriyāt 51:48)

وَالْأَرْضَ مَدَدْنَاهَا وَأَلْقَيْنَا فِيهَا رَوَاسِيَ وَأَنْبَتْنَا فِيهَا مِن كُلِّ شَيْءٍ مَوْزُونٍ

And We have spread the earth out, (like a carpet).[31] (Hijr 15:19)

وَاللَّهُ جَعَلَ لَكُمُ الْأَرْضَ بِسَاطًا

And Allah has made the earth for you in (continuous) expansion.[32]
(Nūh 71:19)

In order to be continuously unrolling and expanding the earth must either be infinitely long, or it must be rounded and "rolling," or rotating, in space. This latter conclusion is supported by another verse:

خَلَقَ السَّمَاوَاتِ وَالْأَرْضَ بِالْحَقِّ يُكَوِّرُ اللَّيْلَ عَلَى النَّهَارِ وَيُكَوِّرُ النَّهَارَ عَلَى اللَّيْلِ وَسَخَّرَ الشَّمْسَ وَالْقَمَرَ كُلٌّ يَجْرِي لِأَجَلٍ مُسَمًّى أَلَا هُوَ الْعَزِيزُ الْغَفَّارُ

He created the heavens and the earth in true (proportions): He rolls[33] *the night into the day and He rolls the day into the night...* (az-Zumar 39:5)

Interestingly, the Qur'ān specified that while the earth is rounded it is not a perfect sphere. Allāh ﷻ said, "*And after that He spread the earth, (to a wide expanse)*" (an-Nāzi'āt 79:30). Here the word translated as "spread," is in fact *dahāhā*, which means that the earth is shaped like an egg, not perfectly round. This is also the view of today's astronomers who describe the earth's shape as an oblong spheroid.

The rotation of the earth gives an explanation of the different references to

---

[30] *Wal arda farashnāhā fa ni'm al-māhidūn.*
Farasha: Roll out, lengthening, laying, unwind, elongation, extension, stretching.
Mahada: Flatten, smoothen, roll.
[31] *Madda*: Stretch out, spread out, sprawl, unwind.
[32] *Basata*: Roll out, spread out, outstretch, unfurl, unfold, unroll, spread, lengthen, unwind.
[33] *Kawwara*—to roll up, to make ball shaped, to wind (a turban).

east and west in the Qur'ān. East and west have been known to all people. The Qur'ān mentions east (*mashriq*, literally the place of the sunrise) and west (*maghrib*, the place of sunset):

$$رَبُّ الْمَشْرِقِ وَالْمَغْرِبِ$$

Lord of the East and the West. (Muzzammil 73:9)

It also mentions the two places of sunrise (*al-maghribayn*—the two easts) and the two places of sunset (*al-mashriqayn*—the two wests):

$$رَبُّ الْمَشْرِقَيْنِ وَرَبُّ الْمَغْرِبَيْنِ$$

Lord of the two Easts and Lord of the two West. (ar-Rahmān 55:17)

If one travels for a distance, the place of sunrise and sunset is changed compared to where they were at one's original position. Thus, for that traveler there are two points of sunrise and sunset. The Qur'ān also mentions the many points of sunrise and many points of sunset.

$$فَلَا أُقْسِمُ بِرَبِّ الْمَشَارِقِ وَالْمَغَارِبِ$$

Lord of all points in the East and all points in the West. (al-Ma'arij 70:40)

The references to the many places of sunrise and sunset indicate that the place of sunrise is constantly moving across the earth as is the place of sunset. The Qur'ān mentioned sunrise and sunset in the singular, reflecting the everyday experience of people. The Qur'ān also mentioned these in the dual: two places of sunrise and two places of sunset, for travelers on a journey. With today's means of travel around the world one may also be in a continuous sunrise or sunset. If one travels westward in an airplane, one may observe the continuously moving sunrise or sunset as it travels around the globe from location to location.[34]

With the constant rotation of the earth a point on the equator moves at 1044 miles per hour around its axis, and there is a continuous sunrise and continuous sunset, and also a continuous wave of Muslims in prayer covering the earth. The *maghrib* (sunset) prayer and the morning prayer before sunrise, the noon prayer, the afternoon prayer, the night prayer are all constantly sweeping over the earth in a never ending cycle of worshipping Allāh ﷻ and praising His Prophet ﷺ.

In addition to describing the shape of the earth and its rotation, the Qur'ān also describes the movement of the sun, moon and the entire universe.

---

[34] This occurs when a plane travels westward, countering the rotation of the earth, which moves the atmosphere, including the plane, eastward.

لا الشَّمْسُ يَنبَغِي لَهَا أَن تُدْرِكَ الْقَمَرَ وَلا اللَّيْلُ سَابِقُ النَّهَارِ وَكُلٌّ فِي فَلَكٍ يَسْبَحُونَ

It is not for the Sun to catch up the Moon nor for the Night to outstrip the
Day: each is swimming in its (assigned) orbit. (Yā Sīn 36:40)

Every heavenly body is swimming in its assigned orbit, perfectly ordered according to Allāh's divine command.

Today's astronomers hold that the earth is traveling at 67,000 miles per hour in its yearly orbit around the sun. The sun in turn also moves continuously in its own orbit although it looks fixed to observers on earth. Allāh ﷻ mentions in the Holy Qur'ān:

وَسَخَّرَ لَكُمُ الشَّمْسَ وَالْقَمَرَ دَائِبَيْنِ وَسَخَّرَ لَكُمُ اللَّيْلَ وَالنَّهَارَ

And He has made subject to you the sun and the moon, both continuously
moving in their orbits; and the night and the day has he (also) made subject
to you. (Ibrāhīm 14:33).

All these speeds are interacting with each other, yet we still do not feel dizzy or perceive this motion in the slightest. Despite hurtling through our galaxy and space at incredible speeds our bodies are still intact. The earth is like a space shuttle on a grand scale, completely equipped with everything we need: food, oxygen, and shelter.

In another verse, Allāh ﷻ says:

وَتَرَى الْجِبَالَ تَحْسَبُهَا جَامِدَةً وَهِيَ تَمُرُّ مَرَّ السَّحَابِ صُنْعَ اللهِ الَّذِي أَتْقَنَ كُلَّ شَيْءٍ إِنَّهُ خَبِيرٌ
بِمَا تَفْعَلُونَ

You see the mountains and think them firmly fixed: but they are moving
quickly as the clouds move quickly: (such is) the creation of Allāh, Who
disposes of all things in perfect order: for He is well acquainted with all that
you do. (an-Naml 27:88)

To the ordinary observer, mountains are stationary, firmly fixed in their places. In this verse, Allāh ﷻ is showing His mercy that despite the mind-boggling speeds of the earth rotating and traveling in its orbit, that its occupants do not even notice this motion, thus the mountains appear fixed. Allāh ﷻ draws attention to the clouds in the sky to show that the mountains are moving quickly through space along with everything else in the universe. Astronomers hold that even the universe itself is not stationary but ever expanding and moving with all of its component planets, stars, and galaxies. [35]

These profound realities of the universe were described in the Qur'ān fourteen hundred years ago.

꧁ ꧂

---

[35] This is confirmed by astronomers today who say that the sun circles the center of our galaxy at about 250 kilometers per second and that our galaxy is moving relative to the 'average velocity of the universe' at 600 kilometers per second:

> Our Earth is not at rest. The Earth moves around the Sun. The Sun orbits the center of the Milky Way Galaxy. The Milky Way Galaxy orbits in the Local Group of galaxies. The Local Group falls toward the Virgo Cluster of Galaxies. But these speeds are less than the speed that all of these objects together move relative to the microwave background. In [the COBE satellite-generated] ...all-sky map, radiation in the Earth's direction of motion appears blueshifted and hence hotter, while radiation on the opposite side of the sky is redshifted and colder. The map indicates that the Local Group moves at about 600 kilometers per second relative to this primordial radiation. This high speed was initially unexpected and its magnitude is still unexplained.

2003. *How did the Known Structure in the Universe Evolve?* [online] Publication information is available. Available from World Wide Web: http://imagine.gsfc.nasa.gov/docs/science/mysteries_l1/structures.html. Energy Astrophysics Science Archive Research Center at NASA's Goddard Space Flight Center.

The Big Bang

The theory that the beginning of the universe issued from an enormous explosion called the Big Bang is something upon which scientists of today generally agree.

وَالسَّمَاءَ بَنَيْنَاهَا بِأَيْدٍ وَإِنَّا لَمُوسِعُونَ

And We have built the sky with mighty power and verify We are expanding (it). (adh-Dhāriyat 51:47)

Centuries before the Big Bang theory, the Qur'ān mentions the skies and universe in continuous expansion, a sign of Allāh's tremendous power and might. More specifically, the Qur'ān describes the shattering explosion from which heavens and earth, which were all one piece, were split apart:

أَوَلَمْ يَرَ الَّذِينَ كَفَرُوا أَنَّ السَّمَاوَاتِ وَالْأَرْضَ كَانَتَا رَتْقًا فَفَتَقْنَاهُمَا

Do not the unbelievers see that the heavens and the earth were joined together before we clove them asunder? (al-Anbyā 21:30)

From Ibn 'Abbās, Mujāhid, and others, the meaning of *ratqan* used in this verse is that the heavens and the earth were stuck together or blended together, and that later they were separated from each other.

The theory holds that out of absolute nothingness there occurred a tremendous blast from wh|ich the entire universe suddenly came into existence. That is, out of nothing or *ex nihilo* the universe appeared just as Imām al- Ghazzālī argued against the philosophers many centuries ago in his famous work *The Incoherence of the Philosophers* (*Tahafut al-falsafa*). Imām al-Ghazzālī in this work glorifed the Divine Will in proving the correctness of Imām Ash'arīs creed ('aqīdah) which advanced against the Mu'tazilites and philosophers the true doctrine of *ithbāt as-siffāt*—the affirmation of Allāh's Attributes. Al-Ghazzālī thus maintained that the universe began only at the exact moment when Allāh willed for it to come into being, as He, the Exalted, says:

إِنَّمَا أَمْرُهُ إِذَا أَرَادَ شَيْئًا أَنْ يَقُولَ لَهُ كُنْ فَيَكُونُ

Verify, when He intends a thing, His Command is, "be," and it is!
(Yā Sīn 36:82)

Moreover, He, the Exalted describes Himself as فَعَّالٌ لِمَا يُرِيدُ —*A Doer of what He wills* (al-Burūj 85:16). Allāh did not pick out a world from non-existents (*m'adūmāt*) to create as the Mu'tazilites claimed, nor did the universe exist from eternity without beginning. For there was no other world before the one He created. For He created the universe *ex nihilo* and at a definite temporal instant.

So out of nothing the universe began its rapid expansion, an expansion that continued for billions of years, forming in its wake countless stars, galaxies and galaxy clusters. Some of these we are able to observe today by means of high powered telescopes. Up until the present moment, there has been no effective disconfirmation of the Big Bang hypothesis. At the same time, it offers an explanation of many of the phenomena we observe in the universe.

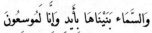

And We have built the sky with mighty power and verify We are expanding (it). (adh-Dhāriyāt 51:47)

This verse describes how the Lord built up the firmament *bi aydin*, literally "by Hand." "Hand" here refers to Allāh's Power. The verse continues, "We are able to keep expanding it." Physicists found vast gatherings of galaxies, each filled with hundreds of millions of stars expanding outward from a point in space—the location of the Big Bang. Physicists and space scientists are stunned when they read that verse of Qur'ān.

According to today's science, if an explosion takes place in the vacuum of free space, i.e. within an environment where there is absolutely no external forces, gravity or otherwise, the exploding object will shatter, and the particles of the object will be flung apart with an equal force on every particle thrusting it away from the core of the explosion. The explosion has a center point—its center of mass. The strongest force of the explosion affects this center. As particles move away from the center, the intensity of the force on them decreases until the particles no longer have a driving force accelerating them but continue moving outward from the center of the blast.

Now empirical observation shows us that the Big Bang occurred. But its expansion did not go on indefinitely. On the face of it, this is puzzling. For the elementary rules of physics hold that an object in motion will continue to remain in motion until acted upon by another opposing force. The laws of physics are not to be applied or ignored arbitrarily. Thus, it is implicit in the sudden explosive creation of the universe and our observation of ordered planets and galaxies that there must have been some force halting the initial immense expansion, and putting it into an ordered state. If there was no opposing force all the parts of the universe, including all atoms of planet Earth, would have kept expanding and separating, in an infinite continuation of that initial impulse from the center of the Big Bang. Instead, they coalesced and formed dense structures: galaxies, stars, gas clouds, nebulae, planets, moons, asteroids and comets.

Let us go back to the verse of the Qur'ān quoted earlier where Allāh says:

إِنَّمَا أَمْرُهُ إِذَا أَرَادَ شَيْئًا أَنْ يَقُولَ لَهُ كُنْ فَيَكُونُ

Verily, when He wills a thing, His Command is, "be" and it is!
(Yā Sīn 36:82)

In Arabic the word for the imperative "be" is *kun* and for "It is!" is *yakūn*. *Kun* is spelled *kāf* (ك) *nūn* (ن). It is said, "*Wa amruhu bayna al-kāf wa an-nūn*—Allāh's order for something 'to be' is between the *kāf* and the *nūn*." Allāh's Order of creation takes place within these two letters. Nothing may happen without Allāh's power, so the creation of the Big Bang came between *kāf* and *nūn*. In between the *kāf* was the driving force outward from the explosion, while the letter *nūn* is the driving force inward.

Nūn symbolizes the Arabic word *nihāya*, for the next letter in the alphabet is *hā* (ه), followed by *wāw* (و)—which may be pronounced as *alif*—and then *yā* (ي). *Nihāya* means "the end" and this caused that explosive shattering action to stop precisely where Allāh ﷻ wanted it to stop. At the right moment, at the right time, at the right space, at the exact place until today every smallest particle and largest galaxy was held in its assigned location. And while continuing some outward motion from the core of the explosion, this opposing force had the effect of preventing the particles of matter from separating from each other forever.[36]

---

[36] Paul Shestople says:

> According to the current variations of the Big Bang theory, the force opposing the expansion of the universe is the mutual gravitational attraction of all the matter in the universe, whose focus is the center of the Big Bang. Scientists believe that the force of gravity is what caused matter to coalesce into galaxies, gas clouds, stars, etc. The question remains however: where did the structure, the variations in density in the exploding matter come from? If the universe after the Big Bang was perfectly symmetrical, then there would have been no point around which galaxies, gas clouds, stars, etc. could coalesce. Thus the fact that we see structure indicates that there must have been structure inherent in the Big Bang itself. This is what Big Bang cosmologists are looking for, and believe they have found, in the minute fluctuations in the Cosmic Microwave Background Radiation (CMBR), which is a theoretical prediction about photons left over from the Big Bang, discovered in the 1960's and mapped out by a team at Berkeley in the early 1990's, and more recently by satellites COBE and WMAP. The latest WMAP composite all-sky image reveals temperature fluctuations believed to be 13 billion years old that scientists believe correspond to the seeds that grew to become cosmic structures. And while gravity, which is slowing down the expansion of the universe, can enhance the tiny fluctuations seen in the early universe, it cannot produce these fluctuations. Cosmologists speculate about the physics needed to produce the primordial fluctuations that formed galaxies.
> It is extremely difficult to model how this clumping may have occurred, but most models agree that it occurred faster than it should have. A possible explanation is that right after the Big Bang the Universe began a period of exaggerated outward expansion, with particles flying outward faster than the current speed of light. This explanation is known as inflation theory, and has widespread advocacy within the astrophysics community because it reconciles theory with

Now the center core of that explosion is the place where the most powerful interactions occur. That center in a real sense should be continuously exploding just as we see in an atomic reaction. The central core is the continuous source of explosive energy that causes the atoms there to maintain an uninterrupted chain reaction. An opposing force will be put in place at a certain time, by which some of these exploding particles will be stopped, becoming fixed, by the driving force of the *nūn*. The remainder continue to expand, because Allāh ﷻ is continuously creating creation through an ongoing outpouring of energy and energized matter in the cosmos.

That chain reaction should continue at the center of this universe, without end. The Big Bang in fact, while reducing in power over time, should not cease. That, in fact, seems to be what is observed. For if the Big Bang had occurred in one short instant and ended, the structure of the universe should be like a shell of matter and energy expanding from a central core, and with nothing in between. For it is understood that the deeper in space one looks, the farther back in time one looks, all the way to the original Big Bang. What we see is that from the beginning up to today, all of space is filled with countless galaxies, clusters of galaxies and star clouds, with no gap in space whatsoever.

Creation is continuous. In theological terms, Allāh's attribute *al-Khāliq*, the Creator, is unchanging and constant. Therefore it must be in continuous effect, i.e. that attribute must manifest in every moment. That is the meaning of *al-Khāliq*—the one who originates from nothingness. Therefore it must be that Allāh's creative power is manifesting somewhere, at every instant, producing something from non-existence.[37]

Still, the question remains: What triggered the Big Bang explosion? From where did the tremendous mass of the universe come? One premise required by the Big Bang theory is that the conditions and materials were, in fact, in place for the Big Bang to occur before it exploded. Yet this premise seems to be accepted on faith. Science does not explain how that came about. But we must ask: How could these trillions upon trillions of particles all be in one place initially? Does it not require energy to put all this matter into a single super-dense location? Did all this simply happen? What tipped everything over into an explosive state? How did this tremendous mass come into existence and what force acted on it to set off the explosion? How did order emerge

---

observation. It should be noted, however, that inflation theory is not directly verifiable.

Big Bang Cosmology Primer, Paul Shestople, 1997.

[37] That the center of the Big Bang is still exploding, producing new matter and energy, cannot be verified by observation. That is because the universe's center is so far away that it is impossible for us to perceive it due to our great distance from it. According to the Inflation theory, this is because of the inflation epoch during which the universe expanded at faster than light speed, after which the laws preventing such speeds came into effect. Thus a ray of light emerging from that center point will never reach us.

from these innumerable particles scattered around the universe?

The answers to these questions can be found in the Qur'ān. Allāh said:

$$وَمَا أَرْسَلْنَاكَ إِلا رَحْمَةً لِلْعَالَمِينَ$$

We sent thee not, but as a Mercy for all creatures. (al-Anbiyā' 21:107)

There are two meanings for the Arabic *'alamīn*. *'Alamīn* can refer to humankind and jinn. It can also mean everyone and everything. Everything that Allāh 🕮 has created is included in *'alamīn*. As Allāh said in the opening of the Qur'ān (*Sūrat al-Fātiha*):

$$الْحَمْدُ لِلّهِ رَبِّ الْعَالَمِينَ$$

All praise is for Allah Lord of the Worlds. (al-Fātiha 1:1)

'Alamīn means Allāh is the Lord of everything. The Prophet 🕮 as a mercy to the worlds (*'alamīn*) is correspondingly sent as a mercy to all of Allāh's creation. Anything and everything that is other than Allāh is a recipient of His mercy and blessings through the Prophet 🕮.

رواه عبد الرزاق بسنده عن جابر بن عبد الله بلفظ قال قلت: يا رسول الله، بأبي أنت وأمي، أخبرني عن أول شيء خلقه الله قبل الأشياء. قال: يا جابر، إن الله تعالى خلق قبل الأشياء نور نبيك من نوره، فجعل ذلك النور يدور بالقدرة حيث شاء الله، ولم يكن في ذلك الوقت لوح ولا قلم ولا جنة ولا نار ولا ملك ولا سماء ولا أرض ولا شمس ولا قمر ولا جني ولا إنسي، فلما أراد الله أن يخلق الخلق قسم ذلك النور أربعة أجزاء: فخلق من الجزء الأول القلم، ومن الثاني اللوح، ومن الثالث العرش، ثم قسم الجزء الرابع أربعة أجزاء، فخلق من الجزء الأول حَمَلَة العرش، ومن الثاني الكرسي، ومن الثالث باقي الملائكة، ثم قسم الجزء الرابع أربعة أجزاء: فخلق من الأول السماوات، ومن الثاني الأرضين، ومن الثالث الجنة والنار، ثم قسم الرابع أربعة أجزاء، فخلق من الأول نور أبصار المؤمنين، ومن الثاني نور قلوبهم وهي المعرفة بالله، ومن الثالث نور إنسهم وهو التوحيد لا إله إلا الله محمد رسول الله. الحديث. كذا في المواهب

It is related that Jābir ibn 'Abd Allāh 🕮 said to the Prophet 🕮, "O Messenger of Allāh, may my father and mother be sacrificed for you, tell me of the first thing Allāh created before all things." He said:

> O Jābir, the first thing Allāh created was the light of your
> Prophet from His light, and that light remained[38] in the midst
> of His Power for as long as He wished, and there was not, at
> that time, a Tablet or a Pen or a Paradise or a Fire or an angel
> or a heaven or an earth. And when Allāh wished to create

---

[38] Literally: "turned"

creation, he divided that Light into four parts and from the first made the Pen, from the second the Tablet, from the third the Throne, then He divided the fourth into four parts [and from them created everything else].[39]

The Prophet ﷺ told Jābir ⧫, "O Jābir! The first thing that Allāh created is the light of your Prophet." If we heed what modern physics is teaching us, then that light must be the source of the great Big Bang. Physicists say that before that event, there was nothing. Then Allāh said, "*Kun—Be!*" and "it was—*fayakūn*." Physicists do not say that—they say there was nothing in existence, when suddenly the Big Bang took place—an immense explosion of energy or light and that light is the essence of the universe.[40]

When the Prophet ﷺ says, "The first thing that Allāh created is my light," and from it whatever else Allāh has created as mentioned in the hadith above. Indeed, Allāh ﷻ has favored everyone by creating them from the light of the Prophet ﷺ. This follows from Allāh's saying, "*We have sent you (O Prophet) not but as a mercy to humanity (or the worlds)*." For from the Light of the Prophet ﷺ, Allāh made the Pen, the Tablet, the Throne, then everything else in material existence.

The Prophet ﷺ said, "That light turned in the midst of His Power for as long as He wished."

Allāh caused that light to turn (*yadurr*) around the Essence of the Divine Attribute of Power—Allāh's Ocean of Power—just as people circumambulate around the Ka'ba, and just as electrons turn around the nucleus of the atom.

When something turns, it generates energy, just as a generator produces electricity when it is turned by the turbine in a hydroelectric plant. As the light of the Prophet ﷺ was turning in the Divine Presence of the Attribute of Power, *bahr al-qudra*, it was accumulating more and more energy. At some point the Light of the Prophet ﷺ was overwhelmed by the immense energy accumulated upon it—to the point that it was essential the energy be released. When the accumulated energy could no longer be contained, Allāh ﷻ ordered it to explode in what is known as the Big Bang.

The expansion of that light and energy of the Big Bang continues even now. And therefore the Prophet Muhammad ﷺ is the center of light. Allāh ﷻ created the light of the Prophet ﷺ, and endowed him with vast energy from

---

[39] 'Abd al-Razzāq (d. 211) narrates it in his *Musannaf*. Bayhaqī (d. 458) narrates it with a different wording in *Dalā'il al-nubūwwa* according to Zurqāni in his *Sharh al-mawāhib* (1:56 of the *Matbā'a al-'amira* in Cairo) and Diyārbakrī in *Tārīkh al-khāmis* (1:20).

[40] In fact, physicists admit that they have no idea what existed before the Big Bang, and most would say that it is a meaningless question in terms of physics because it cannot be deduced from observable phenomena. Some say there were "random fluctuations in the void," and others say there may have been a previous universe which ended in a Big Crunch (opposite of the Big Bang), which then re-exploded to form the current one.

His Ocean of Power. It was through the explosion of that energy that everything in this universe came into existence—all through the agency of the Prophet ﷺ.[41]

If the essence of all creation comes from the Divine Light, then all existence is the result of the Mercy of Allāh ﷻ. Indeed, this follows as a matter of logical necessity because there is no grantor of mercy (*rahmān*) except there also exists a *marhūm*—something which receives mercy. In short, nothing that exists escapes being an object of Divine Mercy. Mercy is the ocean in which all creation swims.

The Ocean of Power is from the Essence—no one knows the reality of this, not even the Prophet ﷺ. This, of course, is the meaning of, *Allāhu waḥdahu lā sharīka lah*—Allāh is One with no partner and,

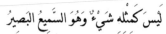

There is nothing whatever like unto Him, and He is the One that hears and sees (all things), (ash-Shūra 42:11)

and,

سُبْحَانَ اللهِ عَمَّا يَصِفُونَ

Glory to Allah. (He is free) from the (sort of) things they attribute to Him!

(al-Muminūn 23:91)

---

[41] Today's physicists agree that Einstein's Special Theory of Relativity, $E=mc^2$ makes light, or its more general form electromagnetic energy, the cornerstone of the universe. Author Lee Baumann says, "…it appears that light has been positioned as the cornerstone of modern physics and natural law." Amit Goswami, author and professor of physics at the University of Oregon concludes in his book *The Self-Aware Universe*, "Light is the only reality." Physicist and author Gerald Schroeder, in noting that one of light's principle characteristics, one in fact quite confounding to even physicists, is that light exists outside of time, says, "Einstein showed us, in the flow of light, the corollary of the Eternal Now: I was, I am, I will be."
To examine the latter concept in depth, consider a particle of light, called a photon. Once it is created, this massless particle travels at the speed of light (299,792 kilometers per second), detemined by Einstein's Theory of Special Relativity to be both the "speed limit" of the universe and a constant—an aspect of light which stills defies imagination. Einstein explained that as an object increases in speed its length in the direction of motion shrinks, its mass increases and time slows. If an object actually reaches lightspeed, distance no longer exists and time stops, and this can only be achieved by a massless particle such as the photon (a corollary of this is that a massless particle always travels at lightspeed and can never go slower). From these fundamental qualities, physicists have determined that light consists of unlimited energy. Lee Baumann states in *God at the Speed of Light*, "One ramification of this is that when physicists attempted to calculate energy calculations of electrons and atoms, the resulting sums were infinite. Based on Einstein's equation , $E=mc^2$ this means the masses of nuclear particles are infinite! Such paradoxes in physics have been "worked around" by mathematical trickery, but remain as stumbling blocks to the limited capacity of the human intellect to grasp the essential nature of physical creation.

Here Allāh 🕮 names the Divine Essence. Allāh 🕮 revealed what He wished of the knowledge of His Attributes, Names and Acts to the Prophet 🕮, but knowledge of His Absolute Essence He did not show to anyone. Thus, He says, *"there is nothing whatever like unto Him, and He is the One that hears and sees (all things),"* asserting the unknowability of His Essence but at the same time affirming His Attributes, some of which knowledge of Himself He, in His Bounty, revealed to humankind through the agency of His Prophet 🕮.

To delve into the spiritual understanding of the Big Bang is to penetrate something of the Muhammadan Reality 🕮. In issuing the command, *"Kun!"* Allāh was giving form to a sound, the very vibrations of which constituted the Prophet 🕮. It is the Divine Speech emanating from Essence to Existence or Reality. Existence, in turn, has been formed from the very Reality that instantiates physical being. The creation of the Muhammadan Reality took place even before the creation of the angels and the reality of that event is something that remains in Allāh's knowledge. Yet at that station of reality, all prophets took up their inheritance.[42] For according to the hadith transmitted on the authority of Ibn 'Abbās, the Muhammadan Reality goes from prophet to prophet (*min nabiyyin ila nabiyyin*) until the moment when Allāh 🕮 causes it to emerge (*akhraja*) as the historical Prophet Muhammad.[43]

In explaining this tremendous aspect of our beloved Prophet Muhammad 🕮, Shaykh 'Abd al-Qādir Jilānī, (d. 561) in his book *Sirr al-asrār fī mā yahtāju ilayh al-abrār* said:

> Know that since Allāh first created the soul of Muhammad 🕮 from the light of His beauty, as He said: I created Muhammad from the light of My Face, and as the Prophet said: The first thing Allāh created is my soul, and the first thing Allāh created is the Pen, and the first thing Allāh created is the Intellect - what is meant by all this is one and the same thing, and that is the *haqīqa muhammadiyya*. However, it was named a light because it is completely purified from darkness, as Allāh said, *"There has come to you from Allāh a Light and a manifest Book."* It was also named an intellect because it is the cause for the transmission of knowledge, and the pen is its medium in the world of letters. The Muhammadan soul (*al-rūh al-*

---

[42]

Behold! Allāh took the covenant of the prophets, saying: "I give you a Book and Wisdom; then comes to you an apostle, confirming what is with you; do ye believe in him and render him help." Allāh said: "Do ye agree, and take this my Covenant as binding on you?" They said: "We agree." He said: "Then bear witness, and I am with you among the witnesses." (āl-'Imrān 3:81)

[43] See Ibn Sa'd *Tabaqāt* (Leiden: 1909) voll. I/1, page 96; Cf. Tabarī, *Tafsīr*, (Cairo: 1323 AH) vol. xxi, page 79.

muhammadiyya) is therefore the quintessence of all created things and the first of them and their origin, as the Prophet said: I am from Allāh and the believers are from me, and Allāh created all souls from me in the spiritual world and He did so in the best form. It is the name of the totality of mankind in that primordial world, and after its creation by four thousand years, Allāh created the Throne from the light of Muhammad himself, and from it the rest of creation.[44]

However, what Allāh created and gave to the Prophet ﷺ at that time no one knows. He said:

اللهُ نُورُ السَّمَاوَاتِ وَالأَرْضِ مَثَلُ نُورِهِ كَمِشْكَاةٍ فِيهَا مِصْبَاحٌ الْمِصْبَاحُ فِي زُجَاجَةٍ الزُّجَاجَةُ
كَأَنَّهَا كَوْكَبٌ دُرِّيٌّ يُوقَدُ مِن شَجَرَةٍ مُّبَارَكَةٍ زَيْتُونَةٍ لا شَرْقِيَّةٍ وَلا غَرْبِيَّةٍ يَكَادُ زَيْتُهَا يُضِيءُ وَلَوْ
لَمْ تَمْسَسْهُ نَارٌ نُّورٌ عَلَى نُورٍ يَهْدِي اللهُ لِنُورِهِ مَن يَشَاءُ وَيَضْرِبُ اللهُ الأَمْثَالَ لِلنَّاسِ وَاللهُ بِكُلِّ
شَيْءٍ عَلِيمٌ

Allah is the Light of the heavens and the earth. The similitude of His light is as a niche wherein is a lamp. The lamp is in a glass. The glass is as it were a shining star. (This lamp is) kindled from a blessed tree, an olive neither of the East nor of the West, whose oil would almost glow forth (of itself) though no fire touched it. Light upon light. Allah guideth unto His light whom He will. And Allah speaketh to mankind in allegories, for Allah is Knower of all things. (an-Nūr 24: 35)

"*Allah is the light of the heavens and the earth,*" means He is the Creator of everything other than Himself. Whatever is other than Allāh is called *mā siwa-Allāh*. Allāh created everything: the Pen, heavens, earth, paradise, angels, universes, galaxies, stars, planets and the smallest objects. "*And the similitude to His light,*" is given by Allāh as an example for us to understand as, "*a niche wherein is a lamp.*" *Mishkāt* is usually translated as niche, but in fact it is a bundle like those in which garlic comes, tied together. "*Mathalu nūrihi ka mishkātin,*" can be translated, "*the example of His light is like a bundle.*" Within the bundle there is a *misbāh*. Misbāh comes from *sabah*, meaning an instrument that produces light, as in His saying to the Prophet Lūt ﷺ:

أَلَيْسَ الصُّبْحُ بِقَرِيبٍ

Is not the light of dawn near? (Hūd 11:81)

---

[44] p. 12-14 of the Lahore edition. This book has now been translated by Shaykh Tosun Bayrak al-Jerrahi as *The Secret of Secrets* (Cambridge: Islamic Texts Society, 1994).

K'ab al-Āhbar ⬥ makes the entire verse refer to Muhammad ⬥—it is a metaphor of the light of Muhammad. The Messenger of Allāh ⬥ is the niche, the lamp is prophethood, the glass is his heart, the blessed tree is the revelation and the angels who brought it, the oil are the proofs and evidence which contain the revelation.[45]

True scholars and *awliyā'* say that this verse refers to the Prophet ⬥. 'Alī al-Qārī in commenting upon the Prophet's title:

a Lamp spreading Light, (al-Ahzāb 33:46)

Muhammad... is a tremendous light and the source of all lights, he is also a book that gathers up and makes clear all the secrets... *sirājan munīran* means a luminous sun, because of His saying:

تَبَارَكَ الَّذِي جَعَلَ فِي السَّمَاءِ بُرُوجاً وَجَعَلَ فِيهَا سِرَاجاً وَقَمَراً مُنِيراً

He hath placed therein a great lamp and a moon giving light
(al-Furqān 25:61).

There is in this verse an indication that the sun is the highest of the material lights and that other lights are outpourings from it: similarly the Prophet is the highest of the spiritual lights and other lights are derived from him by virtue of his mediating connection and pivotal rank in the overall sphere of creation. This is also inferred from the tradition, "The first thing Allāh created is my light."[46]

Allāh is giving an example of His Light—not of His Essence. Allāh here is not describing Himself; for nothing can describe His Essence. Rather, He is describing one of His Attributes—*an-Nūr*—a name that reveals His Light. Here the light of the Prophet ⬥, which was the source of the Big Bang, the source of the light of the heavens and earth, is compared to a lighted bundle holding an instrument that gives light and that light is the Prophet ⬥. "*The lamp is in a glass.*" That light is contained inside the form of glass. "*The glass is as it were a shining star.*" That is not ordinary glass. Rather it is like a star created from *ad-durr,* a very expensive gem, or *lu'lu',* which is a type of pearl. This description is used to accentuate the greatness of that light. He said, "*the lamp is in a glass,*" the lamp is shining in the glass, and "*the glass is as it were a shining star.*" It means that the light within has not yet emerged. Still, that reality of the Prophet, the *haqīqat al-*

---

[45] Al-Qurtubī: *Jam' li-ahkām al-qur'ān*
[46] *Sharh al-shifā'* (1:505).

Muhammadiyya, illumined, pearl-like, a veritable constellation glowing, "*as if it were a shining star*" remains within. That light of the Prophet ﷺ is the light of *Muhammadun rasūlullāh*. That is *al-haqīqat ul-Muhammadiyya*, the Muhammadan Reality, whose internal character signifies that it reflects the Heart of the Essence, since the Prophet's heart moves without restriction in the orbit of the ninety-nine Names and Attributes. He has been blessed by being adorned by the ninety-nine Names inside of which is a glowing pearl not yet come forth. So the Muhammadan Reality has never appeared—it is still hidden and it is not emerging. But what is manifested in this life is *Muhammadun rasūlullāh*.

Thus *Lā ilāha ill-Allāh* in the testimony of faith, represents the Creator and *Muhammadun rasūlullāh* symbolizes the entirety of creation.

The *kāf* in *kun* of Allāh's Order represents *Lā ilāha ill-Allāh* and the *nūn* represents *Muhammadun rasūlullāh* in Allāh's Order which lies between the *kāf* and the *nūn*. Allāh's Order for creation proceeded from the Divine Essence and resulted in the creation of the Muhammadan Reality. Allāh is the One who caused it to expand in the way that He liked. Thus the Prophet's light exists in everything for which Allāh ﷺ said:

$$وَاعْلَمُوا أَنَّ فِيكُمْ رَسُولَ اللهِ$$

And know that within you is Allāh's Messenger. (al-Hujurāt 49:7)

Al-Khāṭib Abū al-Rabʿi Muhammad ibn al-Layth in his book *Shifā' al-sudūr* says:

> The first thing Allāh created is the light of Muhammad ﷺ and that light came and prostrated before Allāh. Allāh divided it into four parts and created from the first part the Throne, from the second the Pen, from the third the Tablet, and then similarly He subdivided the fourth part into parts and created the rest of creation. Therefore the light of the Throne is from the light of the Prophet ﷺ, the light of the Pen is from the light of the Prophet ﷺ, the light of the Tablet is from the light of the Prophet ﷺ, the light of day, the light of knowledge, the light of the sun and the moon, and the light of vision and sight are all from the light of the Prophet ﷺ.[47]

$$عن ابن عباس: إنَّ قريشا (في بعض النسخ: روحه يعني الرسول صلى الله عليه) كانت نورا بين يدي الله تعالى قبل ان يخلق آدم بألفي عام. يسبّح ذلك النور، و تسبّح الملائكة بتسبيحه، فلما خلق الله آدم ألقى ذلك النور في صلبه (ابن أبي عمر العدني في مسنده)$$

<hr>

[47] Cited in Ibn al-Hajj al-Abdarī's (Muhammad ibn Muhammad d. 736) book *al-Madkhal* from 2:34 of the edition published by Dar al-kitāb al-ʿarabī, Beirut.

Ibn 'Abbās ⸙ said:

> Verily the spirit of the Prophet ﷺ was a light in front of Allāh two thousand years before he created Adam. That light glorified Him and the angels joined in its glorification. When Allāh created Adam, he cast that light into his loins.[48]

'Alī ibn al-Husayn ⸙ related from his father, who related from his grandfather said that the Prophet ﷺ said:

> I was a light in front of my Lord for fourteen thousand years before He created Adam.[49]

It is this light, which was sent to this earth, which became manifest when the Prophet was born.

Al-Qurtubī says:

> *"Kindled from a blessed tree, an olive,"* can be taken to refer to the Prophets, in which case Adam would be the blessed tree, or Ibrahim because Allāh called him "blessed."

It is that blessed familial tree from which its most blessed fruit, our master Prophet Muhammad ﷺ was born.

Imām as-Suyūtī said in *al-Riyād al-aniqa*:

> Ibn Jubayr ⸙ and K'ab al-Āhbar ⸙ said, "What is meant by the second light [in *"light upon light"*] is the Prophet ﷺ because he is the Messenger and the Expositor and the Conveyor from Allāh of what is enlightening and manifest." K'ab, referring to *"whose oil would almost glow forth (of itself) though no fire touched it"* said, "Its oil well nigh would shine because the Prophet well nigh would be known to the people even if he did not say that he was a Prophet, just as that oil would send forth light without a fire."

In that regard the Prophet ﷺ said, "The night I was delivered my mother saw a light that lit the castles of Damascus so that she could see them."[50]

---

[48] Suyūtī said in *Manāhil al-safa* (p. 53 #128): "Ibn Abi 'Umar al-'Adanī relates it in his *Musnad*." In *Takhrīj ahādīth sharh al-mawāqif* (p. 32 #12) Suyūtī cites it with the wording: "The Quraysh were a light in front of Allāh."

[49] Something similar is narrated by Imām Āhmad in his *Fadā'il al-sahāba* (2:663 #1130), Dhahabī in *Mīzān al-i'tidāl* (1:235), and al-Tabarī in *al-Riyād al-nādira* (2:164, 3:154).

[50] Narrated by al-Hākim in his *Mustadrak* (2:616-617), Āhmad in his *Musnad* (4:184), and Bayhaqī in *Dalā'il al-nubūwwa* (1:110, 2:8). Ibn al-Jawzī cites it in *al-Wafā'* (p. 91, ch. 21 of Bidāyat nabīyyina sall-Allāhu 'alayhi wa sallam), and Ibn Kathīr in *Mawlid rasūl Allāh* and his *Tafsīr* (4:360). Haythamī cites it in *Majma' al-zawā'id* (8:221) and said Tabarānī and Āhmad narrated it, and Āhmad's chain is fair *(hasan)*. See for Āhmad's complete text *Bishāratu 'Isā* (#454).

The light of the Prophet ﷺ is the source of the light of all believers, for while all things were created from his light, the believers were created in a special way. Al-Qurtubī relates in *Jam' li-ahkām al-qur'ān* from Anas ؓ who said that the Prophet ﷺ said:

> Allāh created me from light and He created Abū Bakr from my light, and He created 'Umar and 'A'isha from the light of Abū Bakr, and He created the male believers of my community from the light of 'Umar and He created the female believers of my community from the light of 'A'isha, Whoever does not love me or love Abū Bakr, 'Umar and 'A'isha has no light.

This hadith explains the tremendous love the Prophet ﷺ bore towards Abū Bakr as-Siddīq ؓ, who was his sole companion when he migrated from Makkah to Madīnah and who was his companion in the cave, for which Allāh revealed:

$$ إِلَّا تَنصُرُوهُ فَقَدْ نَصَرَهُ اللَّهُ إِذْ أَخْرَجَهُ الَّذِينَ كَفَرُوا ثَانِيَ اثْنَيْنِ إِذْ هُمَا فِي الْغَارِ إِذْ يَقُولُ لِصَاحِبِهِ لَا تَحْزَنْ إِنَّ اللَّهَ مَعَنَا $$

If ye help not (your leader), (it is no matter): for Allah did indeed help him, when the Unbelievers drove him out: he had no more than one companion; they two were in the cave, and he said to his companion, "Have no fear, for Allah is with us." (at-Tawbah 9:40)

This magnificent reality applies to those who have no blood relation with the Prophet ﷺ but indicates how close the believers are to him by virtue of their love for him. Through these hadith, the Prophet ﷺ demonstrated his love for those with whom he had no blood connection, but whom he loved for their link to him through spirituality, their piety and their sincerity towards God.

On the other side, in the station of self-sacrifice, was the Prophet's son-in-law to be, and future father of his grandchildren, Sayyidinā 'Alī ؓ. For during the migration from Makkah, when the unbelievers were conspiring to kill the Prophet, Sayyidinā 'Alī ؓ took the Prophet's place in his bed. Sayyidinā 'Alī ؓ willingly accepted to lie down in the Prophet's place—expecting to be killed by the ferocious Quraysh. This spirit of sacrifice was expressed repeatedly by the Family of the Prophet ﷺ throughout the life of the nation (Ummah), up to the present day; for their love of the Prophet ﷺ they bore unfathomable burdens by means of which the Community was relieved, protected and preserved.

And Allāh said in regard to the family of the Prophet ﷺ:

قُل لا أَسْأَلُكُمْ عَلَيْهِ أَجْراً إِلا الْمَوَدَّةَ فِي الْقُرْبَى

Say: I do not ask of you any reward for it but love for my near relatives;

(ash-Shūrā 42:23)

This shows the two sides of love of the Prophet ﷺ—on the one hand love for his family, and on the other hand love for the Ummah, in particular the sincere, guided and perfected ones who hold fast to the Sunnah.

In respect of the first love, the Prophet ﷺ said, "I have left among you two matters by holding fast to which, you shall never be misguided: Allāh's Book and the Sunnah of His Prophet."[51] Another version adds: "And these two shall never part ways until they show up at the Pond."[52]

حدثنا ابن نمير حدثنا عبد الملك بن أبي سليمان عن عطية العوفي عن أبي سعيد الخدري قال
قال رسول الله صلى الله عليه وسلم إني قد تركت فيكم ما إن أخذتم به لن تضلوا بعدي الثقلين
أحدهما أكبر من الآخر كتاب الله حبل ممدود من السماء إلى الأرض وعترتي أهل بيتي ألا وإنهما لن
يفترقا حتى يردا علي الحوض

Other versions state:

> I am leaving among you that which if you hold to it, you shall
> never go astray, one of them greater than the other: Allāh's
> Book—a rope extended down from the heaven to the
> earth—and my mantle (*'itra*), the People of my House. These
> two shall never part ways until they come to me at the Pond.
> Look well to how you act with them after me.[53]

The five mentioned here are known as *Āhl al-'abā'a*, for Jibrīl covered them

---

[51] Narrated from Ibn 'Abbās by al-Bayhaqī in *al-Sunan al-kubrā* (10:114 #20108) and—as part of a longer hadith—by al-Hākim (1:93=1990 ed. 1:171) who declared it *sahīh* and—without chain—by Mālik in his *Muwatta'*.
[52] Narrated from Abū Hurayra by al-Hākim (1:93=1990 ed. 1:172) and al-Bayhaqī in *al-Madkhal*.
[53] Narrated from Zayd ibn Arqam by al-*Tirmidhī* (*hasan gharīb*) and al-Hākim (3:148), the latter with a sound chain as confirmed by al-Dhahabī, but without the last sentence and the words "my mantle"; from Abu Sa'īd al-Khudrī by al-*Tirmidhī* (*hasan gharīb*) and Āhmad with weak chains because of 'Atīyya ibn Sa'd al-Awfī; and from Zayd ibn Thābit by Āhmad and al-Tabarānī in *al-Kabīr* (5:153) with chains containing al-Qāsim ibn Hassan who is passable (*maqbūl*) and not trustworthy, contrary to al-Haythamī's claim in *Majma' al-zawā'id* (1:170). The latter version states: "I am leaving among you two successors (*khalīfatayn*)..." Also narrated from Zayd ibn Arqam by al-Nasā'ī in *al-Sunan al-kubra* (5:45, 5:130) with the wording: "I am leaving among you the two weighty matters..."
Another version states that Jābir ibn 'Abd Allāh said:
> I saw Allāh's Messenger in his Pilgrimage on the Day of 'Arafāt as he was
> mounted on his camel al-Qaswā' addressing the people and I heard him say,
> "O people! I have left among you that which if you hold to it you shall never go
> astray: Allāh's Book and my mantle (*'itra*), the People of my House."
Narrated by al-*Tirmidhī* (*hasan gharīb*) with a weak chain because of Zayd ibn al-Hasan al-Qurashī.

with the cloak (*'abā'a*) of the Prophet, and they were given importance as *Āhl al-Bayt* in two incidents mentioned in the Qur'ān:

حدثنا قتيبة بن سعيد حدثنا حاتم بن إسماعيل عن بكير بن مسمار عن عامر بن سعد عن أبيه

قال

سمعت رسول الله صلى الله عليه وسلم يقول له وخلفه في بعض مغازيه فقال علي أتخلفني مع النساء والصبيان قال يا علي أما ترضى أن تكون مني بمنزلة هارون من موسى إلا أنه لا نبوة بعدي وسمعته يقول يوم خيبر لأعطين الراية رجلا يحب الله ورسوله ويحبه الله ورسوله فتطاولنا لها فقال ادعوا لي عليا فأتي به أرمد فبصق في عينه ودفع الراية إليه ففتح الله عليه ولما نزلت هذه الآية نَدْعُ أَبْنَاءَنَا وَأَبْنَاءَكُمْ دعا رسول الله صلى الله عليه وسلم عليا وفاطمة وحسنا وحسينا فقال اللهم هؤلاء أهلي (مسند أحمد)

'Amir bin Sa'd bin Abī Waqqās reported on the authority of his father that Mu'awīya bin Abī Sufyān appointed Sa'd as the governor and said: "What prevents you from abusing Abū Turāb ('Alī)?" At this he said: "It is because of three things which I remember Allah's Messenger 🕮 having said about him that I would not abuse him and even if I find one of those three things for me, it would be more dear to me than the red camels. ...(The third occasion is) when the (following) verse was revealed: *Let us summon our children and your children.* Allāh's Messenger 🕮 called 'Alī, Fātima, Hasan and Husain and said: O Allāh, they are my family.[54]

It is established that when the verse of mutual invocation of curses (*mubāhala*) was revealed:

فَمَنْ حَاجَّكَ فِيهِ مِنْ بَعْدِ مَا جَاءَكَ مِنَ الْعِلْمِ فَقُلْ تَعَالَوْا نَدْعُ أَبْنَاءَنَا وَأَبْنَاءَكُمْ وَنِسَاءَنَا وَنِسَاءَكُمْ وَأَنْفُسَنَا وَأَنْفُسَكُمْ ثُمَّ نَبْتَهِلْ فَنَجْعَل لَّعْنَةَ اللهِ عَلَى الْكَاذِبِينَ

And whoso disputeth with thee concerning him, after the knowledge which hath come unto thee, say (unto him): Come! We will summon our sons and your sons, and our women and your women, and ourselves and yourselves, then we will pray humbly (to our Lord) and (solemnly) invoke the curse of Allah upon those who lie. (Āl-'Imrān 3:61),

---

[54] *Sahīh Muslim* and another narration in Āhmad's *Musnad*.

the Prophet ﷺ summoned 'Alī, Fāṭima, al-Ḥasan, and al-Ḥusayn, and said: "O Allāh! These are my Family" (*Allāhumā hā'ulā'i Ahlī*).[55]

He repeated this act when the verse of the cleansing of the People of the House was revealed:

$$ إِنَّمَا يُرِيدُ اللَّهُ لِيُذْهِبَ عَنكُمُ الرِّجْسَ أَهْلَ الْبَيْتِ وَيُطَهِّرَكُمْ تَطْهِيرًا ^{56} $$

Allāh only desires to keep away the uncleanness from you, O people of the House! and to purify you a (thorough) purifying, (al-Aḥzāb 33:33)

as mentioned in the following hadith:

قَالَ ابْنُ جَرِيرٍ حَدَّثَنَا ابْنُ الْمُثَنَّى حَدَّثَنَا بَكْرُ بْنُ يَحْيَى بْنِ أَبَانَ الْعَنَزِيُّ حَدَّثَنَا مَنْدَلٌ عَنِ الْأَعْمَشِ عَنْ عَطِيَّةَ عَنْ أَبِي سَعِيدٍ رَضِيَ اللهُ عَنْهُ قَالَ قَالَ رَسُولُ اللهِ صَلَّى اللهُ عَلَيْهِ وَسَلَّمَ نَزَلَتْ هَذِهِ الْآيَةُ فِي خَمْسَةٍ : فِيَّ وَفِي عَلِيٍّ وَحَسَنٍ وَحُسَيْنٍ وَفَاطِمَةَ " إِنَّمَا يُرِيد اللهُ لِيُذْهِبَ عَنكُمُ الرِّجْسَ أَهْلَ الْبَيْتِ وَيُطَهِّرَكُمْ تَطْهِيرًا" قَدْ تَقَدَّمَ أَنَّ فُضَيْلَ بْنَ مَرْزُوقٍ رَوَاهُ عَنْ عَطِيَّةَ عَنْ أَبِي سَعِيدٍ عَنْ أُمِّ سَلَمَةَ رَضِيَ اللهُ عَنْهَا كَمَا تَقَدَّمَ وَرَوَى ابْنُ أَبِي حَاتِمٍ مِنْ حَدِيثِ هَارُونَ بْنِ سَعْدٍ الْعِجْلِيِّ عَنْ عَطِيَّةَ عَنْ أَبِي سَعِيدٍ رَضِيَ اللهُ عَنْهُ مَوْقُوفًا وَاللهُ سُبْحَانَهُ وَتَعَالَى أَعْلَم

Abī Saʿīd ﷺ related that the Prophet ﷺ said:

This verse was revealed regarding five: regarding myself; regarding 'Alī and Ḥassan and Ḥusayn and Fāṭima, *"Allāh only desires to keep away the uncleanness from you, O people of the House! and to purify you a (thorough) purifying."*[57]

Lexically, the term '*itra* was defined as "A man's relatives such as his children, grandchildren, and paternal cousins"[58] while in the context of the present hadiths it was explained to mean "Those of the Prophet's Family who follow his Religion and cling to his commands."[59] What emerges from these meanings together with the two wordings of the hadith "I have left among you two matters" is firm evidence that there is an inseparable connection, until the Last Day, between the Qur'ān, the Sunnah, and the Family of the Prophet.

Know that the light of the Prophet ﷺ is in you, for Allāh said:

$$ وَاعْلَمُوا أَنَّ فِيكُمْ رَسُولَ اللهِ $$

---

[55] Narrated from Saʿd ibn Abī Waqqāṣ by *Muslim, al-Tirmidhī* (*hasan sahīh gharīb*), *al-Ḥākim* and others.
[56] Narrated from Umm Salama by Āḥmad with six chains, *al-Tirmidhī* with several chains (*hasan sahīh*), *al-Ḥākim, al-Ṭabaranī*, and others.
[57] *Mawqūfan* from Abī Saʿīd in Ibn Abī Ḥātim.
[58] *Mu'jam maqayis al-lugha* (4:217).
[59] Al-Taḥāwī, *Sharh mushkil al-athar* (9:88).

. *And know that Allah's Messenger is within you;* (al-Ḥujurāt, 49:7)

Through this verse, and the preceding narrations, we must know that Prophet Muhammad ﷺ was informing us that his light is within every believer; with a particular emphasis on the qualities of perfect character exemplified by Sayyidinā Abū Bakr ﷺ and Sayyidinā 'Umar ﷺ, while those related to the Prophet ﷺ through blood, have the specialty of being from his family, whom Allāh favored in a tremendous way—particularly the descendants of *Ahl al-abā'a*, the children of Sayyidinā 'Alī ﷺ and Sayyida Fāṭima ﷺ. And all will come together with the Prophet ﷺ on the Day of Judgment, meeting at his Pond.

String Network of Matter in the Universe

Fourteen hundred years ago, Allāh ﷻ revealed to Prophet Muhammad ﷺ another verse which describes the universe:

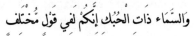

(I swear) by the Sky with its numerous strings, You are certainly at variance with each other (concerning the truth). (adh-Dhāriyāt 51:7-8)

Allāh's mention of strings (*hubuk*)[60] in His mighty oath gives a divine certainty to its reality and importance. He is swearing by the "strings" in the sky, that people are of different opinions about the Prophet ﷺ and the message of Islam that he brought. Previously, Muslim scholars did not fully understand what *hubuk* (strings) referred to, but recent discoveries have shed light on the structure of the universe. Muslims believe with certainty whatever is in the Qur'ān and know that it is the truth. Whatever today's latest understanding is, the theories and discoveries of scientists will culminate in their uncovering the reality and perfect description mentioned fourteen hundred years ago in the Holy Qur'ān.

The Qur'ān mentions the skies (and space) with their strings and consequently knots. With the aid of powerful technology, an understanding of the physical universe has emerged that seems to explain this verse. According to astronomers, the large scale structure of the universe's visible matter follows a filamentous pattern.[61] This web of cosmological strings is evident in both the

---

[60] *Hubuk* are strings or cables. It is derived from the verb root *habaka*: to wind threads into string, spin, weave, knit, tie, tighten, make compact, consolidate, crochet, fasten.

[61] Regarding the large scale structure of the universe Dr. Martin Hendry writes:
    The pattern of ripples which we observe in the Microwave Background radiation provides the seeds of the structure which we see in the universe today. If we measure the positions and distances of galaxies, constructing what cosmologists call a redshift survey, we see that galaxies are not uniformly distributed throughout the universe, but are clustered—arranged in filaments and sheets, the pattern of which tells us a great deal about how such structure formed. …galaxy redshift surveys, revealing clusters, filaments and voids in the galaxy distribution.

Hendry, Martin, 2003. *Dr. Martin Hendry's teaching website* [online]. Publication information is available. Available from World Wide Web:
http://www.astro.gla.ac.uk/users/martin/outreach/lss.html
    Although the clustering of galaxies is now a well-known fact, a complete description of clustering which includes its geometrical features has so far eluded researchers…
    [Models] give rise to the amazing diversity of form, which is characteristic of a highly evolved distribution of matter, and is often referred to as being cellular, filamentary, sheet-like, network-like, sponge-like, a cosmic web etc.
    Most of these descriptions are based either on a visual appearance of large-scale structure… Such distributions display greater connectivity and are sometimes referred to as being network-like.

visible universe and in what astronomers call "dark matter."[62]

It shows not only that the galaxies we see lie within larger dark matter clumps, but that these clumps are connected by "cosmic filaments"—bridges of dark matter that connect the clusters. The existence of these filaments has long been a prediction of the theory of dark matter—that an intricate network of clumps and filaments, the so-called cosmic web, pervades the universe.[63]

Disentangling the Cosmic Web I: Morphology of Isodensity Contours, Schmalzing, Jens; Buchert, Thomas; Melott, Adrian L ; Sahni, Varun; Sathyaprakash, B S ; Shandarin, Sergei F, Astrophys.J. 526 [1999] 568-578.

[62] Regarding dark matter filaments Alan Boyle says:

>...scientists are converging on a consistent view of the basics: a lightweight, accelerating cosmos that's 12 billion to 15 billion years old, dominated by a mysterious "dark energy."

Boyle, Alan. 2003. *A Younger, Lighter Stranger Cosmos* [online]. Publication information is available. Available from World Wide Web: msnbc.com [Technology and Science Space News]. Also:

>Scientists say most of the matter in the universe can't be seen directly. But an international research team is stripping away that cloak of invisibility: The researchers have used an ultrasensitive telescope and heavy-duty computing to chart dark matter's wide-scale effect for the first time.
>The whole point about dark matter is that although it can't be seen, it has a gravitational effect on things we can see. Unless dark matter exists, physicists can't explain why galaxies whirl the way they do or why galaxy clusters stick together.
>The density of dark matter also is a key part of the equations that describe how the universe evolved over billions of years and what might happen to the universe billions of years from now. Thus, determining how much dark matter exists—and what it's made of—are among the most fundamental questions facing astrophysicists. It could be masses of ordinary matter that for some reason doesn't give off light or an exotic type of matter that hasn't yet been detected.
>The first challenge is to figure out where the dark matter is...
>Cosmic cobwebs of dark matter have been detected before on the level of galaxies or even galaxy clusters.
>[A technique of] visualization of a section of sky highlights reddish webs of dark matter, which cannot be observed directly. Instead, the webs are "seen" through their gravitational effect on the light from distant galaxies... [This is] the first effort to detect the gravitational lensing effect for the universe's large-scale structure—that is, the huge filaments of dark matter which are produced after the Big Bang ... the first condensations of matter produced by gravity. ...these filamentary dark matter systems are the witness of the history of the universe...
>So far, the team's findings are consistent with measurements of dark matter conducted by other means, he said: The universe's matter density (known in astrospeak as "omega") seems to be about 35 percent of what would be required for cosmic equilibrium, with a mysterious factor apparently making up the difference. Physicists have given that factor the label of 'dark energy' or the 'cosmological constant'—but the bottom line is that they still don't understand what it is.

Boyle, Alan. 2003. *Astronomers visualize dark matter* [online]. Publication information is available. Available from World Wide Web: msnbc.com [Technology and Science Space News].

[63] The results have been published in the Astrophysical Journal and presented at the UK National Astronomy Meeting in Bristol. The research was performed by Dr. Andrew Taylor of the Royal Observatory, Edinburgh, UK, and Dr. Meghan Gray.

The "Big Bang" happened with all pieces of the universe blasting away from a colossal explosion at tremendous speeds. Somehow all these particles were stopped and held in place, becoming precisely ordered planets and galaxies. Allāh ﷻ caused the contents of the universe to be ordered by a network of strings woven together like a net keeping all the heavenly bodies in their assigned positions.[64]

---

[64] Regarding the formation of structure in the universe NASA says:

The Big Bang is the best theory we have about the origin of the Universe, but this theory is far from complete. For example, in its simplest form, the theory does not explain the origin of the magnificent hierarchy of stars, galaxies, and clusters of galaxies formed from the fiery detritus of that initial spark. Yet clearly the Universe has patches of galaxies and voids of seemingly empty space. How can we account for this?

Cosmologists, who study the origin and evolution of the Universe, hope to augment Big Bang theory to account for the large-scale structure we clearly see today. There are several ideas on the drawing board that work within Big Bang theory to account for the formation of galaxies and other structures. The most popular and best developed idea is called **inflation**: it postulates that the early universe underwent a period of super-rapid expansion that "inflated" an atomic scale piece of the universe to scales larger than the visible universe in a fraction of a second.

Different ideas about how structure first formed—inflation, topological defects, and others—make very specific predictions about the size and location of temperature differences in the Cosmic Microwave Background (CMB). Temperature differences seen today from region to region across the sky point back to the density differences in the early Universe; slightly denser regions then appear as slightly warmer regions now in the CMB. Upon measuring the CMB to the utmost precision, MAP can compare its survey results to these predictions to see which idea is correct. MAP will study the slightest of density differences when the Universe was a thousandth of its current size, about 400,000 years after the Big Bang. Matter and radiation was relatively evenly distributed then, but certain regions had slightly higher or lower densities compared to others. The seeds of structure were thus planted in the earliest moments of the Universe.

The prevailing idea of how structure formed is that density differences appeared and gravity took over. In a classic case of "the rich get richer," regions with slightly higher densities had the gravitational potential to attract more matter, making them denser yet. The region of space that contains our Milky Way galaxy, for example, was only about 0.5% denser than neighboring regions 400,000 years after the Big Bang. About 15 million years later, the present-day Milky Way region was about 5% denser than surrounding regions. (Mind you, our Galaxy still wasn't formed at this point.) A billion years after this, though, our region was about twice as dense as neighboring regions. Cosmologists speculate that the inner part of the Milky Way galaxy began forming at this time.

Structure takes time, as you can imagine. The popular "cold dark matter" theory predicts that exotic dark matter (of a yet unknown and undetectable nature) and a little bit of normal matter (the stuff that the stars and ourselves are made of) clumped together to form long filaments, which were scattered across the Universe creating a web. This was the very first structure. The filaments were a result of millions of years of gravity carving out denser regions of space, leaving voids in its wake. Hydrogen was the predominant gas along these filaments. Hundreds of millions of years went by. Pockets of hydrogen condensed, and galaxies started forming along the filaments like beads on a

꡶ꑰꑯꛍ

string. Stars formed along with galaxies. Where filaments intersected, galaxy clusters arose.
2003. *Formation of Structure in the Universe* [online]. Publication information is available. Available from World Wide Web: http://imagine.gsfc.nasa.gov/docs/features/exhibit/map_structure.html. Energy Astrophysics Science Archive Research Center at NASA's Goddard Space Flight Center.
Explaining the extreme rapidity of the "inflation" of the universe immediately after the Big Bang, which then essentially came to a near "stop" in its current condition, renowned physicist Steven Hawking says:

> The inflation that seems to have occurred in the early unverse ...[involved] an increase in size by a factor of at a least a million million million million million times in a tiny fraction of a second.

Hawking, Steven, *Black Holes and Baby Universes and Other Essays*, New York, Bantam, 1993, p. 96-97.

String Theory and the Ten-Dimensional Universe

In addition to this cosmic web of filaments there is another way that strings are a part of the universe. String theory has come into prominence as a unifying theory of matter in the universe: from large planets to sub-atomic particles. Previously, physicists could not reconcile cosmic physics (dealing with the theory of general relativity and the force of gravity) with quantum physics (dealing with the other three known forces: electromagnetism, strong nuclear forces, and weak nuclear forces). These two theories of macro and micro-physics only worked in their own respective realms and were not compatible with each other.

String theory reconciles these differences and holds that sub-atomic particles are vibrations, or resonances, of minute strings. The vibrations of the strings are like musical notes of a violin with different strings producing different vibrations, or different notes. As Allāh ﷻ said in the Holy Qur'ān:

وَإِن مِّن شَيْءٍ إِلَّا يُسَبِّحُ بِحَمْدَهِ وَلَكِن لَّا تَفْقَهُونَ تَسْبِيحَهُمْ

There is not a thing but celebrates His praise (al-Isrā' 17:44)

A mathematical necessity of string theory is that the universe consists of ten dimensions. Humans are only aware of three visible dimensions and one invisible dimension, time. However, for string theory to explain all of the four forces[65] there must exist six additional unseen dimensions. Theoretical physicist Dr. Michio Kaku says:

> The curious feature of superstrings, however, is that they can only vibrate in 10 dimensions. This is, in fact, one of the reasons why it can unify the known forces of the universe: in 10 dimensions there is "more room" to accommodate both Einstein's theory of gravity as well as sub-atomic physics. In some sense, previous attempts at unifying the forces of nature failed because a standard four dimensional theory is "too small" to jam all the forces into one mathematical framework.

> To visualize higher dimensions, consider a Japanese tea garden, where carp spend their entire lives swimming on the bottom of a shallow pond. The carp are only vaguely aware of a world beyond the surface. To a carp "scientist," the universe only consists of two dimensions, length and width. There is no such thing as "height." In fact, they are incapable of imagining a third dimension beyond the pond. The word "up"

---

[65] That is, gravity, electromagnetism, strong nuclear forces, and weak nuclear forces.

has no meaning for them. (Imagine their distress if we were to suddenly lift them out of their two dimensional universe into "hyperspace," i.e. our world!)

However, if it rains, then the surface of their pond becomes rippled. Although the third dimension is beyond their comprehension, they can clearly see the waves traveling on the pond's surface. Likewise, although we earthlings cannot "see" these higher dimensions, we can see their ripples when they vibrate. According to this theory, "light" is nothing but vibrations rippling along the 5th dimension. By adding higher dimensions, we can easily accommodate more and more forces, including the nuclear forces. In a nutshell: the more dimensions we have, the more forces we can accommodate.

One persistent criticism of this theory, however, is that we do not see these higher dimensions in the laboratory. At present, every event in the universe, from the tiniest sub-atomic decay to exploding galaxies, can be described by four numbers (length, width, depth, and time), not ten numbers. To answer this criticism, many physicists believe (but cannot yet prove) that the universe at the instant of the Big Bang was in fact fully ten-dimensional. Only after the instant of creation did six of the ten dimensions "curl up" into a ball too tiny to observe. In a real sense, this theory is really a theory of creation, when the full power of ten dimensional space-time was manifest....[66]

Today, many physicists believe that we are the carp swimming in our tiny pond, blissfully unaware of invisible, unseen universes hovering just above us in hyperspace. We spend out life in three spatial dimensions, confident that what we can see with our telescopes is all there is, ignorant of the possibility of 10 dimensional hyperspace. Although these higher dimensions are invisible, their "ripples" can clearly be seen and felt. We call these ripples gravity and light.[67]

Strings and even the ten dimensional universe is represented in the Holy Qur'ān, as Allāh ﷻ said:

"وَالسَّمَاءِ ذَاتِ الْحُبُكِ إِنَّكُمْ لَفِي قَوْلٍ مُخْتَلِفٍ"

---

[66] Kaku, Michio. *Black Holes, Worm Holes and the Tenth Dimension.*
[67] Kaku, Michio. *Hyperspace and a Theory of Everything.*

(I swear) by the Sky with its numerous strings, You are certainly at variance with each other (concerning the truth). (adh-Dhāriyāt 51:7-8)

Allāh ﷻ is giving an oath with an emphasis on the greatness of the strings in the sky. The evidence supporting string theory was largely from researchers examining space and the universe.

Thus, string theory has opened a new understanding that the universe actually consists of ten dimensions, adding six unseen dimensions to our ordinary experience of three seen dimensions and one unseen dimension, time. As with the reference to iron in the Qur'ān, there is a numerologic significance to the verse in *Sūrat al-Dhāriyāt* (51:7). 51 numerologically is represented by adding 5 + 1 to give 6. Combining the numerological value of the *Sūrah*, six, with the number of the verse, seven, gives 13 (6+7=13). Thirteen is represented by 1+3 = 4, the number of the four known dimensions. Also, the fifty-first *Sūrah*, numerologically represented by six, the six new unseen dimensions are referenced. Furthermore, it is mentioned in the seventh verse, a remarkable resonance with the total of seven unseen dimensions: time plus the other six dimensions. Seven represents the heavens as mentioned in the Qur'ān:

$$تُسَبِّحُ لَهُ السَّمَاوَاتُ السَّبْعُ وَالْأَرْضُ وَمَن فِيهِنَّ وَإِن مِّن شَيْءٍ إِلَّا يُسَبِّحُ بِحَمْدِهِ وَلَٰكِن لَّا تَفْقَهُونَ تَسْبِيحَهُمْ إِنَّهُ كَانَ حَلِيمًا غَفُورًا$$

*The seven heavens and the earth, and all beings therein, glorify [Allāh]:
Verify everything in existence is celebrating the praise of its Lord but you
do not comprehend their glorification! Verify He is Most Forbearing, Most
Forgiving!* (al-Isrā 17:44)[68]

Thus the seven heavenly dimensions with the three earthly dimensions yields ten. These are the ten dimensions of string theory: three dimensions of our physical world, time is the fourth dimension, and six as-of-yet unknown dimensions.

The fact that there are ten dimensions is also revealing. The number ten is represented by 1+0 which total 1. This is an indication that the One is important and everything else is zero. One and zero are the only numbers in binary code, the type of code running all the computers in the world. When the computer's silicon particles are energized they go from a state of zero energy to an energized moving state, the "one." Through the invention of the computer and through the ten dimensions Allāh ﷻ is showing His signs that He, the One, is the Reality and everything else is nothing, zero.

---

[68] Of note this verse is 17:44 which numerologically breaks down to 1+7 =8 and 4+4 =8; 8 +8 becomes 16, and 1+6 is seven: "The seven heavens..."

There is a new understanding derived from string theory that black holes are not voids but actually connections to other parts of the universe, what theoretical physicists call "worm holes." While this notion is yet to be proven, there in as eloquent hint of this in Allāh's mention of the strings in the sky.

In a verse noted several times above, Allāh ﷻ says:

$$سَنُرِيهِمْ آيَاتِنَا فِي الْآفَاقِ وَفِي أَنْفُسِهِمْ حَتَّى يَتَبَيَّنَ لَهُمْ أَنَّهُ الْحَقُّ$$

*We will (soon) show them Our signs in the universe and in their own souls,
until it will become manifest to them that it is the truth....* (Fussilat 41:53)

Al-āfāq is literally "the horizons," meaning all skies, i.e. the universe. Allāh ﷻ says He will show **them**, not **you**, to indicate that He will show His signs to non-believers in themselves through their research into the nature of the universe, as a means of bringing them to an acceptance of the message of Islam as the truth.

In *Sūrat al-Dhāriyāt*, Allāh ﷻ gives an oath by the strings in the sky that,

$$إِنَّكُمْ لَفِي قَوْلٍ مُخْتَلِفٍ$$

You are certainly at variance with each other (concerning the truth).

(al-Dhāriyāt 51:8)

Humanity is of different opinions about Prophet Muhammad ﷺ and his message, Islam.

$$يُؤْفَكُ عَنْهُ مَنْ أُفِكَ قُتِلَ الْخَرَّاصُونَ$$

*Through which are deluded (away from the Truth) such as would be
deluded. Cursed are the conjecturers.* (al-Dhāriyāt 51:9-10)

These differences of opinion delude people from the truth, but whoever rejects the Messenger ﷺ is wrong. Allāh ﷻ is not pleased with those conjecturing about the Prophet ﷺ without objectively investigating his message. Fourteen hundred years ago Allāh ﷻ revealed this verse, giving an oath by something that was not known at the time. This should indicate to the modern-day scientists and researchers discovering these realities, the greatness of the Prophet Muhammad ﷺ.

The Prophet ﷺ did not mention these things in his time because what he said was enough for his Companions to come to Islam. This information came to light in its own time, when scientific discoveries of these realities emerge to affirm the Qur'ānic reality. The Prophet ﷺ brought such a complete and perfect message from Allāh ﷻ that the words of the Qur'ān are being validated as true today even by non-Muslim scientists. The Qur'ān is *nātiq*, speaking, always bringing its own proofs. Using their own discoveries, Allāh ﷻ is calling the people of the twenty-first century to Islam. When they find these realities in the Qur'ān, many scientists will accept Islam.

عن تميم الداري قال سمعت رسول الله صلى الله عليه وسلم يقول...ولا يترك الله بيت مدر ولا وبر إلا أدخله الله هذا الدين

> As the Prophet ﷺ said, "Islam will enter every house on earth."[69]

And Allāh said:

وَقُلِ الْحَمْدُ لله سَيُرِيكُمْ آيَاتِه فَتَعْرِفُونَهَا

"And say: Praise be to Allāh, Who will (soon) show you His Signs, so that you shall know them..." (an-Naml 27:93)

✽✾❀✾✽

---

[69] Related by Tamīm ad-Dārī in *Musnad Āhmad*, #16344.

Probability in the Qur'ān

E very soul, behavior, discovery, invention, or aspect of life past, present, and future is mentioned in the Qur'ān.

ولَا رَطْبٍ وَلَا يَابِسٍ إِلَّا فِي كِتَابٍ مُّبِينٍ

(There is) naught of wet or dry but (it is noted) in a clear record.

(al-An'am 6:59)

Allāh ﷻ is saying that everything living (wet) or non-living (dry) is mentioned in the Holy Qur'ān. That is, all scientific discoveries, regarding living or non-living things, are mentioned in the Qur'ān, but not everyone can discern them.

A lawyer cannot make scientific discoveries whereas a scientist can. To make discoveries, a scientist works with theories and tests them through experimentation until they are proven to be a fact, or reality. Because the lay person does not make scientific discoveries, it does not follow that these discoveries or realities do not exist. Rather they simply are not known, or accessible, to him.

To someone living in previous times it would have seemed impossible to think that water was composed of gases, but people now have the knowledge to understand this reality. Not everyone could see that ordinary water is composed of two hydrogen atoms and one oxygen atom, but after its composition was discovered it was known and accepted. In chemical symbolism: $2 H_2 + O_2 \rightarrow 2 H_2O$.

When it is said that everything is in the Qur'ān, this does not mean that everyone reading the Qur'ān will find what is in it. Depending on the reader's level of knowledge and understanding he may be able to identify the appropriate verse on a given subject, just as a scientist can identify a particular element or compound in a sample. However, **everything** is in the Qur'ān regardless of whether one can personally ascertain it or not.

Once a great scholar was asked to define internal knowledge as opposed to external knowledge (*'ilm al-bātin* versus *'ilm adh-dhāhir*). He said:

> Whatever one cannot understand is hidden and seems esoteric but to the one who knows something it is external and plain. Internal knowledge cannot be perceived by some people but to us it is a reality. One may think there are two kinds of knowledge, but in actuality there is no difference between external and internal, it is only a question of perception.

The scientific process is the same. Before something is discovered, people deny its existence but then believe it when it becomes known. Nothing has changed, only the willingness and ability to accept the reality. Therefore, it is better not to say that something does not exist just because one does not yet know about it.

Today's scientists say that there were once different species of huge creatures inhabiting the earth called dinosaurs. If one accepts that in the past dinosaurs lived on earth, then one must also ask, why are they no longer in existence today? Today one no longer sees dinosaurs on earth, so one must wonder what became of them. From an Islamic point of view, their time ended. Allāh ﷻ did away with them, and they became extinct. How Allāh ﷻ took them away is a topic of debate even among scientists.

Some pious Muslim scholars say that dinosaurs were present on earth, and most were extremely vicious. Allāh ﷻ changed their physical characteristics, reducing them in size (al-maskh), as a punishment for their incessant horrific fighting and destruction, and their time ended. Even scientifically speaking from the perspective of probability, this is one possibility as to how they disappeared.

When dinosaurs roamed the earth, they may have thought themselves great and powerful, even though there was a probability that they would all be destroyed and made extinct. Even if the probability was small it still existed for them. Whatever event made them become extinct, eventually occurred. Although they were so magnificent in size and strength, they have now disappeared completely from the face of the earth. After them other species have come, also not expecting to be made extinct, although the probability exists for them to be rendered extinct just as it did for the dinosaurs.

Statistics and probability are empirical sciences, branches of mathematics, based on counting the occurrence of something over time. Zero probability means that there is no possibility whatsoever that something will ever happen. A probability of one means there is absolute certainty that something will definitely take place. For any possible event there is a probability between zero and one that it will occur. Someone can estimate or intelligently predict the probability of an event occurring by examining historical patterns. In the past, a certain event happened so many times which leads to the assumption that this will happen again in the future with a certain probability. This science is used in many areas of practical knowledge: quantum physics, chemistry, thermodynamics, weather, population, and even predicting the stock market. Probability is used for predicting the possibility of events for all things which cannot be precisely predicted by a mathematical formula.

If we want to take a scientific or probabilistic approach to the question of man's life on earth, there is a chance that the human race will end. Dinosaurs also faced a probability of extinction and this came to pass. According to paleontologists, there were five massive extinctions throughout the history of the world. Moreover, biologists fear that as many as half of all living species will become extinct within the next century. A recent report of the United Nations predicts that within thirty years almost a quarter of the world's mammals will be in danger of becoming extinct.[70] If so many species are becoming extinct, who is to say that other mammals like human beings will not also face extinction one day? Using probability and logic we may infer that as dinosaurs and other species have came to an end, so too is there a probability that the human race will one day end.

Clear evidence of human existence on earth dates back to around five thousand to seven thousand years ago, and the oldest evidence of apparent human existence to about fifty thousand years ago. The creatures who existed fifty thousand years ago were different from today's humans, and there are no clearly human relics until the Stone Age five thousand to seven thousand years ago. Where are the relics from the creatures of fifty thousand years ago and why did they disappear so suddenly? Humans have lived on earth for a few thousand years, so our probability of disappearing is much higher than it was for the dinosaurs who survived for millions of years.

There is a distinct possibility that man will someday disappear. With extinction, either man will become nonexistent, as scientists and others believe, or as religions say, people are going to face an accounting. If we become extinct then we will be like others before us, but there is a probability that we will face an evaluation, a judgment. Let us take the two cases: either humankind will become extinct, with its existence finally and completely coming to an end, or humankind will come before the Creator and face an accounting. If these are the only two possibilities then all things being equal, the probability is one half, ($\frac{1}{2}$) or fifty percent that one or the other will take place.

If there is a chance that buying a certain stock would make one fabulously rich then many people would buy it, even if the probability was as low as twenty or thirty percent. At fifty percent people would even be willing to borrow money to take a chance on the stock skyrocketing in value. If people are this calculating and clever for the chance to succeed in a worldly venture in which one might lose or gain, then what about a prospect that is "out of this world." Statistically, given a fifty percent chance of the existence of an afterlife, why is no one investing? Even if one lives to be one hundred years old, it is but the blink of an eye compared to the millions and millions of years the earth has been in existence. Comparing one hundred years to eternity is beyond the mind's grasp. If there is no afterlife, one might say he "lost" one hundred years, but if there is an afterlife his gains are infinite. If the eternal afterlife is a reality (and we as Muslims know that it is), then the small investment of one

---

[70] Global Environment Outlook-3 (Geo-3) report of the United Nations Environment Programme (UNEP), Earthscan Publications Ltd, London, 2002.

hundred years is next to nothing.

There have been many inspired people throughout the ages who said, "We are messengers of the Creator, Allāh 🕮," and who told people what was to come in the future and in the afterlife. In many religious traditions there were prophets and messengers who informed us of a coming evaluation, the Day of Judgment. The chance of so many thousands of prophets from different places all coming with the same message is minute. If they were correct and there is an appraisal to be given, one must prepare oneself for that most crucial examination.

Such a proposition of a coming Judgment and Afterlife is not farfetched. Something much more implausible is wholeheartedly accepted without question by most scientists. Today's scientists hold that via random chance and completely accidental occurrences, monkeys transformed into human beings. Using postulates based on purely haphazard events, they were able to elaborate a complex theory which they consider to be an actual fact, although its foundation is built upon sheer probability. Even if the basis for this theory was feasible, the number of mutations needed to randomly occur in an extremely short period of time is all but impossible. Darwin's original theory has been shredded by subsequent scientific discoveries but has been patched together by its proponents with a sort of blind faith that is ironically more consistent with religious belief than science.

Islam has sparked innumerable advances in the sciences and is not in the least antagonistic to scientific inquiry. In fact, Islam encompasses the knowledge of modern sciences and evidence of such was mentioned in the Qur'ān and by Prophet Muhammad 🕮 in hadiths many centuries before the scientific age. For example, scientists of today believe they invented probability, yet it was mentioned fourteen hundred years ago in the Holy Qur'ān:

$$\text{وَمَا يُدْرِيكَ لَعَلَّ السَّاعَةَ قَرِيبٌ} \dots$$

...And what will make you realize that perhaps the Hour is close at hand?

(ash-Shūra 42:17)

The word used here in the Qur'ān, *La'alla* means "perhaps," indicating a possibility or a probability. In Allāh's 🕮 knowledge, the Hour's timing is known precisely, yet in the perfect eloquence of the Qur'ān, Allāh 🕮 uses "perhaps" here, as if to tell today's scientists, "Even if you don't accept it, there is still a possibility that the Judgment Day will occur and it may be very close." For Allāh 🕮, there is no probability. Probability is an empirical tool used to measure the chance of something taking place for those lacking precise knowledge of a thing. For One who has perfect knowledge of what has passed and what is to come, there is no element of chance for it is already known. Allāh 🕮 is *al-'Alīm*, the Absolute Knower, and thus for Allāh 🕮 all things are known with perfect knowledge, precision and certainty.

اللَّهُ يَعْلَمُ مَا تَحْمِلُ كُلُّ أُنْثَى وَمَا تَغِيضُ الْأَرْحَامُ وَمَا تَزْدَادُ وَكُلُّ شَيْءٍ عِندَهُ بِمِقْدَارٍ

Allāh doth know what every female (womb) doth bear, by how much the wombs fall short (of their time or number) or do exceed. Everything is counted and is encompassed in His knowledge. (ar-Ra'd 13:8)

For those to whom Allāh ﷻ reveals these realities, there is also no probability, for they are acting according to certain knowledge. With certain knowledge from Allāh ﷻ, the probability of an event occurring is "one," definite and certain.

Believers know that when Allāh ﷻ says something it will inevitably come to pass, but for modern intellectuals predictions are based on assumptions, not belief. When Allāh ﷻ informed Nūh ﷺ (Noah) that a flood would be coming and that he should prepare a ship in which to escape, he did so based on faith. Through this well-known story, Allāh ﷻ has created a paradigm for the people of later times, including the skeptics of today. Allāh ﷻ is showing them that even without faith, using empirical analysis, there is a chance that a flood would occur and water would reach the ship Nūh ﷺ built. As if to say, "Let us go along with your system and rules of science and probability. Even though there is no way to imagine that the sea will reach that elevated area, probability states that there is a chance, no matter how miniscule, that rivers or springs might overflow and cause the ship to float." As is well-documented, the flood occurred and Nūh's predictions revealed to him by Allāh ﷻ came true.

Similarly for Mūsā ﷺ (Moses), who obeyed Allāh's ﷻ orders to flee towards the sea from Pharoah and his army. Despite knowing that he and the Children of Israel would be cut off by the sea, he put full faith in Allāh's ﷻ Orders that he and his people would be saved. Viewing it within a scientific, probabilistic paradigm, Allāh ﷻ is again showing here that, "Yes, there is a probability, according to the laws of chance, that the sea would part and create a path of escape for Mūsā ﷺ and his people."

Life will not continue forever. As Nūh ﷺ prepared himself for the day of the flood, so must people prepare themselves for their passing from this life. Here Allāh ﷻ is addressing people using their own intellectual methodology demonstrating that there is a possibility of their destruction taking place. Similarly, there is a probability that a Judgment Day will transpire and people will become accountable for their actions in this life. Even if someone does not believe in Allāh ﷻ, statistical science and the laws of probability hold that there is a chance mankind may be brought for judgment. An unexpected event might occur and bring about the complete destruction of mankind who may then come before Allāh ﷻ to account for their actions. Who can say this is impossible when it is demonstrated frequently on a smaller scale by the action of earthquakes, volcanoes, floods and many other acts of God which take place without warning, taking away people, animals and homes. These occurrences are unpredictable, and as unlikely as they may be for a given person, people take out insurance against all these events, for just the same reason Nūh ﷺ built the Ark, seeking protection and safety. If people have not prepared themselves for that day, there will be no escape from the doom that awaits them.

Another element of probability is found in the sayings and predictions of Prophet Muhammad ﷺ. We will describe many of these in greater detail in this book, but in relation to probability let us look at just one example.

وأن ترى الحفاة العراة العالة رعاء الشاء يتطاولون في البنيان (البُخاري كتاب الإيمان)

One of the signs of the Last Days that the Prophet ﷺ mentioned was:

> You will see the barefoot, naked, destitute bedouin shepherds competing in constructing tall buildings.[71]

If we wish to discuss this scientifically, then the probability for this to occur must be analyzed. The chance that someone fourteen hundred years ago would make such a prediction is very remote and the chance it would actually happen is even less likely. Even one hundred years ago such a prediction would have been rejected outright by scientists. How could it happen that barefooted, naked, primitive shepherds would build tall buildings? Yet the prediction was made long before the last century, when it was an even less likely occurrence. Nonetheless, the Prophet ﷺ predicted this implausible event with certainty, saying "you **will** see," not "you **might** see," and no matter how improbable at one time, this has come to pass, exactly as he foretold.

Believers accept these predictions on face value and simply wait for them to transpire. Believers who doubt that the Judgment is near, or say that it is yet far off, or whose faith in that event is weak, should reconsider their expectations. Muslims must know and evaluate the current situation in light of what the Prophet ﷺ said about the signs of the Last Days. If one supposes that skyscrapers being built by bedouins is one of the signs of the Judgment Day, a sign which just took place, then one must admit that Judgment Day is near. Perhaps the remaining signs will take place very quickly, one after the other. Even the science of probability shows that it might happen and at any time. The law of probability says that anything can happen, but the chance of its happening is measured in terms of occurrences within a period of time; if not once in a hundred years, then once in a thousand years, or once in a million years. All people must take heed, and prepare for that Day. The existence of

---

[71] *Sahīh Bukhārī*, "Kitāb al-Īmān."

even the smallest probability that it will occur should be enough to make us take care for the future.

PREDICTIONS

SIGNS OF THE APPROACH OF THE LAST DAYS

Bedouins Compete in Constructing Tall Buildings

In the famous hadith of Jibrīl ﷺ, 'Umar Ibn al-Khattāb ﷺ related that Archangel Jibrīl ﷺ (Gabriel) came to Prophet Muhammad ﷺ and asked him to define Islām, Īmān, and Ihsān.

أخبرنا إسحاق بن إبراهيم قال: حدثنا النضر بن شميل قال: أخبرنا كهمس بن الحسن قال: حدثنا عبد الله بن بريدة عن يحيى بن يعمر، أن عبد الله بن عمر قال: حدثني عمر بن الخطاب قال: بينما نحن عند رسول الله صلى الله عليه وسلم ذات يوم إذ طلع علينا رجل شديد بياض الثياب شديد سواد الشعر، لا يرى عليه أثر السفر، ولا يعرفه منا أحد، حتى جلس إلى رسول الله صلى الله عليه وسلم فأسند ركبتيه إلى ركبتيه ووضع كفيه على فخذيه، ثم قال: يا محمد، أخبرني عن الإسلام، قال: أن تشهد أن لا إله إلا الله وأن محمدا رسول الله، وتقيم الصلاة، وتؤتي الزكاة، وتصوم رمضان، وتحج البيت إن استطعت إليه سبيلا. قال: صدقت، فعجبنا إليه، سأله وبصدقه، ثم قال: أخبرني عن الإيمان، قال: أن تؤمن بالله وملائكته وكتبه ورسله واليوم الآخر والقدر كله خيره وشره. قال: صدقت. قال: فأخبرني عن الإحسان، قال: أن تعبد الله كأنك تراه، فإن لم تكن تراه فإنه يراك (البخاري كتاب الإيمان)

In reply to these questions, the Prophet ﷺ replied:

> Islam is to bear witness that there is no god but Allāh and Muhammad is Allāh's Messenger, prayer, zakāt (charity), fasting in Ramadan, and Hajj al-Bayt for whoever is able to go. Īmān (faith) is to believe in Allāh, His angels, His books, His messengers and the Last Day, and the divine decree (qadar), its good and its evil… Ihsān (the state of excellence or perfection) is to worship Allāh as if you are seeing Him, for if you are not seeing Him, surely He is seeing you. [72]

Then Angel Jibrīl (Gabriel) ﷺ further asked, "When will the Last Day be established?" Allāh's Apostle replied, "The one who is asked does not know better than the one who is asking." Jibrīl ﷺ said, "Then tell me about its signs."

---

[72] Sahīh Muslim, "Kitāb al-Īmān," number 9 and 10.

This hadith mentioned fourteen hundred years ago by Prophet Muhammad ﷺ gives such an eloquent and vivid description of what he was seeing happening today.

... وأن ترى الحفاة العراة العالة رعاء الشاء يتطاولون في البنيان

...and you will see the barefoot, naked, destitute bedouin shepherds competing in constructing tall buildings.[73]

Barefoot and naked (i.e. only covering the private parts) indicates that the shepherds are not from cold climates, but are in hot regions. According to Islamic scholars, the Prophet ﷺ was describing the bedouin Arabs who hail from the desert area of Najd, east of the Hijāz.[74]

The Hijāz area (Western Arabia, where Makka, Madīna, and Jedda are located) contained cities and was the center of Islamic civilization (i.e. not Bedouin-oriented). The Najd area includes the present day cities of Rīyādh, Dhahrān, Dammām, Khobar, and the Gulf region. Before the oil boom the people of Najd lived in tents, and even today the bedouin culture of the region is strong with the people still enjoying recreational desert outings in tents. Thus, the Prophet ﷺ said that in the Last Days the barefoot, naked bedouins of Najd would compete in building tall buildings.[75]

---

[73] "An talida al-amatu rabbataha wa an tara al-hufāt al-'urāt al-'aala ru'ā' ash-shā'ī yatatāwalūna fil-bunyān."

[74] Another version in al-Bukhārī has: "when the barefoot and the naked are the heads of the people." Another version in Muslim says: "when the naked and barefoot are the top leaders of the people." A third version in Bukhārī and Muslim has: "when you see that the barefoot and naked, the deaf and dumb are the kings of the earth." Ibn Hajar said, in commenting on this passage of the hadith in Fath al-bārī:

> It was said that "barefoot and naked," "deaf and dumb" are their attributes by way of hyperbole, showing how coarse they are. That is, they did not use their hearing or sight in anything concerning their Religion even though they are of perfectly sound senses. The Prophet's words: "The heads of the people" means the kings of the earth. Abū Farwa's narration names the kings explicitly. What is meant by them is the people of the desert country, as was made explicit in Sulaymān al-Taymī's and other narrations: "Who are the barefoot and naked?" He answered: "The bedouin Arabs."

[75] Imām Nawawī explains:

> The people of badī'a (the desert bedouins) and their like are indigent. There will come a time in which they become rich and build such structures to demonstrate their wealth.

Tabarānī relates through Abū Hamza, on the authority of Ibn 'Abbās from the Prophet , that "[o]ne of the signs of the change of the Religion is the affectation of eloquence by the rabble and their betaking to palaces in big cities."

Qurtubī said:

> What is meant here is the prediction of a reversal in society whereby the people of the desert country will take over the conduct of affairs and rule every region by force. They will become extremely rich and their primary concern will be to erect tall building and take pride in them.

Al-Hāfiz Ibn Hajar said in the explanation of this hadith, "everyone tries to build a higher building than the other." Imām Āhmad related from Abū 'Amir that the people who construct tall

In all the fourteen hundred years since this hadith was mentioned there have been no skyscrapers in any desert Muslim country.[76] Then, on April 24, 2000 the tallest building was built in the desert. The Faisaliah Building in Rīyādh is 269 meters (882 feet) tall. Yet this did not yet fulfill the conditions described by Prophet Muhammad ﷺ in this hadith, because the Faisaliah was the only skyscraper in the region, and there was no competition. Now in 2003, a new high rise, Kingdom Centre, is being constructed in Rīyādh and is planned to be 300 meters (984 feet), taller than any other building in Najd. This development fulfills the hadith of the Prophet ﷺ because now there is a competition between the inhabitants of Najd to build the tallest building. What the Prophet ﷺ mentioned fourteen hundred years ago as a sign of the Last Days, is appearing today.

The miracle of this prediction is seen in its apparent outward impossibility. One might logically predict that at some point in the future the rulers of a people would build tall buildings. Yet, the Prophet ﷺ specified that the poorest, simplest people of the society, the barefoot naked Bedouin shepherds, would not only build these tall buildings, but would be competing in their construction. Somehow, the poorest, least advanced people, would reach a point when they would be fabulously rich and able to afford the indulgence of competing in construction. The Prophet's ﷺ miraculous vision encompassed the future destiny that the immense wealth of Arabian oil would make possible for the naked, destitute bedouins of Najd.

No prophet ever mentioned what Prophet Muhammad ﷺ foretold fourteen hundred years ago. Furthermore, he gave a precise description with specific details which were not fully understood until their manifestation in the present age. The Prophet ﷺ was explaining what would transpire in the Last Days so that the people witnessing these events could recognize their place in time. The Prophet ﷺ warned that when bedouin Arabs competed in constructing tall buildings in the desert the Judgment Day would be close. Muslims can no longer postpone striving for piety, but must increase their worship and be exemplars of morality following the illustrious example of the

---

buildings will keep building them higher and higher (*Musnad* 4:129). That is, if one builds a structure three stories tall, the next person builds four stories, the next person builds five, etc. Now the buildings are over one hundred stories tall.
In another hadith the Prophet stated: "Whoever builds above ten meters [*fawqa 'ashrati adhru'in*], a caller from the heaven calls out to him: 'Enemy of Allāh! Where are you going with this?'" Narrated from Anas by al-Tabarānī as mentioned in al-Suyūtī's *al-Jami' al-saghīr* (#8569) and al-Munawī's *Fayd al-qadīr*.
The contemporary Saudi Arabian scholar at-Tuwayjirī, holds that the meaning of *yatatāwalūna fil bunyān* is that the number of levels in the homes will increase and be built one above the other. "This happened in our time from the money the barefoot naked bedouins got in the Gulf. And Allāh knows best." (*Ithaf al-jamā'a* (1:471)). Today, people of the desert are building these high structures, and that is Allāh's grant to those people.
[76] Malaysia's Petronas Towers in Kuala Lumpur is the world's tallest building surpassing the Sears Tower in Chicago.

Holy Prophet .

Difficulty and Reward in the Last Days

In the Last Days, those who keep the ways of religion will come under tremendous difficulty. For their patience in these trials, the Prophet ﷺ promised them great rewards from Allāh ﷻ in the afterlife.

حَدَّثَنَا إِسْمَاعِيلُ بنُ مُوسَى الْفَزَارِيُّ بْنُ ابنةِ السُّدَّيِّ الْكُوفِيّ أَخْبَرنا عُمرُ بنُ شَاكرٍ عن أَنسِ ابنِ مالك
قال: قال رَسُولُ الله صَلَى اللهُ عَلَيه وسَلَّمَ يَأتِي عَلَى النَّاسِ زمانُ الصَّابِرِ فيهم عَلى دِينه كَالْقَابِضِ
على الْجَمر (رواه الترمذى في كتاب الفتن)

Anas ﷺ related that the Prophet ﷺ said:

> There will come a time for people that to hold onto one's religion would be like holding a hot coal in one's hand.[77]

وعن أبي هريرة قال: قال رسول الله صلى الله عليه وسلم
ويل للعرب من شر قد اقترب فتنا كقطع الليل المظلم يصبح الرجل مؤمناً ويمسي كافراً يبيع قوم دينهم
بعرض من الدنيا قليل المتمسك بدينه كالقابض على الجمر أو قال على الشوك . وفي رواية بجبط
الشوك (أَحْمَدُ في مُسْنَده)

In another hadith describing the difficulties of the Last Days, Abū Hurayra ﷺ related that the Prophet ﷺ said:

> Woe to the Arabs for a great evil which is nearly upon them: it will be like patches of dark night. A man will wake up as a believer, and be an unbeliever by nightfall. People will sell their religion for a small amount of worldly goods. The one who clings to his religion on that day will be as one who is grasping an ember or thorns.[78]

Because it is so difficult to hold onto faith and religion in these times, Allāh ﷻ is granting untold rewards to those who are keeping to the divine message.

عن ابن عباس قال: أصبح رسول الله صلى الله عليه وسلم يوماً فقال ما من ماء؟ . قالوا: لا فقال
هل من شن . فجاؤوا بشن فوضع بين يدي رسول الله صلى الله عليه وسلم ووضع يده عليه، ثم
فرق أصابعه، فنبع الماء مثل عصا موسى من أصابع رسول الله صلى الله عليه وسلم، فقال يا بلال
اهتف بالناس بالوضوء فأقبلوا يتوضّون من بين أصابع رسول الله صلى الله عليه وسلم، وكانت
همة ابن مسعود الشرب فلما توضؤوا صلى بهم الصبح، ثم قعد للناس فقال يا أيها الناس من

---

[77] Āhmad, *Musnad*. Tirmidhī. "Ya'tī 'alā an-nāsi zamānun al-sābiru 'alā dīnihi kal-qābidi 'alā al-jamr."
[78] (*sahīh*) Āhmad, *Musnad*.

أعجب إيمانا ؟ . قالوا: الملائكة قال وكيف لا تؤمن الملائكة وهم يعاينون الأمر؟ قالوا: فالنبيون يا
رسول الله . قال وكيف لا يؤمن النبيون والوحي ينزل عليهم من السماء . قالوا فأصحابك يا رسول
الله . قال وكيف لا يؤمن أصحابي وهم يرون ما يرون، ولكن أعجب الناس إيمانا قوم يجيئون من
بعدي يؤمنون بي ولم يروني، ويصدقوني ولم يروني، أولئك إخواني
رواه الطبراني في الكبير والأوسط باختصار والبزار باختصار وأحمد

Ibn 'Abbās ⬧ related:

> Once the Prophet ⬧ asked for water and the Companions
> said that there was none. The Prophet ⬧ then asked for a pot,
> and it was brought to him. He put his hand in it and spread
> his fingers. Water filled the pot, gushing from between his
> fingers, as when Mūsā ⬧ struck the rock with his staff. The
> Prophet ⬧ told Bilāl ⬧ to call the people; and everyone came
> to take ablution from this water which emanated from the
> fingers of the Prophet ⬧. Ibn Mas'ūd ⬧ was eager not only to
> make *wudu* but also to drink from that water. The
> Companions performed ablution with that water, and
> everyone prayed.
>
> After the prayer the Prophet ⬧ stood and said, "O my
> Companions! Who is the best in faith?" They said, "The
> angels." And he said, "And how would they not have perfect
> faith when they see paradise?" [i.e. it is simple for them to
> believe]. The Companions then said, "The prophets." And he
> said, "How is it that they would not believe when the
> revelation is coming to them from the heavens?" [i.e. they see
> Angel Jibrīl ⬧ coming to them]. They then said, "Your
> companions." And he said, "How would they not believe
> when they see what they see?" [i.e. they see the Holy Prophet
> ⬧ in person and see such miracles as the water pouring from
> his hand]. They did not speak. He then said, "The best in faith
> are a people who believe in me though they never saw me.
> They are mine, my brothers (*ikhwān*)."[79]

In another hadith on this same incident related from Anas ⬧, the Prophet ⬧
added:

> They are going to see a revealed book and believe in it without
> seeing me during its [period of] revelation. They find it in
> pages, and these are the people with the best of faith.

---

[79] *Tabarānī.*

رواه البزار فقال عن عمر عن النبي صلى الله عليه وسلم أنه قال يؤمنون بي ولم يروني، يجدون
الورق المعلق فيؤمنون به، أولئك أعظم الخلق عند الله منزلة، أو أعظم الخلق إيمانا عند الله يوم
القيامة. وقال الصواب أنه مرسل، عن زيد بن أسلم وأحد إسنادي البزار المرفوع حسن، المنهال بن
بحر وثقه أبو حاتم وفيه خلاف، وبقية رجاله رجال الصحيح

In another hadith from 'Umar, the Prophet ﷺ said:

> They will believe in me without seeing me, they will find
> papers hung and believe in it [the Qur'ān]. They have the
> highest station in Allāh's Presence (or they have the greatest
> faith in Allāh's Presence on Judgment Day).[80]

It is related that the Companions asked if there was anyone more greatly
rewarded than they would be, as they had believed in the Prophet ﷺ and
followed him. He said:

> What prevented you from this when I am among you while
> this revelation is coming down to me? There are a people who
> are coming after me, to whom the Book comes between two
> covers. They believe in it and they act on what is mentioned in
> it. They are more highly rewarded than you.[81]

عن عمر بن الخطاب قال كنت مع النبي صلى الله عليه وسلم جالسا فقال أنبؤوني بأفضل أهل
الإيمان إيمانا ؟ . قالوا يا رسول الله الملائكة، قال: هم كذلك، يحق لهم ذلك، وما يمنعهم من ذلك،
وقد أنزلهم الله المنزلة التي أنزلهم بها؟ قالوا: يا رسول الله الأنبياء الذين أكرمهم الله
برسالته والنبوة. قال "هم كذلك، ويحق لهم وما يمنعهم من ذلك، وقد أنزلهم الله بالمنزلة التي أنزلهم
بها . قالوا يا رسول الله الشهداء الذين استشهدوا مع الأنبياء، قال هم كذلك ويحق لهم، وما يمنعهم
وقد أكرمهم الله بالشهادة، بل غيرهم. قالوا فمن يا رسول الله؟ قال أقوام في أصلاب الرجال يأتون
من بعدي، يؤمنون بي ولم يروني، ويصدقوني ولم يروني، يجدون الورق المعلق فيعملون بما فيه، فهؤلاء
أفضل أهل الإيمان إيمانا .

'Umar Ibn al-Khaṭṭāb ﷺ related that:

> I was sitting with the Prophet ﷺ and he said, "Tell me which
> of the people of faith are the best in all creation?" They said,
> "O Prophet of Allāh, the angels." He said, "So they are. And
> they deserve that, for nothing prevented that from them.
> When Allāh assigned them that station that they are in. No,
> who other than the angels?" They said, "O Prophet of Allāh,

[80] *Bazzār*.
[81] Narrated in *Tārīkh al-Bukhārī* and other books.

the prophets, whom Allāh favored with His Message and Prophecy." He said, "So they are. And they deserve that, for nothing prevented that from them. When Allāh assigned them that station that they are in." They said, "O Prophet, the martyrs who died in the Way of Allāh with the prophets." He said, "So they are. And they deserve that, for nothing prevented that from them when Allāh granted them martyrdom. No, who other than them?" They said, "Who then, O Prophet of Allāh?" The Prophet ﷺ said, "People who are yet seeds in the backs of men, from your offspring, believing in me although they never saw me, testifying to the truth of what I said and accepting it, seeing the paper hanging [the Qur'ān], and acting on what is there. Those are the best of the people of faith."[82]

These hadiths also show another prediction: that the Qur'ān would be compiled in a book form (*mushaf*) and that it would be hanging, as many people hang the Qur'ān on a necklace or on a wall.

أَخْبَرَنَا قُتَيْبَة عن مَالِكَ عَن العلاء بن عَبْد الرَّحْمن عَنْ أبِيه عن أبِي هُرَيْرَةَ أنَّ رَسُولَ اللهِ صَلَّى اللهُ عَلَيه وسَلَم خَرَجَ إلَى المَقْبَرَة فقال السَّلام عَلَيْكُم دار قَوْم مُؤْمِنِين وإنا إنْ شاءَ اللهُ بكُمْ لَاحِقُون وَدِدْتُ أني قدْ رَأيْتُ اخْوانَنا قالوا يا رَسُولَ اللهِ ألَسْنا إخْوانَكَ قال بَلْ أنْتُمْ أَصْحابي واخْوانِي الذِين لَمْ يَأتُوا بَعْدَ وأنا فرطهم على الحَوْض قالوا يا رَسُولَ اللهِ كَيْفَ تَعْرِفُ مَنْ يأتي بَعْدَكَ مِنْ أمَّتِكَ قال أرَأيْتَ لَوْ كان لِرَجُل خَيْل غُر مُحجلة في خيل دهم بهم دهم ألا يَعْرِفُ خَيْلَهُ قالوا بَلى قال فإنهم يأتون يَوْم القيامَة غُرا مُحجلين من الوُضوء وأنا فرطهم على الحَوْض

Abū Hurayra ❀ related that the Prophet ﷺ came to a graveyard and said:

Peace be upon you, O abode of believers! We shall certainly join you, if Allāh wills. How I long to see my brothers! They said, "O Messenger of Allāh, are we not your brothers?" He replied, "You are my Companions! As for our brothers, they are those who have not yet appeared and I shall precede them to my Pond." They said, "How will you recognize those of your Community who had not yet appeared (in your time), O Messenger of Allāh?" He replied, "Suppose a man had horses with shiny white marks on their foreheads and legs: would he not recognize them among other horses which are all black?" They said, "Yes, O Messenger of Allāh!" He continued, "Verily, they (my brothers) shall be coming with shiny bright

---

[82] (*sahīh*) Hākim, *Bazzār*. Suyūtī, *Durr al-Manthūr*.

foreheads and limbs due to their ablutions, and I shall precede them to my Pond."[83]

This is not saying that people of today are higher in rank than angels, or prophets, or the Companions of the Prophet. On the contrary, there is no one who can reach the rank of the Companions who actually saw the Prophet ﷺ in their lifetime. Rather, these hadiths demonstrate that Allāh ﷻ is generously rewarding those who have faith in the days of corruption and darkness, when holding fast to Islam is like holding hot coals.

من أَحْيا سُنَّتِي عِنْد فَسَاد أُمَّتِي فله أَجْر مِنَة شَهيد (البيهقي في الزُّهْد)

The Prophet ﷺ said:

The keeper of my Sunnah at the time my Community has lapsed into corruption will receive the reward of one hundred martyrs.[84]

The Prophet ﷺ is hereby showing that there are some people in the time of corruption and darkness who are keeping the Sunnah and to whom Allāh ﷻ will grant these rewards. The reward of just one martyr is enough to enter Paradise without any accounting. By praying supererogatory Sunnah prayers (nawāfil), wearing loose clothes instead of tight clothes, or wearing a ring, or by simply using the miswāk[85] a believer in these times gets the reward of one hundred martyrs![86] One must marvel at Allāh's mercy and generosity to His servants living in the Last Days. If one performs a Sunnah prayer in these times it will be written as such, and one will receive the reward of one hundred martyrs.[87]

---

[83] Muslim, Nasā'ī, Mālik, and Āhmad.
[84] Narrated from Ibn 'Abbās by al-Bayhaqī in al-Zuhd and cited thus by al-Mundhirī in al-Targhīb. "Man ahyā sunnatī 'inda fasāda ummatī fa lahu ajru mi'ata shahīd."
[85] Miswāk: a natural toothbrush from the root of the 'Arik tree, which the Prophet used to clean his teeth before praying.
[86] The imām of every masjid should encourage the people to use miswāk before every prayer. Because the Prophet said, "Prayer with miswāk is equal to 27 prayers without using miswāk." The Prophet also said that miswāk takes away polytheism and hypocrisy from the heart of the believer. When using miswāk it is Sunnah to say, "Allāhuma tāhhir qalbī min ash-shirki wan-nifāq—Oh Allāh purify my heart from polytheism and hypocrisy."
[87] Shahīd is inadequately translated as a "martyr." Lexically shahīd indicates someone who witnessed an event, and in an Islamic context that event may be a severe sickness, accidentally being burned in a fire, drowning, or dying in face to face combat with a legally defined adversary. People nowadays try to broaden this latter type of shahīd to fit into their ideologies or political goals, but this is not a correct Islamic understanding. Allāh mentioned in the Holy Qur'ān: Those who believe, and migrate (towards goodness, away from evil) and strive in Allāh's way, with their wealth and their selves, have the highest rank in the sight of Allāh... (at-Tawba 9:20). The Prophet allowed four types of striving or jihād: by heart—to empathize with suffering people and make supplication that Allāh helps them; by tongue meaning teaching and education to enjoin goodness and warn against evil; by hand—to distribute food to the poor or even remove a stone from someone's path; by sword—in a situation of legitimate self-defense such as when an intruder enters one's home to rob and

Nowadays in many mosques, people make *iqāma* and pray their obligatory prayer without praying the superogatory prayers. People are neglecting Sunnah prayers, not to mention all of the other Sunnahs the Prophet 🌺 practiced. What would such people say of the Companion 'Abd Allāh Ibn 'Umar 🕸, who used to dismount in order to walk on the exact same spot the Prophet had put his feet although such walking was not part of his lawgiving?[88] The very least that has been said by the scholars of the *Sharī'ah* in this matter is that following the Prophet 🌺 in matters of dress or everyday matters such as eating, walking, and sleeping is a matter of excellence (*ihsān*) and perfection (*kamāl*) and is desirable (*mustahabb*) and part of one's good manners in Religion (*adab*). Every desirable practice performed on the basis of such intention merits a higher degree in paradise, to which the person who neglects it may not attain, and Allāh 🌺 knows best.

༄ ﷽ ༄

---

murder or in a lawful situation of combat between two armies. It is not allowed to kill an innocent person who is not actively engaged in battle. Only an enemy engaged face to face can be fought, and the discipline of combat must be strictly observed. In another verse, Allāh (🌺) mentioned: *"Fight in the way of Allāh those who fight you, but do not transgress limits; for Allāh loves not transgressors."* (al-Baqara 2:190)

Hanzala 🕸 related:
> We went with the Prophet to defend ourselves against the enemy and we came upon a dead woman surrounded by a crowd of people. When the Prophet approached, the people parted for him. He said, **"This was not a combatant!"** (i.e. 'Why was she killed?!') He then dispatched a man to inform the general of the amy, Khalid ibn Walid: **Do not kill a woman or a neutral bystander.**

Abū Dāwūd, "Kitāb al-Jihād" #2663. *Ibn Mājah. Āhmad.*

Anas 🕸 related that the Prophet said:
> Go in the name of Allāh and fight the enemy. But do not kill the elderly, children, or women. Do not be transgressors, for Allāh loves the *muhsinīn*." (Those who keep the highest standards of discipline and do not harm people).

Abū Dāwūd.

During his Caliphate, Abū Bakr as-Siddīq 🕸 advised 'Usāma 🕸 as he was preparing to lead his troops:
> Do not be treacherous, do not backstab, do not transgress, do not mutilate, and do not kill children, the elderly, or women. If people are in their shrines leave them alone." That is, do not harm those in worship or houses of worship.

All of these examples from the Qur'ān, hadith and early generations of Muslims show that Islam places the utmost importance on protecting women, children, the elderly, people in worship and any non-combatant in general. Struggling takes many forms including praying for the suffering, feeding the hungry, and promoting education and learning. Islam allows legitimate self-defense under very strictly defined circumstances and in no way condones violence under the guise of religion.

[88] Bayhaqī, *Sunan al-kubrā* (5:245); Ibn al-Athīr, *Usd al-Ghāba* (3:341); Dhahabī, *Sīyār a'lam al-nubalā'* (3:213); al-Qal'ajī, *Mawsu'āt fiqh Ibn 'Umar* p. 52.

Who Imitates a People is One of Them

A s mentioned previously, to imitate the Prophet ﷺ in his dress or to follow him in any way makes one to be from his group and is a source of blessings, especially in these times.

من تشبه بقوم فهو منهم

(أحمد في مسنده، و أبو دَاود في كتاب اللباس عن ابن عمر، عمر الطبراني في الأوسط عن حذيفة

تصحيح السيوطي حسن)

The Prophet ﷺ said, "Whoever imitates a people is one of them."[89]

One aspect of the above hadith is the undesirability of following un-Islamic ways.

لا تَزَيَّنْ بزينَة أهْل الكُفر (إبن تَيميَّة في إقْتداء الصراط المُسْتَقيم عنْ عمرنُ الخطاب)

'Umar ﷺ related that the Prophet ﷺ said, "Do not dress up like the unbelievers."[90]

حدثنا أحمد بن يونس: حدثنا ابن أبي ذئب، عن المقبري، عن أبي هريرة رضي الله عنه، عن النبي صلى الله عليه وسلم قال لا تقوم الساعة حتى تأخذ أمتي بأخذ القرون قبلها، شبراً بشبر وذراعا بذراع فقيل يا رسول الله، كفارس والروم؟ فقال ومن الناس إلا أولئك (أخْرَجه البخاري في كتاب ال الإعتصام و ابن ماجة في الفتن و أحمَد قي مسنده)

Abū Hurayra ﷺ related that the Prophet ﷺ said:

> The Judgment Day will not come until my Ummah takes up the ways of the nations preceding them, handspan by handspan, armlength by armlength (i.e. completely). The Prophet ﷺ was asked, "Oh Messenger of Allāh, even like the Persians and Romans?" He replied, "Who is there other than they?"[91]

The Prophet ﷺ is showing here that Muslims will imitate the unbelievers in their ways. Romans here signify the nations of the West, while Persians stand for the nations of the East. This means that the Muslims in the Last Days will take up the culture and civilization of non-Muslims, from both the East and

---

[89] Narrated by 'Abd ad-Dīn Ibn 'Umar. (sahīh) Musnad Āhmad (2:50, 92). Abū Dāwūd, "Kitāb al-Libās," "Book of Dress" #4031. "Man tashabah bi qawmin fa hūwa minhum."
[90] Ibn Taymīyya, Iqtidā' al-sirāt al-mustaqīm. "La tatazayyan bi zīnati āhl al-kufr."
[91] Sahīh Bukhārī (8 :151), "Kitāb al-I'itisām":
   Lā taqūmu as-sā'atu hatta tākhudhu ummatī bi mā ākhadh il-qurūnī qabliha, shibran bi shibrin wa dhira'an bi dhira'in. Qīla lahu: Yā Rasūlallāh, ka fārisa war-rūm? Qāla: Wa man in-nāsu illa 'ulā'ik?

the West.

Muslims today follow everything that comes from non-Muslims, whether in fashion, lifestyle, entertainment, cultural values, or ideology. They make it their highest priority and ultimate goal, while putting aside the way of the Qur'ān and the Sunnah. As one can see on Muslim cable television stations, most of the announcers and talk show hosts have markedly un-Islamic appearances which arouse the desire: imitating the unbelievers, wearing excessive makeup and dressing in revealing clothes. They are adopting every style and mannerism that motivates the lower desires, dropping the Sunnah and following the culture of the non-Muslims, leading the Muslims away from the ways of their Prophet ﷺ.

Thus one side of the hadith, "Whoever imitates a people is one of them," is a warning to the Muslims not to imitate the non-Muslims and to be wary of becoming like them. This phenomenon is one of the signs of the Last Days, and to emphasize its inevitability, Imām Bukhārī named one of his chapters after a related hadith.

حدثنا محمد بن عبد العزيز: حدثنا أبو عمر الصنعاني، من اليمن، عن زيد بن أسلم، عن عطاء بن يسار، عن أبي سعيد الخدري، عن النبي صلى الله عليه وسلم قال لتتبعن سنن من كان قبلكم، شبرا بشبر .... (أخرجه البخاري في كتاب أحاديث الأنبياء ومسلم في العلم، باب: اتباع سنن اليهود والنصارى)

The Prophet ﷺ said, "You will certainly follow the ways of those who precede you."[92]

That is to say, that Muslims will observe practices which the non-Muslims engaged in twenty or thirty years earlier and begin to adopt them. Today's Muslims, observing the showy, enticing ways that the non-Muslims have laid out before them, are plunging into following them headlong. People of all nations, including the Muslims, are now following the lifestyles and ways of contemporary society, whether in immodest styles of dress, hairstyles, music (obscene rap music and heavy metal), frequenting bars, discos, nightclubs, theaters, and pornographic movies. There is no religion, in which these things are allowed, including Islam. Nonetheless, Muslims and people from every faith are following these religiously unacceptable ways.

حدثنا قتيبة أخبرنا حماد بن زيد عن أيوب عن أبي قلابة عن أبي أسماء عن ثوبان قال- قال رسول الله صلى الله عليه وسلم: لا تقوم الساعة حتى تلحق قبائل من أمتي بالمشركين (أبو داود في كتاب الفتن والترمذي في كتاب الفتن و مسلم في كتاب الفتن)

Thawban ؓ related that the Prophet ﷺ said:

---

[92] "Latatabi'unna sunan man kāna qablakum shibran bi-shibr."

The Hour will not rise until tribes of my Ummah will follow
the polytheists in everything.[93]

"Tribes" in this narration, indicates a large group of people, which in our
time corresponds to nation's or countries. Among the signs of the End Times
is that Muslim peoples will follow the unbelievers in all aspects of life. No
matter what the unbelievers show them or tell them, Muslims will pursue it,
thinking they are following the best civilization has to offer, and ignoring
Islamic guidance.

The civility of a nation is measured in its high ethics and upright character.
A good nation upholds the best of manners and morality, and when these
diminish corruption spreads, leaving a degraded society.

وقال هشام بن عمار: حدثنا صدقة بن خالد: حدثنا عبد الرحمن بن يزيد بن جابر: حدثنا عطية
بن قيس الكلابي: حدثنا عبد الرحمن بن غنم الأشعري قال: حدثني أبو عامر – أو أبو مالك –
الأشعري، والله ما كذبني. سمع النبي صلى الله عليه وسلم يقول: ليكونَنَّ من أمتي أقوام، يستحلون
الحرَ والحرير، والخمر والمعازف، (البخاري في كتاب الأشربة)

Abū Malik al-'Asharī ﷺ related that the Prophet ﷺ said:

There will be people from my Community who make
permissible fornication and silk and intoxicants and immoral
music.[94]

The Prophet ﷺ is describing the contemporary condition of many
Muslims, who display low morality with their illicit behavior. Mentioned first
are those among the Ummah[95] who allow fornication and adultery: men with
women and women with men. This is exemplified by the numerous Muslim
movements which claim to be in a state of war with non-Muslims. Using this
false platform they twist the Islamic law to suit their desires, stating it is
allowable for them to engage in sexual relations with non-Muslims.

There are also Muslim leaders and entire nations which have declared
conditional (temporary) marriage lawful. Recently, in an Arabic-language
magazine a *fatwā* was published in which the mufti of a large Muslim country
said that conditional marriages are allowed.[96] This trend of legitimizing
otherwise prohibited relations is what the Prophet ﷺ mentioned: **those who
rule that fornication is lawful.** Men and women freely mixing and having

---

[93] *Abū Dāwūd*, "Kitāb al-Fitan" #4252. *Tirmidhī*, "Kitāb al-Fitan" #2177. *Sahīh Muslim*, "Kitāb al-Fitan" #2889. "*Wa lā taqūm as-sā'atu hatta talhaqa qabā'ilun min ummatī bil-mushrikīn.*"
[94] *Sahīh Bukhārī*, (6, 243) "Kitāb al-Ashriba." *Abū Dāwūd*, "Kitāb al-Libās" #4039. "*La-yakūnanna min ummatī aqwāmun yastahillūna al-hira, wal-harīra, wal-khamra, wal-ma'azifa.*"
[95] This hadith refers to *Ummat al-ijāba*—those who heard the Prophet's message and accepted Islam, Muslims. *Ummat al-da'wa*—refers to the non-Muslims.
[96] The mufti who replaced him gave a differing opinion stating that it was not allowed.

relations outside of marriage has now become the norm, and seemingly accepted by a segment of the Muslims. Viewing movies which show people undressed is also commonplace. Adultery is sadly occurring in many homes in Muslim countries. All of these things are examples of how some Muslims are making fornication permissible, or act as if it were.

Also mentioned in the hadith is the wearing of silk by men which in Islam is permitted only for women.[97] Muslim men in every nation now wear silk clothing without a second thought, as if it were not prohibited. Many Muslims also imbibe intoxicants in the form of alcohol or other drugs. In another hadith the Prophet ﷺ mentioned *ghinā al-fāhish*—lewd singing. Music that stirs the desires has become a universal phenomenon, even in Muslim countries. In the discos and night clubs of the modern world we see throngs of Muslims dressing in silk, listening to obscene music, and using alcohol and drugs. These intoxicated men and women dress provocatively and mix freely, predictably falling into fornication. Muslims are running headlong after this lifestyle, ignoring the Islamic position on these matters. They even try to change the understanding of Islam to justify following the promptings of their lustful desires. Such transgressions are known to take place even at Muslim religious gatherings and conferences. This behavior among Muslims is what the Prophet ﷺ unerringly predicted fourteen hundred years ago, and it is one of the clearest signs inidicating that the end of the world is upon us.

---

[97] As with most laws in Islam, there are exceptions to this rule in special circumstances.

Knowledge will be Taken Away

The Prophet ﷺ predicted that in the Last Days of the Ummah, knowledge—in particular knowledge about matters of religion—would decrease.

حدثنا محمود بن غيلان حدثنا النضر بن شميل حدثنا شعبة عن قتادة عن أنس بن مالك أنه قال
أحدثكم حديثا سمعته من رسول الله صلى الله عليه وسلم لا يحدثكم أحد بعدي أنه سمعه من
رسول الله صلى الله عليه وسلم قال قال رسول الله صلى الله عليه وسلم إن من أشراط الساعة
أن يرفع العلم ويظهر الجهل ويفشو الزنا وتشرب الخمر ويكثر النساء ويقل الرجال حتى يكون لخمسين
امرأة قيم واحد

(رواه ابن ماجة في سننه في كتاب الفتن البخاري في كتاب العلم, مسلم في كتاب العلم, الترمذي
في كتاب الفتن)

When his death approached, Anas bin Malik ﷺ said, "Shall I not tell you of a hadith that I heard from the Messenger of Allāh ﷺ, which no one after me will be able to tell you? I heard the Messenger of Allāh ﷺ say:

> Verily, among the signs of the Last Days are that knowledge
> will be taken away, ignorance will appear, intoxicants (wine)
> will be drunk, fornication will be widespread, men will go
> (die), and women will remain to the point that there will be
> fifty women looked after by one man."[98]

There were 124,000 Companions who sat with the Prophet ﷺ and learned his traditions, but few were qualified to give judicial decisions (fatwā). The Prophet ﷺ mentioned that the best generations in faith would be the Companions and the two successive generations.[99] These two generations (the

---

[98] Sahīh Bukhārī, (1:28) "Kitāb al-'ilm." Muslim #2671, "Kitāb al-'ilm," Tirmidhī #2206, "Kitāb al-Fitan":

Alā uhaddithukum hadīthan 'an Rasūlillāhi lā yahaddithukum bihi ahādun 'anhu b'adī annahu sam'ahu min Rasūlillāhi. Qāla: inna min ashrāt is-sā'ati an yurf'a al-'ilmu, wayadhhaba al-jahlu, wa yushrabu al-khamru, wa yafshu az-zinā, wa yadhhaba ar-rijālu, wa yabqā an-nisā'u hatta yakūna li khamsīna imrā'atin qayyimun wāhidun.

[99] In al-Shafi'i's Risāla (p. 286) he quotes the hadith whereby the Prophet said:

Believe my Companions, then those who succeed them, and after that those who succeed the Successors. But after them falsehood will prevail when people will swear to the truth without having been asked to swear, and testify without having been asked to testify. Only those who seek the pleasures of Paradise will keep to the Congregation...

Imām Shafi'i comments:

He who holds what the Muslim Congregation (jamā'a) holds shall be regarded as following the Congregation, and he who holds differently shall be regarded as opposing the Congregation he was ordered to follow. So the error comes

Successors of the Companions and the Successors of the Successors of the Companions) did not overturn previous rulings, but deferred to prior precedents set by the Noble Companions. Only a few hundred notable scholars were able to give verdicts on new issues, and they were highly conscious of their responsibility and were anxious not to make an error. In contrast, it seems that every Muslim nowadays is giving a *fatwā* (religious edict) on every issue. Today, ordinary Muslims feign to be scholars making *fatwas*, and every teenager acts like a mufti.[100] Muslims feel their interpretation and opinion is correct, no matter how uninformed. This lack of knowledge is what the Prophet ﷺ described saying, "Knowledge will be taken away, ignorance will appear."

In the past, education for Muslims used to consist primarily of learning Qur'ān, hadith, Islamic Sharī'ah, purification of the soul, etc., in addition to whatever they learned by way of profession or trade to earn a living. Nowadays, there is little formal instruction in Islam and a lack of access to qualified teachers. Thus, there is much that is not understood. In this time there is no Islamic education to speak of, and ignorance regarding Islam is rampant even among Muslims. In addition to being ignorant of their religion, students today are well-grounded in values which contravene Islam's teachings, primarily learned through their school curricula. Along with the technical knowledge needed to earn a livelihood, the students are indoctrinated in many different ideologies (including atheism) unrelated to their fields of study. Instead of holding a proper Islamic perspective on an issue, these Muslims make decisions according to their education based on secular principles, which inevitably leads to misguidance. From an Islamic understanding this is not education, but the spreading of ignorance.

Nowadays, it seems that some Muslims only contact with Islam or the mosque is at the time of their marriage and their death. This is a common situation in many Muslim countries including those of the Middle East and Central Asia. There is only a nominal Islam in the society, wherein all sorts of unIslamic acts are committed. The hadith continues, "intoxicants [wine] will be drunk—*wa yushrab al-khamr*," stressing that it will become widespread and commonplace, even among Muslims. *Khamr* means any intoxicant and includes the use of drugs, which has become globally pervasive, along with alcohol. Unfortunately, today we see many Muslims who keep their prayers, but also drink alcohol, and there are millions of drug addicts in Muslim countries.

The hadith continues, "Fornication will be widespread." Illicit sex is

---

from separation; but in the Congregation as a whole there is no error concerning the meaning of the Qur'ān, the Sunnah, and analogy (*qīyās*).
[100] The Prophet said in another hadith that knowledge would be taken away by the deaths of scholars (see chapter below "Scholars Replaced by Ignorant Leaders").

everywhere and exeedingly common. Young men and women, driving about in expensive cars, dressed in fine clothing, easily find opportunities for fornication. Forbidden sights and sounds are even more prevalent. In most Muslim countries, it is impossible to walk down the street without encountering forbidden sights, let alone in other countries. With the globalization of entertainment, cable and satellite television networks have made it possible to bring into every Muslim home all sorts of licentious programming, including obscene music videos and pornography. The Prophet ﷺ warned Muslims not to even look at these harmful sights, as this is a sin.

حدثنا إسحاق بن منصور . أخبرنا أبو هشام المخزومي . حدثنا وهيب . حدثنا سهيل بن أبي
صالح عن أبيه، عن أبي هريرة،عن النبي صلى الله عليه وسلم قال كتب على ابن آدم نصيبه من
الزنى . مدرك ذلك لا محالة . فالعينان زناهما النظر . والأذنان زناهما الاستماع واللسان زناه الكلام
واليد زناها البطش والرجل زناها الخطا (رواه مسلم في كتاب القدر و المشكات)

Abū Hurayra ؓ related that the Prophet ﷺ said:

> The fornication of the eyes is the forbidden look, and the fornication of the ears is listening to the forbidden, and the fornication of the tongue is in speaking (about the forbidden), and the fornication of the hand is the forbidden touch, and the fornication of the foot is the step (taking one to fornication).[101]

There are even some Muslims who evade fasting during the month of Ramadan by avoiding the company of other Muslims or by traveling to non-Muslim countries. There they feel free to go anywhere incognito, and easily find forbidden relations.

Such degenerate behavior is against all religions and is displeasing to Allāh ﷻ. Therefore, a disease has emerged to remind people that they are not living as Allāh ﷻ wants them to live. The whole world has been affected by HIV and AIDS and struggles to combat this deadly infection. Many men, especially homosexual men, have died from this disease, and the world's health agencies are trying to reduce the spread of this disease among both men and women. Unfortunately, most preventative programs are not concerned with stopping illicit sex. Instead of encouraging men and women to marry and avoid prohibited sexual relations, they encourage them to continue. As if listening to satanic whisperings in their ears, they promote these acts and teach the people of the world to continue fornicating, only "with protection." This is far from what Allāh ﷻ said in the Holy Qur'ān:

---

[101] *Sahīh Muslim. Miskhāt ul-masabīh*, "Kitāb ul-Qadr" #86:
Al-'aynāni zināhum an-nazharu, wal-udhnāni zināhum al-istimā'u, wal-lisānu zināhu al-kalāmu, wal-yadu zināha al-batshu, war-rijlu zināha al-khutā.

وَلاَ تَقْرَبُوا الزِّنَى إِنَّهُ كَانَ فَاحِشَةً وَسَاءَ سَبِيلاً

And do not come near fornication. Surely it is an indecent abomination and an evil way. (al-Isrā' 17:32)

Allāh is telling humanity not only to avoid fornication, but to not even approach it.

The tradition continues, "Men will die." In the Last Days wars will claim the lives of many. It is significant to note also that this is mentioned right after *zinā* (fornication). This indicates that a number of men will also die from sexually-transmitted diseases. Men will pass away, mainly in wars, "and women will remain—*wa yabqā an-nisā*." Currently women outnumber men in the world, and with the advent of the horrendous wars of the End Times, many more men will die until eventually there will be fifty women for every man.

Time Contracts

The Prophet ﷺ said that in the Last Days time will become very close.

حدثنا أبو اليمان أخبرنا شعيب، عن الزُّهري قال أخبرني حميد بن عبد الرحمن أنَّ أبا هريرة قال

قال رسول الله صلى الله عليه وسلم يتقارب الزمان، وينقص العلم، ويلقى الشح، ويكثر الهرج.

قالوا وما الهرج؟ قال القتل القتل. (رواه البخاري في الكتاب العلم و مسلم في كتاب العلم و ابو داود

في كتاب الفتن)

Abū Hurayra ؓ related that the Prophet ﷺ said:

> Truly among the Signs of the Last Days are that time will
> contract, knowledge will decrease, shortages and miserliness[102]
> will become prevalent, afflictions will appear, and there will be
> much *harj.* The people asked, "O Messenger of Allāh, what is
> *harj?*" He said, "Killing, killing!"[103]

There are many explanations of this hadith. One is that the possibilities and means of travel and communication would be developed to make time contract, so that differences in time would be reduced or eliminated. In the past travel was measured in units of time: days, months or years. Now, a journey is measured by distance: miles or kilometers. If one wanted to visit the neighboring village a few miles away it would take four hours on donkey or an entire day walking to go and return. Now, it takes five minutes to travel the same distance. Traveling to hajj from far off lands such as Southeast Asia or Central Asia would take the pilgrims one year to reach *Madīnat al-munawwara* and *Makkat al-mukarrama.* It would take two years to complete the journey for hajj and return home. As the Last Days draw closer, time shrinks more and more. One year's travel is completed in one month. With the invention of the steamship, the journey of one year shrunk to that of a month. With the invention of trains, cars, and airplanes it shrank even more: from one month to one week; from one week to one day; from one day to one hour. Nowadays to travel from China to the Hijāz takes only a matter of hours.

Time has contracted so much that it is even overlapping. One can take a trans-atlantic flight by supersonic Concorde from London to New York and

---

[102] *Ash-shuhhu*—means that everything will decrease. There will be droughts. There will be less kindness in people's hearts so miserliness will increase. Poor people will find less charity given to them and they will not find food to eat. Wealth will decrease, and economies will be in recession.

[103] *Sahīh Bukhārī,* (1:29), "Kitāb al-'ilm." *Sahīh Muslim,* "Kitāb al-'ilm" #157. *Abū Dāwūd* #4255, "Kitāb al-Fitan":

> *Inna min ashrāt is-sā'ati yan yataqārab az-zamānu wa yanqus ul-'ilm, wa tazhar
> ul-fitanu, wa yulqa ash-shuhhu, wa yakthur ul-harju. Qālū: Ya Rasūlallāh, wa
> mā al-harju? Qāla: al-qatl ul-qatl.*

land an hour before one departed. One can fly from Tokyo to Los Angeles and arrive eight hours before one left while it is already the next day in Tokyo. Time and space have shrunk to an extraordinary degree.

حدثنا عبد الله حدثني أبي حدثنا هاشم حدثنا زهير حدثنا سهيل عن أبيه عن أبي هريرة قال:
قال رسول الله صلى الله عليه وسلم لا تقوم الساعة حتى يتقارب الزمان فتكون السنة كالشهر
ويكون الشهر كالجمعة وتكون الجمعة كاليوم ويكون اليوم كالساعة وتكون الساعة كاحتراق السعفة
الخوصة (رواه أحمد في مسنده، إبن حبان و غيرهما)

Abū Hurayra ﷺ related that the Prophet ﷺ said:

> The Hour will not take place before time shrinks. One year will be like a month, one month will be like a week, a week will be like a day, and a day will be like an hour; and an hour will be like a burning flame.[104]

The Prophet ﷺ is saying in this hadith that time is going to contract even further, to the point that the shortness of time is like the quick burning of a flame, i.e. instantaneous. With the technology of satellites what used to take one year, is now happening in an instant by telephone. One can take a portable phone and speak with China. It is possible to call anywhere in the world, not only by telephone, but via the Internet as well. Now people can speak with each other through email and on the Internet as if they were in the next room. The two parties see each other on the computer screen as if they were face-to-face. With satellites, computers, and the Internet one can see what is going on anywhere. Today, all kinds of information can be bundled and sent all together in one moment. Messages which would previously take years to arrive are sent instantly. This was unimaginable until only very recently.

In the past, scholars of hadith never considered this understanding of the contraction of time. They interpreted it to mean that there will be so much strife in the End Times that the Afterlife would no longer seem far away. They never interpreted it to mean people physically distant, would be as if near each other. Today it is apparent that the satellite and telecommunication systems of today were clearly described by the Prophet ﷺ fourteen hundred years ago. Such is the miraculous knowledge of the Prophet Muhammad ﷺ to speak of such advances fourteen hundred years before their invention. He knew there would be instantaneous global communication. The people of his time could not understand the specifics of how one could talk on a telephone via satellites,

---

[104] (sahīh) Musnad Āhmad (2:537). Sahīh Ibn Hibbān #1887. Albānī, Sahīh al-Jami'a #7422: Lā taqūm us-sā'atu hatta yataqārab uz-zamānu, fatakūn us-sannatu kash-shahri, wa yakūn ush-shahru kal-jumu'ati, wa takūn ul-jumu'atu kal-yawmi, wa yakūn ul-yawmu kas-sā'ati, wa takūnu as-sā'atu ka-htirāq is-sa'afat il-khawaysati.

or land lines, so he explained things in a general way to which the Companions could relate. The Prophet ﷺ said that the Day of Judgement would not come until time shrinks, and this has come to pass.

حدثنا عبد الله بن صبّاح: حدثنا معتمر: سمعت عوفاً: حدثنا محمد بن سيرين: أنه سمع أبا هريرة يقول :قال رسول الله صلى الله عليه وسلم: إذا اقترب الزمان لم تكد رؤيا المؤمن تكذب (رواه البخاري في كتاب التعبير و مسلم في كتاب الرؤيا, الترمذي في كتاب الرؤيا , و ابن ماجة في كتاب تعبير الرؤيا و أحمد في مسنده و مالك في الجامع)

In another hadith related by Abū Hurayra ◈ the Prophet ﷺ said, "When time contracts the *ru'ya*[105] of the believer will not lie."[106]

True dreams are mentioned in the Holy Qur'ān, and there are many accounts in the hadiths about dreams. Notably, the call to prayer (*adhān*) was revealed in a dream to 'Abd Allāh ibn Zayd ◈ who related it to the Prophet ﷺ who approved of it.[107] When time contracts, or when the Last Days approach, there will be no interference in the vision or dreams of the believer, and nowadays many people are seeing things in dreams before they happen.

حدثنا يحيى بن قزعة: حدثنا إبراهيم بن سعد، عن الزهري، عن سعيد بن المسيب، عن أبي هريرة رضي الله عنه: أن رسول الله صلى الله عليه وسلم قال: رؤيا المؤمن جزء من ستة وأربعين جزءا من النبوة (وراه البخاري في كتاب التعبير و مسلم في كتاب الرؤيا, الترمذي في كتاب الرؤيا , و ابن ماجة في كتاب تعبير الرؤيا و أحمد في مسنده و مالك في الجامع)

In the Last Days the believer will see true dreams (or visions) as the Prophet ﷺ said, "The vision (*ru'ya*) of a believer is one of forty six parts of prophethood."[108]

---

[105] *Ru'ya* is a vision or a true good dream inspired by Allāh.
[106] *Sahīh Bukhārī* (8: 76) Chapter on Dreams. *Sahīh Muslim*, #2263. Also found in *Tirmidhī*, and *Abū Dāwūd*.
[107] The dream was also seen by 'Umar ibn al-Khattāb ◈. The hadith is related by *Āhmad, Ibn Mājah*, Ibn Khuzaymah, and *Tirmidhī* who graded it *hasan sahīh*. It is also mentioned in *Fiqh as-sunnah*.
[108] *Sahīh Bukhārī* (9:117), also related by Abū Hurayra ◈.

Scholars Replaced by Ignorant Leaders

The following hadith tells how the affairs of the Muslims will fall into the hands of extremely ignorant people, who have an inadequate understanding of Islam, during the Last Days.

حدثنا هارون بن اسحاق الهمداني، أخبرنا عبدة بن سليمان عن هشام بن عروة، عن أبيه، عن عبد الله بن عمرو بن العاص قال: قال رسول الله صلى الله عليه وسلم: إن الله لا يقبض العلم انتزاعا ينتزعه من الناس ولكن يقبض العلم بقبض العلماء، حتى إذا لم يترك عالما اتخذ الناس رؤوسا جهالا فسئلوا فأفتوا بغير علم فضلوا وأضلوا " . (رواه البخاري في كتاب العلم و مسلم)

'Abd Allāh bin 'Amr Ibn al-'Ās ﷺ related that the Prophet ﷺ said:

> Allāh will not take knowledge from the hearts of the scholars but he takes the scholars (they die). There will be no more scholars to take their place so people will take extremely ignorant leaders. They will be asked questions and will give *fatwas* (legal rulings) without knowledge. They are misguided and they misguide others.[109]

This prediction has been fulfilled, as Muslims presently take leaders who know only the name and description of Islam, and do not know the practice and heart of Islam. For instance, often times a businessman, a doctor, or an engineer becomes the leader of a mosque. These professionals possess no traditional Islamic education. These people did not study *Sharī'ah*, Qur'ānic *asbāb an-nuzūl* (the circumstances of revelation of the Qur'ān), or hadith. They lack the training and knowledge of how to deduce Islamic jurisprudence (*fiqh*), or how to give explanations on topics in Islam. Thus, while working full time in their professions they relegate leadership of the Muslim community to secondary status, like a sort of hobby. These people can legitimately act as imāms and lead the prayer if there is no one more qualified present to do so. However, when these people become a *wa'iz*, (a scholar, speaker, or advisor) they go beyond their capacity and can severely damage the Muslim community.

Such Muslim community leaders transform the mosque into an arena for social dominance rather than a place for religious and spiritual enhancement. This, too, was predicted by the Prophet ﷺ.

---

[109] *Sahīh Bukhārī* 1:33, "Kitāb al-'ilm." *Sahīh Muslim* #157, "Kitāb al-'ilm":
Inna Allāha la yaqbidu al-'ilma intizā'an yantazi'uhu min al-'ibād wa lākin yaqbid ul-'ilma bi qabd il-'ulamā hatta idhā lam yabqā 'aliman itakhada an-nāsu ru'ūsan juhālan fa su'ilu fa aftaw bi ghayri 'ilmin fa dallu wa adallu.

أخبرنا سويد بن نصر قال أنبأنا عبد الله بن المبارك عن حماد بن سلمة عن أيوب عن أبي قلابة عن
أنس أن النبي صلى الله عليه وسلم قال من اشراط الساعة أن يتباهى الناس في المساجد.
(النسائي و إبن ماجة في سننه و أُحمد في مسُنده و الدّارمي في سننه)

Anas ﷺ related that the Prophet ﷺ said:

> Truly one of the signs of the Last Days is when people show
> off in the mosques.[110]

Such showy leaders are unqualified to give decisions on Islamic issues in
general, and in particular, they are not equipped with the experience and
knowledge to deal with the complex challenges faced by the Muslim
communities of modern times. Firmly grounded in secular education but
woefully lacking in Islamic knowledge and training, they may interject some of
their own opinions or egos' whisperings, rendering an Islamically unsound
decision to the detriment of the whole community. Fourteen hundred years
ago the Prophet ﷺ described these ignorant leaders who would be asked about
something and would give a wrong verdict, "They (themselves) are misguided
and they misguide others." When that door of misguidance is opened, Shaytān
enters, and what ensues is a disaster for the entire Muslim community.

It is essential to understand that no one can issue a ruling without
possessing the prerequisite qualifications, and no one can issue a judgment
without such qualifications. Since rulings have a tremendous impact on the life
of society and ruling on the individual, it is essential that those issuing them
have excellent moral character, and most importantly that they are well-
qualified.

Allāh said in the Holy Qur'ān:

قُلْ أَرَأَيْتُمْ مَا أَنْزَلَ اللَّهُ لَكُمْ مِنْ رِزْقٍ فَجَعَلْتُمْ مِنْهُ حَرَامًا وَحَلَالًا قُلْ آللَّهُ أَذِنَ لَكُمْ أَمْ عَلَى اللَّهِ
تَفْتَرُونَ

*Say: Tell me what Allah has sent down for you of sustenance, then you
make (a part) of it unlawful and (a part) lawful. Say: Has Allah
commanded you, or do you forge a lie against Allah? (Yūnus 10.59)*

This verse emphasizes that no one has the right to judge something right
or wrong unless he has complete evidence from the pertinent information as
found in the source texts, from deep discussion among the people who have a
grasp of the issue at hand, and from seeking all meaningful evidence.
Otherwise one should remain silent. To do otherwise would be lying against
Allah and against the religion.

---

[110] Nasā'ī, Āhmad. "In min ashrāt as-sā'ati an yatabāhī an-nāsu fil-masājid."

Imam Shafi'i, founder of one of the four great schools of jurisprudence, said:

> It is not allowed for anyone to give a *Shari'ah* explanation
> (*fatwa*), except one who knows the Holy Qur'ān completely
> including what verses are abrogated and by which verses they
> were abrogated, and which verses resemble each other in the
> Qur'ān and whether a chapter was revealed in Makkah or
> Madīna. He must know the entire corpus of the Hadith of the
> Prophet 鑬, both those which are authentic and those which
> are false. He must know the Arabic language of the time of
> the Prophet 鑬 with its grammar and eloquence as well as
> know the poetry of the Arabs. Additionally he must know the
> culture of the various peoples who live in each different
> nation of the community. If a person has all such attributes
> combined in himself, he may speak on what is permitted
> (*halāl*) and what is forbidden (*harām*). Otherwise he has no
> right to issue a *fatwa*.

It is related from one of the greatest scholars of *Shari'ah*, *al-faqīh* 'Abd al-Rahmān ibn Abī Laila said, "I was able to meet with one hundred and twenty of the Companions of the Prophet. Every one of these companions were asked about specific *Shari'ah* issues, seeking a verdict, but they avoided rendering a decision, instead pointing to another companion to issue the answer. They were afraid to give an answer that would be incorrect for which they would be responsible before God."

That shows that one can be deeply imbued with Islamic knowledge, as were all the Prophet's Companions, and yet still feel unqualified to give a verdict. All one-hundred and twenty of the Prophet's Companions with whom ibn Abī Laila met were hesitant to issue a *fatwa*.

Imām Nawawi—one of the greatest of Islam's later scholars—related that Imām ash-Shu'bi and Hasan al-Basrī and many others of the Successors [generation immediately succeeding the Companions of the Prophet 鑬] said:

> People of today are quick to issue a ruling based on their
> analysis concerning someone. If an answer had been sought
> for that same issue at the time of 'Umar ibn al-Khattāb 鑬
> (second caliph of the Prophet 鑬), he would have gathered all
> the participants of Badr [i.e. 313 of the foremost Companions
> of the Prophet 鑬] in pursuit of the answer.

Unfortunately, today's Islamic leaders, instead of using the mosque as a place of guidance towards goodness and for saving the souls of human beings in the afterlife, use them to discuss this world and its concerns, whether it be politics, fund-raising or encouraging people to spend their time pursuing worldly matters. This was foretold in another hadith in which it is related that the Prophet 襲 said:

> At the end of time will be men who come to the mosques and sit in circles discussing this world and its love. Do not sit with them. Allāh has no need of them.[111]

The eminent Companion Ibn Mas'ūd 鼗 was asked about this hadith. He said the ignorant leaders would be from *asāghir* (those who do not have a thorough or any Islamic education; literally "little ones") and not *akābir* (the scholars who dedicated their lives to learning Islam; literally "great ones, big ones"). *Akābir* are great, educated, literate intellectuals, while *asāghir* are illiterate, the least educated people who scarcely know anything about Islam. The Prophet 襲 said that a sign of the Last Days is when there would be no more knowledge and when knowledge would be taken from *asāghir*, "small ones." Nowadays, our leaders are uneducated in Islam making them "little ones" in terms of religious knowledge despite their advanced age. Moreover, there are literally children on Islamic Internet groups making verdicts on every issue. On the Internet an eighteen year old boy acts like a great scholar issuing edicts, telling his fellow Muslims, "You are wrong! You are an unbeliever!" People raise a major question and everyone types away, giving his uninformed personal opinions based on nonexistent scholarship. People read and follow what these youngsters write. As the Prophet 襲 said, "They (themselves) are misguided and they misguide others."

ﷺ

---

[111] Mentioned by al-Qurtubī in *Jam'li-ahkām al-qur'ān*, in his explanation of *Sūrat an-Nūr* (36).

The Qur'ān is Opened

The Prophet ﷺ predicted a time in which the Qur'ān would be widely available, extensively read, but barely followed.

حدثنا عبد الرحمن بن عثمان ....عن أيوب عن أبي قلابة عن معاذ بن جبل قال تكون فتن يكثر فيها المال ويفتح فيها القرآن حتى يقرأه المؤمن و الكافر والمرأة و الرجل والصغير والكبير فيقرأه رجل فيقول"قرأته علانية فلا أرانى أُتبع فيقعد في بيته و يبني مسجدا في داره ثم يبتدع بما ليس في كتاب الله ولا سنة رسول الله صلى الله عليه وسلم فإياكم و ما ابتدع فانه ضلالة

تقدم هذا الحديث باختلاف يسير في الألفاظ ورد في كتاب السنن الواردة في الفتن وغوائلها والساعة واشراطها المقرى الداني تحقيق ادريس المباركفوري دار العاصمة الرياض صفحة 623 حدثنا أبو خليفة وأحمد بن داود المكي قالا ثنا أحمد بن يحيى بن حميد الطويل حدّثنا حماد بن سلمة عن أيوب عن أبي قلابة عن يزيد بن عميرة عن معاذ بن جبل قال تكون فتن يكثر فيها المال ويفتح فيها القرآن حتى يقرأ الرجل والمرأة والصغير والكبير والمؤمن والمنافق فيقرأه ولا يتبع فيقول والله لأقرأنه علانية ولا يتبع فيقصد مسجدا فيبتدع كلاما ليس من كتاب الله ولا من سنة رسول الله صلى الله عليه وسلم فإياكم وإياها فإنها بدعة ضلالة فإياكم وإياه فإنها بدعة ضلالة فإياكم وإياه فإنها بدعة ضلالة

رواه اللالكائي في شرح أصول اعتقاد أهل السنة(89/1 رقم 117) و أخرجه ابن وضاح في البدع و النهي عنها (ص 26) و الحاكم في المستدرك(466/4) و قال الحاكم هذا حديث صحيح على شرط مسلم". و هو أيضا عند عبد الرزاق في مصنفه (363/11 رقم 20750) و أبي داود في سننه (17/5 رقم 4611) و أخرجه الدارمي في سننه (67/1) من طريق آخر و اسناده صحيح.

On the authority of Mu'ādh ﷺ it is related that the Prophet ﷺ said:

> There will be trials in which large amounts of money will be collected, and the Qur'ān will be opened to the point that it will be read by both the believer and unbeliever, the woman and the man, the young and the old. A man will read it then exclaim, "No one is following me!" So he sits in his home and makes a room like a mosque in his house. Then he will innovate things in the religion which are not found in Allāh's

book nor in the Sunnah of Allāh's Messenger. Be wary of what they innovate for verily it is misguidance![112]

In this hadith and similar narrations, the Prophet ﷺ begins, "There will be trials in which large amounts of money will be collected..." Today, we actually witness this type of confusion. In every mosque, one finds people are donating to fundraising efforts in which millions of dollars are collected, ostensibly for religious causes, yet Allāh alone knows where the funds end up and for what purpose.

The words of the hadith continue, "and the Qur'ān will be opened." The Prophet ﷺ is telling us that in these times the Qur'ān would be opened. Note well he said, "The Qur'ān will be opened" (yuftah). He did not say, "The Qur'ān will be studied" (yudras). "Opened" means "to be made accessible" or "to be made available."

Thus, we see today that many Muslim children memorize the entire Qur'ān in a few years. However, they do not study its meaning. No one sends their children to learn knowledge of the Divine Law ('ilm ash-Sharī'ah). They only send them to learn to recite the Qur'ān by rote from beginning to end.

The hadith continues, "it will be read by both the believer and unbeliever—hatta yaqrā'ahu al-mu'minu wal kāfiru." Here, the Prophet ﷺ predicted that the Qur'ān would be read by both Muslims and non-Muslims.[113] This is something that is happening today on a large scale. Translations of the Qur'ān are available in every bookstore and library, in almost every language. Not only are Muslim authors writing and commenting on the Qur'ān, but so too are many non-Muslims, mainly without any in-depth knowledge or understanding of its contents, context or the meanings contained in its verses.

But the Prophet ﷺ says further, "A man will read the Qur'ān but find that no one is following him." That is because he reads it without religious knowledge and understanding ('ilm). Today's leaders say that one does not need to learn from a scholar ('alim). They say, "Just go and read Qur'ān and hadith by one's self." Mainstream Muslims will not follow this misguidance, so such people will find themselves isolated. He makes a room in his house, like an office, for religious purposes sitting with his prayer carpet and his computer. People today are creating such "rooms" on the Internet, known as Islamic chat rooms and Internet "Mosques."

---

[112] *Takūnu fitanun yaktharu fīha al-māl wa yuftahu fīhā al-qur'ān hatta yaqrā'ahu al-mu'minu wal kāfiru wal mar'atu wa-rajul wa-saghīr wal kabīr. Fa yaqrā'uhu rajulun fa yaqulu: Qarā'atuhu 'alanīyyatin. Fa lā arāni utabi'uh. Fa yaq'udu fi baytihi wa yabnī masjidan fī dārihi. Thumma yabtadi'u bi mā laysa fī kitābillāhi wa lā sunnati rasūlillāh. Fa īyyākum wa ma-btudi'a fa innahu dalāl.* Narrated with slightly different wordings by al-Hākim in *Mustradrak*, who said "authentic (sahīh) based on the rule of Muslim," *Abū Dāwūd*, *Dārimī* from a different way (sahīh), and 'Abd ar-Razzāq in his *Musannaf*.

[113] Another narration reads "until the believer and the hypocrite (munāfiq) will read it..."

Today's Muslim leaders are encouraging Muslims to sit at home and blindly wander though the vast body of knowledge in the Qur'ān and hadith. Today young people, thinking they are experts in Islam from their home study, begin issuing religious edicts through easily accessible chat rooms, email lists and websites.

Today everyone—both Muslim and non-Muslim—is opening the Qur'ān, without studying it in its entirety, picking out one verse and building a case for their verdict around it. Rather than looking to the Qur'ān for guidance on an issue, they begin with their own opinion and then find a verse in the Qur'ān they can use to support their position, right or wrong.

Without knowing what other verses of the Qur'ān may have to say on the issue, or knowing the correct meaning of the verse, or knowing the events and circumstances under which the verse was revealed, these misguided efforts lead into error and innovation in the religion. The Prophet ﷺ described this situation fourteen hundred years ago and strongly warned in this hadith, "Be wary of what they innovate for verily it is misguidance!"

Today everyone has become his own teacher. The teacher-student relationship of Islam of old has almost completely disappeared. Yet, this teacher-student model is the very foundation of Islamic education. The Prophet ﷺ himself mentioned many times that he would study (*yatadaras*) the Qur'ān with Archangel Jibrīl ﷺ. The Prophet ﷺ would recite, and Jibrīl ﷺ would listen. Jibrīl ﷺ brought the Qur'ān to the Prophet ﷺ, and the Prophet ﷺ taught the Qur'ān to his Companions, who in turn taught it to the Successors who taught it to the next generations, and so on, in an unbroken chain.

The relationship of teacher to student has been the keystone of the transmission of Islamic knowledge from the very first moment of the Qur'ān's revelation. After all, was it not possible for Allāh ﷺ to have inscribed the revelation in lights in the sky and the Muslims to read it? Instead, He revealed the Qur'ān and allowed it to be transmitted from an angel to a prophet and further, from one person to another. Revelation occurred in this way for no other reason than to emphasize that an individual must learn from someone who knows. And this is in accordance with the Qur'ānic command:

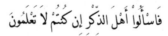

Ask the people of knowledge if you do not know something.
(al-Anbīyā' 21:7)

Today everyone is his own teacher asserting his own views, and rejecting all others, as the Prophet ﷺ predicted, "everyone will be fond of his own opinion." People no longer accept advice and are stubborn in holding to their beliefs, regardless of what they are told.

Today many Muslim lecturers and leaders are concerned primarily with fundraising for religious causes, some of which when examined closely are dubious. In previous times Muslims did not hold fundraising dinners. Now people have begun this practice in order to implement the agenda of whatever group, party or cause they support, all under the name of religion.

It is said that if a religious teacher's lectures are more directed to worldly issues than to the afterlife, then avoid him because his words will only bring darkness to the heart. Listening instead to a teacher who cultivates love of Allāh ﷻ, the Prophet ﷺ and pious people, will bring light into the heart.

Torture Will be Widespread

The Prophet 🌺 described in the following hadith, a time in which some men would have power over others, and would use it to inflict harm on them.

حدثنا ابن نمير حدثنا زيد يعني ابن حباب حدثنا أفلح بن سعيد حدثنا عبد الله بن رافع مولى أم
سلمة قال سمعت أبا هريرة يقول

قال رسول الله صلى الله عليه وسلم يوشك إن طالت بك مدة أن ترى قوما في أيديهم مثل أذناب
البقر يغدون في غضب الله ويروحون في سخط الله (مسلم كتاب الجنة وصفة نعيمها و أهلها و
أحمد في مسنده)

Abū Hurayra ◈ related that the Prophet 🌺 said:

> [O Abū Hurayra], it is imminent and if you live for a while, you will see a people with something in their hands like the tails of oxen. They go out in the morning under the wrath of Allāh and come back in the evening under His curse.[114]

The Prophet's 🌺 saying, "You will see a people with something in their hands like the tails of oxen," means they will have something leather in their hands, like a whip. They will go in the early morning to harm people in disobedience to Allāh, under His displeasure and anger. They go in the morning carrying the whip in their hands against the way of Allāh and against the way of the Prophet 🌺, disobeying Allāh, disobeying the Prophet 🌺. When they come back in the evening (yarūhūna)[115] Allāh 🌺 is disgusted with them. These people are Muslims.

So many centuries ago, the Prophet 🌺 was giving a hint to Abū Hurayra ◈ about such people coming shortly after his lifetime. Although the Prophet 🌺 knew that these people would appear in the Last Days many years after the time of Abū Hurayra ◈, he was emphasizing that the Last Days are not far away in terms of mankind's time on Earth. The Prophet's 🌺 saying, "If you live for a while" is an indication that in reality the Last Days are very near. "I was sent close to the Judgment Day like these two fingers next to each other."[116] Furthermore, the Prophet 🌺 was showing his concern for his Companions, and Muslims of all times, that they prepare themselves for their afterlife which may take place at anytime. Sayyidinā 'Alī ◈ said, "Work for your worldy life as if you will live forever, but work for your afterlife as if you will die tomorrow."

---

[114] Sahīh Muslim. "Yūshiku in tālat bika muddatun an tarā qawman fī aydīhim mithl adhnāb il-baqar. Yaghdūna fī ghadab-illāh. Wa yarūhūna fī sakhat-illāh."
[115] Yarūhūna is derived from rāh—"it went"; it refers to the time of sunset, maghrib, meaning "coming back."
[116] Sahīh Bukhārī, (8:510) "Kitāb al-Tafsīr." Sūrat an-Nāzi'āt.

Believers must always be devout and keep in mind that they will one day face their judgment, because no one knows when they will be called back to their Lord. As Allāh ﷻ mentioned in the Holy Qur'ān:

$$\text{إِنَّ اللَّهَ عِندَهُ عِلْمُ السَّاعَةِ وَيُنَزِّلُ الْغَيْثَ وَيَعْلَمُ مَا فِي الْأَرْحَامِ وَمَا تَدْرِي نَفْسٌ مَّاذَا تَكْسِبُ غَدًا وَمَا تَدْرِي نَفْسٌ بِأَيِّ أَرْضٍ تَمُوتُ}$$

Verily the knowledge of the Hour is with Allah (alone). It is He Who sends down rain, and He Who knows what is in the wombs. Nor does any one know what it is that he will earn on the morrow. Nor does any one know in what land he is to die. (Luqmān 31:34)

In general, people today do not consider that they will be called to account for their actions. Acting contrary to the teachings of all religions, people of today are oppressive and abusive, abusing one another with their bad manners and harshness. Human nature is attracted to the soft and gentle, but there is very little love, peace, or gentleness left among humanity. The Islamic ideal is Prophet Muhammad ﷺ whom Allāh ﷻ described in the Holy Qur'ān:

$$\text{وَإِنَّكَ لَعَلَى خُلُقٍ عَظِيمٍ}$$

Truly you are of the best character and manners. (al-Qalam 68:4)

The Prophet ﷺ exemplified humility and gentleness. Allāh ﷻ says:

$$\text{فَبِمَا رَحْمَةٍ مِّنَ اللَّهِ لِنتَ لَهُمْ وَلَوْ كُنتَ فَظًّا غَلِيظَ الْقَلْبِ لَانفَضُّوا مِنْ حَوْلِكَ}$$

It was by the mercy of Allah that you dealt gently with them. Had you been rough, hard-hearted, they would certainly have dispersed from around you. (Āl-ʿImrān 3:159)

Today Muslims are not following this way, but are rough and hard-hearted. So many people today are rude and stubborn, speaking in a gruff, harsh manner. Muslims repel friends and family and are turning non-Muslims away from the religion. Shaytān uses this rudeness to instigate conflict and even good friends suddenly break off relations as a result.

Another interpretation of this hadith, according to Shalabi,[117] is that leaders will be engaged in widespread torture and human rights abuses to keep themselves in power. This applies to any leader, whether a king, emperor, sultan, president, tribal leader, community leader, political leader, leader of a religious group, or leader of a mosque. People will be tyrants in order to hold onto their positions. Even if there is a group of only three people with one

---

[117] *Sahīh ashrāt as-sā'at*, p 83-84.

person in charge, he will oppress the other two. Everyone in a position of authority will try to retain his position. Such leaders feel no remorse in conspiring against anybody in order to retain their status. They will find any way and use any method or system to maintain their hold on power.

Such leaders have people assigned to help protect their positions. They are assigned to torture people, and as the Prophet ﷺ described, "They go out in the morning under the wrath of Allāh and come back in the evening under His curse." That they leave home in the morning and return in the evening indicates that they are employees. The Prophet ﷺ said these people would be carrying whips in their hands, and today they give all kinds of punishment to innocent human beings. In prisons around the world many innocent prisoners are being whipped and tortured. There are many devious methods of torture, including the cattle prod and electric shock. In the evening the tormentors return home, and Allāh ﷻ hates them for what they did during the day, whipping, beating and torturing people and throwing them in jail without mercy.

Muslims everywhere are under terrible difficulties from these people. The leaders do not let anyone live in peace, and Muslim immigrants see how people "back home" are tortured. The leaders are afraid of anyone unfamiliar to them, so they imprison people indiscriminately. Because of them, a Muslim cannot grow a beard in Muslim countries, and if one wears a cap he will be questioned. If someone prays five times a day they ask to which group he belongs. In some countries there are people with wooden or rubber batons who beat whomever they like. The Prophet ﷺ said these people of the End Times will have whips like the tails of oxen in their hands to torture people, and this is what is happening today. Today there is no place on earth where this kind of torture is not happening in some form. Fourteen hundred years ago the Prophet ﷺ foretold this sad condition which was never as prevalent and widespread as it is today.

Although the Prophet ﷺ was taken to see the inhabitants of Hellfire, two groups were not shown to him because they are the worst of people, at the bottom of Hell. Allāh ﷻ and His Messenger ﷺ are so upset with these people who torture others that they were not shown to the Prophet ﷺ on the Night of Ascension.

حدثني زهير بن حرب حدثنا جرير عن سهيل عن أبيه عن أبي هريرة قال
قال رسول الله صلى الله عليه وسلم صنفان من أهل النار لم أرهما قوم معهم سياط كأذناب البقر
يضربون بها الناس ونساء كاسيات عاريات مميلات مائلات رؤوسهن كأسنمة البخت المائلة لا
يدخلن الجنة ولا يجدن ريحها وإن ريحها ليوجد من مسيرة كذا وكذا (رواه مسلم في كتاب اللباس و
أَحْمَد في مسنده و و مالك في الجامع)

Abū Hurayra ⁓ related that the Prophet ﷺ said:

> There are two types among the people of Hell whom I did not
> see. The first are people who have whips like the tails of oxen,
> with which they beat people...[118]

This hadith further explains the previous hadith in which these people go
in the morning and return home in the evening after spending the day torturing
people. This cruel behavior is not allowed in Islam as no one has authority to
beat and torture people.

حدثنا أبو بكر بن أبي شيبة. حدثنا حفص بن غياث عن هشام بن عروة، عن أبيه، عن هشام بن
حكيم بن حزام. قال:

مر بالشام على أناس، وقد أقيموا في الشمس، وصب على رؤوسهم الزيت. فقال: ما هذا؟ قيل:
يعذبون في الخراج. فقال: أما إني سمعت رسول الله صلى الله عليه وسلم يقول "إن الله يعذب الذين
يعذبون في الدنيا" (روا ه مسلم في كتاب البرّ و أبو داود في سننه و أحمد في مسنده)

In another hadith:

> 'Urwa reported on the authority of his father that Hishām bin
> Hakīm b. Hizām happened to pass by some people in Syria
> who had been made to stand in the sun and olive-oil was
> being poured upon their heads. He said, "What is this?" It was
> said, "They are being punished for (not paying) the *Kharaj* (the
> government revenue)." Thereupon he said, "I heard the
> Messenger of Allāh say, 'Allāh will punish those who torment
> people in this world.'"[119]

The Prophet ﷺ is showing that Allāh ﷻ will take revenge on behalf of any
person who is tortured, whether Muslim or non-Muslim. This hadith shows
that the Prophet ﷺ is, as Allāh ﷻ described:

رَحْمَةً لِّلْعَالَمِين

a mercy to the worlds (al-Anbiyāʾ 21:107)

and:

وَمَا أَرْسَلْنَاكَ إِلَّا كَافَّةً لِّلنَّاسِ بَشِيرًا وَنَذِيرًا

---

[118] *Sahīh Bukhārī. Sahīh Muslim*, #2128 "Kitāb al-Libās." "*Sinfāni min āhl an-nāri lam arahumā: qawmun maʿhum sayāt ka adhnāb il-baqar, yadribūna bihā an-nās...*"
[119] *Sahīh Muslim*, #2613 "Kitāb al-Birr." "*Inna allāha yuʿadhdhibu alladhīnā yuʿadhdhibūna fid-dunyā.*"

We have not sent thee but as a universal (Messenger) to men, giving them glad tidings, and warning them (against sin). (Sabā 34:28)

People are punishing and torturing fellow human beings, but only Allāh ﷻ has the right to punish. People can judge whether something is right or wrong, but they cannot punish according to their opinion or whims. There are very exacting, oftentimes unattainable, conditions which must be fulfilled before anyone can be sentenced to punishment under Islamic *Shari'ah*, but no one is following them today. This discussion is not meant as a political commentary towards any particular regime, but is intended to show that events the Prophet ﷺ foretold would happen in the Last Days are taking place today.

Prophet Muhammad ﷺ mentioned the torture that would occur in the Last Days. Muslims must take a lesson from his warning. Muslims are being tortured in their own countries and being thrown into prisons, oftentimes never to be released. People are constantly in fear that someone may come out of nowhere and subject them to such punishment. With Allāh's mercy, Muslims in some countries are living in peace and are not in such difficulty.

Allāh ﷻ said:

يَا أَيُّهَا الَّذِينَ آمَنُوا أَطِيعُوا اللَّهَ وَأَطِيعُوا الرَّسُولَ وَأُولِي الْأَمْرِ مِنكُمْ

Obey Allāh, obey the Messenger, and those in authority over you.

(an-Nisā' 4:59)

Ordinary people are not leaders, presidents or kings and must follow the rules and laws of the country in which they live. It is not allowed for Muslims to engage in subterfuge or interfere in the affairs of others. The Muslim's duty is to take care of home, family and neighbors, and not to disrupt society. Muslims should prepare themselves to be pious people with whom Allāh ﷻ is pleased and satisfied.

The Prophet ﷺ said, "Whoever knows his limit should stop there."[120]

Muslims must know their limits, know what is incumbent on them, and not step beyond what they are capable, causing society to descend into problems. Muslims must not interfere where they have no permission or authority; else they will bring punishment on all of the Muslims.

---

[120] "Man 'arifa haddahu waqafa 'indahu."

Clothed but Naked

As mentioned previously there were two groups of people in the Hellfire not shown to the Prophet ﷺ, and the second group is the one mentioned here.

حدثني زهير بن حرب . حدثنا جرير عن سهيل، عن أبيه، عن أبي هريرة . قال:
قال رسول الله صلى الله عليه وسلم (صنفان من أهل النار لم أرهما . قوم معهم سياط كأذناب البقر
يضربون بها الناس . ونساء كاسيات عاريات، مميلات مائلات، رؤوسهن كأسنمة البخت المائلة، لا
يدخلن الجنة، ولا يجدن ريحها . وإن ريحها ليوجد من مسيرة كذا وكذا (مسلم في كتاب اللباس و
أحمد في مسنده و مالك في الجامع)

Abū Hurayra ﷺ related that the Prophet ﷺ said:

> There are two types among the people of Hell whom I did not see. The first are people who have whips like the tails of oxen, with which they beat people, and the second are women who are dressed but naked, seductively swaying and dancing about, their heads look (strange) like the humps of camels. They will not enter Paradise or even smell its fragrance, although its fragrance reaches to such a great distance.[121]

The Prophet ﷺ is describing women who are ostensibly wearing clothes, but in reality are undressed. This does not refer to women in today's bathing suits because from an Islamic understanding those women are completely naked. This hadith refers to women who appear to be wearing something, but in reality are exposing everything. The Prophet ﷺ eloquently described them as *kāsīyāt*—clothed, and *āriyāt*, which means naked. Fourteen hundred years ago this seemed like a contradiction, as people could not imagine the styles of today. How could it be that someone is wearing clothes, and at the same time it is as if she is wearing nothing? This means that the clothes are either very tight and revealing or they are transparent through which one can see everything. Many women today put these clothes on and go everywhere, exposing their bodies without shame.

The Prophet ﷺ continued to describe them as, *mumīlātin mā'ilātin*. *Mā'ilāt* literally means tilting right and left, or deviated. They are deviated from the right path of obedience to Allāh ﷺ, and deviated from decency in behavior and

---

[121] *Sahīh Bukhārī, Sahīh Muslim*, #2128 "Kitāb al-Libas":
Sinfāni min āhl an-nāri lam arāhumā: qawmun ma'ahum siyātun ka adhnāb il-baqar, yadribūna biha an-nās. Was nisā'un kāsīyātun 'āriyātun mumīlatun mā'ilātun, ru'ūsuhunna ka asnimat il-bakhti. Al-mā'ilāt lā yadkhulna al-jannata wa lā yajidna rīhaha. Wa inna rīhaha lā tūjadu min masīrati kadha wa kadha.

dress. These women walk like peacocks with their heads high in the air, swinging their shoulders in an exaggerated way to draw men's attention to their shape, for mischief. They sway their hips from side to side when they walk to attract the eyes of men. They use suggestive gestures and mannerisms of speech to draw innocent people to follow their desires. *Mumīlāt* is similar in meaning to *mā'ilāt*, with the stress that such women go further by promoting this degraded style among their friends, roommates, and relations. Not content to be corrupt themselves, they work to spread their disease to other women, teaching them to feel no shyness in walking around unclothed.

The Prophet 襲 continued, "Their heads are something strange," or "They are bad luck, misfortune" *(Ru'ūsuhunna ka asnimat il-bakhti)*. *Bakht* is misfortune, in this hadith meaning that these women are a heap of misfortune. *Asnimat il-bakht*, also means humps of camels, meaning they make their hair stand up high up in the air, or stick out to the side, or wear wigs, or hair extensions; in general showing off their hair. Women with such hairstyles, walking in such a manner, dressed in such clothes are ubiquitous. If a lady tries to dress modestly they dissuade her saying, "That is old fashioned. Come dress like us."

This discussion of the Prophet's 襲 hadith is not aimed at what non-Muslims are doing, rather it is a sad commentary on what Muslim brothers and sisters are doing. In very conservative Muslim countries there are satellite television stations with scantily clad female announcers and talk show hosts. They are seen in Muslim homes around the world, and their provocative style of dress influences the viewers. There is no need to attract sexual interest while reporting the news. This is broadcast from countries that purport to be very religious, claiming to oversee the affairs of Muslims, but they are seemingly blind to what is happening within their own borders. They seem to care little about degrading their Muslim sisters as long as there is a profit to be made.

Worse yet, today we find all manner of cable networks and satellite channels in every part of the globe broadcasting talk shows televising the most lurid content or featuring provocative singers inciting people's sexual desires. Indeed, this global technology is urging people towards their lowest desires in a way unprecedented in human history and never before imagined. Even satellite channels broadcast from Muslim and Arab countries show sexually provocative programs, featuring men and women mixing together in various states of undress. In fact, today's fashion is to wear so little clothing that one is virtually naked. Not so long ago, swimsuits consisted of one piece. Then they became two pieces covering even less of the anatomy. Some beaches now have gone down to only one piece out of the two, while others "boast" no swimsuits at all. Through such influences, people are inflamed by flagrant lustful desire, competing to see who will pay more for misguidance (*dalāla*).

There are some Muslims who will not go to Paradise due to their commiting all kinds of sins. Such people are in the farthest reaches of the

Hellfire and were not shown to the Prophet 鸞 on the Night of Ascension. "They will not enter Paradise or even smell its fragrance, although its fragrance reaches to such a great distance." The scent of Paradise reaches very far; yet those who flaunt themselves in a state of undress will be so far from it as not to be able to smell it. Allāh 鸞 will prohibit them and those who encourage them, using them to corrupt the hearts of innocent Muslims, via the television screen. They are supporting the devil (*Shaytān*), in his evil work. Allāh 鸞 is watching to see who will avoid this temptation and remain constant in faith. The door of repentance is always open for every man and woman. Allāh 鸞 is the most Merciful, and He knows best.

If we use only this hadith for measurement, it is clear how far we have traveled into the signs of the Last Days, and how close we are. From the greatness that Allāh 鸞 gave to Prophet Muhammad 鸞, he was able to describe in detail what we unfortunately are witnessing today.

Open Sexual Relations

The Prophet ﷺ said that one of the Signs of the Last Days is that men and women will have sexual relations (*tasāfud*) in the streets, like donkeys.

وحديث عبد الله بن عمرو " لا تقوم الساعة حتى يتسافد في الطريق تسافد الحمير " أخرجه البزار
والطبراني وصححه ابن حبان والحاكم

'Abd Allāh Ibn 'Umar ؓ related that the Prophet ﷺ said:

The Hour will not come until there are men and women in the streets having sexual relations with each other like donkeys do.[122]

When donkeys want to mate, no one can control them or stop them from jumping on each other. They have sexual relations in plain sight, in the street. The word "tasāfud" means any sexual relation or expression which includes hugging and kissing; even holding hands. For a man and a woman, holding hands is an expression of sexual desire. This is seen everywhere on the streets today. There are many Muslims who express physical affection in public, imitating modern ways. Even Muslims who are married walk holding hands. This is not a sin by itself, but one cannot do that in public. In the Muslim world nowadays there is so much tasāfud happening with both married and unmarried people kissing and hugging each other in the streets, walking hand in hand, and sitting close together.

In previous times this behavior did not exist in Muslim countries, as couples would feel shy to touch each other in public. Touching, although permissible in private, was not allowed in public. It is *harām* (forbidden) to hold hands with one's wife on the street because it might create sinful thoughts in the people watching. It also brings a harmful gaze on one's wife, thus involving the husband in sin on his part. The standards of Islam are a protection, both to keep people from committing sin or even the appearance of sin.

The Prophet ﷺ said that in the Last Days people would be like donkeys, showing everyone what they are doing without any modesty or shyness. It was impossible for the Companions to understand such a thing, yet the Prophet ﷺ told them, "Yes, it will surely happen." This description of conditions in the Last Days did not manifest until very recently. Exactly as the Prophet ﷺ foretold, there are many Muslims holding hands and carrying on immodestly when they go out in public.

The next hadith applies more specifically to Muslims, and as a result Muslims should be very concerned about what is happening today.

---

[122] (*sahīh*) Ibn Hibbān #1889, "Kitāb al-Fitan." Albānī #481, *Silsila sahīha*; he said all of its men are trustworthy on the condition of *Muslim*. "Lā taqūm us-sā'atu hatta yatasāfadu fit-tarīqi tasāfud il-hamīr. Qult inna dhālika la kā'in? Qāla na'm layakūnanna."

عن النبي صلى الله عليه وسلم قال :«والذي نفسي بيده لا تفنى هذه الأمة حتى يقوم الرجل إلى
المرأة فيفترسها في الطريق فيكون خيارهم يومئذ من يقول: لو واريتها وراء هذا الحائط . (مسلم في
كتاب الفتن و الهيثمي في الزوائد ، رواه أبو يعلى ورجاله رجال الصحيح)

On the authority of Abū Hurayra ☙, the Prophet ﷺ said:

> (I swear) by the One in Whose Hand is my soul, this Ummah
> will not vanish until men go to women or women go to men;
> and they have intercourse with each other in the streets. The
> best of them at that time will say, I only wish that I was with
> her behind a wall (in private).[123]

The Prophet ﷺ swears an oath by Allāh ﷻ that in the Last Days the
Ummah will be in such a condition that people will have sexual relations in
public. Here he is speaking about both Muslims and non-Muslims or just
Muslims. This is happening today, especially in France and other European
countries, in public parks, beaches and alleyways. The issue of most concern
for the Muslims comes in the latter part of the hadith, "The best people among
them will say, if only this were happening behind a wall (so that no one could
see me!)."

The best of humanity are the believers because they engage in virtuous
behavior. Believers try to avoid committing sins; they are honest, they pray five
daily prayers, they fulfil their obligations, they fast, pay charity and seek the
good of society. But the Prophet ﷺ said that in the end of time, the believer
would see people having open sexual relations and wish that he was doing the
same thing in private. He will forget about Allāh ﷻ and will say, "If I was with
this woman in private I would have intercourse with her!" and similarly a
woman will think the same about a man. In the time of such open immodesty,
Shayṭān plays with even the believer. The believer cannot commit such an act
openly because he still has some measure of modesty inside of him, and he
does not want people to see him engaged in such behavior. Instead, he wants a
place where no one can see him. Instead of saying, "*Astaghfirullāh,* may Allāh
forgive them (for their public fornication) and forgive me (for desiring it)," he
wishes he was behind a wall with the woman so he could commit the same act.
"Behind a wall," might be in an apartment or anywhere behind closed doors, in
private. The believers in this time see public fornication occurring and say,
"What about us? Let us go behind closed doors."

This is a true hadith from the signs of the Last Days mentioned by

---

[123] (*sahīh*) *Sahīh Muslim* #2137, "Kitāb al-Fitan." Haythamī, *Majma' az-Zawā'id*(7:334). Abū
Y'ala narrated it and its men are *sahīh*. Albānī, *Silsila sahīha* #481:
> *Walladhī nafsī bi yadihi la tafnā hādhihil-ummah hatta yaqūm ur-rajulu ilal-
> mar'ati fayaftarishuhā fī-tarīq fa yakūnu khiyārūhum yawma'idhin man yaqūl
> law ra'aytahā warā hādha al-hā'it.*

Prophet Muhammad ﷺ fourteen hundred years ago. The Prophet ﷺ is the master of psychology, and he knows human nature totally, from beginning to end. He said there will be such people on the streets, but the best people of that time will not engage in sexual relations in public. Rather, they will wish they could do it in private. This was not happening even fifty years ago, but now it is everywhere. Fourteen hundred years ago the Prophet ﷺ said this would happen and it is one of the signs of the Last Days.

Greeting Reserved for Acquaintances

A highly recommended practice for Muslims, both men and women, is to greet any fellow Muslim, known or unknown, by saying, *As-salāmu alaykum*—"peace be upon you." One of the signs of the Last Days is that Muslims will not greet unknown Muslims they encounter. Rather, they will only greet those whom they know.

حدثنا أبو أحمد الزبيري حدثنا بشير بن سلمان عن سيار عن طارق بن شهاب قال كنا عند عبد
الله جلوسا فجاء رجل فقال قد أقيمت الصلاة فقام وقمنا معه فلما دخلنا المسجد رأينا الناس
ركوعا في مقدم المسجد فكبر وركع وركعنا ثم مشينا وصنعنا مثل الذي صنع فمر رجل يسرع
فقال عليك السلام يا أبا عبد الرحمن فقال صدق الله ورسوله فلما صلينا ورجعنا دخل إلى أهله
جلسنا فقال بعضنا لبعض أما سمعتم رده على الرجل صدق الله وبلغت رسله أيكم يسأله فقال
طارق أنا أسأله فسأله حين خرج فذكر عن النبي صلى الله عليه وسلم أن بين يدي الساعة تسليم
الخاصة وفشو التجارة حتى تعين المرأة زوجها على التجارة وقطع الأرحام وشهادة الزور وكتمان
شهادة الحق وظهور القلم (أحمد في مسنده و حاكم)

Imām Āhmad narrated an authentic hadith that the Prophet ﷺ said:

> Verily with the Hour there will be: greetings offered only to acquaintances; an increase in trading and business to the extent that the wife will help her husband in working for money; the cutting of family relations; the bearing of false witness; the concealment of the truth; and the pre-eminence of the pen.[124]

Today, we observe that Muslims only give greetings to their acquaintances. The scenario is, "If I don't know you I will not greet you." This is partly because Muslims are to a large extent unrecognizable as such; there are few outward signs of Islam anymore for Muslims to identify each other. Especially in places where Muslims are a minority, it is important to wear identifiably Islamic apparel, so Muslims can recognize and greet each other.

In the Muslim world, especially in holy cities like Makka and Madīna, Muslim men at minimum wear a headcap. However, outside of these revered places, men do not wear the traditional headcap. Women, on the other hand, are often covered by their headscarves in their daily lives. These women, then,

---

[124] *(sahīh)*. Āhmad, *Musnad* (1:407, 408). Haythamī, *Majma' az-Zawā'id* (7:331). Hākim *Mustadrak* (4:445, 446). Albānī, #647 *Silsila sahīha*. He said al-Bazzār's men are *sahīh*.
Inna bayna yaday is-sā'ati taslīm ul-khāsati wa fashut-tijārati hatta tu'in al-mar'atu zawjaha 'alā at-tijārati wa qat' al-arhāmi, wa shahādat az-zūri wa kitmāna shahādat il-haqqi wa zhuhūr al-qalam.

can be known and receive greetings from their Muslim sisters. It is also commendable for men to show their Muslim identity by wearing a headcap so they can be known and greeted by other Muslims. In this way Allāh ﷻ will be pleased, as He mentioned in the Holy Qur'ān:

وَإِذَا حُيِّيتُم بِتَحِيَّةٍ فَحَيُّوا بِأَحْسَنَ مِنْهَا أَوْ رُدُّوهَا إِنَّ اللَّهَ كَانَ عَلَى كُلِّ شَيْءٍ حَسِيبًا

When you are greeted, respond with a better greeting or at least return it (with an equal greeting).... (an-Nisā' 4:86)

Yet in countries where everyone is Muslim, people also do not greet each other. This is because there is no longer any unity or warmth between Muslims. In Muslim countries one may find hundreds of people passing on the streets, but no one greets each other with *as-salāmu alaykum.* Everyone is busy with his own life. Relationships are no longer based on a divine connection, but are based only on self-interest and worldly connections. This sign of the Last Days predicted by the Prophet ﷺ is a result of a shift in people's priorities.

حدثنا عبد الله حدثني أبي حدثنا ابن نمير عن مجالد عن عامر عن الأسود بن يزيد قال:
أقيمت الصلاة في المسجد فجئنا نمشي مع عبد الله بن مسعود فلما ركع الناس ركع عبد الله
وركعنا معه ونحن نمشي فمر رجل بين يديه فقال: السلام عليك يا أبا عبد الرحمن فقال عبد الله
وهو راكع: صدق الله ورسوله فلما انصرف سأله بعض القوم لِم قلت حين سلم عليك الرجل صدق
الله ورسوله قال: إني سمعت رسول الله صلى الله عليه وسلم يقول: إن من أشراط الساعة إذا
كانت التحية على المعرفة. (أحمد في مسنده)

'Abd Allāh Ibn Mas'ūd ؓ related a similar hadith in which the Prophet ﷺ said:

> Verily from among the signs of the Last Days, is that greetings will only be given to those whom one knows.[125]

If someone encounters a stranger today, they do not care to greet him. This reflects the lack of caring for one's fellow human beings. Even if one's friend or brother is suffering, hardly anyone cares. Everyone is only interested in looking out for himself.

In the past, this was not the case. If one saw a hundred people on the street he would give the greeting of *as-salāmu alaykum* to each of them. One of those greeted might be a pious person, whose *salām,* it is believed, might bring Allāh's mercy on both people. The Companion Sufyan Ibn 'Uyayna ؓ said, "Allāh's mercy descends with the remembrance of pious people—*'Inda dhikr al-sālihīn tatanazzalu al-rahmat.*" Today that practice is gone, and we do not greet

---

[125] *Musnad Āhmad. "Inna min ashrāt as-sā'ati idhā kānat at-tahīyyatu 'alā al-ma'arifah."*

each other. Even if we know someone, we turn our faces away to avoid interacting with each other. For the sake of some worldly agenda we do not want to show that we know this person. Muslims have become separated from each other. The Muslim Ummah cannot be healthy when they are deserting the message of Prophet Muhammad ﷺ.

Another sign of the Last Days mentioned in this hadith is that trade and business will flourish. People will be striving so hard in pursuit of their daily bread that they will set up any kind of work or trade.

The Prophet's ﷺ saying, "The wife will help her husband in working for money," indicates that in the Last Days there would not be adequate sustenance from one income, so that the wife would have to help her husband to provide sufficient support. In previous times, it was not necessary to have two incomes to support a family. Women were active in many endeavors, including caring for their children and families, education, providing medical treatment, farm work and many other activities. Of their own accord, many a woman would help her husband in his work. But previously the wife did not need to leave the house to work an additional job to meet the household expenses. Nowadays out of necessity to provide for the family, both the wife and the husband must go out to work. Everywhere around the world women are working in order to bring money to the household; the family is unable to survive on just the husband's meager income. It is as if the Prophet ﷺ were looking from the distant past at what we are experiencing today.

Cutting Ties of Relationship

The hadith related in the preceding chapter mentions that there would be, *qat'u ul-arhām*—"cutting of family relationships." The close relationship between blood relatives is disappearing, between parents, brothers, sisters, uncles and aunts. Nowadays, children have problems with their parents and as soon as they grow up they leave the family home. One does not see the children anymore, and they do not visit their parents.

In this hadith *"qat'ul-arhām"* also means "to cut the means of continuing the family," namely fertility and childbirth. Today, contraception is widespread, abortions are commonplace, and both men and women are undergoing surgery to prevent fertility. The continuity of the family is being cut in all ways. People are severing the bonds of relationships already established and are failing to bring the next generation of relations, cutting off both past and future family ties.

Another literal manifestation of this hadith, "cutting of the womb—*qat'ul-arhām*," is the actual cutting of the womb (uterus) that is occurring at an unprecedented pace. Routine births are commonly performed via caesarean section, surgically cutting into the uterus to deliver the baby abdominally, often to accommodate the busy schedule of the physician or even the mother. Hysterectomies, actual removal of the uterus, are commonly performed. Surgeries on the uterus are increasing, including intrauterine surgery on the fetus. Recently, in Saudi Arabia, the first attempt at a uterine transplant took place.[126] The Prophet ﷺ foresaw all of these aspects of contemporary life and technology fourteen hundred years ago and foretold that during the end of time the "cutting of the womb" would become commonplace.

[126] W. Fageeh et. al. International Journal of Gynecology & Obstetrics 76 2002, pp. 245-251.

Bearing False Witness

The Prophet ﷺ continued the hadith in the last chapter, saying that in the Last Days there would be "the bearing of false witness—*qawl az-zūr.*" Bearing witness to something false can occur in court when a witness is bribed either with money, or the promise of a position, or pardon by giving certain testimony. Even one politician may conspire against another and bring witnesses to testify against his opponent. There is no nation that does not have such happenings in its courts, where any testimony can be had for a price.

Allāh ﷺ said in the Holy Qur'ān:

$$اجْتَنِبُوا الرِّجْسَ مِنَ الْأَوْثَانِ وَاجْتَنِبُوا قَوْلَ الزُّورِ$$

Shun the abomination of idols, and shun the word that is false.

(al-Hajj 22:30)

Allāh ﷺ mentioned bearing false witness in this verse immediately after idol worship to emphasize its gravity. *Qawl az-zūr* is not limited to giving false testimony in court, but it is generally to put forth any falsehood and lead people to believe it is the truth. On a large scale this is propaganda and brainwashing, not to mention advertising, which falls under the rubric of *qawl az-zūr*. With today's global media of books, magazines, television, and movies any false message can be spread to make the white appear black and the black seem white. This is the propagation of falsehood and the bearing of false witness, *qawl az-zūr*.

Kitmān shahādat al-haqq means is the concealment of the truth. Politicians are notorious for concealing the truth to keep their people pacified and to remain in power. This illness has spread to the common people who nowadays find it easy to lie and conceal the truth. In the global media we find that too often the truth is concealed and falsehood is promoted by reporters. There are too few good, innocent people who remain honest, whether they be journalists in their reporting or politicians conducting the public's business.

Pre-eminence of the Pen

Allāh ﷻ has mentioned the pen in the Holy Qur'ān. The pen is the means of the preservation and transmission of knowledge, i.e. education. *Zuhūr al-qalam* in this hadith is the appearance of widespread knowledge and education. In *Sūrat al-Kahf* we are told that if the oceans were ink and the trees were pens, never would Allāh's words finish, that is knowledge never ends.

قُل لَّوْ كَانَ الْبَحْرُ مِدَادًا لِّكَلِمَاتِ رَبِّي لَنَفِدَ الْبَحْرُ قَبْلَ أَن تَنفَدَ كَلِمَاتُ رَبِّي وَلَوْ جِئْنَا بِمِثْلِهِ مَدَدًا

Say: If the sea were ink with which to write the words of my Lord, verily the sea would be exhausted before the words of my Lord, even if we added another sea like it, for its aid. (al-Kahf 18:109)

It is the greatness of Prophet Muhammad ﷺ to show the importance of education and how the means of education (**the pen**) would be widespread in the Last Days. Throughout Islamic history the pen has been the mechanism by which knowledge was recorded and preserved in manuscripts through writing. As the pen was a known invention during the time of the Prophet ﷺ, the hadith does not mean that the pen will appear, but rather the use of the pen and writing will be pre-eminent. The Prophet ﷺ sought to draw attention not to the pen itself, but to the increase of writings and increase in compiling knowledge that are so prominent today. It is impossible today using a normal pen and paper to keep up with recording and accessing the millions of books and items of knowledge and information. Thus, in this hadith there is a hint from the Prophet ﷺ that there will be something that will be able to facilitate keeping and classifying in archives vast amounts of knowledge and information and bringing them to use in an instant. This is what we are seeing with the fascinating technology of the computer.

Zuhūr al-qalam, (the pre-eminence of the pen, or education, or technology) means that there will be a time when millions and millions of pieces of information will be recorded and accessible to use. We will be able to "download" this information in an instant. We can search huge databases for a word and pull out every place where it appears. For example, we can see every place where the word *'ilm* (knowledge) appears in the Qur'ān, hadiths and Islamic books and instantly pull out each occurrence and its location. The highest level of research has been simplified so that today even a child can use a computer to access this vast array of knowledge. *Zuhūr al-qalam* means the ways and means of knowledge and education will be easy and also widespread, global. The Internet and the computer are a manifestation of this process and the satellite communication system is what has enabled this global phenomenon. This is what the Prophet ﷺ was subtly alluding to in this hadith fourteen hundred years ago. The computer is a manifestation of the *qalam*, and through satellites and the global Internet this has spread all over the world, for good and for bad.

Secrets Laid Bare

In the following hadith, Prophet Muhammad ﷺ prophesied that in the Last Days, wild animals would speak to human beings. We take the literal meaning of the hadith on its face value. In Islamic books human beings are sometimes referred to or classified as *hayawānun nātiq*—the speaking creature. People are speaking creatures, and "wild creatures" in the hadith can also be interpreted to signify a people foreign or unknown.

حدثنا عبد الله حدثني أبي حدثنا يزيد أنبأنا القاسم بن الفضل الحداني عن أبي نضرة عن أبي سعيد الخدري قال:

عدا الذئب على شاة فأخذها فطلبه الراعي فانتزعها منه فأقعى الذئب على ذنبه قال ألا تتقي الله تنزع مني رزقا ساقه الله إلي فقال يا عجبي ذئب مقع على ذنبه يكلمني كلام الإنس فقال الذئب إلا أخبرك بأعجب من ذلك محمد صلى الله عليه وسلم يثرب يخبر الناس بأنباء ما قد سبق قال فأقبل الراعي يسوق غنمه حتى دخل المدينة فزواها إلى زاوية من زواياها ثم أتى رسول الله صلى الله عليه وسلم فأخبره فأمر رسول الله صلى الله عليه وسلم فنودي الصلاة جامعة ثم خرج فقال للراعي أخبرهم فأخبرهم فقال رسول الله صلى الله عليه وسلم صدق والذي نفسي بيده لا تقوم الساعة حتى يكلم السباع الإنس ويكلم الرجل عذبة سوطه وشراك نعله ويخبره فخذه بما حدث أهله بعده (أحمد في مسنده)

Abū Saʿīd ﷺ related a long hadith, in part of which the Prophet ﷺ said:

> By Him in Whose hand is my soul, the Hour will not come
> until wild creatures talk to men, and a man speaks to the end
> of his whip and the straps of his sandals (shoes), and his thigh
> will tell him about what happened to his family after he left.[127]

This hadith signifies that people in the Last Days will talk about someone that they do not know. They will speak about someone they have only heard about somewhere and go into discussions about that person, or his family, or what he has or has not done.

Today there is an entire industry dedicated to publicizing the activities of actors and other famous people. Millions of people buy these magazines and newspapers or watch television programs devoted entirely to reporting what celebrities have done or said. Everything the celebrity does is exposed and discussed by millions of people who have never even seen that person in real life. This is one extreme instance of strangers talking about those they do not know. This hadith is also an indication that backbiting will be prevalent in the

---

[127] Āhmad, *Musnad* (3:84 and 85). Hākim, *Mustadrak* (4:467).

Last Days.[128]

"A man speaks to the end of his whip," indicates that people will speak into something with a cord like speaking into a telephone. Students of physics experiment by oscillating a string to see the resultant waveforms. Also, when one shakes a whip it creates a waveform down the length of the whip. The Prophet ﷺ is showing through the motion of the whip that people in the Last Days will discover a technology using waveforms by which they will speak. This transmission using wavelengths includes all kinds of communications whether radio, television, or satellite. One's cellular telephone in his pocket next to "his thigh will tell him about what happened to his family after he left."

In the Middle East and other places there is a saying that "the walls have ears," i.e. whatever one says and does is known. In this hadith the Prophet ﷺ is saying that there is coming a time where everything one does will be exposed. Even as someone "speaks to his whip," or his shoe, people unknown and unseen will be aware of it. Telecommunications are monitored by computers and people, and every cellular telephone is able to pinpoint its user's location. One's cellular phone will relay information and signals or "speak about him" to unknown observers while he calls his family.

Shoes in this hadith represent what is needed to walk and move about and travel. Today's cars with GPS (global positioning satellite) technology are able to be located at the touch of a button. The location of one's plane high above the clouds is known to unknown air traffic controllers around the world. One's activities on the street are often recorded by security cameras on earth and satellites high in the sky. This hadith is also a warning to Muslims of the Last Days to be pious and virtuous because everything one does today is monitored by unknown people, and everything is exposed.

༺﷽༻

---

[128] Allah ﷻ emphasized that backbiting is a tremendous offense:

O you who believe, avoid most suspicion, verily suspicion in some cases is a sin: And spy not on each other and do not speak badly about people in their absence. Would any of you like to eat the flesh of his dead brother? No, you would abhor it, so be mindful of Allah, verily Allah is Oft-Returning, Most Merciful. (al-Hujurāt 49:12)

This noble verse of the Holy Qur'ān is emphasizing the importance of avoiding suspicions about other people because in some cases these are a sin. According to the famous hadith of 'Umar al-Ibn Khattāb, *"innamā al-'aāmālu bin-niyyāt—actions (are rewarded) according to their intention,"* there is a possibility that one's opinion about someone could be considered meritorious if his intention is good, while if the intention is to demean or speak badly about them then it is a sin. Allāh is giving a vivid example of how horrible backbiting is to both the perpetrator and the victim, *"Would any of you like to eat the flesh of his dead brother?"*

Six Events

The Prophet ﷺ mentioned six tremendous signs that would precede the Day of Judgment.

حدثنا الحميدي: حدثنا الوليد بن مسلم: حدثنا عبد الله بن العلاء بن زبر قال: سمعت بسر بن

عبيد الله: أنه سمع أبا إدريس قال: سمعت عوف بن مالك قال:

أتيت النبي صلى الله عليه وسلم في غزوة تبوك، وهو في قبة من أدم، فقال: (اعدد ستا بين يدي

الساعة: موتي، ثم فتح بيت المقدس، ثم موتان يأخذ فيكم كقعاص الغنم، ثم استفاضة المال حتى

يعطى الرجل مائة دينار فيظل ساخطا، ثم فتنة لا يبقى بيت من العرب إلا دخلته، ثم هدنة تكون

بينكم وبين بني الأصفر، فيغدرون فيأتونكم تحت ثمانين غاية، تحت كل غاية اثنا عشر ألفا

(البخاري في كتاب الجزية و أحمد في مسنده)

'Awf Ibn Mālik ؓ related that the Prophet ﷺ said:

> Count six signs before the Hour: my death; then the opening
> of *Bayt al-Maqdis*; then death in huge numbers, like the plague
> of sheep; then there will be such an excess of money, such
> that a man would give one hundred dinars to a (needy) person
> and he looks at that with disgust; then a confusion that will
> enter every house of the Arabs; then a truce between you and
> the non-Muslims (because) they will be exceedingly powerful
> against you, coming to you with eighty different groups (of
> soldiers or eighty different compelling excuses); under each
> group twelve thousand (soldiers or twelve thousand
> explanations).[129]

One of the first signs of the Last Days occurred with the passing of the Holy Prophet ﷺ from this life. Then the opening of *Bayt al-Maqdis*[130] took place shortly thereafter, during the Caliphate of the Companion 'Umar Ibn al-Khattāb ؓ. The Prophet ﷺ then mentioned that there would be deaths like the plagues of infected animals, *ku'ās al-ghanam*. *Ku'ās* is a disease that comes to sheep, goats or other ruminant animals, and Ibn Hajar explained that it is a

---

[129] *Sahīh Bukhārī*, "Kitāb al-Jihād" (6:198). Āhmad, *Musnad* (6:25 and 27):
'Udud sittan bayna yadayhi as-sā'at: mawtī, thumma fathu bayt il-maqdis,
thumma mūtānun yakhudhu fīkum ka ku'ās il-ghanami, thumma astifādat-ul-
māli hatta y'uti ar-rajulu mi'ata dīnārin fayadhala sākhitan, thumma fitnatun lā
yabqā baytun min al-'arab illa dakhalat-hu, thumma hudnatun takūnu
baynakum wa bayna banī il-asfara fa yaghdurūna fa yā'tūnakum tahta
thamānīna ghāyatin, tahta kulli ghāyatin ithna 'ashara alfa.
Ibn Mājah relates a version of this hadith which mentions an illness which "will purify you of
your deeds."
[130] see further discussion of *Bayt al-Maqdis* in chapter "The Destruction of Yathrib."

sickness that enters through the lungs and results in a discharge from the nose and mouth. Saliva and mucus flow profusely and if the animal is not mercifully slaughtered it dies a miserable death. We have seen this recently in Europe with the outbreak of foot and mouth disease. According to the BBC, over 3.9 million animals were slaughtered by October, 2001. Miraculously, these contemporary events were precisely described by the Prophet ﷺ fourteen hundred years ago.

This hadith mentions that in the Last Days a great number of people will also die in this way, that is by the spread of a harmful substance into the respiratory system. Influenza is spread in this manner and produces similar symptoms. There are yearly epidemics of influenza and occasional pandemics in which a new strain of the virus sweeps over the world, killing millions.[131] In today's world of travelers rapidly criss-crossing the globe a pandemic of influenza could spread like lightning, leaving massive death in its wake.[132] The SARS pandemic is an example of such an outbreak. As of April 2003, the World Health Organization reported nearly 3,000 probable SARS cases worldwide, with four percent resulting in death. At the time of publication, the World Health Organisation's infectious diseases chief said he feared the SARS virus could be carried by people without symptoms.[133]

Contemporary agents of chemical or biological warfare also utilize

---

131

The Spanish Influenza pandemic is the catastrophe against which all modern pandemics are measured. It is estimated that approximately 20 to 40 percent of the worldwide population became ill and that over 20 million people died. Between September 1918 and April 1919, approximately 500,000 deaths from the flu occurred in the U.S. alone. Many people died from this very quickly. Some people who felt well in the morning became sick by noon, and were dead by nightfall. Those who did not succumb to the disease within the first few days often died of complications from the flu (such as pneumonia) caused by bacteria....

Pandemic Influenza, US Centers for Disease Control, National Vaccine Program Office.

132

There's no simple answer to the question of how serious a pandemic might be. It all depends on how virulent (severe) the virus is, how rapidly it can spread from population to population, and the effectiveness of pandemic prevention and response efforts. The 1918 Spanish flu is an example of a worst-case scenario because the strain was highly contagious and quite deadly. This pandemic killed more Americans than all the wars of the 20th century. Since our world today is vastly more populated, and people travel the globe with ease, the spread of a next pandemic could be more rapid than that of previous pandemics.

Pandemic Influenza, US Centers for Disease Control. National Vaccine Program Office.

133 In an April 7 [2003] update published on their web site, the WHO said that SARS diagnostic tests developed so far were problematic. "If there are people who have the virus and don't show symptoms, we are lost, because that would mean it had spread throughout the world, as it is easily contracted," David Heymann [WHO's infectious diseases chief] said in an interview with Spain's El Pais daily.

"That was how AIDS was transmitted before it was discovered. We still don't know if this is the case, that's why we need a test," he added.

airborne transmission of a toxic or infectious agent, leading to a copious discharge of secretions from the nose and mouth, and eventually death. This may also occur with the toxic smoke of a nuclear explosion. The possibility of massive deaths from infections and weapons of mass destruction has never been so great. This is one of the signs of the Last Days mentioned fourteen hundred years ago by Prophet Muhammad ﷺ, and the possibility, or probability, of its occurrence is increasing daily.

The hadith continues that there will be huge amounts of money in the Last Days, *istifādatul-māl.* Today the economy is globalized, with massive amounts of money changing hands, and trade on an unbelievable scale. Huge companies are merging and devouring smaller ones. The Prophet ﷺ said there will be so much trade and inflation around the world that a beggar will consider one hundred *dinārs* (approximately ten dollars) as nothing because it will not be enough to buy anything anymore.[134] *Istifādatul-māl* also means that in the time of Mahdī ﷺ, wealth will be so abundant that one hundred *dinars* will be insignificant.

In the continuation of the hadith the Prophet ﷺ mentioned "a confusion that will enter every house of the Arabs," which represents all of the Muslims. Politicians everywhere in the Muslim world oppress and confuse the people to the point that they no longer know what to do. There is also the confusion of a new ideology and sect in Islam which came to prominence at the beginning of the 20th century.[135] That confusion can be found in every home in the Muslim world, and is causing dissension between children and parents, sister and brother, mother and father, husband and wife. This ideology encourages people to rebel against traditional Islamic teachings.

---

[134] Abū Hurayra related in another hadith that the Prophet said, "There will come a time when people will not care how they make their money, whether from permitted or forbidden means."
It is very rare to find anyone with income that comes completely from permitted means because everything nowadays is corrupted. Most of the money in circulation is from religiously prohibited dealings: whether from criminal enterprises, money laundering, usury, cheating, corrupt deals, gambling, illicit drugs, or weapons.
At the heart of all this is the banking system based on interest which is forbidden in Islam. Even salaries from a decent job which is permitted (*halāl*) still comes through the bank, thereby mixing with the monies of interest. Muslims should not be convinced by claims of "Islamic banking" because these "Muslim banks" work on the institutional level lending to usurious banks and also mixing with interest. Throughout Muslim countries and even in the heart of the Muslim world there are many foreign, non-Muslim bank branches, operating in the same manner that they do in the West. One cannot do anything without banks now, and the credit cards and ATM cards from the banks have replaced carrying currency. Every product and every item of food in the market comes via a letter-of-credit through these banks, with interest paid on it. People still claim to have "*halāl* money" but in fact all the money is mixed with interest. The Prophet foretold that interest would be so ubiquitous like scattered sands leaving nothing untouched. People's lack of concern nowadays with how they obtain their money is one of the signs of the End Times of the world.
[135] This sect uses many pseudonyms: the modernization of Islam, Islamism, Islamic activism, Maudoodism, Qutbism or "Salaf"-ism or Wahhābism. They have rejected all the traditional schools of thought (see also section on Khawārij).

In our time, people speak of a struggle between civilizations, and that is what the Prophet 🌸 mentioned at the end of this hadith.[136] This struggle culminates in a truce between the Muslims and an assemblage of non-Muslims. The non-Muslims will be so powerful at that time, with eighty different excuses and twelve thousand different confusions under each excuse, that the Muslims will be brought to a truce. We can see the evidence of this confusion and the truce it brings looming on the horizon.

حدثنا عبد الرحمن بن إبراهيم الدمشقي حدثنا بشر بن بكر حدثنا ابن جابر حدثني أبو عبد السلام عن ثوبان قال قال رسول الله صلى الله عليه وسلم يوشك الأمم أن تداعى عليكم كما تداعى الأكلة إلى قصعتها فقال قائل ومن قلة نحن يومئذ قال بل أنتم يومئذ كثير ولكنكم غثاء كغثاء السيل ولينزعن الله من صدور عدوكم المهابة منكم وليقذفن الله في قلوبكم الوهن فقال قائل يا رسول الله وما الوهن قال حب الدنيا وكراهية الموت

Thawban narrated that the Prophet 🌸 said:

The people will soon summon one another to attack you as people when eating, invite others to share their dish.

Someone asked: "Will that be because of our small numbers at that time?" He replied: "No, you will be numerous at that time: but you will be like foam that is carried down by a torrent..."[137]

---

[136] Huntington, Samuel P. 1996. *The Clash of Civilizations and the Remaking of World Order.* New York: Simon & Schuster.
[137] *Sunan Abū Dāwūd*, Book 37, Number 4284; a similar narration is found in Āhmad's *Musnad* and mentioned by Haythamī in *Majma' al-zawā'id* (7:287).

West Nile Virus and the Character of Nimrod

Allāh ﷻ described how Mankind foolishly took the Trust from Allāh ﷻ, becoming the deputy (*khalīfa*) of Allāh ﷻ on earth:

إِنَّا عَرَضْنَا الْأَمَانَةَ عَلَى السَّمَاوَاتِ وَالْأَرْضِ وَالْجِبَالِ فَأَبَيْنَ أَن يَحْمِلْنَهَا وَأَشْفَقْنَ مِنْهَا وَحَمَلَهَا
الْآسَانُ إِنَّهُ كَانَ ظَلُومًا جَهُولًا

*We did indeed offer the Trust to the heavens and the earth and the
mountains; but they refused to undertake it, being afraid thereof: but
mankind undertook it; verily he was an oppressor and foolish.*

(al-Ahzāb 33:72)

This undertaking demonstrates a foolish trait which mankind possesses, pride. To voluntarily accept an undertaking which the heavens and the earth refused shows that human beings are prone to an exaggerated self-image. This trait became manifest in the extreme with Pharaoh and Nimrod. Nimrod was given everything in this life, until he became so arrogant and proud of himself that he said, "I am going to kill God in heaven." He built a huge structure, went on top of it, and shot an arrow into the sky. Allāh ﷻ sent an angel with a bird that was struck by the arrow. When the bloodied arrow came down Nimrod said, "Oh, I am everything now! I killed that one in heaven!" He became so arrogant and proud of himself. Today there are a lot of people acting like Nimrod, both men and women. They do not care for their fellow human beings, and think they are the only people that matter. As long as they are sitting on the throne they do not care if the whole country goes up in flames. They are inheriting the character and manners of Shaytān, Iblīs, making them arrogant.

When Nimrod reached the utmost of arrogance, Allāh ﷻ sent him the weakest, frailest creature, a mosquito, in order to show him that he was not so great and in reality was less powerful than a small insect. The mosquito entered through his nose and began to eat his brain. Eating and gnawing away at his brain the mosquito caused Nimrod to have unbelievably severe pain and headaches. The pain of the mosquito devouring his brain was more than anything he could endure, and he was unable to get any relief from this pain except by having his servant beat him on the head. He ordered his servants to repeatedly beat him so he could forget about the pain of the mosquito eating his brain. The tiny mosquito ate away at his brain until it bored through and emerged from the front of his skull, killing Nimrod.

Unfortunately, many Muslims are imitating Nimrod in their manners and behavior. Only because they are from the Community of Prophet Muhammad ﷺ has punishment been mercifully withheld by Allāh ﷻ. If not for their having accepted Islam and Prophet Muhammad 鬱, even if only nominally, Allāh 鬱 would have sent mosquitoes to eat their brains as well. Recently, an extremely rare disease carried by mosquitoes has suddenly come into worldwide prominence. The West Nile Virus (WNV) is carried by mosquitoes and has spread to many countries around the world and is killing men, women, and children. Scientists are amazed at how this diseased mosquito became so prevalent so quickly. Allāh 鬱 is sending that disease to clean the contamination that has appeared from the bad manners and base characters of human beings. Since people are imitating Nimrod and have forgotten that they are weak, Allāh 鬱 has sent the weakest of creatures against them to teach them a similar lesson.

For people who backbite, Allāh 鬱 creates wild animals to attack the body in the grave to punish them, cleanse them, and teach them a lesson. Similarly, from people's bad manners and characters Allāh 鬱 is creating that mosquito to attack them. The prayers of the pious are keeping that virulence contained, but when there are no more pious people in a community, supplications for protection will no longer be accepted. At that time Allāh's punishment may come upon those people.

RELIGION BECOMES STRANGE

THE STRANGENESS OF THE SUNNAH AND ITS ADHERENTS[138]

Islam Began Strange and Will Become Strange

In the Last Days of the Ummah, those who adhere to the Sunnah of the Holy Prophet ﷺ will become rare. On the contrary, those who contravene the Sunnah will be commonplace.

حدثنا محمد بن عباد وابن أبي عمر . جميعا عن مروان الفزاري . قال ابن عباد: حدثنا مروان عن يزيد، يعني ابن كيسان، عن أبي حازم، عن أبي هريرة؛ قال: قال رسول الله صلى الله عليه وسلم: "بدأ الإسلام غريبا وسيعود كما بدأ غريبا . فطوبى للغرباء (مسلم في كتاب الفتن وابن ماجه في كتاب الفتن و أحمد في مسنده)

'Abd Allāh Ibn Mas'ūd ﷺ said the Prophet ﷺ said:

Islam began as something strange, and it will revert to being strange as it was in the beginning, so good tidings to the strangers.[139]

Imām Awzā'i said:

As for this, then it does not mean that Islam will go away, but rather it means that the *Āhl as-Sunnah*[140] will go away, up to the point that there will not remain in a land any of them except one person.

Based on this understanding, there can be found in the statements of the *Salaf* much praise for the Sunnah and their describing it as being strange, and describing its adherents and followers as being few.[141] This is why it has been

---

[138] Excerpts from *Kashf-ul-qurbah fi wasfi hāli āhlil-ghurbah* by Ibn Rajab Hanbalī (d. 795 H). Translation by Dr. Mohammed Fadel.

[139] *Sahīh Muslim*, "Kitāb al-Īmān," Vol. 1 Number 90. *Ibn Mājah*, "Kitāb al-Fitan." We also find in another version in *Sahīh Muslim* narrated by Abū Hurayra that the Prophet said, *"bada' al-islāmu gharīban wa saya'ūdu kamā badā'*—Islam began strange and will return as it began."

[140] What is meant by the term *Āhl as-Sunnah* [or *Āhl as-Sunnati wal-Jamā'ah*] are all the Muslims who follow the Way of the Prophet Muhammad and the Congregation of the Community. They learn it, act upon it, and teach it to others. They consist of the scholars, their students and those that follow in their footsteps.

[141] And as for the complete Sunnah, then it is the path that is free and safe from doubts and desires, as has been stated by Al-Hasan, Yūnus Ibn 'Ubayd, Sufyān, Al-Fudayl and others

mentioned that they are, "A righteous people surrounded by people abounding in much evil. Those who disobey them are greater than those who obey them."[142]

In this is an indication of the smallness of their number and in the number of those who answer and accept their call. We also are made aware of the greatness in number of those who oppose them and disobey them. These strangers are of two categories: the first of them are those who rectify themselves when the people have become corrupt; the second category contains those who rectify what the people have corrupted of the Sunnah; and this latter one is the higher and more virtuous of the two categories.

حدثنا عبد الله بن عبد الرحمن، أخبرنا اسماعيل بن أبي أويس، حدثني كثير بن عبد الله بن عمرو

بن عوف بن زيد بن ملحة عن أبيه عن جده أن رسول الله صلى الله عليه وسلم قال:

إن الدين ليأرز إلى الحجاز كما تأرز الحية إلى جحرها، وليعقلن الدين في الحجاز معقل الأوربة من

رأس الجبل. إن الدين بدأ غريبا وسيعود غريبا فطوبى للغرباء الذين يصلحون ما أفسد الناس من

بعدي من سنتي (الترمذي في كتاب الإيمان)

In another narration 'Amr Ibn 'Awf ﷺ related that the Prophet ﷺ said:

> Truly the religion shall retreat and take refuge in the Hijāz, just like the snake returns to take refuge in its hole. In truth, the religion shall indeed find refuge in the Hijāz in the same manner that mountain-goats find refuge on the tops of mountains. The religion started strange, and it will return as it started. Glad tidings to the strangers. They are those who set right what people have corrupted of my Sunnah after me.[143]

And in another narration:

> The Hour shall not take place until faith returns to take refuge in Madīna just like the snake returning to take refuge in her hole.

Qādī 'Iyād says:

> What the Messenger of Allāh has said about Madīna does not constitute mere praise for a piece of land or a group of houses. On the contrary, it is but praise for the people of that land and these houses, calling attention to the fact that these

---

besides them. Due to this, its adherents are described as strange because of their small number and rarity in the Last Days.

[142] *Musnad Āhmad* (2:177).

[143] *Tirmidhī. Mishkāt ul-masābīh*, #170 "Kitāb ul-Qadr."
   Inna ad-dīna badā'a gharīban wa saya'ūdu kamā badā' fatūbā lil-ghurabā'i, wa hum alladhīna yuslihūna ma afsada an-nāsu min b'adī min sunnatī.

attributes shall endure in them but shall vanish from other than them, at the time when knowledge will be taken back up to the Heavens and removed, so that the people shall take as their leaders ignorant men of whom questions shall be asked and who will answer without means of knowledge. So they will go astray and lead the others astray. Ibn Abī 'Ūways said, "I heard Mālik say regarding the meaning of the hadith, 'Islam began as something uncommon and strange and shall return to be again like it began,' namely it will return to Madīna, just as in Madīna it first began."

Tabarānī and others transmitted the hadith of Abū 'Umāmah ⬥ that the Prophet ⬥ said:

Verily, for every matter there is a progression and a regression. And verily the progression of this Religion is from what you used to be in of blindness and ignorance into what Allāh sent me with. And verily from the progression of this Religion is that the clan was taught (Islam) by its family members, to the point that there was not found amongst them (the tribes) anyone except for one or two evildoers. So these two were oppressed and degraded. When they want to speak they are restrained, subdued and persecuted. And verily from the regression of this Religion is that the tribe acts harshly against its family members, to the point that there is not seen amongst them anyone except one or two *faqihs* (one with understanding). Thus they will both be oppressed and degraded. If they speak and command the good and forbid the evil, they are restrained, subdued and persecuted. And they will not find any supporters or helpers in that matter.

حدثنا أبو النضر قال حدثنا عبد الحميد يعني ابن بهرام قال قال شهر بن حوشب قال ابن غنم لما دخلنا مسجد الجابية أنا وأبو الدرداء لقينا عبادة بن الصامت فأخذ يميني بشماله وشمال أبي الدرداء بيمينه فخرج يمشي بيننا ونحن ننجي والله أعلم فيما نتناجى وذاك قوله فقال عبادة بن الصامت لئن طال بكما عمر أحدكما أو كلاكما ليوشكن أن تريا الرجل من ثبج المسلمين يعني من وسط قرأ القرآن على لسان محمد صلى الله عليه وسلم فأعاده وأبداه وأحل حلاله وحرم حرامه ونزل عند منازله أو قرأه على لسان أخيه قراءة على لسان محمد صلى الله عليه وسلم فأعاده وأبداه وأحل حلاله وحرم حرامه ونزل عند منازله لا يحور فيكم إلا كما يحور رأس الحمار الميت...

And it is recorded that 'Ubādah Ibn Sāmit ⬥, a Companion of the Prophet ⬥, said to one of his companions:

It is imminent that should your life be prolonged for you, you will see a man who recites the Qur'ān with the language of Muhammad ﷺ, repeating it and displaying it, allowing its *halāl* and forbidding its *harām*. He will then be lowered in his status and his position will be neglected amongst you and considered just as the position of a dead donkey.[144]

Indeed, the believer will be debased in the Last Days due to his strangeness in front of the evildoers, from among the people of doubts and desires. Every one of them will hate him and abuse him because of his opposing their way by following his way, and because of the seeking of his goal over their goal, and because of his evidences over what is with them.[145]

Abū Ash-Shaykh Al-Asbahānī reported with a chain connected to the *tab'ī*[146] Hasan al-Basrī, that he said, "If a man from the first generation of Muslims were sent (to us) today, he would not recognize anything from Islam except for this prayer!" Then he said:

> I swear by Allāh, that if he were to live to the time of these evils, he would see the innovator calling unto his innovation, and the individual involved with the worldly life calling unto his worldly affairs. Then Allāh would protect him and his heart would long for the way which the *Salaf as-sālih* (pious predecessors) were on. And so he would follow their footsteps and act according to their ways. For him there will be a great reward.

Ibn Al-Mubārak reported from Al-Fudayl from Al-Hasan ﷺ that he once mentioned the rich and extravagant man who has authority and who amasses wealth claiming that he has no end in it. And then he mentioned the misguided innovator who sets out against the Muslims with an unsheathed sword, changing the meaning of what Allāh ﷻ has revealed concerning the disbelievers in favor of the Muslims.[147] Then he said:

> Your Sunnah, I swear by [Allāh], is between these two: between the self-sufficient one and the hard-hearted, the extravagant one and the ignorant. So have patience with it, for indeed, *Ahl as-Sunnah* are from among the fewest of people, those who do not fall into the category of the extravagant ones in their excessiveness nor do they fall into the category of the innovators in following their own desires. Rather, they

---

[144] *Musnad* of Imām Āhmad.
[145] Today we see traditional Muslim scholars are harassed and persecuted by innovators.
[146] The first generation of Muslims after the Companions of the Prophet.
[147] See also the chapter on Khawārij.

bear with patience following the Sunnah until they meet their Lord. So be on that way, if Allāh wills!

Then he said:

I swear by Allāh, that if a man were to reach these evils, he would hear someone say, "Come over to me!" and someone else say, "Come over to me!" So he would say, "No! I do not want anything but the Sunnah of Muhammad ﷺ," seeking after it and asking questions about it. Indeed this one will be given a great reward. So be on that way, if Allāh wills!

'Abd Allāh bin Mas'ūd ﷺ related that the Prophet ﷺ said:

There will be rulers over you, who will abandon the Sunnah like this, and he pointed to the origin of his finger. If you were to leave these rulers alone, they would bring great affliction and disaster. There has been no previous Ummah except that the first thing they abandoned from their religion was the Sunnah, and the last to be left was the prayer, and were not these rulers shy and afraid of the people, they would not pray.[148]

---

[148] Narrated by Hākim who said this is a sahīh hadith on the condition of Bukhārī and Muslim.

The Truthful One is Rejected

In the Last Days, the one who is trustworthy in keeping the religion will be called a traitor, and the people will look at him as if he had betrayed Islam.

حدثنا عبد الله حدثني أبي حدثنا يونس وسريج قالا حدثنا فليح عن سعيد بن عبيد بن السباق
عن أبي هريرة قال رسول الله صلى الله عليه وسلم: قبل الساعة سنون خداعة يكذب فيها
الصادق ويصدق فيها الكاذب ويخون فيها الأمين ويؤتمن فيها الخائن وينطق فيها الرويبضة قال سريج
وينطق فيها الرويبضة (أحمد في مسنده و إبنُ ماجه في كتاب الفتن)

Abū Hurayra ﷺ related that the Prophet ﷺ said:

> Before the Hour comes, there will be years of deceit, in which the trustworthy one will be said to be a traitor, and the traitor will be trusted and the insignificant will have a say.[149]

The trustworthy one (al-amīn) means the one who is holding fast to the authentic Islamic teachings and traditions from the people of the Sunnah and the main body of Muslims (Āhl as-Sunnah wal Jamā'ah). Not only will people reject the truth and the truthful person, but they will also put their trust and the fate of the Muslims in the hands of someone who is disingenuous: "and the traitor will be trusted." The one who consistently betrays Muslims is considered to be trustworthy, and this is a sign of the Last Days.

حدثنا محمد بن سنان: حدثنا فليح بن سليمان: حدثنا هلال بن علي، عن عطاء بن يسار، عن
أبي هريرة رضي الله عنه قال: قال رسول الله صلى الله عليه وسلم: (إذا ضيعت الأمانة فانتظر
الساعة) . قال: كيف إضاعتها يا رسول الله؟ قال: (إذا أسند الأمر إلى غير أهله فانتظر الساعة
(البخاري في كتاب العلم و أحُمد في مسُنده)

In another hadith Abū Hurayra ﷺ related:

> A bedouin asked the Prophet ﷺ when the Judgement Day would occur. He said, "When the trust (al-amāna) is lost, then wait for the Judgement Day." The bedouin said, "How will it be lost?" The Prophet ﷺ said, "When power and authority comes in the hands of unfit persons, then wait for the Judgement Day."[150]

As the Prophet ﷺ predicted, everything nowadays is upside down. The psychology of people in our time is the opposite of what Islam prescribes, and it is so difficult to find a trustworthy person. Everywhere on earth different

---

[149] Āhmad, Musnad. Ibn Mājah.
[150] Sahīh Bukhārī. Nawawī, #1837, Riyād as-Sālihīn.

groups of Muslims are destroying the religion because they have their own agendas. Muslim groups and individuals slander one another, and through their corrupt behavior support falsehood, while claiming to be believers.

"The trustworthy one will be said to be a traitor," (*yukhawwin ul-amīn*) has another interpretation. *Al-Amīn* is one of the names of Prophet Muhammad ﷺ, and one of the signs of the Last Days is that people will attack Allāh's Messenger.

عَنْ أَبِي هُرَيْرَةَ قَالَ قَالَ رَسُولُ اللهِ صَلَّى اللهُ عَلَيْهِ و سَلَّم لا تَقُوم السَّاعَة حَتَّى يَخْرُج ثَلَاثُون كَذَّابًا رِجَالًا كُلّهم يَكْذِب عَلَى اللهِ عز وَجل وَرسوله صَلَّى اللهُ عَلَيْهِ وسلم (أَبُو داود في كِتَابِ الْمَلَاحِمِ و أَحمد في مُسْنَده)

Abū Hurayra ؓ also related that the Prophet ﷺ said:

The Hour will not come until thirty Dajjāls (liars) appear, all of them lying about Allāh and His Messenger.[151]

These are the smaller *dajjāls* (liars) who will pave the way for al-Masīh ad-Dajjāl, the Anti-Christ. Some non-Muslims may try to demean Prophet Muhammad ﷺ, but when Muslims themselves under the guise of modernism, Islamism, or Wahhābism try to diminish the stature and rank of Allāh's Beloved Prophet ﷺ, it is beyond irreverent and enters the realm of the heretical. They assign little importance to him ﷺ, saying he ﷺ is a mere postman who came, delivered a message, and went away. The importance and exalted rank of the Prophet ﷺ is paramount and fundamental to Islam. One cannot make the canonical prayer or even enter Islam without mentioning his name and status. The first pillar of Islam is to bear witness that there is no god except Allāh and Muhammad is His Messenger: *Lā ilāha illa-Allāh, Muhammadun Rasūlullāh.*

As-Sakhāwī said:

Just as in the testimony of faith (*shahāda*) Allāh ﷻ has placed His Messenger's blessed name next to His Own Sacred Name and has said that he who obeys the Prophet ﷺ obeys Him and he who loves the Prophet ﷺ loves Him, in the same manner He has related our invoking blessings upon the Prophet ﷺ to His Own blessings upon us. Therefore just as Allāh ﷻ said about His remembrance:

فَاذْكُرُونِي أَذْكُرْكُمْ

Remember Me and I will remember you, (al-Baqara 2:152)

[151] *Abū Dāwūd.* Āhmad, *Musnad.*

Likewise is His assurance: Allāh ﷻ sends ten blessings on the one who invokes a single blessing on the Holy Prophet ﷺ, as it is established in the sound hadith.[152]

أخبرنا علي بن حجر قال حدثنا إسماعيل بن جعفر عن العلاء عن أبيه عن أبي هريرة عن النبي
صلى الله عليه وسلم قال: من صلى علي واحدة صلى الله عليه عشرا(مسلم في كتاب الصّلاة و
أحمد في مسنده و في سنن الترّمذي في كتاب الصّلاة و سنن النَّساء في كتاب السّهو و في سنن أبي
داوُد في كتاب الصّلاة)

'Abd Allāh Ibn 'Amr Ibn al-'Ās ؓ related that the Prophet ﷺ said:

> Whoever invokes blessings on me one time, Allāh will send blessings on him ten times.[153]

حدثنا أبو داود سليمان بن سلم المصاحفي البلخي أخبرنا النضر بن شميل عن أبي قرة الأسدي
عن سعيد بن المسيب عن عمر بن الخطاب قال إن الدعاء موقوف بين السماء والأرض لا يصعد
منه شيء حتى تصلي على نبيك صلى الله عليه وسلم.

Another extremely important reason why one must invoke blessings on the Prophet ﷺ is that it is established in the hadith, "The du'a or invocation of the believer is suspended between heaven and earth as long as the invocation of blessings and peace upon your Prophet ﷺ does not accompany it."[154]

Many volumes have been written refuting the claims of the Wahhābis that the Prophet ﷺ is no longer of any benefit to his community. Those who seek to diminish the Prophet ﷺ by claiming he was an ordinary person who came and is now dead, ignore the consensus of Muslim scholars, the hadiths of the Prophet ﷺ and the words of Allāh Almighty in the Holy Qur'ān itself:

ولا تحسبن الذين قتلوا في سبيل الله أمواتا بل أحياء عند ربهم يرزقون

Think not of those who are slain in Allāh's way as dead. Nay, they are alive, receiving their sustenance from their Lord. (Āl-'Imrān 3:169)

Allāh ﷻ is confirming that the *shuhadā'* (martyrs) are alive even after they

---

[152] *Qawl al-Bad'i* p. 132.
[153] *Sahīh Muslim. Riyād as-sālihīn* #1397.
[154] *Tirmidhī* narrates this hadith from 'Umar in the section of his *Sunan* entitled *Sifat al-salāt 'alā an-nabī*, and al-Qadī Abū Bakr Ibn al-'Arabī comments on it thus:
The chain of men who narrate this is sound and both Malik and Muslim have cited it though not *Bukhārī*. Such an utterance on the part of 'Umar can only be a Prophetic legislation because it is not subject to opinion. It is strengthened by Muslim's narration of the Prophet's words: "If you hear the *mu'adhdhin*, repeat his words after him then invoke blessings upon me... then ask Allāh to grant me *al-wasīla* (the station of intercession for the invocation of believers)... *Tuhfat al-ahwādī* (2:273-4).

leave this life. If this is for an ordinary martyr, it is even more certain that prophets are also alive and even more greatly rewarded.

عن أنس بن مالك قال: قال رسول الله صلى الله عليه وسلم: الأنبياء أحياء في قبورهم يصلون
(الهيثمي في الزوند رواه أبو يعلى والبزار ، ورجال أبو يعلى ثقات)

The Prophet ﷺ said, "The prophets are alive in their graves, praying."[155]

During the Night Journey and Ascension the Prophet ﷺ saw Prophet Moses ﷺ praying in his grave. If all other prophets are alive and praying in their graves, there can be no doubt that Prophet Muhammad ﷺ is also alive and praying for his Ummah.

The Prophet ﷺ mentioned numerous hadiths about the continuing good that he gives his Ummah even while in his grave.

عن عبد الله بن مسعود عن النبي صلى الله عليه وسلم قال: إن لله ملائكة سياحين يبلغون عن
أمتي السلام.
" قال: وقال رسول الله صلى الله عليه وسلم: حياتي خير لكم تحدثون ويُحدث لكم، ووفاتي خير
لكم تعرض علي أعمالكم، فما رأيت من خير حمدت الله عليه وما رأيت من شر استغفرت الله
لكم. (رواه البزار ورجاله رجال الصحيح)

Ibn Masʿūd ؓ related that the Prophet ﷺ said:

My life is a great good for you, you will relate about me and it will be related to you. And my passing from this life is a great good for you: your actions will be presented to me, and if I see in them good, I will praise Allāh, and if I see evil I will ask forgiveness of Him on your behalf.[156]

In explaining this hadith the former Grand Mufti of Egypt, Shaykh Hasanayn Muhammad Makhlūf, wrote:

---

[155] Related by Anas. Haythamī, *Majma' az-zawā'id* (8:211). *Bayhaqī* in "The Lives of the Prophets in Their Graves." Ibn Hajr, *Fath al-bārī* (6:487). *"Al-anbīyā' ahyā'un fee qubūrihim yusallūn."*

[156] Narrated from Ibn Masʿūd by al-Bazzār in his *Musnad* (1:397) with a sound chain as stated by al-Suyūtī in *Manāhil al-safā* (p. 31 #8) and *al-Khasā'is al-kubrā* (2:281), al-Haythamī (9:24 #91), and al-ʿIraqī in *Tarh al-tathrīb* (3:297)—his last book, as opposed to *al-Mughnī 'an haml al-asfar* (4:148) where he questions the trustworthy rank of one of the narrators in al-Bazzār's chain. Shaykh ʿAbd Allāh al-Talidī said in his *Tahdhīb al-khasā'is al-kubrā* (p. 458-459 #694) that this chain is sound according to Muslim's criterion, and Shaykh Mahmūd Mamdūh in *Raf'a al-mināra* (p. 156-169) discusses it at length and declares it sound. Their shaykh, al-Sayyid ʿAbd Allāh Ibn al-Siddīq al-Ghumarī (d. 1413/1993) declared it sound in his monograph *Nihāya al-'amal fī dharh wa yashīh hadīth 'ard al-'amal.* (*takhrīj* Dr. Gibril Haddad):
...*wafātī khayrun lakum tu'radu 'alayya 'amālukum famā ra'āytu min khayrin hamadtullāha 'alayh wa mā ra'āytu min sharrin istaghfartullāhu lakum.*

The hadith means that the Prophet ﷺ is a great good for his
Community during his life, because Allāh the Exalted has
preserved the Community, through the secret of the Prophet's
ﷺ holy presence, from misguidance, confusion, and
disagreement, and He has guided the people through the
Prophet ﷺ to the manifest Truth; and that after Allāh took
back the Prophet ﷺ, our connection to the latter's goodness
continues uncut and the extension of his goodness endures,
overshadowing us. The deeds of the Community are shown to
him every day, and he glorifies Allāh for the goodness that he
finds, while he asks for His forgiveness for the small sins, and
the alleviation of His punishment for the grave ones: and this
is a tremendous good for us. There is therefore "goodness for
the Community in his life, and in his death, goodness for the
Community." Moreover, as has been established in the hadith,
the Prophet ﷺ is alive in his grave with a special
"intermediate-life" (ḥayātun barzakhī) stronger than the lives of
the martyrs which the Qur'ān spoke of in more than one
verse. The nature of these two kinds of life cannot be known
except by their Bestower, the Glorious, the Exalted. He is able
to do all things. His showing the Community's deeds to the
Prophet ﷺ as an honorific gift for him and his Community is
entirely possible rationally and documented in the reports.
There is no leeway for its denial; and Allāh guides to His light
whomever He pleases; and Allāh knows best.[157]

The famous story of the bedouin asking for intercession at the Prophet's ﷺ
grave is related by al-'Utbī.

وعن العُتْبيّ ("العتبيّ": هو محمد بن عبيد الله بن عمرو بن معاوية بن عمرو بن عتبة بن أبي سفيان
صخر بن حرب، كان من أفصح الناس، صاحب أخبار ورواية للآداب، حدّث عن أبيه وسفيان
بن عيينة) قال: كنتُ جالسا عند قبر النبيّ صلى الله عليه وسلم فجاء أعرابيّ فقال: السلام
عليك يا رسول الله! سمعتُ اللهَ تعالى يقول: ﴿ وَلَوْ أَنَّهُمْ إِذ ظَّلَمُوا أَنفُسَهُمْ جَاؤُوكَ فَاسْتَغْفَرُوا اللَّهَ
وَاسْتَغْفَرَ لَهُمُ الرَّسُولُ لَوَجَدُوا اللَّهَ تَوَّابًا رَحِيمًا ﴾ (النساء:64) وقد جئتُك مستغفرا من ذنبي،
مستشفعا بك إلى ربي، ثم أنشأ يقول:

يا خيرَ مَنْ دُفنتْ بالقاع أعظُمُه ٭ فطابَ من طيبهنَّ القاع والأكَمُ
نفسي الفداءُ لقبر أنتَ ساكنُهُ ٭ فيه العفافُ وفيه الجودُ والكَرَمُ

---

[157] Fatāwa shar'īyya (1:91-92).

قال: ثم انصرفَ، فحملتني عيناي فرأيت النبيَ صلى الله عليه وسلم في النوم فقال لي: يا عُتْبي،

الحق الأعرابيَ فبشّره بأن الله تعالى قد غفر له

Al-'Utbī said:

> As I was sitting by the grave of the Prophet ﷺ, a bedouin
> Arab came and said: "Peace be upon you, O Messenger of
> Allāh! I have heard Allāh's words:

وَلَوْ أَنَّهُمْ إِذ ظَّلَمُواْ أَنفُسَهُمْ جَآؤُوكَ فَاسْتَغْفَرُواْ اللَّهَ وَاسْتَغْفَرَ لَهُمُ الرَّسُولُ لَوَجَدُواْ اللَّهَ تَوَّابًا

رَّحِيمًا

*If they had only, when they were unjust to themselves, come unto thee and
asked Allāh's forgiveness, and the Messenger had asked forgiveness for
them, they would have found Allāh indeed Oft-returning, Most Merciful,*

(an-Nisā' 4:64)

> So I have come to you asking forgiveness for my sin, seeking
> your intercession with my Lord." Then he began to recite
> poetry:

> O best of those whose bones are buried in the deep earth,
> And from whose fragrance the depth
> And the height have become sweet,
> May I be the ransom for a grave which thou inhabit,
> And in which are found purity, bounty and munificence!

> Then he left, and I dozed and saw the Prophet ﷺ in my sleep.
> He said to me, "O 'Utbī, run after the bedouin and give him
> glad tidings that Allāh has forgiven him."[158]

The Qur'ān was revealed for all people and for all times, and in *Sūrat an-Nisā'* (4:64) Allāh ﷻ encourages every Muslim to come to the Prophet and seek his intercession so that Allāh will grant forgiveness. Those who deny the Prophet's ﷺ status as intercessor in this life and in the next, or in other ways

---

[158] The report is *mashhūr* (well-known) and related by Nawawī, *Adhkār*, Mecca ed. p. 253-254, *al-Majmu'* 8:217, and *al-Idah fī manāsik al-hajj*, chapters on visiting the grave of the Prophet; Ibn Jamā'a, *Hidāyat al-sālik* 3:1384; Ibn 'Aqil, *al-Tadhkira*; Ibn Qudāma, *al-Mughnī* 3:556-557; al-Qurtubī, *Tafsīr* of 4:64 in "Ahkām al-Qur'ān" 5:265; Samhūdi, *Khulāsat al-wafā* p. 121 (from Nawawī); Dahlān, *Khulāsat al-kalām* 2:247; Ibn Kathīr, *Tafsīr* 2:306, and *al-Bidāyat wa al-nihāyat* 1:180; Abū al-Faraj ibn Qudāma, *al-Sharh al-kabīr* 3:495; al-Bahūtī al-Hanbalī, *Kashshāf al-qinā'* 5:30; Taqī al-Dīn al-Subkī, *Shifā' al-Siqam* p. 52; Ibn al-Jawzī, *Muthīr al-gharām al-sākin ila ashraf al-amākin* p. 490; al-Bayhaqī, *Shu'ab al-īmān* #4178; Ibn 'Asākir, *Mukhtasar tārīkh dimashq* 2:408; Ibn Hajar al-Haytami, *al-Jawhar al-munazzam* [commentary on Nawawī's *Idāh*]; Ibn al-Najjār, *Akhbār al-madīna* p. 147. A similar report is cited through Sufyān ibn 'Uyayna (Imām Shafi'i's shaykh), and through Abū Sa'īd al-Sam'anī on the authority of 'Alī.

demean him by claiming he has no power to observe his Ummah from the grave, or to intercede on their behalf, are increasingly common in these times.[159] They should take heed of the Prophet's warning in the following hadith.

حَدَّثَنَا مَحمُودُ بنُ غَيلانَ أَخبَرَنَا أَبو داوُدَ أَنبَأَنَا شُعبَةُ عَن سِمَاكِ بنِ حَربٍ قال سَمِعتُ عَبدَ الرَّحمَنِ

بنَ عبدِ الرَّحمَنِ بنِ عبدِ اللهِ بنِ مسعودٍ يُحَدِّثُ عَن أَبيه قال: سَمِعتُ رَسُولَ اللهِ صَلَّى اللهُ عَلَيه

وسَلَّمَ يَقول إنَّكم مَنصُورونَ ومُصيبُونَ ومَفتُوحٌ لَكم فَمَن أَدرَكَ ذاكَ مِنكُم فَليَتَّقِ اللهَ وليَأمُر بالمَعروف

وليَنهَ عَن المنكَرِ ومَن يَكذِب عَلَيَّ مُتَعَمِّدا فَليَتَبَوَّأ مَقعَدَهُ مِنَ النَّارِ (هذا حَديثٌ حَسَنٌ صَحيحٌ

،البُخاري في كِتابِ العِلمِ و مُسلِم في مُقَدِّمَة و أَبو داوُد, التِّرمذيِ، أَحمد و الدَّارِمي)

---

[159] It is our belief as confirmed by both the Qur'ān and the hadith, that the Prophet was aware not only in his time, but before it, and he is aware after it. Allāh described him as *shāhid* and *shahīd* meaning that he is *hādir* (present spiritually and physically in being) and *nādhir* (to see or behold with ones own eyes, near or far), which together define him as *shahīd*. Both of these attributes (*hādir* and *nādhir*) have to be present, because if there is one without the other, it is clear he could not be *shahīd*.

The presence and the awareness of the Prophet is a fact. Allāh said in the Qur'ān: *"O Prophet, We have sent You as a Witness"* (al-Ahzāb 33:45) and *"Then how shall it be, when We bring up a witness from each nation and O beloved Messenger, We will bring You as a Witness and Guardian against all people."* (an-Nisā' 4:41)

'Allāma Āhmad Qastallānī writes in his book *Al-Mawāhib al-ladunnīya* and Imām Muhammad Ibn Hajar Makkī writes in his book *Madkhal*: "There is no difference between the states of life and death of the Prophet, in his seeing His entire Ummah and recognizing their states, their intentions, and their minds, and all this is clear to him, there is no secret thereof to him."

Qādī 'Iyād in his *Ash-Shifā'* said: "Whenever there is nobody present in the home and when you enter the home recite, *as-salāmu 'alayka ayyuhan-Nabī wa rahmatullāhi bārakātuh."*

And on this Mullā 'Alī al-Qārī in his *Sharh ash-shifā'* about the above: "The reason (for saluting the Prophet) in the present tense is that the Holy Prophet's soul is *hādir* (Present) in every household."

Al-Ghazzālī said in *Mirqat sharh mishkāt*: "When you go into a masjid then say *salām* to the Prophet because the Prophet is present (*hādir*) in masājid."

Also from al-Ghazzālī as reported in the tafsīr *Rūh al-bayān* said, "The Holy Prophet and His Companions' souls have been given the right to travel the world and many *awliyā'ullāh* have seen the Prophet."

And again al-Ghazzālī says in his *Ihyā*: "And believe that the Holy Prophet is pesent (*hādir*) and then you say, *As-salāmu 'alayka, ayyuhan-Nabī."*

Imām Suyūtī says in his *Intibāhul azkīyyā*:
> To keep watch of his own followers' work and pray for their forgivness; to pray for their abstention from bad deeds; to come and go in all parts of the world to give auspiciousness; if a pious person dies from His followers then to come and attend his Janāza; all this is done by the Holy Prophet.

And even before the time of the Prophet, he is *shahīd* when Allah says: *"(O Prophet) Have You not seen how Your Lord dealt with the owners of the Elephant?"* (al-Fīl 105:6) This is an event which happened many years before the Birth of the Prophet. And an event that happened centuries before the Prophet: *"(O Prophet) Have You not seen how Your Lord dealt with (the people) of Aad?"* (al-Fajr 89:9)

And we have related the hadith regarding the awareness of the Prophet after his passing from this worldly life (though his time is until the Day of Judgement).

These hadiths can be found in *Encyclopedia of Islamic Doctrine*, Shaykh Muhammad Hisham Kabbani.

'Abd ar-Rahmān ibn 'Abd ar-Rahmān ibn 'Abd Allāh ibn Mas'ūd from his father that he heard the Prophet 鏖 say, "Whoever purposely tells a lie about me, let him prepare himself for his seat in the Fire."[160]

---

[160] Narrated from 'Abd Allāh Ibn 'Amr Ibn al-'Āas by *Bukhārī, Tirmidhī, Āhmad,* and *Darimī.*

Khawārij

The sect of the Kharijites, or Khawārij, existed in the time of the Successors of the Companions. They were a large group of several tens of thousands of Muslims, composed mostly of individuals who had memorized the Qur'ān and who devoted themselves to much worship, prayer and fasting. They declared the totality of the Companions of the Prophet ﷺ and whoever of the Muslims were with them to be apostate, disbelievers, and took up arms against them. The practices of declaring other Muslims apostate (takfīr) and of taking armed action against the central Muslim authority, the Caliphate, became and continue to be the hallmark of the Khawārij past and present.

Imām Bukhārī in his Sahīh mentioned people who improperly applied verses of Qur'ān, which had been revealed about unbelievers, against Muslims with whom they disagreed.

وقول الله تعالى: ﴿ وما كان الله ليضل قوماً بعد إذ هداهم حتى يبين لهم ما يتقون ﴾ التوبة: 115 وكان ابن عمر يراهم شرار خلق الله، وقال: إنهم انطلقوا إلى آيات نزلت في الكفار، فجعلوها على المؤمنين (باب الخوارج في صحيح البخاري)

Ibn 'Umar would see them as the worst of Allāh's creation and say, "Verily they used verses revealed for unbelievers against the believers."[161]

In our time, this armed rebellion and takfīr took place in northeastern Arabia at the turn of the nineteenth Century CE as mentioned by the scholars of Islam:

> The name of Khawārij is applied to those who part ways with the Muslims and declare them disbelievers, as took place in our time with the followers of Ibn 'Abd al-Wahhāb who came out of Najd and attacked the Two Noble Sanctuaries.[162]

The scholar al-Sāwī said:

> The Khawārij altered the interpretation of the Qur'ān and Sunnah, on the strength of which they declared it lawful to kill and take the property of Muslims as may now be seen in their modern counterparts, namely, a sect in the Hijāz called Wahhābis.[163]

The above excerpts are nothing new. The categorization of the Wahhābis

---

[161] Sahīh Bukhārī (12: 283). Chapter on "Fighting the Khawārij"
[162] Ibn 'Abidin, Radd al-muhtār 'alā al-durr al-mukhtār (3:309), "Bāb al-Bughāt" [Chapter on Rebels].
[163] Al-Sāwī, Hāshīya 'alā tafsīr al-jalālayn (v. 58:18-19) in the Cairo, 1939 al-Mashhad al-Husaynī edition. (3:307-8) repr. Dār Ihyā' al-Turāth al-'Arabī in Beirut.

as Kharijites has been a a dominant recurring thematic feature of Sunni heresiography for the past 200 years. Only recently has it become politically incorrect among some 'ulama to criticize the Wahhābi/"Salafi" sect.

The exercise of takfīr is the chief mark by which the neo-Khawārij can be recognized in our time. They are those who address the Muslims with the libelous chants of: kufr! (unbelief), bid'a! (innovation), shirk! (idolatry), harām! (forbidden), without proof or justification other than their own vain lusts, and without solutions other than exclusionism and violence against anyone with whom they disagree. Their consciences do not cringe at the applying of capital punishment to their charges of takfīr, and so they make light of the sanctity of life and the honor of their brethren. As Shaykh al-Islam Imām Nawawī said: "Extremists are fanatic zealots who exceed bounds in words and deeds" and are "bigots."[164]

To perpetrate takfīr of the Muslims today makes one a Kharijite, regardless of whether one calls oneself "Salafī", Shi'ī, or Sūfī. It is very disheartening to see people today telling their Muslim brother, "Ya Kāfir!—O unbeliever!"

حدثنا يحيى بن يحيى التميمي، ويحيى بن أيوب، وقتيبة بن سعيد، وعلي بن حجر، جميعا عن إسماعيل بن جعفر. قال يحيى بن يحيى: أخبرنا إسماعيل بن جعفر عن عبدالله بن دينار؛ أنه سمع ابن عمر يقول: قال رسول الله صلى الله عليه وسلم: أيما امرئ قال لأخيه: يا كافر. فقد باء بها أحدهما. إن كان كما قال. وإلا رجعت عليه (مسلم في كتاب الإيمان)

'Abd Allāh Ibn 'Umar ﷺ related that the Prophet ﷺ said:

> Whoever calls his brother "unbeliever" it is true of one of them. Either it is as he said, or if not, that epithet comes back on him.[165]

If that person is not an unbeliever that harmful saying will come back against the accuser. Ironically, the young Khawārij of today and their leaders often maintain good relations with non-Muslims, yet they feel no shame in condemning fellow Muslims as enemies and unbelievers. They are busy condemning mankind to hell, including most of the Muslims.

حدثنا أبو بكر بن أبي شيبة. حدثنا علي بن مسهر عن الشيباني، عن يسير بن عمرو. قال: سألت سهل بن حنيف: هل سمعت النبي صلى الله عليه وسلم يذكر الخوارج ؟ فقال: سمعته (وأشار بيده نحو المشرق)

---

[164] Nawawī, Sharh sahīh muslim (16:220 and 7:214).
[165] Sahīh Bukhārī, "Kitāb al-Adab" (7:96). Sahīh Muslim, "Kitāb al-Īmān" # 60. Imām Mālik, Muwatta, "Kitāb al-Kalām" (2:984). "Ayyu'mrin qāla li-akhīhi 'kāfirun' faqad ba'a bihā āhaduhumā, in kāna kamā qāl. Wa il-lā raj'at 'alayh."

"قوم يقرأون القرآن بألسنتهم لا يعدوا تراقيهم . يمرقون من الدين كما يمرق السهم من الرمية." (مُسْلِم فب باب الخوارج وحدثناه أبو كامل . حدثنا عبدالواحد . حدثنا سليمان الشيباني، بهذا الإسناد . وقال: يخرج منه أقوام

Yāsir Ibn 'Amr reported that he inquired of Sahl Ibn Hunayf:

> Did you hear Allāh's Messenger ﷺ make mention of the Khawārij? He said, "I heard him say (as he pointed with his hand towards the east) that these would be a people who would recite the Qur'ān but it would not go beyond their throat. They would pass straight through the religion just as the arrow passes through its prey."[166]

That is, they pass so quickly through the religion that they do not grasp any of it. This description of the Khawārij (who appeared in the time of the Successors to the Companions) is echoed in another hadith describing the Khawārij of the Last Days.

حدثنا عمر بن حفص بن غياث: حدثنا أبي: حدثنا الأعمش: حدثنا خيثمة: حدثنا سويد بن غفلة: قال علي رضي الله عنه:

إذا حدثتكم عن رسول الله صلى الله عليه وسلم حديثاً، فوالله لأن أخرَّ من السماء، أحب إلي من أن أكذب عليه، وإذا حدثتكم فيما بيني وبينكم، فإن الحرب خدعة، وإني سمعت رسول الله صلى الله عليه وسلم يقول: (سيخرج قوم في آخر الزمان، أحداث الأسنان، سفهاء الأحلام، يقولون من خير قول البريَّة، لا يجاوز إيمانهم حناجرهم، يمرقون من الدين كما يمرق السهم من الرميَّة، فأينما لقيتموهم فاقتلوهم، فإن في قتلهم أجرا لمن قتلهم يوم القيامة (البخاري في كتاب إسْتَابة المرْتدين و مسلم في الزكاة و النسائ في تحْريم الدَّم ، أبو داود و أحْمد)

...the Prophet ﷺ said:

> There will appear a group of people at the end of time who are young[167] and have foolish dreams. They speak from the words of the Best of Creation (i.e. the Qur'ān and the Prophet Muhammad's ﷺ hadith). Their faith does not even reach their throats and they pass out of the religion like an arrow passes through its prey...[168]

---

[166] *Sahīh Muslim.*
[167] Literally: "with newly erupted teeth."
[168] *Sahīh Bukhārī* (8:51), Chapter on the Repentance of the Apostates (*istitābat al-murtad-dīn*); *Sahīh Muslim* #1066; and many others:
> Sayakhruju qawman fī akhir iz-zamāni ihdāth al-asnān sufahā al-ahlām, yaqulūna min qawli khayr il-barrīyati, yaqrā'ūna al-qur'ān, lā yujāwizu

The Prophet ﷺ said that at the end of time (*ākhir az-zamān*) there would appear a group of young people with foolish dreams. Their desciption of having newly emerged teeth indicates that they are quite young, as the last molars come in at around ten to twelve years of age and the wisdom teeth in the late teens. These youths are brainwashed at this impressionable age through *qawl az-zūr*,[169] by media, television, books, and indoctrinated in a cultural, national, or religious ideology.

The Prophet ﷺ said that they have crazy dreams, foolish aspirations, and fanciful imaginations (*sufahā al-ahlām*), which means that they have disturbed minds and a lack of understanding. Despite this intellectual deficiency they speak from the sayings of the Prophet ﷺ and they recite the Qur'ān. People are fascinated by their speech, as they recite Qur'ān and hadith for everything.[170] On the Internet they seem like scholars, throwing Qur'ānic verses and hadiths right and left, using them to support their dreams and aspirations, such as the establishment of a utopian society or an Islamic state as they conceive it should be. At the time when the whole world is corrupted during the Last Days, these ignorant young people will come and talk about Islam.

However, they are not wise, intelligent or even good believers. The Prophet ﷺ continued saying: "Their faith does not even reach their throats (i.e. it is nothing) and they pass out of the religion like an arrow passes through its prey." This is what we are experiencing today. These youths recite the Qur'ān and bring hadiths as evidence, but in an incorrect manner, and so derive their own rulings without any knowledge of the subject. They put things together as they like, to fit their needs. They do not have even a rudimentary background in Islamic knowledge and they use verses of the Qur'ān which were meant for unbelievers out of context, applying them to believers. As mentioned before, the Khawārij are not bound to a specific time, but are any and all who fall under that description by going out of the bounds of the religion, declaring Muslims as unbelievers. This is the methodology of the Khawārij, past and present, and the re-emergence of these juvenile, deluded Khawārij in the Last Days was mentioned fourteen hundred years ago by Prophet Muhammad ﷺ.

The Khawārij of today are the followers of the Wahhābi/"Salafi" sect. They are actively promoting the falsehood of their cult with massive propaganda campaigns whether by speakers in mosques, via the Internet, on television, or through the massive distribution of videos, newspapers, books,

---

īmānuhum hanājīrahum. Yumariqūna min ad-dīni kamā yamruqu as-sahm min ar-ramīyyati...
[169] *Qawl az-zūr* is the promotion of false, incorrect ideas, see chapter "Bearing False Witness."
[170] 'Abd Allah Ibn Mas'ūd said:
A time will come upon men when their *fuqahā* (jurisprudents) are few but their Qur'ān reciters are many, when the letters of the Qur'ān are guarded carefully but its limits are lost, when many ask but few give,when they make the sermon long but the prayer short, and put their desires before their actions.

magazines, and pamphlets. All the while they are suppressing and concealing the truths of mainstream classical Islamic teachings, conspiring to silence anyone who speaks against their extremism. They are inheriting the intolerance, and oftentimes violence, seen in the Khawārij of the past, killing Muslims and other innocent people who do not agree with their aberrant beliefs, engaging in subterfuge in various countries where they have no right to do so. These youngsters around the world are brainwashed with *qawl az-zūr*—the bearing of false witness. They apply the verses of Qur'ān and hadiths in the wrong manner, and set off in pursuit of their wild dreams. The Prophet ﷺ described them precisely and foretold that they would reappear in the Last Days and this has come to pass.

حدثنا محمد بن المثنَّى: حدثنا الوليد بن مسلم: حدثنا ابن جابر: حدثني بسر بن عبيد الله الحضرمي: أنه سمع أبا إدريس الخولاني: أنه سمع حذيفة بن اليمان يقول: كان الناس يسألون رسول الله صلى الله عليه وسلم عن الخير، وكنت أسأله عن الشر، مخافة أن يدركني، فقلت: يا رسول الله، إنا كنا في جاهلية وشر، فجاءنا الله بهذا الخير، فهل بعد هذا الخير من شر؟ قال: (نعم) . قلت: وهل بعد ذلك الشر من خير؟ قال: (نعم، وفيه دخن) . قلت: وما دخنه؟ قال: (قوم يهدون بغير هديي، تعرف منهم وتنكر) . قلت: فهل بعد ذلك الخير من شر؟ قال: (نعم، دعاة على أبواب جهنم، من أجابهم إليها قذفوه فيها) . قلت: يا رسول الله صفهم لنا، قال: (هم من جلدتنا، ويتكلمون بألسنتنا) . قلت: فما تأمرني إن أدركني ذلك؟ قال: (تلزم جماعة المسلمين وإمامهم) . قلت: فإن لم يكن لهم جماعة ولا إمام؟ قال: (فاعتزل تلك الفرق كلها، ولو أن تعضَّ بأصل شجرة، حتى يدركك الموت وأنت على ذلك .

Hudhayfa ﷺ related:

> ...the Prophet ﷺ replied [to a question posed by him], "There will be some people who will lead others on a path different from mine. You will see good and bad in them."[171]

I (Hudhayfa) asked, "Will some evil come after that good?" The Prophet ﷺ said, "Some people will be standing and calling at the gates of Hell; whoever responds to their call,

---

[171] The first portion of this hadith reads:
Narrated Hudhayfa bin Al-Yaman: The people used to ask Allah's Prophet about the good but I used to ask him about the evil lest I should be overtaken by them. So I said, "O Messenger of Allah! We were living in ignorance and in an (extremely) evil state, then Allah brought to us this good (i.e., Islam); will there be any evil after this good?" He said, "Yes." I said, 'Will there be any good after that evil?" He replied, "Yes, but it will be tainted (not pure.)" I asked, "What will be its taint?" He replied, "(There will be) some people who will guide others not according to my tradition. You will approve of some of their deeds and disapprove of some others." I asked, "Will there be any evil after that good?" ...

they will throw him into the Fire."
I said, "O Messenger of Allāh, describe them for us."
He said, "They will be of our complexion and speak our very language."
I asked, "What do you advise me to do if I should live to see that?"
He said, "You must stick to the main body (jamāʿah) of the Muslims and their leader (Imām)."
I asked, "What if there is no main body and no leader?"
He said, "Isolate yourself from all of these sects, even if you have to eat the roots of trees until death overcomes you while you are in that state."[172]

---

[172] *Sahīh Bukhārī*, "Kitāb al-Fitan," (9:65). There are many hadith which give evidences of the necessity of keeping with the congregation of Muslims, including:
Inna Allāha la yajmaʿu ummatī—aw qāla: ummata Muhammadin—ʿalā dalālatin wa yadullāhi mʿa al-jamāʿa—"Verily Allāh will not make my community—or Muhammad's community—agree on error, and Allāh's hand is with the largest congregation."
Tirmidhī said: "And the meaning of *jamāʿa* according to the people of knowledge is: the people of jurisprudence, learning, and hadith."
In another hadith the Prophet said, *"Yadullāh ʿalā al-jamāʿa—*Allāh's Hand is over the group."
Munawī said:
"Allāh's Hand is over the group," means His protection and preservation for them, signifying that the collectivity of the people of Islam are in Allāh's fold, so be also in Allāh's shelter, in the midst of them, and do not separate yourselves from them. Whoever diverges from the overwhelming majority concerning what is lawful and unlawful and on which the Community does not differ has slipped off the path of guidance and this will lead him to hell."

Calumny of "Innovation"

The Prophet ﷺ described a time to come in which those who follow the Sunnah would be labeled as "innovators."

بن مسعود قال: كيف عن عبد الله...حدثنا عبد الرحمن بن عثمان قال: حدثنا أحمد بن ثابت

أنتم اذا ظهر فيكم البدع و عمل بها حتى يربو فيها الصغير و يهرم الكبير و يسلم فيها الاعاجم

قالوا متى ذلك؟ يا أبا عبد الرحمن ! قال: " إذا كثرت أمراؤكم حتى يعمل بالسنة فيقال :"بدعة"

وقلت أمناؤكم وكثرت قراؤكم و قلت فقهاؤكم وتفقه لغير الدين وابتغيت الدنيا بعمل الآخرة"

ادرس المباركفوري كتاب السنن الواردة في الفتن وغوائلها والساعة واشراطها المقرى الداني تحقيق

دار العاصمة الرياض صفحة 618 اخرجه نعيم بن حماد (ق5 ب رقم 52) الدارمى فى سننه

(64/1) وابن وضاح في البدع(ص89) وابن عبد البر في جامع بيان العلم وفضله(188/1) وأبو

نعيم في الحلية(136/1)والحاكم في مستدركه (514/4) و ذكر الذهبي أنه على شرط البخارى و

....و يتخذ سنة فان غيرت مسلم .وأخرجه عبد الرزاق في مصنفه(359/11 رقم 20742)

و هو موقوف و اسناده باجتماع يوما قيل هذا منكر..... و هكذا ورد عند الجميع في أوله

الطرق صحيح و الحديث أورده الألباني في صحيح الترغيب(47/1 رقم 106)

Ibn Mas'ūd ؓ said:

> How will it be when innovation is prevalent and the child will be raised in it and the elder will have already become white-haired in it, and your affairs or your leadership will be given to the non-Arabs, until when a man follows the Sunnah, it will be said of him, "Innovation." They said [addressing Ibn Mas'ūd], "Ya Abā 'Abdur Rahmān, when will that happen?" He said, "when your leaders increase and your trustworthy ones will decrease and the number of your Qur'ān reciters increases and the number of your *fuqahā* decreases and they will study [intensively] other than the religion. People will seek the work of *dunyā*, and leave the work of *akhira*."[173]

This hadith refers to a time when the young will have been raised in innovation and the old will have already learned it. Today we see countless forms of innovation, particularly in the many ideologies that have flooded the Muslim nations, from the left to the right; from secularism to nationalism. The

---

[173] Two other narrations are similar:

خبرنا يعلى حدثنا الأعمش عن شقيق قال قال عبد الله

كيف أنتم إذا لبستكم فتنة يهرم فيها الكبير ويربو فيها الصغير ويتخذها الناس سنة فإذا غيرت سنة قالوا غيرت السنة

people following these newly innovated ideologies will tell us that everything that came before is wrong, regressive and backwards.

In that time the affairs of the Muslims (or in another reading, the leadership of the Muslims) will be given to the non-Arabs, meaning that foreigners will control the Muslim community. We see this today, wherein someone appears out of nowhere and suddenly becomes the ruler of a Muslim nation—typically one who has no foundation in religious knowledge and aspires only to power.

At that time, whoever acts according to the Sunnah of the Prophet ﷺ will be considered coming against the ideology of this time and will be told, *bid'a,*—"innovation!"

That was foretold fourteen hundred years ago. And today anyone who practices Islam correctly according to the Sunnah of the Prophet ﷺ is told: *bid'a, bid'a!* This is something everyone has experienced. There is a group of people among the Muslims, who if they don't like what you do, say: *bid'a, bid'a, harām, shirk, kufr!* Today if you enter almost any mosque, you may easily hear these words being spoken.

Years ago that term, *bid'a* was never used commonly in that manner. But the new generation repeats it blindly, applying it to almost anything which in their opinion they consider wrong, for they were raised with that term from the lips of their teachers. They are implementing the actions predicted in the hadith. In truth, this is one of the most problematic issues facing the Muslims today.

Today you can hardly find three persons in one place who follow the same political or religious leader. Each one follows his own leader (*amīr*). If one looks on the Internet you find the followers of one leader giving verdicts on the followers of another leader, aggressively asserting their viewpoint and condemning the views of all others. Each has become a leader in his own right and is unwilling to follow anyone else. Each one issues a verdict based on his own objectives, not on true religious understanding.

Such leaders lack any knowledge of hadith or *fiqh* (Islamic jurisprudence), but are experts in memorizing Qur'ān. In this time we see that people send their children to learn the Qur'ān, but as the hadith says, "your scholars of *fiqh* will decrease." There is no longer any study of Islamic knowledge and sciences (*'ulūm*), and no more *fiqh*. No one is learning the meanings of the Qur'ān, the importance of hadith, or the reasons behind the revelation of each verse—all essentials to issuing juristic verdicts.

...*wa tufaqahu li-ghayri id-dīn*—"and they will study [intensively] other than religion." They learn Qur'ān but leave off learning *fiqh*. Simultaneously there is a great increase in the study of the secular sciences—learning something other than religion.

In the time of the *Sahāba* and the later generations of Islamic civilization that followed, including the Ummayyad dynasty, the Abbāsid dynasty, up through the time of the Ottomans, Muslims eagerly sought Islamic knowledge. Today that is no longer the case. Instead, most people are eagerly chasing the study of every form of secular knowledge while religious study has been all but completely neglected.

"People will seek the work of this life and leave the work of the afterlife." This means that almost no one will be interested in *akhira* while nearly all will be interested in this worldly life and its pleasures.

That narration reflects today's circumstances like a shining mirror. To the current generation every aspect of Islam that earlier generations followed have now become *bid'a*—innovation.

The Destruction of Yathrib

In this hadith the Prophet ﷺ mentions that one of the signs of the Last Days is the building up of *Bayt al-Maqdis* in Jerusalem and that Yathrib (Madīna, the Holy City of the Prophet) will be destroyed.

حدثنا عبد الله حدثني أبي حدثنا زيد بن الحباب حدثنا عبد الرحمن بن ثوبان حدثني أبي عن
مكحول عن معاذ بن جبل قال: قال رسول الله صلى الله عليه وسلم: عمران بيت المقدس خراب
يثرب وخراب يثرب خروج الملحمة وخروج الملحمة فتح القسطنطينية وفتح القسطنطينية خروج
الدجال ثم ضرب على فخذه أو على منكبه ثم قال: إن هذا لحق كما أنك قاعد وكان مكحول
يحدث به عن جبير بن نفير عن مالك بن يخامر عن معاذ بن جبل عن النبي صلى الله عليه وسلم
مثله.

(رواه أبو داود في سننه في كتاب الملحمة و الترمذي في الفتن و أحمد في مسنده)

Mu'ādh Ibn Jabal ﷺ related that the Prophet ﷺ said that among the signs of the Last Days were:

> The restoration of *Bayt al-Maqdis;* the destruction of Yathrib
> **and** the destruction of Yathrib; the appearance of slaughter
> **and** the appearance of slaughter (bloody fight, fierce battle)
> the conquest of Constantinople **and** the conquest of
> Constantinople; (and) the appearance of the Dajjāl (Anti-
> Christ).
>
> Then the Prophet ﷺ struck his hand on (Mu'ādh Ibn Jabal's
> ﷺ) thigh and said, "Verily this is the truth just as you are
> sitting here."[174]

One would think that to build up the city of *Quds* (Jerusalem) there would be tall buildings and the appearance of civilization which we see today, and that in Madīna there would be no such "civilization." Yet, in Madīna there is extensive construction with tall buildings, malls, huge hotels, tunnels going to the mosque, and the great expansion of the mosque. All of this seems to be at odds with the hadith that Madīna will be destroyed.

When one looks deeper into the hadith we see that the Prophet did not mention that the entire city of Jerusalem (*Quds*) would be built up, but that *Bayt*

---

[174] Aḥmad, *Musnad* (5:232 and 245). Abū Dāwūd #4294, "Kitāb al-Malahim." Ibn Kathīr, *Nihāya* (1:59). Suyūṭī, *Jami' al-saghīr*. Mishkāt ul-masābīḥ #5424. Albānī in *Saḥīḥ al-jāmi'a* #3975: *'umrānu bayt ul-maqdisi; kharābu Yathrib wa kharābu Yathrib; khurūj ul-malhamati wa khurūj ul-malhamati; fath ul-qustāntinīyyati wa fath ul-qustāntinīyyat; khurūj ud-dajjāl. Thumma daraba biyadihi 'alā fakhdh-illadhī haddathahu (aw mankibah) thumma qāla: inna hādha lahaqqun, kamā annaka qā'idun hā-hunnā (ya'nī mu'adh ibn jabal).*

al-Maqdis would be restored. *Quds* is the whole city of Jerusalem and *Bayt al-Maqdis* is a specific holy place from which Prophet Muhammad ﷺ ascended on the Night of *Isra'* and *Mi'raj*. The Prophet ﷺ is not referring to all of the buildings of Jerusalem, as the hadith says "the restoration of *Bayt al-Maqdis*," specifically mentioning *bayt* (house) to emphasize a structure that will be preserved and restored, including what is around it: monuments and relics. This area has been maintained over the centuries and has been preserved in its old form. Through the miraculous knowledge with which Allāh ﷻ favored him, Prophet Muhammad ﷺ described these events fourteen hundred years ago.

As mentioned above, the current situation in Madīna with its many modern buildings seems to contradict the hadith that Madīna will be destroyed. Yet upon closer examination one notices that the Prophet ﷺ specifically mentioned that Yathrib, not Madīna, would be destroyed. The Prophet's ﷺ precise wording gives a meaning whose subtlety can be understood in a modern context. Yathrib is the city of the Prophet ﷺ, from which the light of knowledge shone upon the world. It is the site of the first Islamic government and the fountainhead of the many accomplishments of the Companions. *Kharābu Yathrib* means that the civilization of the old city of Madīna (which was formerly known as Yathrib) will be destroyed. The implication is that anything old or traditional in Islam will be destroyed in times before the end of the world.

The destruction will occur by people bringing their own, revamped, version of Islam which discredits and disdains the traditions which preceded it. Today we are witness to the emergence of a group of people coming against every aspect of mainstream, traditional Islam which Muslims have maintained over fourteen centuries. This group wants to change the entire understanding of the religion by promoting their "modernist" Islam. These people make up a very small minority of the Muslim population. Their aberrant ideas were roundly refuted and rejected by the scholars of Islam, as has been well documented.

There is no such thing as modernizing, or improving, or renovating Islam. Islam is perfect as it was brought in its entirety by Prophet Muhammad ﷺ and will continues in its perfection until Judgment Day. As Allāh ﷻ said in the Holy Qur'ān:

$$\text{الْيَوْمَ أَكْمَلْتُ لَكُمْ دِينَكُمْ وَأَتْمَمْتُ عَلَيْكُمْ نِعْمَتِي وَرَضِيتُ لَكُمُ الْإِسْلَامَ دِينًا}$$

This day have I perfected your religion for you, completed My favor upon you, and have chosen for you Islam as your religion. (al-Māida 53)

Islam is the last message and must be able to accommodate all people living until the end of time. Islam can encompass any culture without adding or removing a single word. Therefore, there is no reformation, no renovation, no additions, and no subtractions. While there is no such thing as reforming Islam, there is such a thing as reforming Muslims, making them understand and practice Islam correctly. In its perfection the religion of Islam is like the full moon: Nothing can be taken from it or added to it. *Kharābu Yathrib* is mentioned twice in the hadith at hand. The first time is the destruction of the civilization of the knowledge of the Prophet 變, ruining the religion by deviating from the Prophet's message. The self-styled "renovators of Islam" want to come up with something new to replace and eliminate whatever is old and traditional. From Muhammad Ibn 'Abd al-Wahhāb to Jamaluddin Afghani to Mawdoodi to Syed Qutb and others, these "modernists" are changing the whole Islamic tradition which was taught and exemplified by the Holy Prophet 變 in Yathrib.

The Wahhābi sect first brought a completely new understanding of Islam under the guise of "purifying" Islam. This new Wahhābi ideology destroyed traditional Islam under the guise of "purifying" Islam, as if all Muslims before the advent of Muhammad Ibn 'Abd al-Wahhāb had been astray. He brought not the purification, but the destruction of centuries-old Islamic knowledge and practices. What was accepted by the Prophet 變 himself and all subsequent generations of Muslims was suddenly branded as a form of idol worship (*shirk*) to be destroyed. Muslims on the *hajj* (pilgrimage) are exposed to their literature and propaganda and become concerned that their traditional beliefs and practices are somehow against Islam. The Wahhābi sect casts doubts on fourteen hundred years of scholarly tradition by its outlandish claims of *kufr, shirk, bid'a, harām* (unbelief, idolatry, innovation, forbidden) in reference to a multitude of traditional practices and understandings.[175]

The first destruction of Yathrib (*kharābu Yathrib*) was when Muhammad Ibn 'Abd al-Wahhāb destroyed the knowledge of Islam by poisoning the Muslims' understanding of their religion. *Kharābu Yathrib* mentioned again signifies the physical destruction of the buildings and monuments dating to the time of the Prophet 變 in old Madīna, Yathrib.[176] In Madīna there has actually

---

[175] The chief brand of New Khārijism distinguishes itself by three main principles:
1. **Attributing a body to the object of Islamic worship**, i.e. anthropomorphism of the Deity.
2. **Harming the Prophet** through disrespect of: his noble person; his blessed Mosque; his Holy grave; his vestiges; his Family and Companions; those who visit, love, and praise him; disparaging or disdaining his intercessor-status.
3. **Dismantlement of the Schools and methods of the Sunni Imāms of the Muslims** past and present, including:
(a) The Imāms of Sunni doctrine ('aqīda): al-Ash'arī and al-Matūridī, and their Schools.
(b) The Imāms of Sunni jurisprudence (fiqh): Abū Hanīfa, Malik, al- Shafi'ī, Āhmad, and their Schools or madhāhib, sing. madhhab.
(c) The Imāms of Sunni morals (akhlāq) known as the Poles (aqtāb, sing. qutb) of the science of soul-purification: al-Junayd, al-Gilanī, al-Shādhilī, al- Rifa'ī, al-Chishtī, al-Suhrawardī, Shah Naqshband, al-Tijanī, and their Schools, known as Paths (turuq, sing. tariqa).
[176] Dr. Muhammad Sa'id al-Būtī says:

been an expansion of the *Haram*, the Sanctuary of the Mosque, but this does not contradict *kharābu Yathrib* because the hadith refers to the **old** city of Madīna known as Yathrib and all that it represents. Everything relating to the Prophet's 襤 life was preserved by Muslims over the years, whether old mosques, relics from buildings, or burial places of the Prophet's 襤 Companions, children, and wives. Although Muslims for centuries agreed that this was an essential part of Islamic history and tradition, it was all destroyed by the Wahhābi sect under the false pretext that "this is not Islam anymore." Their narrow understanding of Islam led to widespread destruction of innumerable relics and monuments. *Kharāb* is "to destroy," but the word contains the shade of meaning "to ruin." There are still pockets of those old traditions, which Muslims want to restore, but they are prevented from doing so. Only the ruins of those traditional relics and buildings remain.

No one anymore knows where the graves of many of the Companions are located. At Jabal Uhud, a mountain near Madīna, one can see a ruined building that used to be a beautiful tomb with domes and ornaments. With all their graves clearly marked, the shrine commemorated the Companions who died with Hamza 襤 at Jabal Uhud.[177] Now there are only a few broken walls which go unnoticed by the casual observer. Similarly, there is no longer any indication of the graves of the Companions who died at Badr. Also, there are no longer any markings at the grave of the Prophet's wife, Sayyidā Khadījat al-Kubrā 襤, in Makka in Jannat al-Mu'ala. In Jannat al-Baqī' (the graveyard next to the Prophet's 襤 grave and mosque in Madīna) the burial places of 'Uthmān 襤, Sayyidā 'A'isha 襤 and numerous Companions were preserved by the Ottomans until the early twentieth century, but their markers have since been removed. There remain only a few elderly people who still know where these sites are located. This is the physical destruction of the Islamic civilization as it was during the time of the Prophet 襤 at Yathrib. Slowly and quietly the followers of the Wahhābi sect have been removing anything related to the Prophet 襤 and traditional Islam, until now almost nothing is left.[178]

Next to the Ka'ba in *Makkat al-Mukārrama* there is *Maqām Ibrāhīm*, which

---

The strangest thing in all this is that they [Wahhābi scholars] see very well the extent to which the Islamic World disapproves of this and its profound anger at this innovation that looks down upon the early Consensus of the Muslims and makes light of the symbols of their faith. They see this, yet they do not turn to address the Muslims with one word by which they might try to justify their actions and explain their viewpoint.

[177] To build a mosque at the site of pious people is recommended as mentioned in the Holy Qur'ān, "... *(Some) said, 'Construct a building over them': Their Lord knows best about them: those who prevailed over their affair said, 'Let us surely build a masjid over them.'"* (al-Kahf 18:21)

[178] As-Sayyid Yūsuf al-Rifā'i in his 1999 book *Advice to the Scholars of Najd* addressing the Wahhābi scholars "You tried and continue to try—as if it were your goal in life—to destroy the last remnants of the historical vestiges of the Messenger of Allāh...."

houses the footprint of Prophet *Ibrāhīm* ﷺ as he built the Ka'ba. Allāh ﷻ says in the Holy Qur'ān:

وَإِذْ جَعَلْنَا الْبَيْتَ مَثَابَةً لِّلنَّاسِ وَأَمْنًا وَاتَّخِذُوا مِن مَّقَامِ إِبْرَاهِيمَ مُصَلًّى

And take Maqam Ibrahim (the Station of Abraham) as a place of prayer.

(al-Baqara: 2:125)

Nonetheless, the Wahhābi/"Salafi" religious authorities over Makka once tried to have *Maqām Ibrāhīm* removed. This happened during the lifetime of the late Shaykh Mutwallī Sha'rāwī of Egypt who informed King Faisal of their plans and he ordered them to leave it in place. He stood up against them on one crucial issue, but there are so many similar issues that it is almost impossible to stop this flood of destruction of Islamic relics and traditions.

Until the 1960's in Madīna the grave of the Prophet's ﷺ father was marked with a plaque on the wall of a house, near the Prophet's Mosque but it has since been removed. At the Prophet's ﷺ Mosque in Madīna, all of the walls and pillars were covered with Islamic poetry in praise of the Prophet ﷺ. The followers of the Wahhābi/"Salafi" sect took these down, either replacing the marble or polishing it down until no traces of the poetry remained. The only thing they could not remove was in front of the *minbar* at the *mihrab* (prayer niche) wherein are written praises of the Prophet ﷺ and 200 of his names. In 1936, the Wahhābis even tried to separate the *Masjid* of the Prophet ﷺ from his grave, but in a rare victory the Muslim countries all stood against this and prevented it.

On the Gate to the Prophet's Noble Grave (*Muwājihā ash-Sharīfa*) it used to read: *Yā Allāh! Yā Muhammad!* The Wahhābi sectarians removed the letter *yā* (ى) in *Yā Muhammad* so that there was only an *alif* left, *Ā Muhammad,* or just *Muhammad.* Recently, they have gone one step further by replacing the *Yā* of *Yā Muhammad,* by also adding a dot under the *hā* (ﺣ) to make *jīm* (ج) and adding two more dots after it to form a *yā* (ى). In doing so they have changed the name of *Muhammad* to read *Majīd,* one of Allāh's Attributes. It now reads: *Yā Allāh! Yā Majīd!* Just as they have already erased the graves of his companions and family, they have now erased the name of the Prophet ﷺ from his own grave. This is contrary to how Allāh Himself honored the Prophet by placing the Prophet's name with His name in the testimony of faith, *Lā ilāha illa Allāh Muhammadun rasūlullah.*

Kharabu Yathrib mentioned twice in the hadith has been accomplished first ideologically by Muhammad Ibn 'Abd al-Wahhāb and his adherents, and then by their ongoing physical destruction of the remnants of traditional Islam. The restoration of *Bayt al-Maqdis* (*'umrānu bayt ul-maqdis*), mentioned once in the hadith, is also in progress. The latter sees the restoration of the old relics in Jerusalem while the former is the destruction of the old ways and vestiges of

Yathrib (the City of the Prophet ﷺ, Madīna).

Rejection of Hadith

Allāh ﷻ gave the Prophet ﷺ the great foresight to describe fourteen hundred years ago the situation in which we find ourselves today. He saw the people who claim to follow only the Qur'ān, and who ignore the hadith, or the Sunnah of Prophet Muhammad ﷺ, which embodies all his actions and sayings, and the actions and sayings by others of which he approved.

حدثنا قتيبة، أخبرنا سفيان بن عيينة، عن محمد بن المنكدر، وسالم أبي النضر عن عبيد الله بن أبي رافع، عن أبي رافع وغيره رفعه قال:

لا ألفين أحدكم متكئا على أريكته يأتيه أمر مما أمرت به أو نهيت عنه فيقول لا أدري، ما وجدنا في كتاب الله اتبعناه". هذا حديث حسن. وروى بعضهم عن سفيان عن ابن المنكدر، عن النبي صلى الله عليه وسلم مرسلا. وسالم أبي النضر عن عبيد الله بن أبي رافع عن أبيه عن النبي صلى الله عليه وسلم. وكان ابن عيينة إذا روى هذا الحديث على الانفراد بين حديث محمد بن المنكدر من حديث سالم أبي النضر، وإذا جمعها روى هكذا وأبو رافع مولى النبي صلى الله عليه وسلم اسمه أسلم حاكم ، بن (حنان ، بن ماجه في المقدمة)

Abū Rafi ؓ narrated that the Prophet ﷺ said:

> You are going to encounter a people sitting on lofty
> cushioned chairs. My order comes to them from what I was
> ordered (by Allāh ﷻ) to command or forbid. They say, "We
> do not know about that. We follow only what we find in
> Allāh's Book (the Qur'ān)."[179]

The Prophet ﷺ described those who disregard the hadith as sitting on their lofty chairs or cushions, considering themselves to be very high. When the Prophet's ﷺ order or prohibition comes to them, these people will reject it. They say, "We only follow the Qur'ān and we do not know or care about what the hadith says." Today such people are sitting, just as the Prophet ﷺ mentioned, claiming to only follow the Qur'ān, and rejecting the hadith. These people are not educated in Islamic knowledge, and they are not authentic scholars. They have taken their positions by force, not merit, and then claim to represent the Muslims. Ironically, these unqualified people have become the self-appointed spokespeople for the Muslims, while denying the hadith of the Prophet of Islam, the Prophet Muhammad ﷺ.

It is much more difficult to deny the Qur'ān because then they would be

---

[179] Narrated in *Musnad Āhmad*, (4:130), *Sunan Abū Dāwūd*, *Tirmidhī* in "Bab al-'Amal," *Hākim*, *Ibn Hibbān*, *Ibn Mājah*:
   Lā alfi'anna ahadukum mutaki'an 'alā arrīkatihi yā'tihi amrun mimmā ummirtu bihi aw nuhītu 'anhu fa-yaqūlu lā adrī, ma wajadnā fī kitābillāhi it-taba'na'.

coming directly against Allāh ﷻ. Instead, they subversively demean the station and honor of the Prophet ﷺ in order to discredit the hadith literature, saying, "The Prophet was an ordinary person like us. He came, delivered the message of the Qur'ān, and went. He is finished now. We only follow Allāh's Book, not the hadith." They forget that Allāh ﷻ speaks of the Prophet ﷺ in a lustrous and timeless sense; the Prophet ﷺ is:

$$وَمَا أَرْسَلْنَاكَ إِلَّا رَحْمَةً لِّلْعَالَمِينَ$$

A mercy for all creation. (al-Anbiyā' 21:107)

Furthermore, Allāh confirmed that the Prophet ﷺ does not speak on his own.

$$وَمَا يَنطِقُ عَنِ الْهَوَى$$

Nor does he say (aught) of (his own) desire. (an-Najm 53:3)

The Prophet ﷺ never spoke from his own thoughts, ideas, whims, or desire, whether a good desire or a bad desire.

$$إِنْ هُوَ إِلَّا وَحْيٌ يُوحَى$$

It is naught but revelation that is revealed to him. (an-Najm 53:4)

This means that the hadiths of the Prophet ﷺ are revelations to his heart directly from Allāh ﷻ. For every single event that happened in his lifetime Allāh ﷻ revealed to his heart what to say, what to do and the explanation of each action.

حدثنا عبد الله حدثني أبي حدثنا عبد الرحمن وزيد بن الحباب قالا حدثنا معاوية بن صالح عن الحسن بن جابر قال زيد في حديثه حدثني الحسن بن جابر قال سمعت المقدام بن معدي كرب يقول: حرم رسول الله صلى الله عليه وسلم يوم خيبر أشياء ثم قال يوشك أحدكم أن يكذبني وهو متكئ على أريكته يحدث بحديثي فيقول بيننا وبينكم كتاب الله فما وجدنا فيه من حلال استحللناه وما وجدنا فيه من حرام حرمناه ألا وإن ما حرم رسول الله صلى الله عليه وسلم مثل ما حرم الله (أحمد، أبو داود في كتاب المقدّمة، الترمذي في كتاب العلم و الدّارمي في المقدّمة)

And it is narrated from Muqdām Ibn Ma'dī Karb ؓ who related that the Prophet ﷺ said:

> It is imminent that a person will be sitting on a lofty cushioned chair, in a group of people, speaking of one of my hadiths and he says, "Between us and you is Allāh's Book (the Qur'ān). Whatever we found in it as permitted we made it

permissible. What we found mentioned as forbidden in it we forbade it."[180] [The Prophet asks], "Is not what Allāh's Messenger forbade the same as what Allāh forbade?"[181]

The people who reject the hadiths and claim to only follow the Qur'ān are in reality completely ignorant of the Qur'ān. There are many clear evidences in the Holy Qur'ān itself of the necessity of following the Prophet ﷺ and his Sunnah. There is no separation of the Qur'ān and Sunnah, as they complement each other, and are utilized together. This is established in numerous verses of the Qur'ān including:

وَمَا آتَاكُمُ الرَّسُولُ فَخُذُوهُ وَمَا نَهَاكُمْ عَنْهُ فَانْتَهُوا

And whatever the Messenger gives you, take it. And whatever he forbids
you avoid it. (al-Hashr 59:7)

يَا أَيُّهَا الَّذِينَ آمَنُوا أَطِيعُوا اللَّهَ وَأَطِيعُوا الرَّسُولَ وَأُولِي الأَمْرِ مِنكُمْ

O you who believe! Obey Allah, and obey the Messenger, and those in
authority among you. (an-Nisā' 4:59)

وَأَطِيعُوا اللَّهَ وَالرَّسُولَ لَعَلَّكُمْ تُرْحَمُونَ

And obey Allah and the Messenger so that you may receive mercy.
(Āl-Imrān 3:132)

قُلْ إِن كُنتُمْ تُحِبُّونَ اللَّهَ فَاتَّبِعُونِي يُحْبِبْكُمُ اللَّهُ وَيَغْفِرْ لَكُمْ ذُنُوبَكُمْ وَاللَّهُ غَفُورٌ رَحِيمٌ

Say: "If you (truly) love Allah, Follow me: Allah will love you and forgive
you your sins: For Allah is Oft-Forgiving, Most Merciful."
(Āl-Imrān 3:31)

لَقَدْ كَانَ لَكُمْ فِي رَسُولِ اللَّهِ أُسْوَةٌ حَسَنَةٌ لِمَن كَانَ يَرْجُو اللَّهَ وَالْيَوْمَ الآخِرَ وَذَكَرَ اللَّهَ كَثِيرًا

You have indeed in the Messenger of Allah a beautiful pattern (of conduct)
for any one whose hope is in Allah and the Final Day, and who engages
much in the Remembrance of Allah. (al-Ahzāb 33:21)

---

[180] That is, "we only use the Qur'ān to decide what is right and wrong, not the hadith."
[181] Narrated in *Musnad Āhmad*, *Sunan Abū Dāwūd*, and by *Tirmidhī*, *Hākim*, *Ibn Hibbān*, and *Ibn Mājah*:
> Yūshiku an yaq'uda ar-rajulu mutaki'an 'ala arrīkatihi, yuhaddithu bi-hadīthin min hadīthee fa-yaqūl 'baynanā wa baynakum kitāballāh. Fa mā wajadnā fīhi min halāl istahlalnāh wa mā wajadna fīhī min harām harramnāh.' alā wa inna mā harrama Rasūlallāhi mithla mā harram-Allāh?

قال عمر بن الخطاب سمعت أنَّ رسول الله صلَّى الله علىُّ و سلم قال تركتُ فيكم أمرين لنْ تضلُّوا
ما تمسكتمْ بهما كتاب الله و سنة نبيَّه (رواه ملك في كتاب الجامع و البيهقي في سنن الكبرى)

The Prophet ﷺ said:

> I have left among you two matters, as long as you hold fast to
> them, you shall never be misguided: Allāh's Book and the
> Sunnah of His Prophet.[182]

Those who reject hadith do not follow Islamic knowledge from its
traditional authentic sources. From the beginning of Islamic history there has
been the *'ijāza* system of learning and authorization. This system involves
learning from a qualified teacher who authorizes his student when he has
achieved mastery of the subject.[183] The teacher in turn was deemed qualified by
his own teacher, who had been qualified by his teacher and so on in a line of
transmission that ultimately reaches back to one of the Companions, who was
taught by the Prophet ﷺ himself. There is a great emphasis placed on having a
proper teacher of religion. In the book of Hafiz Ibn 'Alī, *Kanz al-'ummāl,* the
following important hadith is found.

The Prophet ﷺ said:

> O 'Umar, your religion is your flesh and blood. Look at those
> from whom you take your religion; take it from those who are
> on the right path and do not take it from those who deviated.

---

[182] Narrated from Ibn 'Abbās by Bayhaqī in *Sunan al-kubrā* (10:114 #20108) and—as part of a
longer hadith—by Hākim (1:93, 1990 ed. 1:171) who declared it *sahīh* and by Mālik in his
Muwattā'.
In another hadith Zayd ibn Arqam narrated:
> The Prophet stood among us at a brook named Khumm between Makkah and
> Madīna [three miles from al-Juhfā]. He praised Allāh and glorified Him, then
> said:
> To proceed. O people! Truly I am now only waiting for a messenger [of death]
> sent by my Lord so that I may respond. Therefore I am leaving among you the
> two weighty matters: Allāh's Book—in it is the guidance and the light, therefore
> hold fast to Allāh's Book, and conform to it!
> And he encouraged people to do so, and urged them. Then he said:
> And the people of my House (Āhli Baytī). I remind you of Allāh concerning the
> people of my House! I remind you of Allāh concerning the people of my House!
> I remind you of Allāh concerning the people of my House!
(Found in *Sahīh Muslim,* and in *Āhmad* with the addition of the words, "I am only a human
being," Dārimī, Tahawī in *Mushkil al-athar* (9:89 #3464), Ibn Abī 'Asim in *al-Sunnah* (#1550),
Tabarānī (#5028), and others.)
[183] This is similar to the way that surgeons or other specialized professionals learn to practically
apply principles found in books under the guidance and tutelage of a qualified practioner. As
the wise person will not go to a doctor who has no license in healing, so the Muslim must find a
teacher who has received the license ('ijāza) from his teacher. The Islamic knowledge is most
important since it affects not only our daily life but our eternal afterlife. Thus it is of the utmost
significance to have Islamic teachers who are qualified to guide us correctly in finding answers
to the issues we face.

Imām Muslim said, "This great knowledge (of the self) is by itself the religion. So you have to know from whom you take your religion." A scholar said, "Knowledge is a spirit which is blown into the hearts, not philosophy or pretty tales to be written. So be very careful from whom you take it."

The people the Prophet ﷺ described as rejecting the hadith have no such intact, traceable lineage of scholarship back to the Prophet ﷺ via one of his Companions and one of the four Imāms of jurisprudence certifying their qualifications and knowledge *('ijāza)*.[184] Now Muslims have broken that lineage and take knowledge without an intact chain of transmission. What they are learning is at best questionable and at worst contrary to the understanding of fourteen centuries of Islamic scholarship. There are even some Muslims learning about Islam in secular universities from non-Muslim professors who argue that there is no reliable hadith evidence. These Orientalists reject the hadiths, saying they are fabricated, and in doing so poison the minds of Muslims. Muslims learn from these people and think they are being educated in Islam. They begin to parrot their teachers and say, "We only read the Qur'ān," and they completely ignore the hadith. Allāh ﷻ said in the Holy Qur'ān:

$$فَلَا وَرَبِّكَ لَا يُؤْمِنُونَ حَتَّى يُحَكِّمُوكَ فِيمَا شَجَرَ بَيْنَهُمْ ثُمَّ لَا يَجِدُوا فِي أَنْفُسِهِمْ حَرَجًا مِمَّا قَضَيْتَ وَيُسَلِّمُوا تَسْلِيمًا$$

But nay, by your Lord! they will not believe (in truth) until they make you (O Muhammad) judge of what is in dispute between them and find within themselves no dislike of that which you decide, and submit with full submission. (an-Nisā' 4:65)

Throughout their history, Islamic peoples have never accepted only the Qur'ān while rejecting hadith. It is amazing to see some Muslim leaders, and those on the Internet who follow them, rejecting the hadiths. Even fifty years ago this was unheard of, and now this ideology can be found in most of the mosques in the West and around the world. There are many people rejecting the Prophetic Hadith and Sunnah, and this did not happen until the present time. The Prophet ﷺ said these people would appear in the Last Days and this has come to pass, as manifest in the following extraordinary Companion

---

[184] We reference hadiths with their chain of transmission back to a Companion who heard it from the Prophet. Similarly with Islamic knowledge we must have a chain of transmission which reaches back to one of the four Imāms of jurisprudence (Abū Hanīfa, al-Shafi'ī, Mālik, Āhmad Ibn Hanbal) who were living near to the time of the Prophet and could integrate all branches of Islamic knowledge into a comprehensive approach to the Qur'ān and Sunnah. All four Imāms are regarded as correct and differences of opinion only show the breadth of Islam. Al-Khattābī said in *Gharīb al-hadīth*:

> ... In the different rulings of the branches of the law (*ahkām al-furu'*): Allāh has made them mercy and generosity for the scholars, and that is the meaning of the hadith, "Difference of opinion in my Community is a mercy."

report.

حدثني أبو بكر محمد بن أحمد بن بالويه، حدثنا عبد الله بن أحمد بن حنبل، حدثني أبي، حدثنا
عبد الرحمن بن مهدي، حدثنا عكرمة بن عمار، عن حميد بن عبد الله الفلسطيني، حدثني عبد
العزيز ابن أخي حذيفة، عن حذيفة رضي الله تعالى عنه- قال:

أول ما تفقدون من دينكم الخشوع، وآخر ما تفقدون من دينكم الصلاة، ولتنقضن عرى الإسلام
عروة عروة، وليصلين النساء وهن حيض، ولتسلكن طريق من كان قبلك حذو القذة بالقذة،
وحذو النعل بالنعل، لا تخطئون طريقهم، ولا يخطأنكم حتى تبقى فرقتان من فرق كثيرة .فتقول
إحداهما: ما بال الصلوات الخمس، لقد ضل من كان قبلنا، إنما قال الله -تبارك وتعالى-: ﴿أقم
الصلاة طرفي النهار وزلفا من الليل ﴾ [هود: 114]. لا تصلوا إلا ثلاثا. وتقول الأخرى: إيمان
المؤمنين بالله كإيمان الملائكة، ما فينا كافر ولا منافق، حق على الله أن يحشرهما مع الدجال.

هذا حديث صحيح الإسناد، ولم يخرجاه . المستدرك على الصحيحين،الإصدار للإمام محمد بن عبد
الله الحاكم النيسابوري. وجدت في: الجلد الرابع .كتاب: الفتن، والملاحم.

A narration from Hudhayfa al-Yamānī ﷺ states:

The first thing you will lose from your religion is humility (*khushuʿ*) and the last, prayer (*salāt*). You shall certainly undo the bonds of Islam one by one. Women shall be praying while in menses.[185] You shall certainly walk the road of those that came before you as closely as the arrow-feather and the sandal-span, not missing a step of the way, nor shall their way be any different from yours. In the end two out of many [wayward] sects shall remain. The first shall say: "What are these five prayers? Surely those that came before us went astray. Allāh only said: *Establish worship at the two ends of the day and in some watches of the night* (Hūd 11:114). Do not pray except three prayers!" The other sect shall say: "The faith of the believers in Allāh is just like the faith of the angels. There is not, among us, a single apostate nor dissimulator!" It shall be right that Allāh raise them together with the Antichrist.[186]

---

[185] The precedent has already been introduced in such new-fangled *fatāwā* as those by Abd al-ʿAzīz bin Bāz permitting women in menses to recite, read and even touch the *mushaf*. See: Muhammad bin Abd al-ʿAzīz Al-Musnad, *Islamic Fatawa Regarding Women*, translated by Jamaal Al-Din Zarabozo.

[186] Narrated by al-Hākim (4:469=1990 ed. 4:516) who declared its chain *sahīh* and al-Dhahabī confirmed it. Although the chain of this *mawqūf* narration is not raised up to the Prophet nevertheless its status is that of a Prophetic hadith as it pertains to unseen matters which are not subject to the Companion's opinion and which he can only have said upon hearing them from the Prophet.

TRIBULATIONS

KILLING AND DESTRUCTION

Armageddon

In the chapter "The Destruction of Yathrib" the hadith of Mu'ādh Ibn Jabal
🙵 describes a tremendous battle to occur at the time of the conquest of
Constantinople(Istanbul) and the emergence of the Dajjāl, the Anti-Christ:

حدثنا عبد الله حدثني أبي حدثنا زيد بن الحباب حدثنا عبد الرحمن بن ثوبان حدثني أبي عن
مكحول عن معاذ بن جبل قال: قال رسول الله صلى الله عليه وسلم: عمران بيت المقدس خراب
يثرب وخراب يثرب خروج الملحمة وخروج الملحمة فتح القسطنطينية وفتح القسطنطينية خروج
الدجال ثم ضرب على فخذه أو على منكبه ثم قال: إن هذا لحق كما أنك قاعد وكان مكحول
يحدث به عن جبير بن نفير عن مالك بن يخامر عن معاذ بن جبل عن النبي صلى الله عليه وسلم
مثله .

(رواه أبو داوُد في سننه في كتاب الملحمة و الترمذي في الفتن و أحمد في مسنَده)

Mu'ādh Ibn Jabal 🙵. related that the Prophet 🕌 said:

> ...the appearance of the fierce and bloody battle **and** the
> appearance of the fierce and bloody battle; the conquest of
> Constantinople **and** the conquest of Constantinople; (and) the
> appearance of the Dajjāl (Anti-Christ).

In the past there was a great battle between the Muslims and the
Byzantines (*Rūm*) at Constantinople in the time of the great Companion Abū
Ayyūb al-Ansārī 🙵. The Muslims were unable to conquer the city. The Prophet
🕌 predicted that Abū Ayyūb al-Ansārī 🙵 would die in the cold (an unusual
prediction in the hot climate they lived in), and Abū Ayyūb 🙵 did, in fact, pass
away in the cold during that siege (672 CE).

حدثنا عبد الله حدثني أبي حدثنا عبد الله بن محمد بن أبي شيبة وسمعته أنا من عبد الله بن
محمد ابن أبي شيبة قال:
حدثنا زيد بن الحباب قال حدثني الوليد بن المغيرة المعافري قال حدثني عبد الله بن بشر الخثعمي
عن أبيه أنه سمع النبي صلى الله عليه وسلم يقول لتفتحن القسطنطينية فلنعم الأمير أميرها ولنعم

الجيش ذلك الجيش قال فدعاني مسلمة بن عبد الملك فسألني فحدثته فغزا القسطنطينية . (رواه
أحمد في مسنده)

Many years later, Muhammad Fātih conquered Constantinople, as was predicted by the Prophet ﷺ in another hadith:

> Constantinople will surely be conquered. What a most splendid leader is the leader of the army that does so, and most splendid is that army.[187]

The conquest of Constantinople by the Ottoman Sultan Muhammad Fātih in 1453 CE, is a sign of the Last Days according to the hadith of the Prophet ﷺ. However, the Prophet ﷺ mentioned it would be conquered twice, meaning that Constantinople will again come to prominence. As mentioned in the hadith of Muʿādh Ibn Jabal ﷺ this occurs after an enormous battle with many casualties (khurūj ul-malhama),[188] and is further described in this hadith.

حدثنا أبو اليمان: أخبرنا شعيب: حدثنا أبو الزناد، عن عبد الرحمن، عن أبي هريرة:
أن رسول الله صلى الله عليه وسلم قال: لا تقوم الساعة حتى تقتل فئتان عظيمتان، يكون بينهما
مقتلة عظيمة، دعوتهما واحدة. وحتى يبعث دجالون كذابون، قريب من ثلاثين، كلهم يزعم أنه
رسول الله، وحتى يقبض العلم وتكثر الزلازل، ويتقارب الزمان، وتظهر الفتن، ويكثر الهرج، وهو
القتل. وحتى يكثر فيكم المال، فيفيض حتى يهم رب المال من يقبل صدقته، وحتى يعرضه، فيقول
الذي يعرضه عليه: لا أرب لي به. وحتى يتطاول الناس في البنيان. وحتى يمر الرجل بقبر الرجل
فيقول: يا ليتني مكانه. وحتى تطلع الشمس من مغربها، فإذا طلعت ورآها الناس - يعني - آمنوا
أجمعون، فذلك حين: ﴿ لا ينفع نفساً إيمانها لم تكن آمنت من قبل أو كسبت في إيمانها خيراً ﴾.
ولتقومن الساعة وقد نشر الرجلان ثوبيهما بينهما، فلا يتبايعانه ولا يطويانه. ولتقومن الساعة وقد
انصرف الرجل بلبن لقحته فلا يطعمه. ولتقومن الساعة وهو يليط حوضه فلا يسقي فيه، ولتقومن
الساعة وقد رفع أكلته إلى فيه فلا يطعمها ((رواه البخاري في كتاب (الفتن و مُسلم في كتاب الإيمان
و الفتن و أحمد في مسنده)

Abū Hurayra ﷺ related that the Prophet ﷺ said, "The Hour will not appear until there will be two enormous groups

---

[187] *Sahīh Bukhārī*. *Sahīh Muslim*. Āhmad, *Musnad* (4:236). Hākim, *Mustadrak* (4:422), Dhahabi, Suyūtī, and Haythamī. "*La-tuftahanna al-qustāntinīyyatu. Fala-ni'am al-amīru amīruhā wa la-ni'am al jayshu dhālika al-jaysh*"

[188] *Malhama* is a fierce clash between two huge parties with tremendous bloodshed, a bloodbath.

fighting each other in a colossal battle, (and) their issue is
one."...[189]

حدثنا الحميدي: حدثنا الوليد بن مسلم: حدثنا عبد الله بن العلاء بن زبر قال: سمعت بسر بن

عبيد الله: أنه سمع أبا إدريس قال: سمعت عوف بن مالك قال:

أتيت النبي صلى الله عليه وسلم في غزوة تبوك، وهو في قبة من أدم، فقال: (اعدد ستا بين يدي

الساعة: موتي، ثم فتح بيت المقدس، ثم موتان يأخذ فيكم كقعاص الغنم، ثم استفاضة المال حتى

يعطى الرجل مائة دينار فيظل ساخطا، ثم فتنة لا يبقى بيت من العرب إلا دخلته، ثم هدنة تكون

بينكم وبين بني الأصفر، فيغدرون فيأتونكم تحت ثمانين غاية، تحت كل غاية اثنا عشر ألفا

(البخاري في كتاب الجزية و أحمد في مسنده)

'Awf Ibn Mālik ﷺ related that the Prophet ﷺ said:

Count six signs before the Hour: my death; then the opening
of *Bayt al-Maqdis*; then death in huge numbers, like the plague
of sheep; then there will be such an excess of money, such
that a man would give one hundred dinars to a (needy) person
and he looks at that with disgust; then a confusion that will
enter every house of the Arabs; then a truce between you and
the non-Muslims (because) they will be exceedingly powerful
against you, coming to you with eighty different groups (of

---

[189] *Sahīh Bukhārī*, "Kitāb al-Fitan" (13:8). *Sahīh Muslim*, "Kitāb al-Fitan" (1:57). The full text
reads:

The Hour will not appear until there will be two enormous groups fighting each
other in a colossal batte and their issue is one ("*Lā taqūmu as-sā'atu hatta
taqtatila fi'atāni 'azhīmatāni. Yakūnu baynahumā maqtalatun 'azhīmatun
da'wāhumā wāhidah*"); till about thirty Dajjals (liars) appear, and each one of
them will claim that he is Allah's Apostle; till the religious knowledge is taken
away (by the death of religious scholars); earthquakes will increase in number;
time will pass quickly; afflictions will appear; al-Harj, (i.e., killing) will increase;
till wealth will be in abundance—so abundant that a wealthy person will worry
lest nobody should accept his Zakāt, and whenever he will present it to
someone, that person (to whom it will be offered) will say, "I am not in need of
it,"; till the people compete with one another in constructing high buildings; till a
man when passing by a grave of someone will say, "Would that I were in his
place"; and till the sun rises from the West. So when the sun will rise and the
people will see it (rising from the West) they will all believe (embrace Islam) but
that will be the time when: (As Allah said), *"No good will it do to a soul to
believe then, if it believed not before, nor earned good (by deeds of
righteousness) through its Faith."* (al-An'am 6, 158) And the Hour will be
established while two men spreading a garment in front of them but they will
not be able to sell it, nor fold it up; and the Hour will be established when a
man has milked his she-camel and has taken away the milk but he will not be
able to drink it; and the Hour will be established before a man repairing a tank
(for his livestock) is able to water (his animals) in it; and the Hour will be
established when a person has raised a morsel (of food) to his mouth but will
not be able to eat it.

soldiers or eighty different compelling excuses); under each group twelve thousand (soldiers or twelve thousand explanations).[190]

These hadiths thus indicate that there will be a huge, bloody battle (*malhama*), which will take place between two gigantic groups having the same goal. This leaves many to expect that a great war (perhaps a nuclear war) between two powers will erupt in that region over a common interest and benefit in that part of the world, whether Central Asia, the Gulf region or the Middle East.

This war will result in a huge bloodbath with many casualties, and it will affect Constantinople. This might happen in the future, and it is one of the most significant signs of the Last Days, known as Armageddon in all holy books. The hadith indicates that this will be very close to the time of the appearance of the Dajjāl, Anti-Christ. The first hadith mentions that the Prophet ﷺ hit the thigh of Mu'ādh Ibn Jabal ؓ and said, "This is the truth (*haqq*) just as you are sitting here." Hitting his thigh was to emphasize its reality, meaning, "It is going to happen; do not think it too strange."

---

[190] *Sahīh Bukhārī*, "Kitāb al-Jihād" (6:198). Āhmad, *Musnad* (6:25 and 27):
'Udud sittan bayna yadayhi as-sā'at: mawtī, thumma fathu bayt il-maqdis, thumma mūtānun yakhudhu fīkum ka ku'ās il-ghanami, thumma astifādat-ul-māli hatta y'uti ar-rajulu mi'ata dinārin fayadhala sākhitan, thumma fitnatun lā yabqā baytun min al-'arab illa dakhalat-hu, thumma hudnatun takūnu baynakum wa bayna banī il-asfara fa yaghdurūna fa yā'tūnakum tahta thamānīna ghāyatin, tahta kulli ghāyatin ithna 'ashara alfa.
Sahīh Bukhārī, "Kitāb al-Jihād" (6:198). Āhmad, *Musnad* (6:25 and 27).

Thirty Liars

There have been many liars and false prophets, from Mūsāylima the Liar (in the time of the Prophet Muhammad ﷺ) up to the present day.

حدثنا عبد الله حدثني أبي حدثنا محمد بن جعفر قال حدثنا شعبة قال سمعت العلاء ابن عبد
الرحمن يحدث عن أبيه عن أبي هريرة عن النبي صلى الله عليه وسلم أنه قالا
-لا تقوم الساعة حتى يظهر ثلاثون دجالون كلهم يزعم أنه رسول الله ويفيض المال فيكثر وتظهر
الفتن ويكثر الهرج قال قيل وأيما الهرج قال القتل القتل ثلاثا . (مسلم ، البخاري و ابو داود)

Abū Hurayra ؓ related that the Prophet ﷺ said:

> The Hour will not come until thirty liars (Dajjāls) emerge each of them claiming to be a messenger of Allāh. And (the Hour will not come) until there will be a great increase in money, and tribulations will appear, and there will be much *harj*.
>
> The Prophet ﷺ was asked, "What is *harj*?" He said, "Killing, killing," three times.[191]

Among the signs of the Last Days mentioned in this hadith is that there would be liars claiming to be messengers from Allāh ﷻ after Prophet Muhammad ﷺ. Another sign of the Last Days that this hadith speaks of is the corrupt leadership of our time awash in "dirty money," causing dissension, and taking their communities and nations down the road to bloodshed, violence, and wars, not leaving a single home without fear. The Prophet ﷺ then mentioned that *harj* would occur, which is widespread, indiscriminate killing. This is happening so much that it is not even unusual anymore, and today there is not a single country which is safe from the killing of innocent people.

يكثر الهرج و المرج (مسلم و البخاري)

This sign of the Last Days was mentioned by the Prophet Muhammad ﷺ in another hadith,

> "There will be much slaughter and killing."[192]

People are being killed everywhere in wars, and even in countries without war people are killing each other in robberies, petty squabbles, and oftentimes senselessly. Many people involved in blood feuds have long forgotten why they

---

[191] *Sahīh Muslim* (4:2240) "Kitāb al-Fitan." *Sahīh Bukhārī*, al-Manāqib #3609. *Sunan Abū Dāwūd*, #4333:
  Lā taqūm us-sā'atu hatta yakhruju thalathūna dajjālūna kulluhum yaz'amu annahu rasūlullāh. Hatta yafīd al-mālu; wa tazhar ul-fitanu; wa yakthur ul-harju.
  Qālu wa mā al-harju ya Rasūlallāhi? Qāl: al-qatl, ul-qatl.
[192] *Sahīh Bukhārī* and *Sahīh Muslim*. "Yakthuru al-harju wal-marju."

began fighting in the first place. Gangs, organized to commit violence against one another, are a manifestation of this widespread killing. There are countless innocent bystanders who are killed in this plague of violence.

وحدثنا عبدالله بن عمر بن أبان وواصل بن عبدالأعلى . قالا: حدثنا محمد بن فضيل عن أبي إسماعيل الأسلمي، عن أبي حازم، عن أبي هريرة، قال: قال رسول الله صلى الله عليه وسلم "والذي نفسي بيده ! لا تذهب الدنيا حتى يأتي على الناس يوم، لا يدري القاتل فيما قتل . ولا المقتول فيم قتل" (رواه مسلم في كتاب الفتن)

Abū Hurayra ﷺ related that the Prophet ﷺ said:

> By Him in Whose Hand is my life, the world will not perish until a time will come when the murderer would not know why he has committed the murder, and the victim would not know why he has been killed.[193]

This chaotic violence and carnage will make people long for their deaths.

حدثنا عبدالله بن عمر بن محمد بن أبان بن محمد بن صالح ومحمد بن يزيد الرفاعي (واللفظ لابن أبان) . قالا: حدثنا ابن فضيل عن أبي إسماعيل، عن أبي حازم، عن أبي هريرة، قال: قال رسول الله صلى الله عليه وسلم "والذي نفسي بيده ! لا تذهب الدنيا حتى يمر الرجل على القبر فيتمرغ عليه، ويقول: يا ليتني كنت مكان صاحب هذا القبر . وليس به الدين إلا البلاء" (رواه المسلم في كتاب الفتن)

Abū Hurayra ﷺ related that the Prophet ﷺ said:

> By Him, in Whose hand is my life, the world will not perish until a man passes by someone's grave, would roll over it and say, "Would that I were in his place!" He does not say this for the sake of his religion, but because of the calamities around him.[194]

These tribulations will destroy people both physically and spiritually. They will be so severe that they can change someone from belief to unbelief in a single day or night.

حدثنا عبد الله حدثني أبي حدثنا عبد الصمد حدثنا أبي قال حدثنا محمد بن جحادة عن عبد الرحمن بن ثروان عن هزيل بن شرحبيل عن أبي موسى قال: قال رسول الله صلى الله عليه وسلم إن بين يدي الساعة فتنا كقطع الليل المظلم يصبح الرجل فيها مؤمنا ويمسي كافرا ويمسي مؤمنا ويصبح كافرا القاعد فيها خير من القائم والقائم فيها خير من

---

193 Sahīh Muslim.
194 Sahīh Bukhārī, "Kitāb al-Fitan."

الماشي والماشي فيها خيرٌ من الساعي فاكسروا قسيكم وقطعوا أوتاركم واضربوا بسيوفكم
الحجارة فإن دُخِل على أحدكم بيته فليكن كخير ابني آدم. (رَوَاهُ أبو داود في كتاب الفتن)

Abū Mūsā al-Ashʿarī ﷺ related that the Prophet ﷺ said:

> Before the Last Hour there will be afflictions like patches of a
> dark night in which a man will be a believer in the morning
> and an unbeliever in the evening, or a believer in the evening
> and an unbeliever in the morning. He who sits during them
> will be better than he who stands, and he who walks during
> them is better than he who runs. So break your bows, cut your
> bowstrings and strike your swords on stones. If people then
> come in to one of you, let him be like the better of Adam's
> two sons (i.e. death is better than getting involved in the
> *fitna*).[195]

فتنة الأحلاس هرب وحرب ثم فتنة السراء دخنها من تحت قدم رجل من أهل بيتي يزعم أنه مني
وليس مني وإنما أوليائي المتقون ثم يصطلح الناس على رجل كورك على ضلع ثم فتنة الدهيماء لا
تدع أحدا من هذه الأمة إلا لطمته لطمة فإذا قيل: انقضت تمادت يصبح الرجل فيها مؤمنا ويمسي
كافرا حتى يصير الناس إلى فسطاطين: فسطاط إيمان لا نفاق فيه، وفسطاط نفاق لا إيمان فيه فإذا
كان ذاكم فانتظروا الدجال من يومه أو غده .

(أخرجه أبو داود كتاب الفتن باب ذكر الفتن ودلائلها رقم (4224)، وقال في عون المعبود:
(312/11) أخرجه الحاكم وصححه وأقره الذهبي ص) .

'Abd Allāh ibn 'Umar ﷺ said: We were sitting with the
Messenger of Allāh ﷺ when he mentioned the many
tribulations. He spoke at length about many of them until he
mentioned the "strife of the saddle-blankets" (*fitnat al-Ahlās*).
He said the latter was all flight and war. Then he mentioned
the "strife of prosperity" (*fitnat al-sarra'*). He said, "Its heat and
smoke (*dakhan*) would seep in from under the feet of a man
from my family—he will claim that he descends from me but
he does not descend from me. My relatives are only those
who fear God." Then [the Prophet said] the people will rally
around a man like a rib-bone on top of a hip-bone [ie. a
temporary, impermanent arrangement]. Then will come the
"pitch-dark, blind strife" (*al-fitnat al-duhayma'*). "It will leave
alone none of this Ummah except it will smite him. When
they think it is over it will linger some more. At that time, a
man will rise a believer in the morning and will reach night a

---

[195] *Sunan Abū Dāwūd*, "Kitāb Al-Fitan Wa Al-Malāhim" #4246.

disbeliever. People will eventually take two sides—the rallying-place of belief which will contain no hypocrisy; and the rallying-place of hypocrisy which will contain no belief. When you see this, expect the appearance of the Anti-Christ (Dajjāl) from one day to the next." [196]

In this hadith we hear a description of the peoples' condition during the Last Days when the one sitting is better than the one who is standing; and better yet than going outside to be entangled in problems and dissension. It is a difficult time in which those who moving about fall into afflictions, while those who stay home remain out of harm's way.

The Prophet ﷺ issued a stern warning to those would live to see such tribulations: do not to involve oneself in these miseries and confusing affairs.

حدثنا محمد بن عبيد الله: حدثنا إبراهيم بن سعد، عن أبيه، عن أبي سلمة بن عبد الرحمن، عن أبي هريرة

قال إبراهيم: وحدثني صالح بن كيسان، عن ابن شهاب، عن سعيد بن المسيَّب، عن أبي هريرة قال:

قال رسول الله صلى الله عليه وسلم: (ستكون فتن، القاعد فيها خير من القائم، والقائم فيها خير من الماشي، والماشي فيها خير من الساعي، من تشرَّف لها تستشرفه، فمن وجد فيها ملجأً، أو معاذاً، فليعذ به (رواه مسلم و البخاري في كتاب الفتن)

Abū Hurayra ؓ related that the Prophet ﷺ said:

Whoever exposes himself to these afflictions, will be destroyed by them. So whoever can find a place of protection or refuge from them, should take shelter in it.[197]

Allāh ﷻ mentioned in the Holy Qur'ān:

فَأْوُوا إِلَى الْكَهْفِ يَنشُرْ لَكُم رَّبُّكُم مِّن رَّحْمَتِهِ وَيُهَيِّئْ لَكُم مِّنْ أَمْرِكُم مِّرْفَقًا

Betake yourselves for refuge to the cave; your Lord will shower His mercies on you and dispose of your affair towards comfort and ease.

(al-Kahf 18:16)

In another hadith of Abū Mūsā al-Ash'arī ؓ, the Prophet ﷺ advised, "At that time be the saddle-cloths of your houses."[198]

This means Muslims should stay at home and not go about. So many

---

[196] *Abū Dāwūd* in his *Sunan* and *Aḥmad* in his *Musnad* narrated that.
[197] *Saḥīḥ Muslim*, Chapter "the Descent of Afflictions like Rainfall." ("Nuzul al-fitan ka mawāqi' al-qatar").
[198] Narrated by *Aḥmad*. *Al-ahlās* means saddle-cloth.

Muslims are going around needlessly to coffee houses, restaurants, and malls. One should not go out without a good reason. It is advisable to go directly to and from work without unnecessary delays or stops. In these trying times, it is best to sit at home and look after one's family. The Prophet ﷺ is telling the Muslims that in the Last Days, when one is powerless to overcome these enormous difficulties and unable to change anything, not to mix anywhere, not to be a part of anything, not to interfere in fighting or politics. Muslims should break the arrows of anger, cut the bowstrings with which they fling retorting barbs in response to harsh taunts, and false accusations and dull the swords of self-defense by words and pens, breaking their egoes on the stones of hardship borne with patience.

When tribulations are rife it is better to stay home and increase one's worship: praying, reading Qur'ān and hadith, remembering Allāh ﷺ.

حَدَّثَنَا قُتَيْبَةُ أَخْبَرَنَا حَمَّادُ بْنُ زَيْدٍ عَنِ المُعَلَّى بْنِ زِيَادٍ رَدَّهُ إِلَى معاوية بْنِ قُرَّةَ رَدَّهُ إِلَى مَعْقِلِ بْنِ يسارٍ رَدَّهُ إِلَى النَّبِيِّ صَلَّى اللهُ عَلَيهِ وسَلَّم قال: العبادةُ فِي الهَرجِ كهِجرةٍ إلَيَّ (رواه مسلم في كتاب الفتن .هذا حديثٌ صحيحٌ غريبٌ إنما نعرفُهُ من حديثِ المُعلى بن زياد)

Ma'qil Ibn Yasār ؓ related that the Prophet ﷺ said:

Worshipping during the period of widespread turmoil is like emigration towards me.[199]

To keep away from these difficulties Muslims are advised to recite special forms of *tasbīh*, every day. See Chapter, "Daily Recitations for Protection from Tribulations," on page 287.

༻⁕❁⁕༺

---

[199] *Sahīh Muslim.* "Kitāb al-Fitan."

Sanctions on Iraq and Shām

The Prophet Muhammad ﷺ foretold sanctions on Iraq and Syria which would take place in the Last Days.

حدثنا زهير بن حرب وعلي بن حجر (واللفظ لزهير) . قالا: حدثنا إسماعيل بن إبراهيم عن الجريري، عن أبي نضرة، قال: كما عند جابر بن عبدالله فقال: يوشك أهل العراق ألا يجبى إليهم قفيز ولا درهم. قلنا: من أين ذاك؟ قال: من قبل العجم. يمنعون ذاك . ثم قال: يوشك أهل الشام أن لا يجبى إليهم دينار ولا مدي. قلنا: من أين ذاك؟ قال: من قبل الروم. ثم أسكت هنية . ثم قال: قال رسول الله صلى الله عليه وسلم "يكون في آخر أمتي خليفة يحثي المال حثيا . لا يعده عددا (مسلم في كتاب الفتن)

Abū Nadra ﷺ narrated:

We were with Jābir Ibn 'Abd Allāh ﷺ who said, "It is iminent that the people of Iraq will not receive a single *qafīz*[200] nor *dirham*." We said, "Who would be responsible for it?" He said, "The *'Ajam* (non-Arabs) would prevent it." He (Jābir) then said, "It is imminent that the people of Shām (Syria) will not receive a single *dīnār* nor *mudd*."[201] We said, "Who would be responsible for it?" He said, "*Rūm* (Romans or Byzantines)." He (Jābir Ibn 'Abd Allāh ﷺ) kept quiet for a while and then reported that Allāh's Messenger ﷺ said, "There will be a caliph in the Last Days who will freely give handfuls of wealth to the people without counting it."[202]

Among the Signs of the Last Days is that the Iraqi people will be under sanctions from the non-Arabs (*'Ajam*). Abū Nadhra ﷺ related that Jābir ﷺ said[203] that there will come a time when the people of Iraq will be so poor that

---

[200] As there were no scales at that time in 'Iraq, the *qafīz* or *mikyān* (a unit of measure like a pot) was used, it is approximately 5 kg.

[201] *Mudd* is double the *qafīdh*, about 10 kg.

[202] *Sahīh Muslim* #2913. Al-Jurayrī (who narrated this hadith from Abū Nadra) asked Abū Nadra and Abū 'Alā, "Do you think it means 'Umar Ibn 'Abd al-'Azīz?" They said: "No":

Yūshiku āhl al-'irāqi an lā yujbā ilayhim qafīdhun wa lā dirham. Qulnā: wa min ayna dhāk? Qāla: min qibal il-'ajami. Yamna'ūna dhāka. Thumma qāla: yūshiku āhl ash-shāmi an lā yujba ilayhim dīnārun wa lā muddyun. Qulnā: min ayna dhāk? Qāla: min qibal ir-rūmi. Thumma asqata hunyatan. Thumma qāla: Qāla Rasūlullāhi sall-Allāhu 'alayhi wasallam, Yakūnu fī akhir iz-zamāni khalīfatun yahth il-māla hathyan wa lā ya'uddu lahu 'addadan…. Qāl: atarāyāni annahu 'Umar ibn 'Abd al-'Azīz? Faqalā: Lā.

[203] Jābir is relating what he learned from the Prophet describing the sanctions in his explanation of the hadith of the Prophet mentioned at the end of the narration, "There will be a caliph in the Last Days…" There are similar hadiths of the Prophet such as *Sahīh Muslim* #6923 in which Abū Hurayra ﷺ related that the Prophet said:

they will not even have enough to weigh one *qafīdh*; that is, they will have nothing. The Prophet ﷺ gave an eloquent hint: that they cannot measure even five kilograms, indicating that trade will be stopped. The *'Ajam* will prevent this by placing sanctions on them and stopping the entire nation from receiving anything. As there is no trade there is no money in the economy, and the dinar will not reach them either. The people will not be able to buy anything in their markets, even goods worth the value of a penny (*dirham*).

This is going to happen from the *'Ajam*, in general any non-Arabic speaking people, and specifically Persians. This gives a clue that the sanctions against Iraq would originate after a conflict with the Persians, which was seen with the Iran-Iraq war during the 1980's. Iraq had problems first with the Persians, and then with Kuwait, which resulted in restrictive sanctions imposed by the U.N.[204] The sad consequence of this is that there are massive numbers of dead children, as if the nation had been struck by a plague. The total number of dead from the sanctions alone reaches at minimum 1.5 million people.[205] The implementation of these sanctions is one of the signs of the Last Days miraculously foretold by Prophet Muhammad ﷺ.

The Prophet ﷺ predicted that after the sanctions on Iraq, the *dīnār* and the *mudd* would be withheld from the people of Shām (greater Syria). The cause of the sanctions in this instance would be *ar-Rūm*. *Rūm* indicates the People of the Book of the local denominations, extending from Russia all the way to the Syrian border, and also in general refers to the non-Muslims of the West. Already there is a trade problem. Even today in Shām, there are shortages, and the people have few dīnārs to buy fuel and other essentials. As Iraq had a conflict with the al-'Ajam, Syria may have a difference of opinion with the non-Muslims of the West (*ar-Rūm*) and also end up under sanctions. This work is not concerned with the political aspects of these events but in the analysis of these modern-day events in light of the predictions of Prophet Muhammad ﷺ. The Prophet ﷺ predicted today's situation, and told the Companions about it fourteen hundred years ago.

All of the foregoing Jābir ؓ learned from the Prophet ﷺ, and he related these events to give the background to the crucial end of this narration: "There will be a caliph in the Last Days who will freely give handfuls of wealth to the people without counting it." The Prophet ﷺ said that in the Last Days there

---

Iraq would withhold its *dirhams* and *qafīz*; Syria would withhold its mudd and *dīnār* and Egypt would withhold its *irdab* and *dīnār* and you would recoil to that position from where you started and you would recoil to that position from where you started and you would recoil to that position from where you started, the bones and the flesh of Abū Hurayra would bear testimony to it.

[204] U.N. Resolution 661 of August 6, 1990, imposed comprehensive economic sanctions on Iraq exempting food and medicine and established the 661 Committee to oversee implementation of the sanctions.

[205] According to UNICEF reports, 600,000 of the dead are children under five years of age.

would be a caliph (*khalīfa*), or ruler, for all Muslims. This leader is Mahdī ﷺ, who comes with heavenly support from Allāh ﷻ, filling the earth with justice and removing killing and oppression. He is not a prophet but a *khalīfa* who will pass out wealth without counting it, meaning that there will be sufficient provision for everyone. Before Mahdī's ﷺ time, sanctions will leave people unable to utilize the wealth and resources in their lands, and governments will be unable to collect revenues as there will be nothing to tax. There will be no funding for schools, hospitals, or money for fuel, electricity and water. Without the essentials of survival people will become desperate and there will be general instability in society with the law of the jungle the order of the day.

All this will change in the time of Mahdī ﷺ when the earth will bring forth its treasures with Mahdī's ﷺ supplications to Allāh ﷻ, and there will be overflowing wealth and prosperity. This will be a big opening to relieve (*faraj*) the Muslims. At that time people will not be lacking money, as it will be so abundant that money from the state's coffers will be given to the people without counting.

᠁᠁᠁

Tribulations from the East/Najd

The Prophet ﷺ mentioned the dissensions and problems that would come from the area of Najd, which is the area east of Hijāz.

حدثنا عبد الله بن أبي مسلمة، عن مالك، عن عبد الله بن دينار، عن عبد الله بن عمر رضي الله عنهما قال:

رأيت رسول الله صلى الله عليه وسلم يشير إلى المشرق، فقال: (ها إن الفتنة ها هنا، إن الفتنة ها هنا، من حيث يطلع قرن الشيطان. (البخاري في كتاب الفتن، مسلم في كتاب الفتن و الحافظ في كتاب الفتن)

> Ibn 'Umar ﷺ related, "I saw the Messenger of Allāh ﷺ pointing to the East and he then said, 'Look! The dissension is from here, the dissension is from here. From there will arise the horn of Shaytan.'"[206]

In another well authenticated hadith, the Prophet ﷺ did not pray for the people of Najd when requested to do so.

حدثنا محمد بن المثنى قال: حدثنا حسين بن الحسن قال: حدثنا ابن عون، عن نافع، عن ابن عمر قال:

اللهم بارك لنا في شامنا وفي يمننا . قال: قالوا: وفي نجدنا ؟ قال: قال: (اللهم بارك لنا في شامنا وفي يمننا) . قال: قالوا: وفي نجدنا . ؟ قال: قال: (هناك الزلازل والفتن، وبها يطلع قرن الشيطان (الخاري في كتاب الفتن، بن حبّان، مسلم، التّرمذي)

حدثنا عبد الله حدثني أبي حدثنا أبو عبد الرحمن حدثنا سعيد حدثنا عبد الرحمن بن عطاء عن نافع عن ابن عمر أن رسول الله صلى الله عليه وسلم قال

اللهم بارك لنا في شامنا ويمننا مرتين فقال رجل وفي مشرقنا يا رسول الله فقال رسول الله صلى الله عليه وسلم من هنالك يطلع قرن الشيطان ولها تسعة أعشار الشر . (الترمذي)

> Ibn 'Umar ﷺ related that the Prophet ﷺ said, "O Allāh! Bless us in our Shām and our Yemen!" They said, "O Messenger of Allāh! And our Najd!" He did not reply, but again said, "O Allāh! Bless us in our Shām and our Yemen!" They said, "O Messenger of Allāh! And our Najd!" He did not reply, but again said, "O Allāh! Bless us in our Shām and our Yemen!"

---

[206] Sahīh Bukhārī, "Kitāb al-fitan" (8:95) #7118. Sahīh Muslim, "Kitāb al-fitan" # 2095. Al-Hāfizh, "Bāb al-fitan" #1347. "Alā inna al-fitnata hā-hunna. Alā inna al-fitnata hā-hunna (yushīru il-al-mashriqi) min haythu yatla'u qarn ush-Shaytān."

They said, "O Messenger of Allāh! And our Najd!" He said,
"Thence shall come great upheavals and dissensions, and
from it shall issue the horn of Shaytān." One narration has the
addition, "And in it [Najd] are nine tenths of all evil."[207]

رواه الطبراني في الأوسط واللفظ له، وأحمد ولفظه: إن رسول الله صلى الله عليه وسلم قال:
"اللهم بارك لنا في شامنا ويمننا". – مرتين – فقال رجل: وفي مشرقنا يا رسول الله؟ فقال رسول
الله صلى الله عليه وسلم: "من هنالك يطلع قرن الشيطان وبه تسعة أعشار الشر

In an almost identical hadith the Prophet ﷺ interposes *mashriq* (East) for
Najd. The Prophet ﷺ said:

> "O Allāh! Bless us in our Shām and our Yemen!" A man said:
> "And our East (*mashriq*), O Messenger of Allāh!" The Prophet
> ﷺ repeated his invocation twice, and the man twice said: "And
> our East (*mashriq*), O Messenger of Allāh!,' whereupon the
> Prophet ﷺ said: "Thence shall issue the horn of *Shaytān*. In it
> are nine tenths of disbelief. In it is the incurable disease."[208]

حدثنا يحيى بن يحيى. أخبرنا هشيم عن داود بن أبي هند، عن أبي عثمان، عن سعد بن أبي
وقاص. قال:
قال رسول الله صلى الله عليه وسلم "لا يزال أهل الغرب ظاهرين على الحق حتى تقوم
الساعة."(أخرجه مسلم كتاب الإمارة)

The Prophet ﷺ said, "The people to the west will be
preeminent until Judgment Day."[209]

In the Arabic usage, the people of the *maghrib* (west), or the people to the
west, refers to the inhabitants of Shām and those in its proximity. The people
of the *mashriq* (east) are the people of Najd and Iraq.[210]

ال الخطابي: نجد من جهة المشرق ومن كان بالمدينة كان نجده بادية العراق ونواحيها وهي مشرق
أهل المدينة (الباري)

Khattābi said:

---

[207]Narrated from Ibn 'Umar in *Sahīh Bukhārī* (4:390), *Sahīh Ibn Hibbān* (16:290), *Sahīh Muslim*,
Tirmidhī, and *Āhmad* with three chains, one of which with the addition: "And in it [Najd] are nine
tenths of all evil."
[208] Narrated from Ibn 'Umar ☀ by Tabarānī in *al-Awsat* (2:529 #1910) with a sound chain as
indicated by Haythamī in *Majma' al-zawā'id*(3:305).
[209] "Lā yazālu āhl ul-maghribi (aw al-gharb) dhāhirīn hatta taqūm as sā'ah."
[210] Hadith and discussion found in *Manāqib ash-shām wa āhlihi* p. 76 as referenced in *Al-Fitan
wa ghawā'ilūha* p 754.

Jihat al-mashriq (the direction of the east) equals Najd, and to those who are in Madīna, their Najd is the desert of Iraq and its vicinities, which all lie east of the people of Madīna.[211]

This includes the modern day Gulf area: Kuwait, Khobar, Dhahrān, Rīyādh, etc. Imām Nawawī said, "Najd is the area that lies between Jurash (in Yemen) all the way to the rural outskirts of Kūfa (in Iraq), and its Western border is the Hijāz."[212] Similarly Ibn Hajar related that Dawūdī said, "Najd lies in the direction of Iraq."[213] In the following hadith the Prophet 鐄 uses *mashriq* (east) and Iraq interchangeably.

حدثنا محمد بن علي المروزي ثنا أبو الدرداء عبد العزيز بن المنيب ثنا إسحاق بن عبد الله بن
كيسان عن أبيه عن سعيد بن جبير عن بن عباس قال دعا نبي الله صلى الله عليه وسلم فقال اللهم
بارك لنا في صاعنا ومدنا وبارك لنا في مكنا ومدينتا وبارك لنا في شامنا ويمننا فقال رجل من
القوم يا نبي الله وعراقنا فقال إن بها قرن الشيطان وتهيج الفتن وإن الجفاء بالمشرق (رواه الطبراني
في الكبير ورجاله ثقات ، الطبراني في الكبير و أبو نعيم في حلية الأولياء)

The Prophet 鐄 said:

> O Allāh! Bless us in our *sāʿa* and in our *mudd* (i.e. in every measure)! Bless us in our Makka and our Madīna! Bless us in our Shām and our Yemen! A man said, "O Prophet of Allāh, and our Iraq!" The Prophet 鐄 said, "In it is the horn of *Shaytān*. In it shall dissensions heave. Verily, disrespect (*al-jafāʾ*) lies in the East."[214]

The foregoing examples illustrate that the East (*mashriq*), Najd, and Iraq are often synonymous, as "east" for someone in Madīna (in the Hijāz) is towards the direction of both Najd and Iraq. Some people mistakenly apply the hadiths of Najd exclusively to Iraq, which is incorrect,[215] as Najd at that time included not only Iraq but also, as in our present time, everything east of Madīna, especially the regions south of Iraq.[216] Throughout Islamic history there have been many well recorded events in that region from the eighth and ninth

---

[211] Khattābi in *Fath al-bārī* (13:47). Found in *Sahīh Ibn Hibbān* (16 : 291-292).

[212] Al-Nawawī in *Tahrīr al-tanbīh* (p. 157, *s.v.* "najd").

[213] Ibn Hajar, *Fath al-bārī* (1959 ed. 13:48).

[214] Narrated from Ibn 'Abbās by Tabarānī in *al-Kabīr* (12:84 #12553) with a sound chain as indicated by Haythamī in *Majmaʿ al-zawāʾid*(3:305). Abū Nuʿaym narrates something similar in the *Hilya* (1985 ed. 6:133).

[215] Cf. al-Rabaʾi, *Fadāʾil al-shām wa dimashq* (p. 6, 27).

[216] This is confirmed by *Bukhārī*'s narration in seven places and *Muslim*'s in six, from Ibn 'Umar, that the East (*al-Mashriq*) is the origin of dissension and the place where the horn of *Shaytān* (or two horns in one narration of *Muslim*) would appear, as cited previously. The fact that *Muslim* narrated that Salim Ibn 'Abd Allāh Ibn 'Umar applied this hadith to the people of Iraq does not limit its meaning to them. It only confirms that the Prophet foresaw the dissensions from the East such as the false prophet Musaylima the Liar, the Khawārij and others.

century *Hijrī* to the present era which have born out the prediction of the Prophet ﷺ that this region would be mired in many difficulties and problems.

ﷺ

Fire from Hijāz

The predictions of the Prophet ﷺ at times impress the reader with not only their precision, but with the precision of their description of events. Many who read the following hadith find remarkable its vivid yet concise depiction of events which are fresh in our minds today.

حدثني حرملة بن يحيى . أخبرنا ابن وهب . أخبرني يونس عن ابن شهاب . أخبرني ابن المسيب؛
أن أبا هريرة أخبره؛ أن رسول الله صلى الله عليه وسلم قال حدثني عبدالملك بن شعيب بن
الليث . حدثنا أبي عن جدي . حدثني عقيل بن خالد عن ابن شهاب؛ أنه قال: قال ابن المسيب:
أخبرني أبو هريرة؛
أن رسول الله صلى الله عليه وسلم قال "لا تقوم الساعة حتى تخرج نار من أرض الحجاز، تضيء
أعناق الإبل ببصرى (رواه مسلم في كتاب الفتن و البخاري)

Abū Hurayra ﷺ related that the Prophet ﷺ said:

> The Hour will not be established until a fire emerges from the land of Hijāz which will light up the necks of the camels in Basra.[217]

For the people of Madīna east is towards Najd and Iraq. For the people of Basra and Iraq, west is the direction of Najd and the Hijāz. Thus, the camels in Basra will be craning their necks to see a fire coming from the direction of Hijāz to the west, the same direction for them as Najd. This huge fire is one of the afflictions from Najd, and might arise from burning oilfields. This may also indicate a huge conflict in the area. This hadith shows that this conflagration will be enormous, dwarfing the burning oilfields of 1991. When that inferno takes place, no place on earth will be safe except for Makka, Madīna and Shām.

Other hadith describe a great conflict which will engulf the region of Basra, and the land of the two rivers, the Tigris and the Euphrates. These hadith could well refer to the area of Baghdad today, which was established by the Abbasid Dynasty in the eighth-century by the caliph Mansūr.

حدثنا أبو النضر هاشم بن القاسم حدثنا الحشرج ابن نباتة القيسي الكوفي حدثني سعيد بن جمهان
حدثنا عبيد الله بن أبي بكرة حدثني أبي في هذا المسجد يعني مسجد البصرة قال
قال رسول الله صلى الله عليه وسلم لتنزلن طائفة من أمتي أرضا يقال لها البصرة يكثر بها عددهم
ويكثر بها نخلهم ثم يجيء بنو قنطوراء عراض الوجوه صغار العيون حتى ينزلوا على جسر لهم يقال
له دجلة فيتفرق المسلمون ثلاث فرق فأما فرقة فيأخذون بأذناب الإبل وتلحق بالبادية وهلكت

---

[217] Sahīh Muslim # 6935 and Sahīh Bukhārī. "Lā taqūm us-sā'atu hatta takhruja nārun min ard il-Hijāz tudī'u a'nāq ul-ibli bi basrā."

وأما فرقة فتأخذ على أنفسها فهذه وتلك سواء وأما فرقة فيجعلون عيالهم خلف ظهورهم
ويقاتلون فقتلاهم شهداء ويفتح الله على بقيتها
حدثنا سرج حدثنا حشرج عن سعيد عن عبد الله أو عبيد الله بن أبي بكرة قال حدثني أبي في
هذا المسجد يعني مسجد البصرة فذكر مثله

Narrated Abū Bakrah:

The Prophet of Allāh said: Some of my people will alight on low-lying ground, which they will call al-Basrā, beside a river called Dajla (the Tigris) over which there is a bridge. Its people will be numerous and it will be one of the capital cities of immigrants (or one of the capital cities of Muslims, according to the version of Ibn Yahyā who reported from Abū Ma'mar). At the end of time the descendants of Qantūrā'[218] will come with broad faces and small eyes and alight on the bank of the river. The town's inhabitants will then separate into three sections, one of which will follow cattle (or in one version camels) and (live in) the desert and perish, another of which will seek security for themselves (in one version: and fall into *kufr*) and perish, and a third who will put their children behind their backs and fight the invaders; those who are killed will be martyrs; the remainder will be granted victory by Allāh.[219]

---

[218] Qantūrā' was one of of Sayyidinā Ibrāhīm's Canaanite wives whom he married after the deaths of Sārah and Hājar, or a concubine, who came from Central Asia. She bore him three sons whom Sayyidinā Ibrāhīm sent to Khorasān. They complained of this, saying that Isma'il had been sent to a holy place and Ishāq was kept beside him, but they were sent to Khorasān. Sayyidinā Ibrāhīm taught them an invocation. When they experienced a drought in Khorasān, these three sons were sought by the people of the area to relieve the drought, for that invocation was always accepted. They prayed and it began to rain and the drought ended. Following that their descendants were addressed as "Khan"—a title of importance to the Turks (who inhabited Khorasān at that time). The people would not touch this tribe, out of respect and reverence, even to the point of avoiding one drop of their drop of their blood to fall on the earth in fear that would bring about Allah's revenge. Because of this tremendous respect, if a descendant of Qantūrā' committed a capital crime he could not be punished by the sword, which is the tradition of the Turks. Instead a bowstring would be used to throttle the guilty, in order to prevent his blood from falling on the ground, and this was a tradition of the descendants of Ibrāhīm. This practice spread among all the Turks.
Imām Munawī said that Banī Qantūrā could be the cousins of Yā'jūj and Mā'jūj, and he quoted Ibn Dahīyya saying that they were the ones who were absent when the remaining Yā'jūj wa Mā'jūj were barred by Dhul-Qarnayn. Munawī also cites Ibn Dahīyya as saying that from them were the Tatars; and then others came from them who fought the Umayyads, and from them were those who caused the destruction of Baghdad (and it is possible this hadith refers to that event) and the killing of al-Mu'tasim (the 'Abbasid caliph), and that from them came Tamerlame, who assisted in the destruction of Damascus. Afterwards they spread throughout the world.
[219] 'Abd Allāh ibn Mas'ūd and Abd Allāh ibn 'Abbās related that a tent was erected during the battles of Badr and the Trench called the Tent of the Turks, built by Turkic Muslims who had

Another hadith describes a huge fire coming from Hadramawt, Yemen, indicating that there will be conflict in that area as well.

حدثنا أحمد بن منيع حدثنا حسين بن محمد البغدادي حدثنا شيبان عن يحيى بن أبي كثير عن

أبي قلابة عن سالم بن عبد الله بن عمر عن أبيه قال

قال رسول الله صلى الله عليه وسلم ستخرج نار من حضرموت أو من نحو بحر حضرموت قبل يوم

القيامة تحشر الناس قالوا يا رسول الله فما تأمرنا قال عليكم بالشام

قال أبو عيسى وفي الباب عن حذيفة بن أسيد وأنس وأبي هريرة وأبي ذر وهذا حديث حسن

غريب صحيح من حديث ابن عمر

(الترمذي وأحمد في مسنده)

---

settled in Madīna. The Prophet assisted in putting up that tent. The Prophet commanded the Muslim army from that tent. At one point, as he sat under the tent, the Prophet said, "You will conquer Constantinople and what a noble commander is that commander and what a noble army is that army." Thus the "Tent of the Turks" came to serve as a command center and a place for tribes to come together to draw up agreements or to ally themselves against an enemy. Thus is became a Sunnah to make such tribal alliances under a tent called Qubbat al-Turki.

Narrated Zainab bint Jahsh: That the Prophet came to her in a state of fear saying, "None has the right to be worshiped but Allah! Woe to the Arabs because of evil that has come near. Today a hole has been made in the wall of Gog and Magog as large as this." pointing with two of his fingers making a circle. Zainab said, "I said, 'O Allah's Apostle! Shall we be destroyed though amongst us there are pious people? ' He said, 'Yes, if evil increases." Narrated Umm Salama: The Prophet woke up and said, "Glorified be Allah: What great (how many) treasures have been sent down, and what great (how many) afflictions have been sent down!" (narrated by Bukhārī). At that time the Turks under the Sultan of Gokturk were defeated in a tremendous and important battle against the Chinese. The result of this battle was that instead of maintaining a defensive posture, the Chinese began to surround the lands of the Turks and restrict their movements to a small area west of the Great Wall of China.

Later in 630 AD, at the battle of Talas, the Arabs and some Turkish Khanates allied to fight the Chinese in the area of Turkestan and defeated them. This brought an end to the invasive encroachments of the Chinese and the rest of the Turks began to enter Islam. Most Turkish tribes had accepted Islam by ~800 AD.

It is related that the Persian Emperor at that time was Nushrevan, renowned for his great justice. The daughter of the Turkish Hakkān Gokturk (sultan) of that time married the Emperor and bore him three daughters. When the Sassānids lost the war to the Muslim armies, the three daughters were brought to Sayyidina 'Umar as prisoners of war. Seeing them, he felt great sympathy for them. One of the three, Banū Ghazal, was married to Sayyidinā Husayn bin 'Alī and from them came Sayyidinā Zayn al-Abidīn. The second daughter married Sayyidinā 'Umar's grandson Salim and from their marriage was born the fifth rightly-guided caliph, known as the "second 'Umar" for his justice, 'Umar ibn 'Abd al 'Azīz. The third daughter married Sayyidinā Abū Bakr's son Muhammad and from their union came the great walī Qāssim bin Muhammad bin Abū Bakr as-Siddīq. Sayyidinā al-Qāssim was fourth in the Naqshbandi Golden Chain. He was raised with Salmān Fārsī when he was very young. At Karbala all of Sayyidinā al-Husayn's sons were martyred except Sayyidinā Zayn al-Ābidīn. He was very sick at the time and the enemy thinking he was dead did not kill him. From him sprang the entire lineage of the Āhl al-Bayt descendants of Sayyidinā al-Husayn, for which he was known as Nūh of the Sayyids. He was taken to Shām after Karbala and treated for his illness.

The Prophet ﷺ said:

A huge fire will issue from Hadramawt (or: from the direction of the Sea of Hadramawt) before the Day of Resurrection, which will cause a great movement of people.

They said, "O Messenger of Allāh! What do you order us to do at that time?" He said, "You must go to Shām."[220] Which indicates that the region of the Arabian Penninsula will not be safe.

---

[220] From Ibn 'Umar by Tirmidhī, Āhmad and others.

Shām and the Abdāl

The Prophet ﷺ encouraged his Companions to go to Shām and asked Allāh to bless it.

عن ابن عمر قال: صلى رسول الله صلى الله عليه وسلم اللهم بارك لنا في شامنا وفي يمننا (رواه مسلم من حديث طويل و البخاري،الترمذي و أحمد في مسنده)

The Prophet ﷺ said, "O Allāh! Bless us in our Shām and our Yemen!"[221]

The Prophet ﷺ said:

O Allāh! Bless us in our *sāʿa* and in our *mudd* (i.e. in every measure)! Bless us in our Makka and our Madīna! Bless us in our Shām and our Yemen![222]

حدثنا عبد الله حدثني أبي حدثنا حيوة بن شريح ويزيد بن عبد ربه قالا حدثنا بقية قال حدثني بحير بن سعد عن خالد بن معدان عن أبي قتيلة عن ابن حوالة أنه قال: قال رسول الله صلى الله عليه وسلم سيصير الأمر إلى أن تكون جنود مجندة جند بالشام وجند باليمن وجند بالعراق فقال ابن حوالة خر لي يا رسول الله إن أدركت ذاك قال عليك بالشام فإنه خيرة الله من أرضه يجتبي إليه خيرته من عباده فإن أبيتم فعليكم بيمنكم واسقوا من غدركم فإن الله عز وجل قد توكل لي بالشام وأهله. (رواه أبو داود و أحمد في مسنده)

The Prophet ﷺ said:

Go to Shām, for it is the cream of Allāh's lands on this earth. Allāh has chosen the best of his creation to reside there... If you do not wish to go there, then go to your Yemen and drink from its streams. Allāh has vouchsafed for me the safety of Shām and its people.[223]

Imām Nawawī, in his book *Fadā'il Shām* (The Merits of Shām), mentioned forty hadiths of the Prophet ﷺ praising the immense merits of Shām. In his

---

[221] Narrated from Ibn 'Umar as part of a longer hadith in *Sahīh Bukhārī* (4:390), *Sahīh Ibn Hibbān* (16:290), *Sahīh Muslim, Tirmidhī*, and *Āhmad* (see section "Tribulations from the East/Najd.").

[222] Narrated from Ibn 'Abbās by Tabarānī in *al-Kabīr* (12:84 #12553) with a sound chain as indicated by Haythamī in *Majma' al-zawā'id* (3:305). Abū Nu'aym narrates something similar in the *Hilyā* (1985 ed. 6:133).

[223] *Sunan Abū Dāwūd. Musnad Āhmad. Sahīh Ibn Hibbān* (16:295). Hākim, *Mustadrak* (4:510). Bayhaqī, *Sunan al-kubrā* (9:179):
'Alaykum bish-shāmi fa innahā safwatu bilādillāh. Yaskunuhā khīratuhu min khalqihi. Fa man abā fal yalhaq bi-yamanihi. Wal yasqī min ghudrihi. Fa-inna Allāha 'azza wa jalla takaffal lī shāmi wa āhlih.

book *The Importance of Living in* Shām, al-ʿIzz Ibn ʿAbd al-Salām said that ten thousand Companions went to Shām due to the recommendation of the Prophet ﷺ.

عَنْ عَبْد الله بْنِ العاصِقِ قال قال النَّبِيِّ صلى الله عَلَيْهِ و سلم لا لِيَأْتِيَنَّ على الناس زمانٌ لا يَبْقى
على الأَرْضِ مُؤْمِن إلا لَحِقَ بالشام (حاكم)

ʿAbd Allāh Ibn ʿAmr Ibn al-ʿĀs ؓ related that the Prophet ﷺ said, "There will come a time for humanity when every believer will certainly go to Shām."[224]

That is, the believer will leave everything and go to Shām.

عن أبي الدرداء قال: قال رسول الله صلى الله عليه وسلم "بينا أنا نائم رأيت عمود الكتاب احتمل
من تحت رأسي فظننت أنه مذهوب به فأتبعته بصري فعمد به إلى الشام ألا وإن الإيمان حين تقع
الفتن بالشام
(رواه البزار ورجاله رجال الصحيح غير محمد بن عامر الأنطاكي وهو ثقة)

The Prophet ﷺ said:

> Indeed when the trials and tribulations befall (when the Dajjāl appears), safety (or faith) is in Shām.[225]

The Anti-Christ will cover all the world, but he cannot enter three places: Makka, Madīna and Shām. Shām is protected by angels, and it is the place where the Resurrection will take place.

الشام أَرْضُ المَحْشَرِ و المَنْشَرِ

Abū Dharr ؓ related that the Prophet ﷺ said, "The land of Shām is the place of Resurrection and Judgment."[226]

حدثنا عبد الله حدثني أبي حدثنا يزيد أنبأنا بهز عن أبيه عن جده قال: قلتُ يا رَسُولَ الله أَيْنَ
تأمُرُني قال-ها هُنا ونحا بِيَدِه نحو الشّام قال إنكُم مَحْشُورُونَ رِجَالًا ركبانا وتجرون
على وجوهكم. (رَوَاهُ أَحْمَدُ في مُسْنَدِه)

The Prophet ﷺ also said:

[224] Hākim (4:457). Sahīh on the conditions of Sahīh Bukhārī and Sahīh Muslim. "Layatīyanna ʿalā an-nāsi zamanun la yabqā ʿalā al-ardi mu'minun illa lāhiqa bi ash-shām."
[225] Tabarānī. "Alā wa inna al-īmānu hīna taqa'u al-fitan bi ash-Shām."
[226] Āhmad, Musnad. Ibn Mājah. Albānī, Sahīh al-jami'a #3620. "Ash-shāmu ard al-mahshar wal-manshari."

You are going to be resurrected, men (and women) some on
foot and some riding. And you are going to be pulled here on
your faces. (And he pointed with his hand towards Shām).[227]

Shām is the place of the Resurrection, and is a special place of safety and
security when there is confusion and chaos around the world. The Prophet ﷺ
mentioned many hadiths specifically on the merits of Shām, thousands of
Companions migrated there, and many saints (awliyā') are there, including the
Abdāl (Substitutes). While there are no more prophets, there are always saints
(awliyā') as Allāh ﷻ described them in the Qur'ān:

$$أَلَا إِنَّ أَوْلِيَاءَ اللهِ لَا خَوْفٌ عَلَيْهِمْ وَلَا هُمْ يَحْزَنُونَ$$

*Behold! Verily, for Allah's saints (awliya') there is no fear nor shall they
grieve.* (Yūnus 10:62)

حدثني محمد بن عثمان بن كرامة: حدثنا خالد بن مخلد: حدثنا سليمان بن بلال: حدثني شريك
بن عبد الله بن أبي نمر، عن عطاء، عن أبي هريرة قال:
قال رسول الله صلى الله عليه وسلم: إن الله قال: من عادى لي وليا فقد آذنته بالحرب، وما تقرب
إلي عبدي بشيء أحب إلي مما افترضت عليه، وما يزال عبدي يتقرب إلي بالنوافل حتى أحبه، فإذا
أحببته: كنت سمعه الذي يسمع به، وبصره الذي يبصر به، ويده التي يبطش بها، ورجله التي يمشي
بها، وإن سألني لأعطينه (رواه البخاري)

Abū Hurayra ؓ related that the Prophet ﷺ said that Allāh ﷻ said in a
hadith *qudsī*:

> Whoever shows enmity to My saint (*walī*), I declare war on
> him. My servant draws close to Me with what has been
> enjoined on him and draws even closer with the superogatory
> (*nawāfil*) acts of worship until I love him. When I love him I
> become his hearing with which he hears, and his vision with
> which he sees, and his hand with which he holds, and his foot
> with which he walks. If he asks Me, I give to him and if he
> seeks refuge I protect him.[228]

---

[227] (sahīh). Āhmad, *Musnad* (5:3, 5). *Tirmidhī*, in "Qiyāma" #2426. It was related by Bahz bin
Hakīm who heard it from his father who heard it from his grandfather:
*Innakum mahshūrūn rijālun wa rukbānun. Wa tujarūna 'alā wujūhikum hā-
hunnā. (Wa awma'a biyaddihi nahwa ash-shām).*

[228] Sahīh Bukhārī, (8:509). Also cited and accepted by Ibn Taymīyya:
*Man 'adā lī walīyyan faqad ādhantuhu bil-harb... Fa idhā ahbabtuhu kuntu
sam'ahu alladhī yasma'u bihi wa basarahu alladhī yubsiru bihi wa yadahu allatī
yabtushu bihā wa rijlahu allatī yamshī bihā. Wa in sa'alanī 'ataytuhu wa la'in
ista'ādhanī la-ut'iannahu.*

Allāh ﷻ said:

$$وَلَوْلَا دَفْعُ اللهِ النَّاسَ بَعْضَهُمْ بِبَعْضٍ لَّفَسَدَتِ الأَرْضُ$$

And if Allāh had not repelled some men by others the earth would have been corrupted. (al-Baqara 2:251)

In his explanation of this verse Ibn Kathīr mentioned the following hadith.

حدثنا عبد الله حدثني أبي حدثنا عبد الوهاب بن عطاء أنبأنا الحسن بن ذكوان عن عبد الواحد بن قيس عن عبادة بن الصامت عن النبي صلى الله عليه وسلم أنه قال:
-الأبدال في هذه الأمة ثلاثون مثل إبراهيم خليل الرحمن عز وجل كلما مات رجل أبدل الله تبارك وتعالى مكانه رجلا (أَخْرَجَهُ أحمد في مسنده ، حاكم و الترْمذي في في نوادر الأصُول، الجلال في كرامات الأولياء)

The Prophet ﷺ said:

The Substitutes (Abdāl) in this Community are thirty men like *Ibrāhīm* ﷺ, the Friend of the Merciful. Every time one of them dies, Allāh substitutes another one in his place.[229]

$$عن عبادة بن الصامت قال قالَرَسُولُ اللهِ صلى الله عليه و سلم بهم تَقُومُ الأَرْضُ و بهم تُمطَرُونَ و بهم تُنصَرُونَ(الطبراني في الكبير)$$

Another version adds:

By means of them the world turns *(bihim taqūm al-ard)*, you receive rain, and you achieve victory.[230]

عن أنس قال: قال رسول الله صلى الله عليه وسلم:
"ن تَخلو الأرض من أربعين رجلاً مثل خليل الرحمن، فبهم تُسقون، وبهم تُنصرون، ما مات منهم أحد إلا أبدل الله مكانه آخر".
قال سعيد : وسمعت قتادة يقول: لسنا نشك أن الحسن منهم . رواه الطبراني في الأوسط وإسناده حسن

The Prophet ﷺ said:

---

[229] Narrated from 'Ubāda Ibn Sāmit by Āhmad in his *Musnad*, *Hākim*, Tirmidhī in *Nawādir al-usūl*, Ibn Mardūyah, and Khallal in *Karamāt al-awliyā'*. Haythamī in *Majma' al-zawā'id*(10:62) indicated that Āhmad's chain was sound, and Suyūtī declared it *sahīh* in *Jami' al-saghīr*.
[230] Tabarānī in *al-Kabīr* and Bazzār from 'Ubāda Ibn Sāmit. Suyūtī declared it *sahīh* in *Jami' al-saghīr* and Munawī did not contradict him in *Fayd al-qadīr*. Tabarānī in *al-Kabīr* (10:181) also narrates from Ibn Mas'ūd a similar narration mentioning the number forty.

The earth will never lack forty men similar to the Friend of the Merciful [*Ibrāhīm* ﷺ], and through them people receive rain and are given help. None of them dies except Allāh substitutes another in his place.

Qatāda said, "We do not doubt that al-Hasan is one of them."[231]

حدثنا عبد الله حدثني أبي حدثنا أبو المغيرة حدثنا صفوان حدثني شريح يعني ابن عبيد قال: ذكر أهل الشام عند علي بن أبي طالب رضي الله عنه وهو بالعراق فقالوا: إلعنهم يا أمير المؤمنين قال: لا إني سمعت رسول الله صلى الله عليه وسلم يقول: -الأبدال يكونون بالشام وهم أربعون رجلا كلما مات رجل أبدل الله مكانه رجلا يسقى بهم الغيث وينتصر بهم على الأعداء ويصرف عن أهل الشام بهم العذاب (أخرجه الإمام أحمد في مسنده الهيثمي في الزوائد و غيرهم)

Shurayh Ibn 'Ubayd ﷺ said that the people of Shām were mentioned in front of 'Alī Ibn Abū Tālib ﷺ while he was in Iraq, and some people said to him, "Curse them, O Commander of the Believers." He replied:

No, I heard the Messenger of Allāh say, "The Substitutes (al-Abdāl) are in Shām and they are forty men, every time one of them dies, Allāh substitutes another in his place. By means of them Allāh brings down the rain, gives us victory over our enemies, and averts punishment from the people of Shām."[232]

---

[231] Narrated from Anas by Tabarānī in *al-Awsat* as stated in *Majma' al-zawā'id*(10:63).

[232] Narrated by Āhmad in his *Musnad* and *Fadā'il al-sahāba* (2:906) with a sound chain as indicated by Sakhāwī in *al-Maqāsid*, Haythamī in *Majma' al-zawā'id*, Munawī in *Fayd al-qadīr*, Suyūtī in *Khabar al-dāll*, and Ghumārī in his notes on the latter who all declared its narrators trustworthy. Suyūtī similarly declared it sound in *Jami' al-saghīr*.
Sakhāwī cited Shurayh Ibn 'Ubayd's narration as the strongest report on the *Abdāl* and said in *Maqasid al-hasana* (p. 33 #8):
>What makes this hadith stronger and indicates its currency among the Imāms is the statement of our Imām, al-Shafi'ī, concerning a certain man, "We considered him one of the *Abdāl*" and Bukhārī's words concerning another, "They did not doubt that he was one of the *Abdāl*," and other than these two among the highly meticulous scholars, hadith masters, and Imāms also used this description for other people, stating that they were of the *Abdāl*.
Abū Hātim said of 'Abd al-Kabīr Ibn Mu'afī that he was considered one of the *Abdāl*. Abū Dāwūd in the *Sunan* narrates the same from Muhammad Ibn 'Isā about 'Anbasa al-Qurashī. Ibn Mājah in his *Sunan* states the same of Yahyā Ibn 'Uthman al-Himsī, al-Khatīb in *Jami' li akhlāq al-rawī* (2:229) of Abū 'Umar al-Khawlanī, Bayhaqī in the *Shu'ab* (4:137) of Jābir Ibn Marzūq, Daraqutnī in *al-'Ilal* (6:63) of Nadr Ibn Kathīr al-Sa'dī, Nawawī in *Bustān al-'arifīn* (p. 31) of the hadith master Hammād Ibn Salāma Ibn Dīnār (d. 167), Fattānī in his *Tadhkira* of Hubaysh Ibn Dīnār, etc. (*takhrīj* Dr. Gibril Haddad).

لا تَسُبُّوا أَهْلَ الشَّامِ وَ لكِنْ سُبُّوا شِرارَهُم فَإِنَّ فِهم الأَبْدالُ . . . .

(أَخْرَجَهُ الحاكِم وَ صَحَّحَهُ وَ ذَهَبَ الذَّهَبِي فِي مُختَصِرِه)

The Prophet ﷺ said on the authority of 'Alī Ibn Abi Tālib ؓ:

> Do not curse the people of Shām but curse their injustice. For
> among them are the Abdāl.[233]

لا تَسُبُّوا أَهْلَ الشَّامِ فَإِنَّ فِهم الأَبْدالِ وَ سُبُّوا ظُلْمَتَهُم (أَخْرَجَهُ الحاكِم وَ صَحَّحَهُ وَ ذَهَبَ الذَّهَبِي فِي
مُختَصِرِه)

Another narration states that 'Alī Ibn Abī Tālib ؓ said to the people of
Iraq:

> Do not curse the people of Shām, for among them are the
> Substitutes (al-Abdāl), but curse their injustice.[234]

Suyūtī, in Ta'aqqubāt 'al al-mawdū'at, asserted that the Prophetic report of
the existence of the Abdāl is sahīh and its general meaning is mutawātir (widely
known and accepted).[235] This is confirmed by the hadith master al-Kattanī in
his Nazm al-mutanathir (p. 220-221). Suyūtī's position is supported by the fact
that the pious Muslims of the first three centuries after the Hijra believed in the
existence of the Abdāl, and Ibn Taymiyya himself included such belief into his
Islamic creed entitled al-'Aqīda al-wāsitiyya!

---

[233] Narrated as part of a longer hadith from 'Alī by Tabarānī in al-Awsat, Nu'aym and ibn
Asākir.

[234] Narrated by Hākim who graded it sound (sahīh), and Dhahabī concurred.

[235] A hadith is said to be mutawātir (lit. repeated successively or by one after another) when it is
reported by such a large number that it is impossible that they should have agreed upon
falsehood, so that the very fact that it is commonly accepted makes its authority
unquestionable. To this category belong hadiths that have been accepted by every generation
of Muslims from the time of the Holy Prophet. (Ibn Hajar al-'Asqalānī in Sharh nukhbat al-fikr)

Westerners Enter Islam

The Prophet gave an indication in the following hadith, that in the Last Days of this world the people of the West (al-maghrib) would enter Islam in large numbers.

حدثنا عبدالملك بن شعيب بن الليث. حدثني عبدالله بن وهب. أخبرني الليث بن سعد .

حدثني موسى بن علي عن أبيه، قال: قال المسؤرد القرشي، عند عمرو بن العاص:

سمعت رسول الله صلى الله عليه وسلم يقول "تقوم الساعة والروم أكثر الناس". فقال له عمرو:

أبصر ما تقول. قال: أقول ما سمعت من رسول الله صلى الله عليه وسلم. قال: لئن قلت ذلك، إن

فيهم لخصالا أربعا: إنهم لأحلم الناس عند فتنة. وأسرعهم إفاقة بعد مصيبة. وأوشكهم كرة بعد

فرة. وخيرهم لمسكين ويتيم وضعيف. وخامسة حسنة وجميلة: وأمنعهم من ظلم الملوك (مسلم في

كتاب الفتن)

Mustawrid al-Qūrashi ☙ narrated the following hadith to 'Amr Ibn al-'Ās ☙ when he visited the latter's home:

> Mustawrid al-Qūrashi ☙ said that he heard the Prophet ﷺ saying, "(When) the Hour (Last Days) comes the *Rūm* will be the majority of people." When 'Amr Ibn al-'Ās heard this he said in astonishment, "Watch what you are saying!" Mustawrid al-Qūrashi ☙ said, "I am saying what I heard from Allāh's Messenger ﷺ." 'Amr Ibn al-'Ās ☙ said, "If you say this is true, then it is believeable in that they have four particular good qualities: They are the most calm and patient people in the face of trials and tribulations. They restore themselves to their senses after trouble (to try to solve the problem). They attack again after flight. They are good to the needy, the orphans and the weak. A fifth good quality in them is that they do not stand for the oppression of tyrants."[236]

This is a very interesting hadith of the Prophet ﷺ which many people in the past glossed over because, until recently, it was not well understood. Muslims accord little importance to this hadith although it is very well documented and accepted even by the late "Salafi" writer Nāsir al-Dīn Albānī

---

[236] *Sahīh Muslim*, "Kitāb al-Fitan" #2898, and mentioned by Albānī's student Mustafa Shalabī in his *Sahīh ashrāt as-sā'at*, p. 179:

> Taqūm as-sā'atu war-rūmu akthar un-nāsi... Qāl la'in qulta dhālika inna fīhim la-khisālan arba'an: Innahum la-ahlamu an-nāsi 'inda fitnatin: wa asrā'uhum ifāqatan ba'da musībatin. Wa awshakuhum karratan ba'da farratin. Wa khayrūhum li miskīnin wa yatīmin wa da'īfin. Wa khāmisatu hasanatun jamīlatun: Wa amnā'uhum min dhulm il-mulūki.

who rejected so many other hadiths. Albānī tried to whittle down the hadith body as much as he could, yet when he "corrected" the books of *sahīh* hadiths to take out the narrations which he thought were false he could not reject this hadith. To survive such a process whereby many other sound and established hadiths were rejected indicates that this hadith is especially strong and unquestionably valid. Despite the fact that this hadith is accepted by all scholars and is mentioned in *Sahīh Muslim*, Muslims all too easily have ignored it. Because the significance of this hadith was not understood, Muslims of the past did not appreciate how clearly it reveals the greatness of the Prophet 鑾. Today the meaning has become clear. Before entering into the discussion of this hadith, let us reiterate that this is only an explanation of the Prophet's 鑾 hadith without any implications of support or criticism for any political regime.

Al-Qurashi 鑾 mentioned to 'Amr Ibn al-'Ās鑾 that the Prophet 鑾 said that "*ar-Rūm* will be the majority of people." In the past non-Muslims were referred to as *'Ajam* (Persians) and *Rūm* (Romans). Any people from Europe or other areas outside the Arabian Penninsula were referred to as *Rūm*. In fact *ar-Rūm* has two meanings, one of which is the those *Āhl al-Kitāb* (People of the Book), and in this particular case such as live in Eastern Europe. The second meaning, to which this hadith apparently refers, is those of Constantinople (modern day Istanbul), the European peoples and Western civilization in general. The Prophet 鑾 is speaking about *ar-Rūm* who will be the largest group and the majority of people in the Last Days. Today, there are 1.2 billion Muslims, but all the *Āhl al-Kitāb* combined are more numerous than that. The Prophet 鑾 said that *ar-Rūm* would be the most numerous when the Hour took place. This is a very moving statement for Muslims because it indicates that the Hour is near.

The Prophet 鑾 also said that Islam will enter every home on earth, so when Mustawrid al-Qūrashi 鑾 related the hadith of the *Rūm* being the majority to 'Amr Ibn al-'Ās 鑾 he was surprised, saying, "What are you saying? Be careful! This contradicts the hadith of the Prophet 鑾 that Islam will enter every home." Al-Qūrashi 鑾 replied, "I am saying what I heard the Prophet 鑾 say." 'Amr Ibn al-'Ās 鑾 then agreed and described the good qualities of the *Rūm*, which indicated that they were people who would easily come into Islam. They are the most calm and patient people in the face of tribulation and confusion. That is, they keep their wits about them and try to find a solution to the problem at hand. They restore themselves to their senses after trouble, and quickly recover to a normal state after a tragedy. Along similar lines, they try to make people around them aware of the problem in order to solve it. They attack again after the retreat. They are good to the needy, the orphans and the weak, as they support humanitarian causes around the world. The fifth good quality mentioned is that they do not stand for the tyranny of leaders over the people, which means they support human rights.

Imām Bukhārī comments that this hadith of *ar-Rūm* being the majority indicates that "in the Last Days *ar-Rūm* will enter Islam. Because these good qualities are only found in people with faith (*Īmān*) (*hadhā yadullu, wa Allāhu 'alam, inn ar-rūma sayaslamūna fī ākhir iz-zamān...*)."

حدثنا علي بن حجر حدثنا عبد الله بن جعفر حدثني ثور بن زيد الديلي عن أبي الغيث عن أبي هريرة قال

كنا عند رسول الله صلى الله عليه وسلم حين أنزلت سورة الجمعة فتلاها فلما بلغ ﴿وآخرين منهم لما يلحقوا بهم﴾ قال له رجل يا رسول الله من هؤلاء الذين لم يلحقوا بنا فلم يكلمه قال وسلمان الفارسي فينا قال فوضع رسول الله صلى الله عليه وسلم يده على سلمان فقال والذي نفسي بيده لو كان الإيمان بالثريا لتناوله رجال من هؤلاء

قال أبو عيسى هذا حديث حسن وقد روي من غير وجه عن أبي هريرة عن النبي صلى الله عليه وسلم وأبو الغيث اسمه سالم مولى عبد الله بن مطيع مدني (يعني الفارس و الروم) (في سنن الترمذي في كتاب المناقب و البخاري في كتاب تفسير القرآن و أحمد في مسنده

Imām Bukhārī supports this conclusion with another hadith in which the Prophet 🌿 said:

> I swear by the One in Whose Hand is my soul (Allāh), if faith
> were in the skies (heavens) the first people to go catch it
> would be the Rūm and Persians.[237]

That is, the non-Muslims will be running to catch faith (Islam) even if it is in the heavens. Thus, the Prophet 🌿 predicted fourteen hundred years ago that the Western peoples would enter Islam in the Last Days and this is what we are seeing today. Despite all the obstacles they face, Westerners are entering Islam in droves by Allāh's grace. This is not difficult for Allāh as:

وَلَكِنَّ اللَّهَ يَهْدِي مَن يَشَاءُ

Allah guides whomever He wishes. (al-Qasas 28:56)

---

[237] *Sahīh Bukhārī*, (6: 63) in the explanation of *Sūrat al-Jumū'ah* and in *Sahīh Muslim* #2546: *Wa alladhī nafsī bi yadihi law kāna al-īmān bi thuraya latanāwaluhu rijālun min hā'ula (y'anī faris wa rūm).*

Islam Enters Every House

Allāh ﷺ mentioned in the Holy Qur'ān:

فَأَقِمْ وَجْهَكَ لِلدِّينِ حَنِيفاً فِطْرَةَ اللهِ الَّتِي فَطَرَ النَّاسَ عَلَيْهَا لَا تَبْدِيلَ لِخَلْقِ اللهِ ذَلِكَ الدِّينُ
الْقَيِّمُ وَلَكِنَّ أَكْثَرَ النَّاسِ لَا يَعْلَمُونَ

*So set thou thy face steadily to the true way, the state of innocence in which
Allah has created all human beings. There is no change in Allah's creation,
that state (Islam) is the upright religion. But most among mankind
understand not.*

(ar-Rūm 30:30)

حدثنا عبدان: أخبرنا عبد الله: أخبرنا يونس، عن الزهري قال: أخبرني أبو سلمة بن عبد الرحمن:
أن أبا هريرة رضي الله عنه قال: قال رسول الله صلى الله عليه وسلم ما من مولود إلا يولد على
الفطرة، فأبواه يهودانه، أو ينصرانه، أو يمجسانه، (مسلم في كتاب الجنائز و الترمذي في كتاب القدر،
و أحمد في مسنده و غيرهم)

Abū Hurayra ﷺ related that the Prophet ﷺ said:

> Every single child is born in a state of innocence (*fiṭra*). His
> parents make him [one faith or another].[238]

The Prophet ﷺ did not say that one's parents make him Muslim because
everyone is born Muslim, in a state of Islam. Thus, children born to Muslim
parents remain Muslim. Someone may be raised by parents with beliefs that
alter the person's religion, but the reality of the original state of innocence,
Islam, is present in everyone and never disappears. Non-Muslim parents may
change the child's intrinsic naturally-held beliefs, but the light of faith in the
heart cannot be extinguished, and may be brought out at any time. This is
evidenced today by the thousands of people from diverse backgrounds who
become Muslim. As the time of the Last Days approaches, Allāh ﷺ is sending
His guidance (*hidāya*) to lead non-Muslims back to their spiritual origins and
people are returning to Islam, the primordial religion of humankind and its
natural state.

The fact that this verse occurs in the *Sūrah* named for people of the West,
Rūm, appears to confirm the proclivity of those people towards the faith of
Islam, i.e. *that state of innocence in which Allah has created all human beings....*
Additionally, the *Sūrah* begins:

---

[238] *Saḥīḥ Bukhārī* and *Saḥīḥ Muslim*. "*Mā min mawlūdin illa yūladu 'alā al-fitrati fa abawāhu
yuhawwidānihi aw yunasirrānihi aw yumajjisānihi...*"

الم(1) غُلِبَتِ الرُّومُ(2) فِي أَدْنَى الأَرْضِ وَهُم مِّن بَعْدِ غَلَبِهِمْ سَيَغْلِبُونَ(3) فِي بِضْعِ سِنِينَ لِلَّهِ الأَمْرُ مِن قَبْلُ وَمِن بَعْدُ وَيَوْمَئِذٍ يَفْرَحُ الْمُؤْمِنُونَ(4) بِنَصْرِ اللَّهِ يَنصُرُ مَن يَشَاءُ وَهُوَ الْعَزِيزُ الرَّحِيمُ(5)

Alif. Lam. Mim. The Romans are vanquished, In the nearer land, and they, after their defeat will be victorious within ten years - Allah's is the command in the former case and in the latter - and in that day believers will rejoice in Allah's help to victory. He helpeth to victory whom He will. He is the Mighty, the Merciful. (ar-Rum 30:1-5)

These verses were revealed when the Persians defeated the Byzantines, in Shām, Greater Syria. At the time the believers had hoped for the victory of the Byzantines, for they were People of the Book (*Āhl al-kitāb*), in preference to the idolatrous Persians. Later, when the prediction of Rūm's victory was borne out nine years after these verses were revealed, the believers rejoiced. This shows the affinity of the Muslims towards the People of the Book rather than the idolaters. It is therefore not hard to understand from this, a premonition of good fortune for the people of ar-Rūm, and what greater goodness than the guidance of their hearts to the faith of Islam, as confirmation of Allāh's good pleasure and a completion of their faith. For this reason we see a greater tendency of the people of the West towards Islam, who see it as a completion of the heavenly messages in the Bible and the Torah, and a completion of that message.

Islam, as a religion of goodness, will constantly strive against evil wherever it is. Islam seeks every opportunity to sympathize with the needy from the human family, and to help them, whomever and wherever they are. The real promoters of Islam pursue the love of their Lord, and the promotion of that love among all of humanity. They do not seek power or politics. They always show humility before their Lord, and its traces are evident on their faces. Their faces reflect their inner state of humility and servanthood to their Creator.

Allāh ﷻ said in the Holy Qur'ān:

هُوَ الَّذِي أَرْسَلَ رَسُولَهُ بِالْهُدَى وَدِينِ الْحَقِّ لِيُظْهِرَهُ عَلَى الدِّينِ كُلِّهِ وَكَفَى بِاللَّهِ شَهِيدًا

It is He Who has sent His Messenger with guidance and the religion of Truth to make it pre-eminent over all religions; and enough is Allah for a Witness. (al-Fath 48:28)

This verse shows that it is from the divine disposition of events that Allāh ﷻ has sent the Prophet ﷺ with guidance and the Religion of Truth for all humanity. The miraculous spread of Islam by the Holy Prophet ﷺ is evidence of its truth and its far reaching character, for there is nothing which it has not influenced. According to the explanation of this verse by mainstream scholars, Islam will be everywhere on earth. In another verse, Allāh 🕮 said in the Holy Qur'ān:

إِنَّ الدِّينَ عِندَ اللَّه الإِسْلاَم

Religion for Allah is Islam. (Āl-'Imrān 3:19)

Allāh's religion is Islam and therefore no one can prevent its promulgation except as Allāh 🕮 wills. Allāh 🕮 promises that He will protect the religion of Islam and that it will continue until Judgement Day:

إِنَّا نَحْنُ نَزَّلْنَا الذِّكْرَ وَإِنَّا لَهُ لَحَافِظُونَ

We have revealed the dhikr (Qur'an, Islam) and We are protecting it...

(al-Ḥijr 15:9)

حدثنا أبو المغيرة قال حدثنا صفوان بن سليم قال حدثني سليم بن عامر عن تميم الداري قال
سمعت رسول الله صلى الله عليه وسلم يقول ليبلغن هذا الأمر ما بلغ الليل والنهار ولا يترك الله
بيت مدر ولا وبر إلا أدخله الله هذا الدين بعز عزيز أو بذل ذليل عزا يعز الله به الإسلام وذلا
بذل الله به الكفر
وكان تميم الداري يقول قد عرفت ذلك في أهل بيتي لقد أصاب من أسلم منهم الخير والشرف والعز
ولقد أصاب من كان منهم كافرا الذل والصغار والجزية.'' (أَخْرَجَهُ أحمد في مسنده، الهيثمي في
الزوائد، البخاري في التاريخ و غيرهم)

The Prophet 🕮 said:

This great cause will reach wherever the night and the day reach. Allāh will not leave a single house[239] nor tent[240] (i.e. no city nor remote area) except He will cause this Religion to enter it, raising and honoring some while humbling and lowering others. He will raise and honor Islam while humbling and lowering disbelief.[241]

---

[239] *Madar*—literally a mud house; indicating cities and towns.

[240] *Wabar*—a tent from animal skins or a cave; indicating unpopulated areas.

[241] Narrated from Tamīm al-Dārī by Aḥmad in his *Musnad* with a chain of *saḥīḥ* narrators cf. al-Haythamī, *Majma' al-zawā'id* (6:14, 8:262); *Bukhārī* in *Tārīkh al-kabīr* (2:150 #2016); Taḥawī, *Shark Mushkil al-āthār,* Tabarānī, *al-Kabīr* (2:58 #1280) and *Musnad al-shāmiyyīn* (2:79 #951); Ibn Mandah, "Kitāb al-Īmān" (2:982 #1085); Ḥākim in the *Mustadrak* (4:330=1990 ed. 4:477 "*Saḥīḥ* per the criterion of *Bukhārī* and *Muslim*," al-Dhahabī concurring); and Bayhaqī, *Sunan al-kubrā* (9:181). Also narrated from Miqdād ibn al-Aswad by Aḥmad with a strong chain. Albānī also said it was *saḥīḥ* in *Silsila saḥīḥa* page 173:

Layablughanna hādha al-amru mā balagha al-laylu wan-nahār. Wa lā yatruku Allāhu bayta madarin wa lā wabarrin illa adkhalahu Allāhu hādha ad-dīn. Bi

As night and day are everywhere, Islam, the religion of Allāh ﷻ, will be everywhere. With His Majestic command, Allāh ﷻ will cause Islam to enter every house in every place on earth. Allāh ﷻ will elevate the dignity of believers and bring down oppressors and evildoers. When Nimrod came against Prophet Abrāham ﷺ, Allāh ﷻ humiliated Nimrod while honoring the Prophet Abrāham ﷺ and making him victorious. The same thing happened when Pharoah opposed the Prophet Moses ﷺ. Pharaoh was drowned in the sea and Moses ﷺ was victorious. When idol-worshippers opposed Prophet Muhammad ﷺ, they failed and the Prophet ﷺ was triumphant, for Allāh ﷻ said:

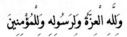

Strength and Dignity are for Allah and for His Messenger, and for the Believers. (al-Munafiqūn 63:8)

Allāh ﷻ may try the believers with hardships but ultimately truth will prevail over falsehood as Allāh ﷻ and His Prophet ﷺ have promised.

What the Prophet ﷺ predicted fourteen hundred years ago about the spread of Islam is now coming true. Islam has spread far and wide and has become known around the world, despite continuous, concerted efforts to stem the flow of people entering Islam. Although millions of dollars are spent to convert people away from Islam, it is still the fastest growing religion in the world. Muslims and non-Muslims are now seeking to learn more about Islam. The Qur'ān is in libraries, bookstores, and in the homes of many non-Muslims. The Holy Book of Islam has been spread far and wide, and after reading it, many people enter Islam.

Islam has also spread to the four corners of the earth via television and global satellite broadcasts. News organizations have brought Islam into homes around the world. Although these networks were not formed with this intention, Allāh's Wisdom has allowed them to come into being so that the message of Islam could reach every home, fulfilling this prediction of the Prophet ﷺ.

Allāh ﷻ says in the Holy Qur'ān:

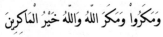

They plotted and planned, and Allah too planned, and Allah is the best of planners. (Āl-'Imrān 3:54)

Allāh's plan must come to pass no matter what human beings may do.

'*izzin 'azīzin aw bi dhillin dhalīlin, 'izzan yu'izzu Allāhu bihi al-Islāma, wa dhillan yudhillu bihi kufra.*

Islam is spreading everywhere and even leaders of non-Muslim countries are defending the religion, testifying to the fact that Islam is a religion of peace and tolerance.

Someone living one hundred years ago or even twenty years ago would have never believed that Islam would be on every tongue, as it is today. Islam is the hottest topic around the world, and even at the North Pole, the Eskimos know of Islam, while a visitor to the South Pole also speaks about it as well.[242] That prophecy has been fulfilled that Islam will enter every house. This is yet another example that the Prophet 襤 speaks only what Allāh 襤 reveals to him to say.

وَمَا يَنطِقُ عَنِ الْهَوَى إِنْ هُوَ إِلَّا وَحْيٌ يُوحَى

Nor does he say (aught) of (his own) desire. It is naught but revelation that is revealed (to him). (Najm 53:3-4)

The hadith is also a revelation from Allāh 襤,[243] and what Allāh 襤 revealed to his Prophet 襤 to so many years ago has come to pass. Such is the greatness of Prophet Muhammad 襤 that Allāh 襤 honored him with such miraculous knowledge which no one has been able to rival before or after.

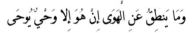

---

[242] Antarctica is an unpopulated, international zone, the only place where anyone may go without a visa. Even in this remotest part of the world a visitor knows about Islam.
[243] See also section "Rejection of Hadith."

The Anti-Christ (Dajjāl)

Like all prophets and messengers before him, Prophet Muhammad ﷺ predicted the coming of the anti-Christ as one of the final signs before the coming of the Day of Judgment.

حدثنا علي بن محمد حدثنا عبد الرحمن المحاربي عن إسماعيل بن رافع أبي رافع عن أبي زرعة
السيباني يحيى بن أبي عمرو عن عمرو بن عبد الله عن أبي أمامة الباهلي قال
خطبنا رسول الله صلى الله عليه وسلم فكان أكثر خطبته حديثًا حدثناه عن الدجال وحذرناه
فكان من قوله أن قال إنه لم تكن فتنة في الأرض منذ ذرأ الله ذرية آدم أعظم من فتنة الدجال
وإن الله لم يبعث نبيا إلا حذر أمته الدجال وأنا آخر الأنبياء وأنتم آخر الأمم......(روى في
سنن إبن ماجة في كتاب الفتن)

The Prophet ﷺ said:

> O people! There has been no tribulation on the earth since the
> time of Adam عليه السلام greater than the tribulation of the anti-
> Christ (Dajjāl). Verily, every prophet sent by Allāh warned his
> community about the Dajjāl. I am the Last Prophet and you
> are the Last Ummah...[244]

Prophet Muhammad ﷺ is the prophet for all people, both Muslims and non-Muslims. The Prophet ﷺ directed this hadith to all of humanity saying, "O human beings!" (*nās*) not "O Muslims!" or "O believers!" The appearance of Masīh ad-Dajjāl (Dajjāl, False Messiah or Anti-Christ) is a truly fearsome event for all people on earth, and it will happen in the Last Days. He will move about the earth "spreading corruption right and left"[245] and terrorize the believers, changing them from faith to unbelief. Even the Companions of the Prophet ﷺ were fearful about the coming of the Dajjāl fourteen hundred years ago.

The Dajjāl will appear between Shām and Iraq, and some other hadiths say he will emerge from Khorasan, Iran and will move quickly and cover the whole earth.

---

[244] (*sahīh*). *Ibn Mājah* #4128 "Kitāb al-Fitan." Hākim, *Mustadrak* (4:436 and 437). Suyūtī, *Jami'*
al-saghīr #4752. Albānī, *Silsila sahīha* #2457:
> Yā ayyuhā an-nās innahā lam takun fitnatin 'alā wajh al-ard mundhu dharā
> dhurrīyata ādam 'azham min fitnat id-dajjāl. Inna Allāha ('azza wa jall) lam
> yab'ath nabīyyan illa hadhar ummatahu min al-dajjāl. Wa anā ākhir ul-anbiyā'a
> wa antum ākhir ul-umam...
[245] Ibid. (*sahīh*). *Ibn Mājah* #4128 "Kitāb al-Fitan." Hākim, *Mustadrak* (4:436 and 437). Suyūtī,
Jami' al-saghīr #4752. Albānī, *Silsila sahīha* #2457.

حدثنا الوليد بن مسلم. حدثنا عبدالرحمن بن يزيد بن جابر عن يحيى بن جابر الطائي، عن عبدالرحمن بن جبير بن نفير، عن ابيه، جبير بن نفير، عن النواس بن سمعان، قال: ذكر رسول الله صلى الله عليه وسلم الدجال ذات غداة. فخفض فيه ورفع. حتى ظنناه في طائفة النخل. فلما رحنا اليه عرف ذلك فينا. فقال «ما شانكم؟» قلنا: يا رسول الله! ذكرت الدجال غداة. فخفضت فيه ورفعت. حتى ظنناه في طائفة النخل. فقال «غير الدجال اخوفني عليكم. ان يخرج، وانا فيكم، فانا حجيجه دونكم. وان يخرج، ولست فيكم، فامرؤ حجيج نفسه. والله خليفتي على كل مسلم. انه شاب قطط. عينه طافئة. كاني اشبهه بعبدالعُزَّى بن قطن. فمن ادركه منكم فليقرا عليه فواتح سورة الكهف. انه خارج خلة بين الشام والعراق. فعاث يمينا وعاث شمالا. يا عباد الله! فاثبتوا» قلنا: يا رسول الله! وما لبثه في الارض؟ قال «اربعون يوما. يوم كسنة. ويوم كشهر. ويوم كجمعة. وسائر ايامه كايامكم» قلنا: يا رسول الله! فذلك اليوم الذي كسنة، اتكفينا فيه صلاة يوم؟ قال «لا. اقدروا له قدره» قلنا: يا رسول الله! وما اسراعه في الارض؟ قال «كالغيث استدبرته الريح. فياتي على القوم فيدعوهم، فيؤمنون به ويستجيبون له. فيامر السماء فتمطر. والارض فتنبت. فتروح عليهم سارحتهم، اطول ما كانت ذرا، واسبغه ضروعا، وامده خواصر. ثم ياتي القوم. فيدعوهم فيردون عليه قوله. فينصرف عنهم. فيصبحون ممحلين ليس بايديهم شيء من اموالهم. ويمر بالخربة فيقول لها: اخرجي كنوزك. فتتبعه كنوزها كيعاسيب النحل. ثم يدعو رجلا ممتلئا شبابا. فيضربه بالسيف فيقطعه جزلتين رمية الغرض ثم يدعوه فيقبل ويهلل وجهه. يضحك. فبينما هو كذلك اذ بعث الله المسيح ابن مريم. فينزل عند المنارة البيضاء شرقي دمشق. بين مهرودتين. واضعا كفيه على اجنحة ملكين. اذا طاطا راسه قطر. واذا رفعه تحدر منه جمان كاللؤلؤ. فلا يحل لكافر يجد ريح نفسه الا مات. ونفسه ينتهي حيث ينتهي طرفه. فيطلبه حتى يدركه بباب لد. فيقتله. ثم ياتي عيسى ابن مريم قوم قد عصمهم الله منه. فيمسح عن وجوههم ويحدثهم بدرجاتهم في الجنة. فبينما هو كذلك اذ اوحى الله الى عيسى: اني قد اخرجت عبادا لي، لا يدان لاحد بقتالهم. فحرز عبادي الى الطور. ويبعث الله ياجوج وماجوج. وهم من كل حدب ينسلون. فيمر اوائلهم على بحيرة طبرية. فيشربون ما فيها. ويمر اخرهم فيقولون: لقد كان بهذه، مرة، ماء. ويحصر نبي الله عيسى واصحابه. حتى يكون راس الثور لاحدهم خيرا من مائة دينار لاحدكم اليوم. فيرغب نبي الله عيسى واصحابه. فيرسل الله عليهم النغف في رقابهم. فيصبحون فرسى كموت نفس واحدة. ثم يهبط نبي الله عيسى واصحابه الى الارض. فلا يجدون في الارض موضع شبر الا ملاه زهمهم ونتنهم. فيرغب نبي الله عيسى واصحابه الى الله. فيرسل الله طيرا كاعناق البخت. فتحملهم فتطرحهم حيث شاء الله. ثم يرسل الله مطرا لا يكن منه بيت مدر ولا وبر. فيغسل الارض حتى يتركها كالزلفة. ثم يقال للارض: انبتي ثمرك، وردي بركك. فيومئذ تاكل العصابة من الرمانة.

ويستظلون بقحفها . ويبارك في الرسل . حتّى ان اللقحة من الابل لتكفي الفئام من الناس . واللقحة
من البقر لتكفي القبيلة من الناس . واللقحة من الغنم لتكفي الفخذ من الناس . فبينما هم كذلك اذ
بعث الله ريحا طيبة . فتأخذهم تحت اباطهم . فتقبض روح كل مؤمن وكل مسلم . ويبقى شرار
الناس، يتهارجون فيها تهارج الحمر، فعليهم تقوم الساعة".

(مسلم كتاب في الفتن، أبو داود في كتاب الفتن و الترمذي في كتاب الفتن)

Nawwās Ibn Sam'ān ﷺ reported that Allāh's Messenger ﷺ
made a mention of the Dajjāl one day in the morning. He
sometimes described him to be insignificant and sometimes
described (his turmoil) as very significant and we felt as if he
were in the cluster of the date-palm trees. When we went to
him (to the Holy Prophet) in the evening and he read (the
signs of fear) in our faces, he said, "What is the matter with
you?" We said, "Allāh's Messenger, you made a mention of
the Dajjāl in the morning (sometimes describing him) to be
insignificant and sometimes very important, until we began to
think as if he were present in some (near) part of the cluster of
the date palm trees." Thereupon he said, "I harbor fear in
regard to you in so many other things besides the Dajjāl. If he
comes forth while I am among on, I shall contend with him
on your behalf, but if he comes forth while I am not amongst
you, a man must contend on his own behalf and Allāh would
take care of every Muslim on my behalf (and safeguard him
against his evil). He (Dajjāl) would be a young man with
twisted, contracted hair, and a blind eye. I compare him to
'Abd-ul-'Uzza bin Qatān. He who amongst you would survive
to see him should recite over him the opening verses of *Sūrat
al-Kahf*. He would appear on the way between Syria and Iraq
and would spread mischief right and left. O servant of Allāh!
Adhere (to the path of Truth)." We said, "Allāh's Messenger,
how long would he stay on the earth?" He said, "For forty
days, one day like a year and one day like a month and one day
like a week and the rest of the days would be like your days."
We said, "Allāh's Messenger, would one day's prayer suffice
for the prayers of day equal to one year?" Thereupon he said,
"No, but you must make an estimate of time (and then
observe prayer)." We said, "Allāh's Messenger, how quickly
would he walk upon the earth?" Thereupon he said, "Like
cloud driven by the wind. He would come to the people and
invite them (to a wrong religion) and they would affirm their
faith in him and respond to him. He would then give

command to the sky and there would be rainfall upon the
earth and it would grow crops. Then in the evening, their
posturing animals would come to them with their humps very
high and their udders full of milk and their flanks stretched.
He would then come to another people and invite them. But
they would reject him and he would go away from them and
there would be drought for them and nothing would be left
with them in the form of wealth. He would then walk through
the wasteland and say to it: Bring forth your treasures, and the
treasures would come out and collect (themselves) before him
like the swarm of bees. He would then call a person brimming
with youth and strike him with the sword and cut him into
two pieces and (make these pieces lie at a distance which is
generally) between the archer and his target. He would then
call (that young man) and he will come forward laughing with
his face gleaming (with happiness) and it would be at this very
time that Allāh would send Christ, son of Mary, and he will
descend at the white minaret in the eastern side of Damascus
wearing two garments lightly dyed with saffron and placing his
hands on the wings of two Angels. When he would lower his
head, there would fall beads of perspiration from his head,
and when he would raise it up, beads like pearls would scatter
from it. Every non-believer who would smell the odour of his
self would die and his breath would reach as far as he would
be able to see. He would then search for him (Dajjāl) until he
would catch hold of him at the gate of Ludd and would kill
him. Then a people whom Allāh had protected would come to
Jesus, son of Mary, and he would wipe their faces and would
inform them of their ranks in Paradise and it would be under
such conditions that Allāh would reveal to Jesus these words:
'I have brought forth from amongst My servants such people
against whom none would be able to fight; you take these
people safely to Tūr, and then Allāh would send Gog and
Magog and they would swarm down from every slope. The
first of them would pass the lake of Tiberias and drink out of
it. And when the last of them would pass, he would say,
'There was once water there.' Jesus and his companions would
then be besieged here (at Tūr, and they would be so severely
pressed) that the head of the ox would be dearer to them than
one hundred dinārs and Allāh's Apostle, Jesus, and his
companions would supplicate Allāh, Who would send to them
insects (which would attack their necks) and in the morning
they would perish like one single person. Allāh's Apostle,

Jesus, and his companions would then come down to the earth and they would not find in the earth as much space as a single span which is not filled with their putrefaction and stench. Allāh's Apostle, Jesus, and his companions would then again beseech Allāh, Who would send birds whose necks would be like those of bactrian camels and they would carry them and throw them where God would will."

Then Allāh would send rain which no house of clay or (the tent of) camel's hairs would keep out, and it would wash away the earth until it could appear to be a mirror. Then the earth would be told to bring forth its fruit and restore its blessing and, as a result thereof, there would grow pomegranate [so large] that a group of persons would be able to eat that, and seek shelter under its skin and milch cow would give so much milk that a whole party would be able to drink it. And the milch camel would give such (a large quantity of) milk that the whole tribe would be able to drink out of that and the milch sheep would give so much milk that the whole family would be able to drink out of that and at that time Allāh would send a pleasant wind which would soothe (people) even under their armpits, and would take the life of every Muslim and only the wicked would survive who would commit adultery like asses and the Last Hour would come to them. [246]

This hadith relates that the Dajjāl walks upon the earth like a cloud driven by the wind.

حدثنا إبراهيم بن المنذر: حدثنا الوليد: حدثنا أبو عمرو: حدثنا إسحق: حدثني أنس بن مالك رضي الله عنه، عن النبي صلى الله عليه وسلم قال ليس من بلد إلا سيطؤه الدجال، إلا مكة والمدينة، ليس له من نقابها نقب إلا عليه الملائكة صافين يحرسونها، ثم ترجف المدينة بأهلها ثلاث رجفات، فيخرج الله كل كافر ومنافق (مسلم في أشراط الساعة)

Anas ﷺ related that the Prophet ﷺ said, "There will be no place that the Dajjāl will not enter except Makka and Madīna...."[247]

حدثنا يحيى بن سليمان قال: أخبرني ابن وهب قال: حدثني عمر ابن محمد: أن أباه حدثه، عن ابن عمر رضي الله عنهما قال:

كنا نتحدث بحجة الوداع، والنبي صلى الله عليه وسلم بين أظهرنا، ولا ندري ما حجة الوداع،

---

[246] *Ibid. Sahīh Muslim*, #2937 "Kitāb al-Fitan." *Abū Dāwūd, Sunan* #4321, "Kitāb al-Malāhim." *Tirmidhī* #2241 "Kitāb al-Fitan.
[247] *Sahīh Muslim*, "Kitāb Ashrāt as-Sā'at."

فحمد الله وأثنى عليه، ثم ذكر المسيح الدجال فأطنب في ذكره، وقال: (ما بعث الله من نبي إلا
أنذره أمته، أنذره نوح والنبيون
من بعده، وإنه يخرج فيكم، فما خفي عليكم من شأنه فليس يخفى عليكم: أن ربكم ليس على ما
يخفى عليكم – ثلاثا – إن ربكم ليس بأعور، وإنه أعور العين اليمنى، (البخاري في كتاب المغازي)

Ibn 'Umar ◈ related that the Prophet ﷺ said:

> I warn you against him (the Dajjāl) and there was no prophet
> but warned his nation against him. No doubt, Noah warned
> his nation against him, but I will tell you something about him
> which no prophet told his nation before me. You should
> know that he is one-eyed, and Allāh is not one-eyed.[248]

حدثنا عبد الله حدثني أبي حدثنا محمد بن جعفر وروح قالا حدثنا شعبة عن حبيب بن الزبير
قال سمعت عبد الله بن أبي الهذيل قال روح، العنزي يحدث عن عبد الرحمن بن أبزي عن عبد الله
بن خباب عن أبي بن كعب وقال روح في حديثه، أن عبد الله بن خباب حدثه عن أبي بن كعب
عن النبي صلى الله عليه وسلم- .أنه ذكر الدجال عنده فقال: عينه خضراء كالزجاجة فتعوذوا
بالله من عذاب القبر. (أحمد في مسنده)

Abū bin K'ab ◈ related that the Prophet ﷺ said, "The Anti-
Christ's eye is green like glass."[249]

حدثنا محمد بن المثنى ومحمد بن بشار . قالا: حدثنا محمد بن جعفر . حدثنا شعبة عن قتادة،
قال: سمعت أنس بن مالك قال:
قال رسول الله صلى الله عليه وسلم "ما من نبي إلا وقد أنذر أمته الأعور الكذاب. ألا إنه أعور .
ولإن ربكم ليس بأعور . ومكتوب بين عينيه ك ف ر (مسلم في كتاب الفتن و البخاري في كتاب
الفتن)

Anas Ibn Malik ◈ related that the Prophet ﷺ said:

> There has never been a Prophet who did not warn his people
> against that one-eyed liar. Verily he is one-eyed and verily your
> Lord is not one-eyed. Between his eyes will be written the
> letters Kāf, Fa, Ra (kafara).[250]

On the Anti-Christ's forehead will be written the letters ka, fa, ra (i.e.
kafara ك ف ر). The Prophet ﷺ said that this will be seen only by true believers,
whom Allāh ﷺ wants to save from the tribulation of the Dajjāl. The Dajjāl is

---

Sahīh Bukhārī.
[249] *Musnad Āhmad.* "Ad-dajjāl 'aynuhu khadra kaz-zujāj"
[250] *Sahīh Muslim*, "Kitāb al-Fitan." *Sahīh Bukhārī*, "Kitāb al-Fitan."

not an organization made under the name *kafara*, nor is it a community or a country. The Anti-Christ is a man. The Prophet ﷺ was informing us that in the Last Days there would be someone who would deceive all of humanity. The Dajjāl will possess power over this world (*dunyā*). Thus, Muslims must be careful not to have the love of the world in their hearts so they won't leave their religion and follow him. [251] He will be able to heal the sick by wiping his hand on them, like Jesus ﷺ did, but with this deceit the Dajjāl will lead people down the path to Hell. Thus, the Dajjāl is the False Messiah, or Anti-Christ (*Massīh ad*-Dajjāl). He will pretend to be the Messiah, and deceive people by showing them amazing powers.

حدثنا يحيى بن بكير: حدثنا الليث، عن عقيل، عن ابن شهاب قال: أخبرني عبيد الله بن عبد الله بن عتبة: أن أبا سعيد الخدري رضي الله عنه قال:

حدثنا رسول الله صلى الله عليه وسلم حديثًا طويلا عن الدجال، فكان فيما حدثنا به أن قال: (يأتي الدجال، وهو محرم عليه أن يدخل نقاب المدينة، بنزل بعض السباخ التي بالمدينة، فيخرج إليه يومئذ رجل هو خير الناس، أو من خير الناس، فيقول: أشهد أنك الدجال، الذي حدثنا عنك رسول الله صلى الله عليه وسلم حديثه، فيقول الدجال: أرأيت إن قتلت هذا ثم أحييته هل تشكون في الأمر؟ . فيقولون: لا، فيقتله ثم يحييه، فيقول حين يحييه: والله ما كنت قط أشد بصيرة مني اليوم، فيقول الدجال: أقتله فلا أسلط عليه

(رَوَاهُ البُخَارِي و مسلم في كِتَاب الفِتَنِ)

The Prophet ﷺ said:

> The Dajjāl will come wearing the clothes of a pilgrim (*ihrām*) to the gate of Madīna. One of its best people will come forth and say, "I bear witness that you are the Dajjāl who was mentioned by the Prophet ﷺ." The Dajjāl will say to his

---

[251] Once the Prophet called his Companions when the sun was rising and told them to run towards a mountain (Jabal Uhud) with the sun at their backs and catch their shadows. Whoever caught their shadow would be rewarded with the Prophet's robe. They did not ask why he was saying this, rather they left that up to the Prophet, and they all ran after their shadows. As they ran with the sun at their backs, their shadows were running away from them. Although logically one can predict that it is impossible to catch a shadow, the Companions did not evaluate the Prophet's orders with their minds. They used their intelligence to help them fulfill an order but they would not evaluate whether or not an order should be followed. They knew that he was the Prophet who did not say a single word from his own desires, but he only spoke what Allāh revealed to him to say. Sadly, Muslims of today are very far from that love and belief in the Prophet and they often do the opposite of what he commanded. When they reached the mountain he told them to turn around and, "Run towards me." Then the shadows were running behind after them as they ran to the Prophet. He said, 'O my Companions, whoever is running after this worldly life is like one running after his shadow, and he will never get it. Whoever is running towards *ākhira* (towards me and the message that I brought from Allāh) this world will run after him like your shadow was running after you.' It is said, *"ad-dunya jīfatun wa tulābuhā kilābuhā*—the world is a carcass and those who run after it are like dogs."

followers, "If I kill him and bring him back to life will you believe in me?" They say, "Yes." The Dajjāl kills him then brings him back to life. When the man is alive again he says, "(I swear) by Allāh, I am positive that you are the Dajjāl!" The Dajjāl will then kill him....[252]

The Dajjāl will come with the powers of the devil. He will terrorize the Muslims into following him, converting them into unbelief. He will conceal the truth and bring forth falsehood. The Prophet ﷺ said that the Dajjāl will have the power to show the image of one's dead ancestors on his hand, like a television screen. The relative will say, "Oh my son! This man is correct. I am in Paradise because I was good and I believed in him." In reality that relative is in Hell. If the relative says, "Believe in this man, I am in Hell because I didn't believe," one must say to the Dajjāl, "No, he is in Paradise. This is false."

حدثنا علي بن محمد حدثنا عبد الرحمن المحاربي عن إسمعيل بن رافع عن أبي رافع عن أبي زرعة السيباني يحيى بن أبي عمرو عن عمرو بن عبد الله عن أبي أمامة الباهلي قال خطبنا رسول الله صلى الله عليه وسلم فكان أكثر خطبته حديثًا حدثناه عن الدجال وحذرناه فكان من قوله أن قال إنه لم تكن فتنة في الأرض منذ ذرأ الله ذرية آدم أعظم من فتنة الدجال وإن الله لم يبعث نبيا إلا حذر أمته الدجال وأنا آخر الأنبياء وأنتم آخر الأمم وهو خارج فيكم لا محالة وإن يخرج وأنا بين ظهرانيكم فأنا حجيج لكل مسلم وإن يخرج من بعدي فكل امرئ حجيج نفسه والله خليفتي على كل مسلم وإنه يخرج من خلة بين الشام والعراق فيعيث يمينا ويعيث شمالا يا عباد الله فاثبتوا فإني سأصفه لكم صفة لم يصفها إياه نبي قبلي إنه يبدأ فيقول أنا نبي ولا نبي بعدي ثم يثني فيقول أنا ربكم ولا ترون ربكم حتى تموتوا وإنه أعور وإن ربكم ليس بأعور وإنه مكتوب بين عينيه كافر يقرؤه كل مؤمن كاتب أو غير كاتب وإن من فتنته أن معه جنة ونارا فناره جنة وجنته نار فمن ابتلي بناره فليستغث بالله وليقرأ فواتح الكهف فتكون عليه بردا وسلاما كما كانت النار على إبراهيم وإن من فتنته أن يقول لأعرابي أرأيت إن بعثت لك أباك وأمك أتشهد أني ربك فيقول نعم فيتمثل له شيطانان في صورة أبيه وأمه فيقولان يا بني اتبعه فإنه ربك وإن من فتنته أن يسلط على نفس واحدة فيقتلها وينشرها بالمنشار حتى يلقى شقتين ثم يقول انظروا إلى عبدي هذا فإني أبعثه الآن ثم يزعم أن له ربا غيري فيبعثه الله ويقول له الخبيث من ربك فيقول ربي الله وأنت عدو الله أنت الدجال والله ما كنت بعد أشد بصيرة بك مني اليوم

Abū Umāma al-Bāhilī ﷺ related that the Prophet ﷺ said:

> ...the Dajjāl will say to a bedouin Arab, "What will you think if I bring your father and mother back to life for you? Will you bear witness that I am your lord?" The bedouin will say,

---

[252] *Saḥīḥ Bukhārī* (8:103) and *Saḥīḥ Muslim* #2938.

"Yes." So two devils will assume the appearance of his father and mother, and say, "O my son, follow him for he is your lord..."[253]

Whatever the Anti-Christ shows will be the opposite of the truth.

حدثني محمد بن رافع. حدثنا حسين بن محمد. حدثنا شيبان عن يحيى، عن أبي سلمة، قال: سمعت أبا هريرة قال:

قال رسول الله صلى الله عليه وسلم "ألا أخبركم عن الدجال حديثًا ما حدثه نبي قومه؟ إنه أعور. وإنه يجيء معه مثل الجنة والنار. فالتي يقول إنها الجنة، هي النار. وإني أنذرتكم به كما أنذر به نوح قومه" (البخاري في كتاب أحاديث الأنبياء و مسلم في كتاب الفتن)

Abū Hurayra ☙ related that the Prophet ﷺ said:

Shall I tell you something about the Dajjāl which no prophet has ever told his people before me? The Dajjāl is one-eyed and will bring with him something which will resemble Paradise and Hell; but that which he calls Paradise will in fact be Hell. I have warned you against him as Noah warned his people against him.[254]

حدثنا أبو بكر بن أبي شيبة. حدثنا يزيد بن هارون عن أبي مالك الأشجعي، عن ربعي بن حراش، عن حذيفة، قال:

قال رسول الله صلى الله عليه وسلم "لأنا أعلم بما مع الدجال منه. معه نهران يجريان. أحدهما، رأى العين، ماء أبيض. والآخر، رأى العين، نار تأجج. فإما أدركن أحد فليأت النهر الذي يراه نارا وليغمض. ثم ليطأطئ رأسه فيشرب منه. فإنه ماء بارد. وإن الدجال ممسوح العين. عليها ظفرة غليظة. مكتوب بين عينيه كافر. يقرؤه كل مؤمن، كاتب وغير كاتب (مسلم في كتاب الفتن، البخاري في كتاب الفتن و أبو داود)

Hudhayfah ☙ related that the Prophet ﷺ said:

I know more about the powers which the Dajjāl has than he knows himself. He will have two flowing rivers: one will appear to be crystal clear water, and the other will appear to be flaming fire.[255] Whosoever lives to see that, let him choose the river which seems to be fire, then let him close his eyes,

---

[253] Sunan Ibn Majāh #4067, "Kitāb al-Fitan."
[254] Sahīh Bukhārī (4:104). Sahīh Muslim #2936.
[255] Like a welder's torch requires a mask to use, the Dajjāl's river of fire is so hot that it makes the eyes water to look at it.

lower his head and drink from it, for it will be cold water.[256]
The Dajjāl will be one-eyed; the place where one eye should
be will be covered by a piece of skin (mamsūha). Between his
eyes will be written the word kāfir (unbeliever) and every
believer[257] will be able to read it even if he is illiterate.[258]

The coming of the Anti-Christ must occur in the Last Days. This dreadful
event is approaching, and in that time only three cities will be safe: Makka,
Madīna, and Shām (Damascus). If anyone wants safety in that time he will have
to run to one of these three cities.

حدثني أبو بكر بن إسحق أخبرنا أبو اليمان أخبرنا شعيب عن الزهري قال أخبرني عروة بن الزبير
أن عائشة زوج النبي صلى الله عليه وسلم أخبرته أن النبي صلى الله عليه وسلم كان يدعو في
الصلاة اللهم إني أعوذ بك من عذاب القبر وأعوذ بك من فتنة المسيح الدجال وأعوذ بك من فتنة
المحيا والممات اللهم إني أعوذ بك من المأثم والمغرم قالت فقال له قائل ما أكثر ما تستعيذ من المغرم
يا رسول الله فقال إن الرجل إذا غرم حدث فكذب ووعد فأخلف
(رواه المسلم)

Sayyidā 'A'isha ❀ related a supplication that the Prophet ❀ would recite in
prayer:

> O Allāh! I seek refuge in You from the torture of the grave
> and from the tribulation of the Anti-Christ!...[259]

The Prophet ❀ and his Noble Companions were concerned about the
appearance of the Anti-Christ. Muslims of today must certainly take heed of
what the Prophet ❀ mentioned about the Anti-Christ (Dajjāl) and seek Allāh's
protection from this tremendous evil.

The Prophet ❀ strongly recommended Muslims to keep their state of wudu'
at all times. The Prophet ❀ himself would make a new ablution for prayer even
when he had not broken the old ablution because it is nūrun 'ala nūr (light upon
light). On the Day of Judgment the light of the wudu' will be shine forth from
the believers. It is also a protection against devils in this world, as the Prophet
❀ said, "wudu' is the weapon of the believer." In times when one's faith is
under strong attack it is important to keep wudu' at all times, and quickly renew
one's ablution when it is lost, to keep evil and devils away.

---

[256] The Prophet warned in another hadith not to drink from the river that appears to be water,
because whoever drinks from it will fall into corruption and confusion.
[257] Allāh will give every believer, literate or illiterate, the ability and knowledge to recognize the
Anti-Christ, Dajjāl.
[258] Sahīh Muslim, #2934 "Kitāb al-Fitan." Sahīh Bukhārī (8:101) "Kitāb al-Fitan." Abū Dāwūd
#4315.
[259] Sahīh Bukhārī and Sahīh Muslim.

The Prophet ﷺ also recommended that certain verses of the Qur'ān be recited for protection from the Dajjāl.

حدثنا حفص بن عمر حدثنا همام حدثنا قتادة عن سالم بن أبي الجعد عن معدان بن أبي طلحة عن حديث أبي الدرداء يرويه عن النبي صلى الله عليه وسلم قال من حفظ عشر آيات من أول سورة الكهف عصم من فتنة الدجال

قال أبو داود وكذا قال هشام الدستوائي عن قتادة إلا أنه قال من حفظ من خواتيم سورة الكهف و قال شعبة عن قتادة من آخر الكهف

Abū Darda ؓ related that the Prophet ﷺ said:

> Whoever memorizes the first ten verses[260] of *Sūrat al-Kahf* (and in another version, the last ten verses[261]) is protected from the tribulation of the Dajjāl.

وأخرج أبو عبيد وابن مردويه عن أبي الدرداء، عن النبي صلى الله عليه وسلم قال: "من حفظ عشرة آيات من أول سورة الكهف، ثم أدركه الدجال، لم يضره. ومن حفظ خواتيم سورة الكهف، كانت له نورا يوم القيامة" (درر المنثور للإمام السيوطي وأخرج أبو عبيد وابن مردويه)

In another hadith related by Abū Dardā' ؓ, the Prophet ﷺ said:

> If the Dajjāl comes upon someone who has memorized the first ten verses of *Sūrat al-Kahf* he cannot harm him. And whoever memorized the last verses of *Sūrat al-Kahf* will have light on the Day of Judgment.[262]

For these verses of protection see Chapter "Verses of Sūrat al-Kahf," on page 284.

---

[260] This was related in *Sahīh Muslim*, "Kitāb al-Salāt," "Chapter on the Excellence of *Sūrat al-Kahf* and *Ayat al-Kursī*," and by *Āhmad, Abū Dāwūd, Tirmidhī, Nasā'ī, Ibn Hibbān, Hākim*, and *Bayhaqī*.

[261] *Sunan Abū Dawūd*, "Chapter on the Appearance of the Anti-Christ", *Sahīh Muslim*, "Kitāb al-Salāt," "Chapter on the Excellence of *Sūrat al-Kahf* and *Ayat al-Kursī*," and by *Āhmad* and *Nasā'ī*.

[262] Suyūtī, *Durr al-Manthūr*.

The Mahdī ﷺ

I n the present era, many people do not believe in the coming of the *Mahdī al-Muntadhar* (Awaited Savior) ﷺ in the Last Days. However, the Prophet ﷺ foretold the appearance of the Mahdī ﷺ, and emphasized the inevitability of his arrival, to his Companions. In ignorance, some people assert that the Mahdī ﷺ is a Shi'a concept, and not part of traditional Sunni Islamic beliefs. On the contrary, the coming of the Mahdī ﷺ is established doctrine for both Sunni[263] and Shi'a Muslims, and indeed for all humanity. According to the pertinent religious texts, he is considered to be coming as a leader for the believers and good people in all the nations around the world. The arrival of the Mahdī ﷺ is confirmed by many authentic narrations (hadith). Muslims, then, should not worry about whether or not the Mahdī ﷺ is coming, but when, and what they have prepared for that time.

Due to the lack of religious education, many Muslims today know little or nothing about Mahdī ﷺ. Mahdī ﷺ is a powerful figure, whose arrival must occur before Judgment Day.

حدثنا مسدد أن عمر بن عبيد حدثهم ح و حدثنا محمد بن العلاء حدثنا أبو بكر يعني ابن عياش ح و حدثنا مسدد حدثنا يحيى عن سفيان ح و حدثنا أحمد بن إبراهيم حدثنا عبيد الله بن موسى أخبرنا زائدة ح و حدثنا أحمد بن إبراهيم حدثني عبيد الله بن موسى عن فطر المعنى واحد كلهم عن عاصم عن زر عن عبد الله

عن النبي صلى الله عليه وسلم قال لو لم يبق من الدنيا إلا يوم قال زائدة في حديثه لطول الله ذلك اليوم حتى يبعث فيه رجلا مني أو من أهل بيتي يواطئ اسمه اسمي واسم أبيه اسم أبي زاد في حديث فطر يملأ الأرض قسطا وعدلا كما ملئت ظلما وجورا وقال في حديث سفيان لا تذهب أو لا تنقضي الدنيا حتى يملك العرب رجل من أهل بيتي يواطئ اسمه اسمي

قال أبو داود لفظ عمر وأبي بكر بمعنى سفيان (رواه أحمد في مسنده و الترمذي في سننه)

The Prophet ﷺ said about him:

> If this world has just one day remaining Allāh will extend that
> day until a man comes. He is from me, (or from my family).
> His name is like my name, (i.e. Muhammad), his father's name
> is like my father's name (i.e. 'Abd Allāh). He fills the earth
> with equality and justice, as it has been filled with injustice and
> oppression.[264]

---

[263] Traditional Muslims of *Āhl as-Sunnat wal Jamā'ah*.

[264] *Sahīh* hadith according to *Tirmidhī* in al-Fitan #2231 and #2232. Ibn Taymiyya *Minhāj as-Sunnah* (4:211). *Abū Dāwūd*, "Kitāb al-Mahdī" #4282. Albānī, *Silsila sahīha* #1529:

This hadith is an extremely well authenticated (*sahīh*) hadith, which even Ibn Taymīyya and al-Albānī[265] accepted. The Prophet ﷺ said that even if there were just one day left in the world, Allāh ﷻ would extend it for the Mahdī ﷺ to appear.

The Mahdī ﷺ is coming to remove evil and bring peace in the world. Muslims and Christians have heard about and anticipate the return of Jesus ﷺ, but many Muslims do not consider his arrival to be imminent. Jews are waiting for the Messiah, Christians are waiting for Jesus ﷺ, and Muslims are waiting for both the Mahdī ﷺ and Jesus ﷺ. All religions have described them as men coming to save the world. Allāh ﷻ said:

$$وَقُلْ جَاءَ الْحَقُّ وَزَهَقَ الْبَاطِلُ إِنَّ الْبَاطِلَ كَانَ زَهُوقًا$$

Say, "Truth has come and falsehood is vanquished." (al-Isrā 17/81)

They will not use guns and weapons, but will have a spiritual support, and all believers will follow them. During the same period, the unbelievers will ally themselves with the Anti-Christ, Dajjāl, and form the army of evil.

The Mahdī ﷺ is a caliph *(khalīfa)* for all Muslims. Many, nowadays, are calling for the establishment of a Caliphate; the Prophet also warned that before Mahdī's ﷺ appearance there would come 40 false caliphs. Anyone calling for Caliphate is, in theory, correct. However, most do not understand the true meaning of the "caliphate," thinking it is a political movement or the "modernization" of Islam. Caliphate is for none other than the Mahdī ﷺ, who is one of the Prophet's ﷺ descendants and who is coming with divine support.

حدثنا أحمد بن إبراهيم، ثنا عبد الله بن جعفر الرَّقي، ثنا أبو المليح الحسن بن عمر، عن زياد بن بيان، عن عليّ بن نُفيل، عن سعيد بن المسيّب، عن أُمّ سلمة قالت: سمعت رسول الله ـصلى الله عليه وسلم ـ يقول: المهديُّ من عترتي من ولد فاطمة (أخرجه أبو داود في سننه في كتاب المهدي و ابن ماجه)

Umm Salama ؇ said the Prophet ﷺ said, "The Mahdī is from my family, from the descendants of Fātima."[266]

---

[265] *Law lam yabqā min ad-dunyā illa yawmun wāhidun latawwal Allāha dhālik al-yawm hatta yab'ath Allāh fīhī rajulan minnī (aw min āhli baytī) yuwātīu ismuhu ismī wa ism abihī ism abī yamla al-ard qistan wa 'adlan kamā muli'at zhulman wa jūra.*

[265] Both these two scholars are very "strict" about accepting hadiths.

[266] (*sahīh*) Abū Dāwūd, "Kitāb al-Mahdī," #3603. *Ibn Mājah*, (4:135). "Al-mahdīyu min 'itratī, min waladi Fātima."

حدثنا عبد الله حدثني أبي حدثنا فضل بن دكين حدثنا ياسين العجلي عن إبراهيم بن محمد بن
الحنفية عن أبيه عن علي رضي الله عنه قال: قال رسول الله صلى الله عليه وسلم: المهدي منا
أهل البيت يصلحه الله في ليلة (اخرجه أحمد في مسنده)

'Alī Ibn Abū Tālib ﷺ related that the Prophet ﷺ said:

> The Mahdī is from us, Āhl al-Bayt (the Family of the Prophet);
> Allāh will prepare him in one night.[267]

He will come suddenly during the Last Days.

ابن ماجه عن أبي سعيد أن النبي صلى الله عليه وسلم قال يكون في أمتي المهدي أن قصد فسبع
وإلا فتسع فتنعم فيه أمتي نعمة لم يسمعوا بمثلها قط يؤتي أكلها ولا تدخر عنهم شيئًا والمال يومئذ
كدوس فيقوم الرجل فيقول يا مهدي أعطني فيقول خذوا . وأخرج ابن أبي شيبة ونعيم بن حماد في
الفتن وابن ماجه وأبو نعيم عن ابن مسعود قال بينما نحن عند رسول الله صلى الله عليه وسلم إذ
أقبل فتية من بني هاشم فلما رآهم النبي صلى الله عليه وسلم اغرورقت عيناه وتغير لونه فقلت ما
نزال نرى في وجهك شيئًا نكرهه فقال إنا أهل بيت اختار الله لنا الآخرة على الدنيا وإن أهل بيتي
سيلقون بعدي بلاء وتشريدا وتطريدا حتى يأتي قوم من قبل المشرق معهم رايات سود فيسألون
الحق فلا يعطونه فيقاتلون فينصرون فيعطون ما سألوا فلا يقبلونه حتى يدفعوها إلى رجل من أهل
بيتي فيملأها قسطا كما ملؤوها جورا فمن أدرك ذلك منكم فليأتهم ولو حبوا على الثلج فأنه
المهدي .

'Abd Allāh ibn Mas'ūd ﷺ is reported to have said:

> Once we were in the company of Allāh's Messenger ﷺ, when
> some youths belonging to Banū Hāshim came (to him). As the
> Holy Prophet ﷺ saw them, his eyes were welled up with tears
> and his color changed. He ('Abd Allāh) stated, "I said: We do
> not cease to see something on your face which we dislike."
> Upon this he said, "We are the People of the House (and)
> Allāh has chosen for us the hereafter against the (material)
> world; and my family will meet with calamity, expulsion (exile)
> and attack after me; until a people will come from the east and
> with them would be black flags. They will ask for a justice but
> they will not be granted that. Then they will fight and they will
> be helped. Then they will be granted what they would ask
> for." But they would not accept that till they would hand over
> this (treasure) to a person of my household and it would be

---

[267] (sahīh) Āhmad. Albānī, Sahīh al-jami' #6735. "Al-mahdīyu minna āhl il-bayt yaslahahu
Allāhu fī laylah."

filled with justice just as it was filled with wrong. Whosoever of you finds this (situation), should go to those even crawling on the snow (or ice).[268]

In this extraordinary hadith, the Prophet ﷺ predicted what would happen to his children, grand children and his family after him. He accurately foretold that the People of the House (*Āhl al-Bayt*) would face tremendous trials: that they would be killed; that they would face terrible difficulties and they would be exiled. He predicted that his noble family would become fugitives from the people, hiding themselves, as people sought to kill them. "Until from the east," and the Prophet ﷺ gestured towards the east, "will be coming people with black flags. They will ask for the righteous deeds and for justice (*al-haqq*). They will not be given to them. They will fight and they will be victorious. They will be given what they have asked but at that time they will not accept it." Other hadith indicate that black flags coming from the area of Khorasān will signify the appearance of the Mahdī ﷺ is nigh. Khorasān is in today's Iran, and some scholars have said that this hadith means when the black flags appear from Central Asia, i.e. in the direction of Khorasān, then the appearance of the Mahdī ﷺ is imminent.

وأخرج ابن ماجه والحاكم وصححه وأبو نعيم عن ثوبان قال قال رسول الله صلى الله عليه وسلم
يقتل عند كنزكم ثلاثة كلهم ابن خليفة ثم لا تصير إلى واحد منهم ثم تطلع الرايات السود من قبل
المشرق فيقتلونكم قتلا لم يقتله قوم ثم يجيء خليفة الله المهدي فإذا سمعتم به فأتوه فبايعوه ولو حبوا
على الثلج فإنه خليفة الله المهدي. (أحمد في مسنده)

Thawbān ؓ related that the Prophet ﷺ said:

> If you see him, go and give him your allegiance, even if you have to crawl over ice, because he is the Viceregent (*Khalīfa*) of Allāh, the Mahdī.[269]

This hadith shows that the knowledge of the Prophet ﷺ encompassed cold climates, or countries of "ice," which were unknown to the Arabs. It also shows his foreknowledge that Islam's message would reach to these far-away lands.

ابن أبي شيبة وأحمد وأبو داود أبو يعلى والطبراني عن أم سلمة عن النبي صلى الله عليه وسلم
يكون اختلاف عند موت خليفة فيخرج رجل من أهل المدينة هاربا إلى مكة فيأتيه ناس من أهل

---

[268] *Abū Na'īm* and *Ibn Mājah*, "Kitāb al-Fitan." Al-Hākim has transmitted it in *al-Mustadrak* from the channel of 'Umar bin Qays on the authority of al-Hakam who narrates from Ibrāhīm. According to *al-Zawā'id*, its chain of transmission is *da'īf* because of the weakness (*du'f*) of Yazīd bin Abī Zīyād al-Kūfī. But Yazīd bin Abī Zīyād is not singular to transmit it on Ibrāhīm's authority.

[269] *Ibn Mājah*, "Kitāb al-Fitan" #4084

مكة فيخرجونه وهو كاره فيبايعونه بين الركن والمقام ويبعث إليه بعث من الشام فيخسف بهم

بالبيداء بين مكة والمدينة فإذا رأى الناس ذلك أتاه ابدال الشام وعصائب أهل العراق فيبايعونه ثم

ينشأ رجل من قريش أخواله كلب فيبعث إليهم بعثًا فيظهرون عليهم وذلك بعث كلب والخيبة لمن لم

يشهد غنيمة كلب فيقسم المال ويعمل في الناس بسنة نبيهم صلى الله عليه وسلم ويلقي الإسلام

بجرانه إلى الأرض يلبث سبع سنين ثم يتوفى ويصلي عليه المسلمون . (أخرجه إبن حبان)

Umm Salama ؇ related that the Prophet ؄ said:

> Strife shall take place after the death of a Caliph. A man of the
> people of Madīna will come forth flying to Makka. Some of
> the people of Makka will come to him, bring him out against
> his will and swear allegiance to him between the Corner (of
> the Ka'ba) and the Maqām (Station of Abrāham, next to the
> Ka'ba). An army will then be sent against him from Shām but
> will be swallowed up in the desert between Makka and
> Madīna. When the people see that, the Abdāl[270] (Substitutes)
> of Shām and the best people of Iraq will come to him and
> swear allegiance to him between the Corner and the Maqām.
> Then there will arise a man of the Quraysh whose maternal
> uncles belong to the tribe of Kalb. He will send an army
> against them. They (the Mahdī and the believers) will destroy
> them and they will be victorious, and he will divide the
> rewards among the people. He will establish and practice the
> Sunnah of the Prophet ؄ among them. Islam will spread all
> over the earth. He will stay seven years with them. Then he
> will pass away and the Muslims will pray [the funeral prayer]
> over him.[271]

أحمد ومسلم عن أبي سعيد وجابر عن رسول الله صلى الله عليه وسلم قال يكون في آخر الزمان

خليفة يقسم المال ولا يعده . وأخرج أبو نعيم عن أبي سعيد عن النبي صلى الله عليه وسلم قال

يكون في أمتي المهدي إن قصر عمره فسبع سنين وإلا فثمان وإلا فتسع سنين تنعم أمتي في زمانه

نعيما لم يتنعموا مثله قط في البر والفاجر يرسل الله السماء عليهم مدرارا ولا تدخر الأرض شيئًا من

نباتها .

وأخرج أبو نعيم عن أبي سعيد عن النبي صلى الله عليه وسلم أنه قال

تملأ الأرض ظلما وجورا فيقوم رجل من عترتي فيملأها قسطا وعدلا يملك سبعا أو تسعا .

وأخرج أحمد وأبو نعيم عن أبي سعيد قال قال النبي صلى الله عليه وسلم

---

[270] These are a group of awliyā' (saints) that the Prophet mentioned in many hadiths. (See chapter "Shām and the Abdāl.")
[271] Sahīh Ibn Hibbān #6757.

لا تنقضي الدنيا حتى يملك الأرض رجل من أهل بيتي يملأ الأرض عدلاً كما ملئت جوراً يملك سبع سنين .

وأخرج أبو نعيم والحاكم عن أبي سعيد أن رسول الله صلى الله عليه وسلم قال يخرج المهدي في أمتي يبعثه الله غياثاً للناس تنعم الأمة وتعيش الماشية وتخرج الأرض نباتها ويعطي المال صحاحا .

يخرج في آخر أمتي المهدي، يسقيه الله الغيث، وتخرج الأرض نباتها، ويعطى المال صحاحا، وتكثر الماشية، وتعظم الأمة، يعيش سبعا أو ثمانيا.

ك – عن ابن مسعود) (أخرجه الحاكم في المستدرك (4/558) وقال صحيح ووافقه الذهبي وعن أبي سعيد الخدري. ص.

Abū Saʿīd al-Khudrī ؓ related that the Prophet ﷺ said:

> In the Last Days of my Ummah, the Mahdī will appear. Allāh will give him power over the wind and rain and the earth will bring forth its foliage. He will give away wealth profusely, flocks will be in abundance, and the Ummah will be large and honored. He will live seven or eight years....[272]

At that time Allāh ﷻ will cause the heavens to open, turning deserts into veritable paradises for the sake of the Mahdī ﷺ by means of abundant rainfall.

حدثنا قتيبة بن سعيد حدثنا يعقوب وهو ابن عبد الرحمن القاري عن سهيل عن أبيه عن أبي هريرة أن رسول الله صلى الله عليه وسلم قال لا تقوم الساعة حتى يكثر المال ويفيض حتى يخرج الرجل بزكاة ماله فلا يجد أحدا يقبلها منه وحتى تعود أرض العرب مروجا وأنهارا. (أخرجه مسلم في كتاب الزكاة و أحمد في مسنده)

In another hadith, Abū Hurayra ؓ related that the Prophet ﷺ said:

> The Hour will not come until wealth will be plentiful amongst you and overflow in abundance; and until a man goes out to pay his poor-due and he will not find anyone to accept it from him; and until the land of the Arabs is filled with flowing with rivers once again.[273]

---

[272] (sahīh) Hākim, Mustadrak (4:557 and 558). Albānī, Silsila sahīha, #711. Other narrations shown here are not translated but are similar in import:
Yakhruju fī ākhiri ummatī al-Mahdī yusqīhi allāhu al-ghaytha wa tukhrij al-ardu nabātuhā wa y'utī al-māla sihāhan wa takthuru al-māshīyyat wa tan'um ul-ummah ya'iyshu sab'an aw thamānīyyan.
[273] Sahīh Muslim, "Kitāb al-Zakāt" #157. Āhmad, Musnad #8819:
Lā taqūm us-sā'atu hatta yakthura fīkum al-māla wa yafīdu, wa hatta yukhrij ar-rajulu bizakāti mālihi falā yajidu āhadan yaqbaluhā minhu, wa hatta ta'ūda ard ul-'arabī murūjan wa anhāra.

With the Mahdī's arrival, Allāh ﷻ will send heavy showers, both heavy rains and abundant spiritual sustenance. Then, the earth will put forth its full capacity to produce plants. Some descriptions say that the earth will yield watermelons of such strength that they will no longer grow on the ground, but on trees. Al-Mahdī ﷺ will give money in abundance, and flocks will be plentiful. It will be the Golden Age, the best time for the Ummah. He will live seven or eight years, and when he passes away 'Isā ﷺ (Jesus) will lead his funeral prayer.

Ibn Kathīr said:

> I think that [Mahdī's] appearance will be before the descent of
> 'Isā bin Maryam ﷺ as the hadiths indicate.[274]

حدثنا ابن بكيرٍ: حدثنا الليث، عن يونس، عن ابن شهاب، عن نافع مولى أبي قتادة الأنصاري: أن
أبا هريرة قال:
قال رسول الله صلى الله عليه وسلم كيف أنتم إذا نزل ابن مريم فيكم، وإمامكم منكم . (أخرجه
البخاري و مسلم)

The Prophet ﷺ mentioned:

> How will you be when the son of Maryam ('Isā, Jesus)
> descends upon you and your Imām (Mahdī) is among you
> (leading the prayer)?[275]

---

[274] Abū Dāwūd, "Kitāb al-Fitan wal-Malāhīm" (1:55).
[275] Sahīh Bukhārī and Sahīh Muslim. "Kayfa antum idha nazala ibnu maryama fīkum wa imāmukum minkum!"

Return of Jesus Christ ('Isā ibn Maryam ﷺ)

The return of Jesus Christ ﷺ to earth from heaven is mentioned in many hadith of the Prophet ﷺ.

عَنْ إِبْنِ سَمْعَانَ قَالَ ذَكَرَ رَسُولَ اللهِ صلى الله عليه وسلم فَيَنْزِلُ عِنْدَ الْمَنَارَةِ الْبَيْضَاءِ شَرْقِي دِمَشْقَ . بَيْنَ مَهْرُودَتَيْنِ . وَاضِعًا كَفَيْهِ عَلَى أَجْنِحَةِ مَلَكَيْنِ . إِذَا طَأْطَأَ رَأْسَهُ قَطَرَ . وَإِذَا رَفَعَهُ تَحَدَّرَ مِنْهُ جُمَانٌ كَاللُّؤْلُؤِ . فَلَا يَحِلُّ لِكَافِرٍ يَجِدُ رِيحَ نَفَسِهِ إِلَّا مَاتَ . وَنَفَسُهُ يَنْتَهِي حَيْثُ يَنْتَهِي طَرْفُهُ (اخرجه مسلم في كتاب الفتن)

Nawās Ibn Sama'ān ﷺ related that the Prophet ﷺ said

> [Jesus Christ, son of Mary] will descend at the white minaret on the eastern side of Damascus... placing his hands on the wings of two Angels. When he lowers his head, drops of perspiration will fall from his head, and when he raises it up, beads like pearls will scatter from it. Every non-believer who smells the fragrance of his breath will die and his breath will reach as far as he is able to see.[276]

The Prophet ﷺ describes the coming of Jesus ﷺ to the White Minaret, in the eastern part of Damascus. It is part of what is known as the *Masjid al-Umawī*.[277] From there, Jesus ﷺ, along with the Mahdī ﷺ, will lead the believers against the Dajjāl, the Anti-Christ.

حَدَّثَنِي زُهَيْرُ بْنُ حَرْبٍ . حَدَّثَنَا مُعَلَّى بْنُ مَنْصُورٍ . حَدَّثَنَا سُلَيْمَانُ بْنُ بِلَالٍ . حَدَّثَنَا سُهَيْلٌ عَنْ أَبِيهِ، عَنْ أَبِي هُرَيْرَةَ؛ أَنَّ رَسُولَ اللهِ صلى الله عليه وسلم قَالَ "لَا تَقُومُ السَّاعَةُ حَتَّى يَنْزِلَ الرُّومُ بِالْأَعْمَاقِ، أَمْ بِدَابِقٍ . فَيَخْرُجُ إِلَيْهِمْ جَيْشٌ مِنَ الْمَدِينَةِ . مِنْ خِيَارِ أَهْلِ الْأَرْضِ يَوْمَئِذٍ . فَإِذَا تَصَافُّوا قَالَتِ الرُّومُ: خَلُّوا بَيْنَنَا وَبَيْنَ الَّذِينَ سَبَوْا مِنَّا نُقَاتِلْهُمْ . فَيَقُولُ الْمُسْلِمُونَ: لَا . وَاللهِ ! لَا نُخَلِّي بَيْنَكُمْ وَبَيْنَ إِخْوَانِنَا . فَيُقَاتِلُونَهُمْ . فَيَنْهَزِمُ ثُلُثٌ لَا يَتُوبُ اللهُ عَلَيْهِمْ أَبَدًا . وَيُقْتَلُ ثُلُثُهُمْ، أَفْضَلُ الشُّهَدَاءِ عِنْدَ اللهِ . وَيَفْتَحُ الثُّلُثُ . لَا يُفْتَنُونَ أَبَدًا . فَيَفْتَتِحُونَ قُسْطَنْطِينِيَّةَ . فَبَيْنَمَا هُمْ يَقْتَسِمُونَ الْغَنَائِمَ . قَدْ عَلَّقُوا سُيُوفَهُمْ بِالزَّيْتُونِ، إِذْ صَاحَ فِيهِمُ الشَّيْطَانُ: إِنَّ الْمَسِيحَ قَدْ خَلَفَكُمْ فِي أَهْلِيكُمْ . فَيَخْرُجُونَ . وَذَلِكَ بَاطِلٌ . فَإِذَا جَاءُوا

---

[276] *Muslim*, "Kitāb al-Fitan." Part of a long hadith:
... *fayanzilu 'inda al-minārat-il-bayda sharqi id-dimashq.... Wādihan kafayyhi 'alā ajnihati malikayn. Idhā tā'tā' rāsuhu qatara. Wa idhā rafa'hu tahadara minhu jumānun kal-lu'lu. Fa lā yahillu li-kāfirin yajidu rīha nafasihi illa māt. Wa nafasahu yantahī haythu yantahī tarfuh...*
[277] Showing the tolerance of Islam, in the time of the second Caliph 'Umar ibn al-Khattāb ﷺ the building was shared between the Muslims and the Christian and Jewish worshippers.

الشام خرج. فبينما هم يعدون للقتال، يسوون الصفوف، إذ أقيمت الصلاة. فينزل عيسى ابن مريم
صلى الله عليه وسلم. فأمهم. فإذا رآه عدو الله، ذاب كما يذوب الملح في الماء. فلو تركه لاذاب
حتى يهلك ولكن يقتله الله بيده فيريهم دمه في حربته (أخرجه مسلم في كتاب الفتن و الذهبي في
التذكرة)

In another hadith, the Prophet ﷺ said:

> (The Muslims) will be straightening their lines to pray. 'Isā ibn
> Maryam will descend and lead them. When the cursed enemy
> of Allāh, Dajjāl, (Anti-Christ) sees him, he will dissolve as the
> salt dissolves in water. If ('Isā) leaves him (to continue like
> this), he will dissolve completely (and die), but Allāh will cause
> 'Isā to kill him by his hand. Then he will show the people his
> blood on his spear.[278]

عن جابر قال، قال رسول الله صلى الله عليه وسلم،
لا تزال أمتي ظاهرين على الحق حتى ينزل عيسى بن مريم فيقول إمامهم تقدم فيقول أنت أحق
بعضكم أمراء على بعض أمر أكرم به هذه الأمة (أخرجه مسلم في كتاب الإيمان و الهيثمي في
الزوائد)

Jābir Ibn 'Abd Allāh ﷺ related that the Prophet ﷺ said:

> 'Isā ﷺ will descend on them and their leader (the Mahdī) will
> say to him, "Lead the prayer for us." And he will say "No,
> some of you are leaders over others, by this Allāh has honored
> this Ummah."[279]

Ibn Qayyim mentioned in *Manar al-munīf* that the leader in this hadith is the
Mahdī ﷺ who will request Jesus ﷺ to lead the Muslims in prayer. Jesus ﷺ
will remain on earth, not as a prophet, but as one of the Community of
Prophet Muhammad ﷺ. Muslims will follow him as their leader. According to
Shalabi, the Mahdī ﷺ will lead the Muslims in prayer, and Jesus ﷺ will rule
the Muslims according to the Divine Law (*Sharī'ah*).[280] Imām Muslim stressed
that Jesus ﷺ would rule according to the Islamic Divine Law in his chapter
entitled: The Descent of Jesus son of Mary to rule with the Divine Law of our
Prophet Muhammad ﷺ. In fact the Prophet ﷺ mentioned that Jesus ﷺ would

---

[278] *Muslim*, "Kitāb al-Fitan" #2897. Part of a long hadith:
... *yusawūn as-sufūf idh uqīmat as-salāt fa yanzilu 'Isā ibn Maryam fa-
ammahum fa idhā ra'ā 'adūwallāhi dhāba kamā yadhūbu al-milhu fil-mā'i. Fa
law tarakahu landhaba wa lākin yaqtuluhu-Llāhu biyadih. Fayurīhim dammahu
fī harbatih.*

[279] *Sahīh Muslim* #157 "Kitāb al-Īmān," "Chapter on the Descent of 'Isā ibn Maryam to Rule with
the Divine Law of our Prophet Muhammad."

[280] *Sahīh ashrāt as-sā'at* (p 258)

perform the hajj (greater pilgrimage), and on his journey would stop to visit the Prophet ﷺ in Madīna.

عن أبي هريرة قال قال رسول الله صلى الله عليه و سلم ليهبطن الله عيسى ابن مريم حكمًا عدلًا
و إمامًا مقسطًا فليسلكن فج الروحاء حاجًا أو معتمرًا و ليقعن على قبري فيسلمن علي و لأردن
عليه (الحاكم في المستدرك)

Abū Hurayra ؓ related that the Prophet ﷺ said:

> Verily, 'Isā ibn Maryam ﷺ shall descend as an equitable judge and fair ruler. He shall tread his path on his way to *hajj* (pilgrimage) and come to my grave to greet me, and I shall certainly answer him![281]

Allāh ﷻ mentioned in the Holy Qur'ān:

وَإِن مِّنْ أَهْلِ الْكِتَابِ إِلَّا لَيُؤْمِنَنَّ بِهِ قَبْلَ مَوْتِهِ وَيَوْمَ الْقِيَامَةِ يَكُونُ عَلَيْهِمْ شَهِيدًا

> *There is not one of the People of the Scripture but will believe in him ('Isa, Jesus) before his death, and on the Day of Resurrection he will bear witness for them. (an-Nisā' 4:159)*

Like all prophets, Prophet Jesus ﷺ came with the divine message of surrender to God Almighty, which is Islam. This verse shows that when Jesus ﷺ returns he will personally correct the misrepresentations and misinterpretations about himself. He will affirm the true message that he brought in his time as a prophet, and that he never claimed to be the Son of God. Furthermore, he will re-affirm in his second coming what he prophesized in his first coming bearing witness to the Seal of the Messengers, Prophet Muhammad ﷺ. In his second coming many non-Muslims will accept Jesus ﷺ as a servant of Allāh Almighty, as a Muslim and a member of the Community of Muhammad ﷺ (Ummah).

Ibn 'Abbās ؓ said:

> At the time 'Isā ﷺ descends there shall not remain on the face of the earth... anyone who worships [any diety] other than Allāh, [except] all believing in 'Isā ﷺ and following him as the spirit from Allāh and His Word, His servant and Messenger.[282]

On the Day of Resurrection, Jesus ﷺ will bear witness that in his second coming those people of the Scripture (non-Muslims) did indeed come to

---

[281] Hākim, *Mustadrak* (2:651) #4162. Dhahabī concurred it was sound.
[282] Cited by Ibn al-Jawzī (d. 597) in his *Tafsīr* (2:247-248), in which he said, "This is the position of Qatāda, Ibn Zayd, and Ibn Qutayba, and Ibn Jarīr al-Tabarī chose it."

correctly believe in him and in Prophet Muhammad 鐵. Conversely, Jesus العظيم
will bear witness against those who denied his correct teachings, who altered
his teachings by considering him the Son of God, and those who denied
Prophet Muhammad 鐵 as the Seal of the Messengers.

Jesus العظيم will rule for forty years and the earth will be full of peace and
happiness.

Abu Su'ud in his commentary on the Qur'ān said:

> ...at which time there will be but one community on earth,
> lions and tigers and wolves shall graze side by side with the
> camels and cattle and sheep, etc. for forty years, after which
> 'Isā العظيم shall die and be buried.[283]

فيَمْكُثُ في الأَرْضِ أَرْبَعِين سنة ثمَّ يَتَوفَّى فيُصَلِّي عليه المُسْلِمُونَ (أَخْرَجه أَحْمد في مُسْنده و أبو

داود في كتاب الملاحم)

Abū Hurayra ﷺ related that the Prophet 鐵 said:

> ('Isā) will stay on earth for forty years then he will die and the
> Muslims will pray (the funeral prayer) over him.[284]

Ten years after he passes away, the earth will be filled with corruption such
that there will be no one left who even says, *Lā ilāha ill-Allāh* (there is no god
except God), i.e. there will be no more monotheists. When iniquity comes back
on the earth, it will be very close to the Judgment Day. Allāh 鐵 will send a
beautiful, fragrant breeze from Paradise to take the souls of the believers.

---

[283] Abu al-Su'ud (d. 951) in his *Tafsīr* (2:252).

[284] (*sahīh*) Abū Dāwūd, "Kitāb al-Malāhīm" (3:24). Suyūtī, *Jami' al-saghīr*, (5:265). *"Thumma
yamkuthu fil-ardi arba'īna sannatin thumma yatawafā wa yusalli 'alayhi al-muslimūn."*

The Beast of the Earth

One of the signs of the Last Days mentioned in this hadith is the emergence of the "Beast of the Earth" (*Dābbat al-Arḍ*). Allāh ﷻ mentioned it in the Holy Qur'ān:

وَإِذَا وَقَعَ الْقَوْلُ عَلَيْهِمْ أَخْرَجْنَا لَهُمْ دَابَّةً مِنَ الْأَرْضِ تُكَلِّمُهُمْ أَنَّ النَّاسَ كَانُوا بِآيَاتِنَا لَا يُوقِنُونَ

And when the Word is fulfilled against them, we shall produce from the earth a beast for them: He will speak to them, for that mankind did not believe with certainty in Our Signs. (an-Naml 27:82)

The Beast is also mentioned in hadith of the Prophet ﷺ.

حدثنا أبو خيثمة، زهير بن حرب وإسحاق بن إبراهيم وابن أبي عمر المكي واللفظ لزهير (قال إسحاق أخبرنا، وقال الآخران حدثنا) سفيان بن عيينة عن فرات القزاز، عن أبي الطفيل، عن حذيفة بن أسيد الغفاري قال اطلع النبي صلى الله عليه وسلم علينا ونحن نتذاكر فقال ما تذاكرون؟ قالوا نذكر الساعة قال إنها لن تقوم حتى ترون قبلها عشر آيات فذكر الدخان، والدجال، والدابة، وطلوع الشمس من مغربها، ونزول عيسى ابن مريم صلى الله عليه وسلم، ويأجوج ومأجوج. وثلاثة خسوف خسف بالمشرق، وخسف بالمغرب، وخسف بجزيرة العرب وآخر ذلك، نار تخرج من اليمن، تطرد الناس إلى محشرهم (أخرجه مسلم في كتاب الفتن و أبو داود في سننه)

Hudhayfa ﷺ related that the Prophet ﷺ said:

> (The Hour) will not come until you see ten signs: the smoke, the Dajjāl, the Beast (of the Earth), the rising of the sun from the west, the descent of Jesus son of Mary عليه السلام, Gog and Magog, and land-slidings (or earthquakes) in three places, one in the east, one in the west and one in Arabia at the end of which fire would burn forth from the Yemen, driving people to the place of their assembly.[285]

Ibn Jarīr ﷺ related from Alī ﷺ that the words of this verse of Qur'ān, *For that mankind did not believe with certainty in Our Signs,* will be those spoken by the Beast of the Earth in his address to mankind. It will sort people into two categories and will brand every person on their forehead as either believer or unbeliever.

---

[285] *Saḥīḥ Muslim*, "Kitāb al-Fitan" #6931.

حدثنا يزيد أخبرنا حماد بن سلمة وعفان حدثنا حماد أخبرنا علي بن زيد عن أوس بن خالد عن
أبي هريرة

عن النبي صلى الله عليه وسلم قال تخرج الدابة ومعها عصا موسى عليه السلام وخاتم سليمان
عليه السلام فتخطم الكافر قال عفان أنف الكافر بالخاتم وتجلو وجه المؤمن بالعصا حتى إن أهل
الخوان ليجتمعون على خوانهم فيقول هذا يا مؤمن ويقول هذا يا كافر (مسند أحمد)

Abū Hurayra ﷺ related that the Prophet ﷺ said, "The Beast of the Earth
will emerge, and will have with it the rod of Moses and the ring of
Solomon."[286]

حدثنا عبد الله حدثني أبي حدثنا علي بن بحر حدثنا أبو تميلة بالمثناة يحيى بن واضح الأزدي
أخبرني خالد بن عبيد أبو عصام حدثنا عبد الله بن بريدة عن أبيه قال:
-ذهب بي رسول الله صلى الله عليه وسلم إلى موضع بالبادية قريبا من مكة فإذا أرض يابسة
حولها رمل فقال رسول الله صلى الله عليه وسلم تخرج الدابة من هذا الموضع فإذا فتر في شبر
(أخرجه ابن ماجه في كتاب الفتن)

Barīdah ﷺ related, "The Prophet ﷺ took me to a place in the desert, near
Makka. It was a dry piece of land surrounded by sand. The Prophet ﷺ said,
'The Beast will emerge from this place.' It was a very small area."[287]

---

[286] *Tirmidhī* and *Musnad Āhmad*.
[287] *Ibn Mājah*, "Kitāb al-Fitan."

Rising of the Sun from the West

Another one of the Signs of the Last Days is the rising of the sun from the west.

حدثنا موسى بن إسماعيل،حدثنا عبد الواحد،حدثنا عمارة، حدثنا أبو زرعة، حدثنا أبو هريرة رضي الله عنه قال:

قال رسول الله صلى الله عليه وسلم، (لا تقوم الساعة حتى تطلع الشمس من مغربها، فإذا رآها الناس آمن من عليها، فذاك حين، لا ينفع نفسا إيمانها لم تكن آمنت من قبل (أخرجه البخاري في كتاب التفسير)

Abū Hurayra ❀ related that the Prophet ﷺ said:

The Hour will not come until the sun rises from the West. When the people see it, whoever is living on earth will believe, but that will be the time when: *No good will it do to a soul to believe in them then, if it believed not before.* (al-An'am 6:158)[288]

This was explained by the scholars, including Ibn Kathīr, that faith or repentance would not be accepted at that time. The door of faith and the door of repentance will be closed with this tremendous sign.

---

[288] *Sahīh Bukhārī*, "Kitāb at-Tafsīr."

Smoke Covers the Earth

Allāh ﷻ said:

فَارْتَقِبْ يَوْمَ تَأْتِي السَّمَاءُ بِدُخَانٍ مُبِينٍ يَغْشَى النَّاسَ هَذَا عَذَابٌ أَلِيمٌ

That day when a manifest smoke (dukhan mubeen) will come from the skies, covering humanity. They will say, "This is a painful punishment"

(ad-Dukhān 44:10-11)

In 1945, Islamic scholars thought that this verse might refer to the atomic explosion at Hiroshima. At the time its mushroom cloud was the greatest cloud of smoke to date, but today's nuclear weapons can produce explosions which are thousands of times greater. Not only are these weapons much more powerful, but today there is also a potential for rapid, numerous, missile launches in reponse to an attack, or even in response to a false alarm. Further, this verse refers not to a single explosion, but to a smoke that is manifest (*mubin*), and can be easily seen by everyone around the world. Thus, it will not be limited to a single city or country. The smoke will encompass the entire globe, indicating mass destruction.[289]

حدثنا هاشم بن مرثد الطبراني ثنا محمد بن إسماعيل بن عياش حدثني أبي حدثني ضمضم بن زرعة عن شريح بن عبيد عن أبي مالك الأشعري أن رسول الله صلى الله عليه وسلم قال إن الله عز وجل أجاركم من ثلاث خلال ان لا يدعو عليكم نبيكم فتهلكوا جميعا وأن لا يظهر أهل الباطل على أهل الحق وان لا تجتمعوا على ضلالة فهؤلاء أجاركم الله منهن وربكم أنذركم ثلاثا الدخان يأخذ المؤمن منه كالزكمة ويأخذ الكافر فينتفخ ويخرج من كل مسمع منه والثانية الدابة والثالثة الدجال (أخرجه الطبراني في الكبير و في الزَّوائد)

Abū Malik al-Ashʿarī ﷺ related that the Prophet ﷺ said:

> Your Lord has warned you about three things. Smoke that affects the believer like a catarrh[290] and will affect the unbeliever by inflating him until it comes pouring out of his

---

[289] "Scientific analysis shows that if you drop 1,000 bombs on 100 cities, you'll create such a pall of black, radioactive, oily smoke, it will cover the earth for a year, block out the sun, and produce nuclear winter..."
Helen Caldicott, M.D.
[290] An illness which causes inflammation of the mucous membrane chronically affecting the human nose and air passages.

eardrums. Secondly, the Beast of the Earth. Thirdly, the Dajjāl.[291]

In this hadith the Prophet ﷺ says that there will be an enormous amount of smoke coming at the end of the Last Days. When a believer breathes this smoke he will feel its effect as a flu-like illness. This indicates that it is a toxic substance which will affect all believers, but not kill them. The Prophet ﷺ did not say one believer, or a limited area of believers, but "believers" in general (everywhere) will have a runny nose and flu-like symptoms when they inhale the smoke. This is another indication by the Prophet ﷺ of the widespread nature of the smoke; that when it appears it will overtake the whole earth. Such a tremendous amount of smoke could come from several sources: volcanoes' noxious sulfur smoke; smoke from burning oil; or from a nuclear explosion.

In contrast to the believers, unbelievers will be inflated, will then burst and die. Contemporary science shows that in a severe blast injury, such as from a nuclear explosion, the body's solid organs, as well as the blood and other fluids, expand from the pressure of the blast wave. With this increased pressure, they enlarge and compress the air-filled organs (like the ears) until they burst as the Prophet ﷺ said, "Inflating him until it comes pouring out of his eardrums."[292] This phenomenon was not mentioned by any other prophet, so in this hadith we see another example of the miraculous knowledge of the Prophet ﷺ.

As a mercy from Allāh ﷻ, believers will be spared. Allāh ﷻ does as He wishes, and whoever He wants to save will be saved. In the time of Nūh ﷺ one elderly lady was not on Nūh's ark yet she was not drowned by the flood. When Sayyidinā Nūh ﷺ landed with his ship he asked her how she survived the flood that had engulfed the whole earth. She said, "What flood? I only remember that one day one of my cows came back from grazing with mud on its legs and this had never happened before."

This shows us that whomever Allāh ﷻ wishes to protect will be protected, and no harm will come to him or her. In the next life, Allāh will save anyone who testified to His Unity, by saying the testimony of faith (*shahāda*): *ashaddu an lā ilāha ill-Allāh wa ashaddu anna Muhammadun rasūlullāh*. The mercy shown to the Ummah of Prophet Muhammad is from the Allāh's special love for the Prophet, for he is *habībullāh*—the Beloved of Allāh ﷺ—making this a Nation

---

[291] Ibn Hājar, *Fath* (8:571). Narrated by Tabarānī and Ibn Jarīr. Ibn Kathīr said its *isnad* is sound. Commenting on *Sūrat al-Dukhān* in another narration, 'Alī Ibn Abū Tālib ؓ confirmed the smoke and its effect on believers and unbelievers:

Inna rabbakum indharakum thalāthan: ad-dukhān yākhudh ul-mu'mina kaz-zukmati, wa yākhudh ul-kāfira fa yantafikhu hatta yakhruja min kulli masma'in minhu. Wa thānīyatu: ad-dābbatu. Wa thālithatu: ad-dajjāl.

[292] In some cases the force of the blast wave can be significant enough to force air bubbles into the blood stream (air emboli), quite literally "blowing him up" or "inflating him" with air.

bestowed with Mercy (*Ummatan marhūma*). Because of Allāh's love for the most beloved of His creation, Allāh ﷻ will send **all** the believers to Paradise.

حدثنا عثمان بن أبي شيبة حدثنا كثير بن هشام حدثنا المسعودي عن سعيد بن أبي بردة عن أبيه عن أبي موسى قال، قال رسول الله صلى الله عليه وسلم أمتي هذه أمة مرحومة ليس عليها عذاب في الآخرة عذابها في الدنيا الفتن والزلازل والقتل (سنن أبي داود)

Abū Mūsā ؓ narrated that the Prophet ﷺ said:

> This people of mine is one to which mercy is shown. It will have no punishment in the next world, but its punishment in this world will be trials, earthquakes and being killed.[293]

٭٭٭

---

[293] *Sunan Abū Dawūd*, Book 35, #4265:

Gog and Magog (Yā'jūj and Mā'jūj)

I n the Holy Qur'ān, Allāh ﷻ has related:

حَتَّى إِذَا بَلَغَ بَيْنَ السَّدَّيْنِ وَجَدَ مِن دُونِهِمَا قَوْمًا لَا يَكَادُونَ يَفْقَهُونَ قَوْلًا قَالُوا يَا ذَا الْقَرْنَيْنِ إِنَّ
يَأْجُوجَ وَمَأْجُوجَ مُفْسِدُونَ فِي الْأَرْضِ فَهَلْ نَجْعَلُ لَكَ خَرْجًا عَلَى أَن تَجْعَلَ بَيْنَنَا وَبَيْنَهُمْ سَدًّا
قَالَ مَا مَكَّنِّي فِيهِ رَبِّي خَيْرٌ فَأَعِينُونِي بِقُوَّةٍ أَجْعَلْ بَيْنَكُمْ وَبَيْنَهُمْ رَدْمًا آتُونِي زُبَرَ الْحَدِيدِ حَتَّى
إِذَا سَاوَى بَيْنَ الصَّدَفَيْنِ قَالَ انفُخُوا حَتَّى إِذَا جَعَلَهُ نَارًا قَالَ آتُونِي أُفْرِغْ عَلَيْهِ قِطْرًا فَمَا
اسْطَاعُوا أَن يَظْهَرُوهُ وَمَا اسْتَطَاعُوا لَهُ نَقْبًا قَالَ هَٰذَا رَحْمَةٌ مِّن رَّبِّي فَإِذَا جَاءَ وَعْدُ رَبِّي
جَعَلَهُ دَكَّاءَ وَكَانَ وَعْدُ رَبِّي حَقًّا

Until, when he reached (a place) between two mountains, he found, before them a people who scarcely understood a word. They said: O Dhul-Qarnayn! Gog and Magog are making great mischief on earth: shall we then render you a tribute in order that you might erect a barrier between us and them?

He said: (The power) in which my Lord has established me is better (than tribute). Help me therefore with strength (and labor). I will erect a strong barrier between you and them. Bring me blocks of iron. At length, when he had filled up the space between the two steep mountainsides, He said, "Blow (with your bellows)." Then, when he had made it (red) as fire, he said: Bring me, that I may pour over it, molten copper. Thus (Gog and Magog) were made powerless to scale it or to dig through it. He said: This is a mercy from my Lord. But when the promise of my Lord comes to pass, He will make it into dust; and the promise of my Lord is true.

(al-Kahf 18:93-98)

The Prophet ﷺ said that there will come a time after 'Isā عليه السلام when there will be no more problems or hatred in the world. Then a tremendous enemy, Gog and Magog (Yā'jūj and Mā'jūj), will come and spread everywhere on earth as mentioned in the verses above. Imām Suyūtī described these people in his *tafsīr ad-Durr al-manthūr*. They have small eyes, and red or yellowish hair. Some have ears so large that they can use one ear as a mattress and the other ear like a blanket. They have hair on their bodies to protect them from extremes of temperature. Their height and width are equal. Some are the size of a man or smaller and of equal width. Some are one-hundred twenty arms-lengths in height and girth. Nothing can stand in front of them, neither man nor mountain. They will come from every direction and invade the earth.

حدثنا يحيى بن بكير: حدثنا الليث، عن عقيل، عن ابن شهاب، عن عروة بن الزبير: أن زينب
بنت أبي سلمة حدثته، عن أم حبيبة بنت أبي سفيان، عن زينب بنت جحش رضي الله عنهن:
أن النبي صلى الله عليه وسلم دخل عليها فزعا يقول لا إله إلا الله، ويل للعرب من شر اقترب، فتح
اليوم من ردم يأجوج ومأجوج مثل هذه وحلق بإصبعه الإبهام والتي تليها، قالت زينب بنت جحش
فقلت يا رسول الله، أنهلك وفينا الصالحون؟ قال نعم، إذا كثر الخبث(البخاري في أحاديث
الأنبياء)

Zaynab bint Jahsh, *Umm ul-Mu'minīn* (Mother of the Believers)
related that the Prophet 喿 once came to her shaking in a state
of fear and said, "There is no god but Allāh! Woe unto the
Arabs from a danger that has come near. An opening has
been made in the wall of Gog and Magog like this," making a
circle with his thumb and index finger. She said, "O Allāh's
Messenger! Shall we be destroyed even though there are
(some) pious persons among us?" He said, "Yes, when
corruption[294] is widespread."[295]

Fourteen hundred years ago there was only a small opening in the barrier
of Gog and Magog and the Prophet 喿 was trembling at the tremendous
calamity coming to his community from their invasion. Muslims today are so
much closer to the time of Gog and Magog, yet they are heedless, unconcerned
with their arrival.

Many Muslims just sit, relaxed and happy in front of their televisions,
forgetting Allāh 喿 and heedless of their Afterlife. This heedlessness has
reached the extent that when prayer time comes, some Muslims leave their
televisions on so as not to miss any of the show they are watching while they
are praying. Instead of concentrating on their prayer, they pay attention to their
television. On television all kinds of corruption (*khubth*) and obscenity are
being broadcast, with people provocatively dressed—even boasting on talk
shows about how much fornication they have done. People are proud of this
degraded behavior. This is the corruption the Prophet 喿 said would happen
before the appearance of Yā'jūj and Mā'jūj. In the time of the Prophet 喿 the
hole through which Yā'jūj and Mā'jūj will break through was opened slightly,
so with the ubiquitous fornication (*zinā*) of today it must have spread wide
allowing them to burst forth. Such behavior is an invitation for Yā'jūj and
Mā'jūj to overwhelm humanity.

In the Holy Qur'ān it is mentioned that Dhul-Qarnayn 喿 has made a wall

---

[294] *Khubth*—specifically fornication, *zinā*.
[295] *Sahīh Bukhārī*, "Kitāb al-Fitan."

to prevent Yā'jūj and Mā'jūj from coming out.[296] Imām Suyūtī in his explanation of *Sūrat al-Kahf* (chapter 18) relates that the wall is one hundred miles long and two hundred and fifty yards high. That wall will be destroyed, and Yā'jūj and Mā'jūj will appear and devour the whole world. They are going to drink all the water on earth, consume everything on earth, and not leave anything. Yā'jūj and Mā'jūj are behind the barrier, trying to break through every day. One day they will say, *inshā'Allāh* we will break through tomorrow,' and with the blessing of saying *inshā'Allāh* (God willing) they will be allowed to go through.

حدثنا محمد بن بشار وغير واحد – المعنى واحد – واللفظ لمحمد بن بشار، قالوا أخبرنا هشام بن عبد الملك، أخبرنا أبو عوانة عن قتادة عن أبي رافع عن حديث أبي هريرة عن النبي صلى الله عليه وسلم في السد قال

يحفرونه كل يوم حتى إذا كادوا يخرقونه قال الذي عليهم ارجعوا فستخرقونه غدا، قال، فيعيده الله كأمثل ما كان حتى إذا بلغ مدتهم وأراد الله أن يبعثهم على الناس قال الذي عليهم ارجعوا فستخرقونه غدا إن شاء الله، واستثنى، قال: فيرجعون فيجدونه كهيئته حين تركوه، فيخرقونه ويخرقونه ويخرجون على الناس فيستقون المياه، ويفر الناس منهم فيرمون بسهامهم إلى السماء فترجع مخضبة بالدماء، فيقولون: قهرنا من في الأرض وعلونا من في السماء قسوة وعلوا، فيبعث الله عليهم نغفا في أقفائهم فيهلكون . قال فوالذي نفس محمد بيده إن دواب الأرض تسمن وتبطر وتشكر شكرا من لحومهم (الترمذي في أبواب التفسير– سورة الكهف)

Abū Hurayra ⸰ related that the Prophet ⸰ said:

> Every day Gog and Magog are trying to dig a way out through the barrier. When they begin to see sunlight through it, their leader says, "Go back, you can continue digging tomorrow," and when they come back the barrier is stronger than it was before. This will continue until their time comes and Allāh wishes to send them forth. They will dig until they begin to see sunlight, then the one who is in charge of them will say, "Go back, you can continue digging tomorrow, *in sha'Allāh*." In this case he will make an exception by saying *insha'Allāh*, thus relating the matter to Allāh's will. They will return on the following day, and find the hole as they left it. They will continue digging and come out against the people. They will drink all the water, and the people will hide themselves in their fortresses. Gog and Magog will fire their arrows into the sky, and they will fall back to earth bloodied. Gog and Magog will say, "We have defeated the people of earth, and overcome the

---

people of heaven." Then Allāh will send a kind of worm in
the napes of their necks, and they will be killed by it. By Him
in Whose hand is the soul of Muhammad, the beasts of the
earth will become plump.[297]

The Prophet ﷺ mentioned that when Yā'jūj and Mā'jūj appear they will
descend on humanity. At that time Sayyidinā 'Isā عليه السلام will be gone, (or in some
narrations he will still be present on earth), and the believers will flee to their
homes to escape from Yā'jūj and Mā'jūj. Their massive troops will come upon
Lake Tiberias and drink it dry. Yā'jūj and Mā'jūj are millions strong, moving
together. After they have killed everything and drunk all the water there will be
some Muslims hiding in their homes. Yā'jūj and Mā'jūj will say, "We have
finished with the people of the earth. Now we have to finish with the people of
heaven." Like Nimrod they will shoot at the heavens, and Allāh ﷻ will make
them see their arrows fall down bloodied. Then they will say, "We have
finished the heavens." Yā'jūj and Mā'jūj will first finish with the Muslims then
direct their attack to the heavens, directly against Allāh ﷻ. While this will
physically take place in the future, the ideological attack has already begun.
Atheists are openly attacking religion, religious people, and even coming
directly against Allāh Almighty.

أخرج نعيم بن حماد في الفتن وابن مردويه بسند واه، عن ابن عباس رضي الله عنهما قال، قال
رسول الله صلى الله عليه وسلم بعثني الله ليلة أُسري بي إلى يأجوج ومأجوج، فدعوتهم إلى دين الله
وعبادته فأبوا أن يجيبوني، فهم في النار مع من عصى من ولد آدم وولد إبليس" (درر المنثور)

The Prophet ﷺ said that on the night of *Isra'* and *Mi'raj*, he was sent as a
messenger to Gog and Magog:

> I called them to Islam and to Allāh and they refused. They are
> going to be in Hellfire with those who disobeyed from the
> children of Adam عليه السلام and the children of Satan (*Iblīs*).[298]

---

[297] *Tirmidhī*, "Abwāb Tafsīr," *Sūrat al-Kahf*.
[298] Suyūtī, *Durr al-Manthūr*, explanation of *Sūrat al-Kahf*.

The Destruction of the Ka'ba

After the appearance of Yā'jūj and Mā'jūj, one of the signs of the Last Days mentioned in the books of authentic hadiths is the destruction of the Ka'ba, its decorations and the removal of its covering, *kiswa*. This will happen both figuratively and literally, with the final stage being the physical dismantlement of the Ka'ba. The Ka'ba is the focal point from whence Islam originated. Unfortunately, the physical structure of the building is all that remains today from that time. All the relics of the Ka'ba from the time of the Companions and their Successors have been removed by the followers of the Wahhābi ideology. There was even an attempt to remove *Maqām Ibrāhīm*. The Wahhābi sect has also dismantled the ideological foundations of Islam and destroyed the Ka'ba's essence, which is the authentic understanding and teachings of Islam. The following is an introduction to the coming, actual demolition of the Ka'ba by *Dhu-Suwayqatayn*, who comes in the Last Days.

A man from Ethiopia, called *Dhu-Suwayqatayn*, which means a man with very thin weak legs, will destroy the Ka'ba.

حدثنا علي بن عبد الله: حدثنا سفيان: حدثنا زياد بن سعد، عن الزهري، عن سعيد بن المسيب، عن أبي هريرة رضي الله عنه، عن النبي صلى الله عليه وسلم قال يخرب الكعبة ذو السويقتين من الحبشة من الحبشة (أخرجه الترمذي)

Abū Hurayra ﷺ related that the Prophet ﷺ said, "*Dhu-Suwayqatayn* from Ethiopia will demolish the Ka'ba."[299]

The Prophet ﷺ described his appearance in detail.

حدثنا عمرو بن علي: حدثنا يحيى بن سعيد: حدثنا عبيد الله بن الأخنس: حدثني ابن أبي مليكة، عن ابن عباس رضي الله عنهما، عن النبي صلى الله عليه وسلم قال كأني به أسود أفحج، يقلعها حجرا حجرا (أخرجه البخاري في كتاب الحج)

Ibn 'Abbās ﷺ said he heard the Prophet ﷺ saying, "It is as if I am seeing him, he is black, bow-legged and he will dismantle (the Ka'ba) stone by stone."[300]

Allāh's revenge came on Abrāha when he tried to destroy the Ka'ba in the time of the Prophet's grandfather. Allāh ﷺ mentioned this in the Holy Qur'ān:

---

[299] *Tirmidhī*. Another version is narrated by 'Abd Allāh Ibn 'Amr Ibn al-'As, Āhmad in his *Musnad* (2:220). Haythamī, *Majma' az-zawā'id*(3:301). "*Yakhrub al-Ka'bata dhu-suwayqatayni min al-habasha.*"

[300] *Sahīh Bukhārī*, (2:59) "Kitāb al-Hajj," Chapter on the Destruction of the Ka'ba. "*Ka-annī bihi aswadun afhajun yaqlā'uha hajjaran hajjara [ya'nī al-Ka'bata].*"

أَلَمْ تَرَ كَيْفَ فَعَلَ رَبُّكَ بِأَصْحَابِ الْفِيلِ أَلَمْ يَجْعَلْ كَيْدَهُمْ فِي تَضْلِيلٍ وَأَرْسَلَ عَلَيْهِمْ طَيْرًا
أَبَابِيلَ تَرْمِيهِم بِحِجَارَةٍ مِّن سِجِّيلٍ فَجَعَلَهُمْ كَعَصْفٍ مَّأْكُولٍ

Did you not see how your Lord dealt with the Companions of the
Elephant? Did He not make their treacherous plan go astray? And He
sent against them Flights of Birds. Striking them with stones of sijjeel. Then
did He make them like an empty field of stalks and straw, which has been
eaten up. (al-Fīl 105:1-5)

Allāh ﷻ sent birds from heaven carrying small burning pebbles from Hellfire (*sijjīl*), which were like asteroids or lasers. A large stone may knock someone dead, but a small pebble from a bird cannot do the same damage. Yet, these searing hot, explosive pebbles from Hellfire completely annihilated Abrāha's army. As soon as these stones hit the ground they destroyed Abrāha's army, disintegrating them from their intense heat. There were thousands of soldiers, but not one was buried because there were no remains left. They came to demolish the Ka'ba, and Allāh ﷻ destroyed them. Finally, in the Last Days, Allāh ﷻ will allow the Ka'ba to be dismantled.

JUDGMENT DAY

THE APPROACH OF THE HOUR

Final Events

In the previous sections we have discussed the signs of the Last Days as described by Prophet Muhammad ﷺ and their manifestations in recent times. The Prophet ﷺ told us of the signs of the Last Days, but exactly when the Judgment Day will occur is known only to Allāh ﷻ. These signs are indicators that the Judgment Day is near, when Allāh ﷻ will judge all of humanity. As Allāh ﷻ said in the Holy Qur'ān:

يَسْأَلُونَكَ عَنِ السَّاعَةِ أَيَّانَ مُرْسَاهَا قُلْ إِنَّمَا عِلْمُهَا عِندَ رَبِّي لاَ يُجَلِّيهَا لِوَقْتِهَا إِلاَّ هُوَ ثَقُلَتْ فِي السَّمَاوَاتِ وَالأَرْضِ لاَ تَأْتِيكُمْ إِلاَّ بَغْتَةً يَسْأَلُونَكَ كَأَنَّكَ حَفِيٌّ عَنْهَا قُلْ إِنَّمَا عِلْمُهَا عِندَ اللهِ وَلَكِنَّ أَكْثَرَ النَّاسِ لاَ يَعْلَمُونَ

They ask thee about the (final) Hour, when will be its appointed time? Say:
"The knowledge thereof is with my Lord (alone): none but He can reveal as
to when it will occur. Heavily will it weigh on the heavens and the earth. It
will come to you suddenly." They ask you as if you were eager in search
thereof. Say: The knowledge thereof is with Allāh (alone), but most men
know not. (al-A'rāf 7:187)

يَسْأَلُونَكَ عَنِ السَّاعَةِ أَيَّانَ مُرْسَاهَا(42) فِيمَ أَنتَ مِن ذِكْرَاهَا(43) إِلَى رَبِّكَ مُنتَهَاهَا(44) إِنَّمَا أَنتَ مُنذِرُ مَن يَخْشَاهَا(45) كَأَنَّهُمْ يَوْمَ يَرَوْنَهَا لَمْ يَلْبَثُوا إِلا عَشِيَّةً أَوْ ضُحَاهَا(46)

They ask you about the Hour, 'When will be its appointed time?' Wherein
are you (concerned) with the declaration thereof? With your Lord is the
limit fixed thereof. Thou art but a warner for such as fear it. The Day they
will see it, (it will be) as if they had tarried but a single evening, or (at most
till) the following morn!
(an-Nāzi'āt 79:42-46)

Even if someone were to live for a hundred years his life will be as a dream when the Hour comes to pass. Some think that there is no Day of Reckoning, and that this world will keep going for millions of years. However, these verses explain that Judgment Day will come suddenly, at a time which only Allāh ﷻ

knows. The small signs of the Last Days (*'alamāt as-sughra*) mentioned by the Prophet ﷺ have occurred, so every Muslim and truly every human being must take notice.

ه حدثنا أحمد بن المقدام: حدثنا الفضيل بن سليمان: حدثنا أبو حازم: حدثنا سهل بن سعد
رضي الله عنه قال:
رأيت رسول الله صلى الله عليه وسلم قال بإصبعيه هكذا، بالوسطى والتي تلي الإبهام: (بعثت أنا
والساعة كهاتين (أخرجه البخاري في كتاب التفسير)

One cannot suppose that it is very far off because the Prophet ﷺ said, "I was sent so close to the Judgment Day like these two fingers (and he held up the forefinger and the middle one)."[301]

Indeed, in every prayer Muslims read *Sūrat al-Fatiha*, in which Allāh ﷺ is referred to as *"Owner of the Judgment Day"* (*māliki yawm id-dīn*). Despite this, Muslims act as if it will not happen.

اقْتَرَبَ لِلنَّاسِ حِسَابُهُمْ وَهُمْ فِي غَفْلَةٍ مَّعْرِضُونَ

Closer and closer to mankind comes their Reckoning: yet they heed not and they turn away. (Al-Anbiyā' 21:1)

The Prophet ﷺ said that Islam will slowly disappear. At the end of time, people will no longer know what kind of prayer they are performing, or be cognizant of their fasting, and charity will not be given.

حدثنا علي بن محمد حدثنا أبو معاوية عن أبي مالك الأشجعي عن ربعي بن حراش عن حذيفة
بن اليمان قال
قال رسول الله صلى الله عليه وسلم يدرس الإسلام كما يدرس وشي الثوب حتى لا يدرى ما
صيام ولا صلاة ولا نسك ولا صدقة وليسرى على كتاب الله عز وجل في ليلة فلا يبقى في الأرض
منه آية وتبقى طوائف من الناس الشيخ الكبير والعجوز يقولون أدركنا آباءنا على هذه الكلمة لا إله
إلا الله فنحن نقولها
فقال له صلة ما تغني عنهم لا إله إلا الله وهم لا يدرون ما صلاة ولا صيام ولا نسك ولا صدقة
فأعرض عنه حذيفة ثم ردها عليه ثلاثا كل ذلك يعرض عنه حذيفة ثم أقبل عليه في الثالثة فقال يا
صلة تنجيهم من النار ثلاثا (أخرجه ابن ماجه في كتاب الفتن)

Hudhayfa Ibn al-Yaman ﷺ related that the Prophet ﷺ said:

---

[301] *Sahīh Bukhārī*, (8:510) "Kitāb al-Tafsīr." *Sūrat an-Nazi'āt*.

Islam will have deteriorated like clothes deteriorate, until there will be no one who knows what fasting, prayer, charity and rituals are. The Qur'ān will disappear in one night, and no verse of it will be left on earth. Some groups of old people will be left who will say, "We heard our fathers saying *Lā ilāha illa Allāh,* so we repeated it." Silah asked Hudhayfa ◈, "What will saying *Lā ilāha illa Allāh* do for them when they do not know what prayer, fasting, ritual and charity are?" Hudhayfa ◈ ignored him; then Silah repeated his question three times, and each time Hudayfa ◈ ignored him. Finally he answered, "O Silah, it will save them from Hell," and said it three times.[302]

حدثنا عبد بن حميد . أخبرنا عبدالرزاق . أخبرنا معمر عن ثابت، عن أنس، قال: قال رسول الله صلى الله عليه وسلم:

لا تقوم الساعة على أحد يقول الله الله (أخرجه مسلم في كتاب الإيمان)

The Prophet ﷺ said, "Judgment Day will not come on anyone who is saying 'Allāh, Allāh.'"[303]

This means that the Judgment Day will only come when no one is calling on his Lord. That is, there will only be unbelievers left on earth.

Allāh ﷻ said in the Holy Qur'ān:

وَيَوْمَ يُنفَخُ فِي الصُّورِ فَفَزِعَ مَن فِي السَّمَاوَاتِ وَمَن فِي الْأَرْضِ إِلَّا مَن شَاءَ

And the Day when the Trumpet will be sounded, then will be smitten with terror those who are in the heavens, and those who are on earth, except such as Allāh will please (to exempt)... (an-Naml 27/87)

When Allāh ﷻ orders Angel Isrāfīl ﷺ to blow the Trumpet everything in this world will disappear. Even inhabitants of the heavens *(samāwāt)* will also completely vanish, except for those whom Allāh ﷻ wishes to remain. Angel Isrāfīl ﷺ will sound the first blast of the Trumpet, causing complete destruction. The whole earth will shake and disintegrate into dust, and there will be nothing left except what Allāh ﷻ wills.

Allāh ﷻ will order Isrāfīl ﷺ to blow the Trumpet again, but instead of destruction, the second blast will resurrect all creation. Allāh ﷻ is showing His Power and Greatness that with the same Trumpet He can make everyone die and make everyone alive again.

---

[302] *Ibn Mājah. Albānī, Silsila sahīha,* # 87.
[303] *Muslim,* "Kitāb al-Īmān."

وَمَا قَدَرُوا اللَّهَ حَقَّ قَدْرِهِ وَالْأَرْضُ جَمِيعاً قَبْضَتُهُ يَوْمَ الْقِيَامَةِ وَالسَّمَاوَاتُ مَطْوِيَّاتٌ بِيَمِينِهِ سُبْحَانَهُ وَتَعَالَى عَمَّا يُشْرِكُونَ(67) وَنُفِخَ فِي الصُّورِ فَصَعِقَ مَنْ فِي السَّمَاوَاتِ وَمَنْ فِي الْأَرْضِ إِلَّا مَنْ شَاءَ اللَّهُ ثُمَّ نُفِخَ فِيهِ أُخْرَى فَإِذَا هُمْ قِيَامٌ يَنْظُرُونَ(68) وَأَشْرَقَتِ الْأَرْضُ بِنُورِ رَبِّهَا وَوُضِعَ الْكِتَابُ وَجِيءَ بِالنَّبِيِّينَ وَالشُّهَدَاءِ وَقُضِيَ بَيْنَهُمْ بِالْحَقِّ وَهُمْ لَا يُظْلَمُونَ

No just estimate have they made of Allah, such as is due to Him: On the Day of Judgment the whole of the earth will be but His handful, and the heavens will be rolled up in His right hand: Glory to Him! High is He above the Partners they attribute to Him! The Trumpet will (just) be sounded, when all that are in the heavens and on earth will swoon, except such as it will please Allah (to exempt). Then it will be sounded another time, and, behold, they will all be standing and looking on! (az-Zumar 39:67-69)

The Coccyx Remains

The Prophet ﷺ gave an indication about how people will be re-created at the Resurrection, and this has been confirmed with the help of modern technological advances.

حدثنا عمر بن حفص: حدثنا أبي قال: حدثنا الأعمش قال: سمعت أبا صالح قال: سمعت أبا
هريرة، عن النبي صلى الله عليه وسلم قال:
بين النفختين أربعون. قالوا يا أبا هريرة، أربعون يوما ؟ قال أبيت، قال أربعون سنة ؟ قال أبيت، قال
أربعون شهرا ؟ قال أبيت وبلى كل شيء من الإنسان إلا عجب ذنبه، فيه يُركب الخلق (أخرجه
البُخاري في كتاب تفسير القرآن)

Abū Hurayra ؓ related that the Prophet ﷺ said:

Between the two blasts of the Trumpet there will be forty.
The people said, "O Abū Hurayra! Forty days?" He refused to
reply. They said, "Forty years?" He refused to reply and
added: "Everything of the human body will decay except the
coccyx and from that bone Allāh will reconstruct the whole
body."[304]

حدثنا عبد الله حدثني أبي حدثنا علي بن حفص أنبأنا ورقاء عن أبي الزناد عن الأعرج عن أبي
هريرة قال قال رسول الله صلى الله عليه وسلم
-كل ابن آدم تأكله الأرض إلا عجب الذنب فإنه منه خلق ومنه يركب. (أخرجه الإمام مالك في
الجنائز و غيره)

Abū Hurayra ؓ also related that the Prophet ﷺ said:

The earth eats all of the human being except the coccyx. He
was created from it, and on it he is built.[305]

Fourteen hundred years ago the Prophet ﷺ said that with death, the whole body is consumed by the earth, except for the coccyx. Muslim scientists could not understand this hadith in the past, because when a grave was opened they would not find the coccyx bone as all the remains were disintegrated. Scientists were finally able to unravel the secret behind this hadith of the Prophet ﷺ using the sophisticated techniques of DNA analysis. Scientists took a sample of the coccyx and subjected it to the most severe stresses imaginable. They crushed it under high pressure, boiled it, and even cremated it, yet no matter what they did it was impossible to destroy the DNA contained in the coccyx.

---

[304] *Sahīh Bukhārī* (6:338).
[305] Imām Mālik's *Muwatta*, Book 16.

Under conditions which annihilate all other bones and cells, the remnant of the coccyx somehow survived thereby preserving the DNA of that person. Each cell of the human body contains the entire genetic blueprint for the whole body, and this microscopic remnant of the coccygeal DNA contains sufficient information to recreate the entire human being.

Such information, bestowed by Allāh on the Prophet so many centuries ago, show Allāh's Greatness, our smallness and are a powerful evidence to believers that their time would be better spent in seeking the benefit of the afterlife with the fervour most spend in pursuing the interests and pleasures of this temporary life.

The Coccyx and Embryology

The last hadith mentions that the human being is "constructed" from the coccyx, "He was created from it, and on it he is built." An examination of this in light of modern embryological findings is revealing. At approximately two weeks of age, the developing embryo separates from the placenta until there is no contact between the two except via a connecting stalk at the embryo's caudal-most end which is the future location of the coccyx.[306] This stalk is the precursor to the umbilical cord, which will connect the developing embryo to its nourishment from the placenta. Not only is the source of nutrition coming into the embryo from the caudal end (coccyx), but the embryo's formation also progresses from the starting point of the coccyx.

The embryo's orientation and subsequent development begins when a line called the "primitive streak" forms at the caudal end (coccyx) of the embryo and proceeds towards the cranial end (head). Development proceeds from this point, and the final phase of the neural tube closure is again at the caudal end—at the area of the coccyx—from whence it began. Fourten hundred years ago the Prophet ﷺ described the coccyx and human development, saying mankind "was created from it, and on it he is built."

Such discoveries are enough, O mankind, to realize the Glory of He Whose Greatness knows no bounds and Whose Superiority over His Creation is incomprehensible. It is sufficient as confirmation that we are endlessly in need of His forgiveness, His love and His tender mercy.

٭﷽٭

---

[306] Early Embryogenesis. Dr. David Rapaport. UCSD Department of Surgery, Division of Anatomy.

The Coccygeal Remnant and the Resurrection

With the first trumpet blast Allāh ﷻ destroys everything, and with the second trumpet blast human beings and creation will be brought back to life. Then Allāh ﷻ will send a rain for forty days which reaches the height of seventy arm-lengths.

حدثنا أبو كريب، محمد بن العلاء . حدثنا أبو معاوية عن الأعمش، عن أبي صالح، عن أبي هريرة،
قال:

قال رسول الله صلى الله عليه وسلم ما بين النفختين أربعون قالوا يا أبا هريرة أربعون يوما ؟ قال
أبيت .قالوا أربعون شهرا ؟ قال أبيت قالوا أربعون سنة؟ قال أبيت ثم ينزل الله من السماء ماء
فينبتون كما ينبت البقل ، قال وليس من الإنسان شيء إلا بلى إلا عظما واحدا وهو عجب
الذنب ومنه يركب الخلق يوم القيامة (أخرجه البخاري في كتاب تفسير و مسلم في كتاب الفتن)

Abū Hurayra ؆ related that the Prophet ﷺ said:

> ...Allāh will send down rain that makes the people grow like vegetables. Every part of the human body will be destroyed except the coccyx. By it Allāh will reconstruct the whole body.[307]

Every drop of that rain will be composed of sperm which will connect to the "egg" of each person—that being the remains of the coccyx—in order to re-create that person.

Allāh ﷺ said in the Holy Qur'ān:

وَمِنْ آيَاتِهِ أَنَّكَ تَرَى الْأَرْضَ خَاشِعَةً فَإِذَا أَنزَلْنَا عَلَيْهَا الْمَاءَ اهْتَزَّتْ وَرَبَتْ إِنَّ الَّذِي أَحْيَاهَا
لَمُحْيِي الْمَوْتَى إِنَّهُ عَلَى كُلِّ شَيْءٍ قَدِيرٌ

And among His Signs is this: thou seest the earth barren and desolate; but when We send down rain to it, it is stirred to life and yields increase. Truly, He Who gives life to the (dead) earth can surely give life to (people) who are dead. For He has power over all things. (Fussilat 41:39)

Allāh ﷺ said:

إِذَا زُلْزِلَتِ الْأَرْضُ زِلْزَالَهَا وَأَخْرَجَتِ الْأَرْضُ أَثْقَالَهَا

---

[307] *Sahīh Bukhārī. Sahīh Muslim* (9:p. 92). *Riyād as-sālihīn* #1836:
Wa yablā kullu shay'in min al-insāni illa 'ajb adh-dhanab fīhī yurakkab ul-khalq. Thumma yunazzilu Allāhu min as-samā'i mā'an, fayanbutūna kamā yanbut ul-baql.

When the earth is shaken to its (utmost) convulsion, and the earth brings forth its burdens (from within).... (al-Zalzala 99:1-2)

The way a sieve is shaken to separate different sized particles, the earth will shake and bring out the coccygeal remnants. Allāh ﷻ will bring out all these remnants by sifting the whole earth so that each one may meet its destined raindrop. Allāh ﷻ will recreate the earth and bring back each man, woman, and child as they were.

Events of Judgment Day

B ecause the advent of the resurrection will occur so suddenly, mankind will be amazed at how they have been brought back..

وَنُفِخَ فِي الصُّورِ فَإِذَا هُم مِّنَ الْأَجْدَاثِ إِلَى رَبِّهِمْ يَنسِلُونَ قَالُوا يَا وَيْلَنَا مَن بَعَثَنَا مِن مَّرْقَدِنَا هَذَا مَا وَعَدَ الرَّحْمَنُ وَصَدَقَ الْمُرْسَلُونَ

The trumpet shall be sounded, when behold! They will hasten forth from their graves to their Lord! They will say: Ah! Woe unto us! Who has raised us up from our place of sleep? (Yā Sīn 36: 51-52)

In other verses Allāh ﷻ says:

فَإِذَا نُقِرَ فِي النَّاقُورِ فَذَلِكَ يَوْمَئِذٍ يَوْمٌ عَسِيرٌ عَلَى الْكَافِرِينَ غَيْرُ يَسِيرٍ

For when the Trumpet is sounded, surely that day will be a day of anguish, for the unbelievers, anything but easy. (al-Muddaththir 74:8-10)

وَقَالَ الْإِنسَانُ مَا لَهَا يَوْمَئِذٍ تُحَدِّثُ أَخْبَارَهَا بِأَنَّ رَبَّكَ أَوْحَى لَهَا

And the human being cries (distressed): "What is the matter with it?" On that day [the earth] shall tell its news, for that your Lord will have inspired it. (az-Zalzala 99:3-5)

Allāh ﷻ will reveal to the earth to report what everyone did in this life.

فَمَن يَعْمَلْ مِثْقَالَ ذَرَّةٍ خَيْراً يَرَهُ وَمَن يَعْمَلْ مِثْقَالَ ذَرَّةٍ شَرّاً يَرَهُ

Whoever has done an atom's weight of good will see it then, and whoever has done an atom's weight of evil shall see it. (az-Zalzala 99:6-8).

On that day some faces will be enlightened from Allāh's mercy because of their good deeds and some faces are going to be darkened with Allāh's punishment from their evil deeds.

وُجُوهٌ يَوْمَئِذٍ مُّسْفِرَةٌ ضَاحِكَةٌ مُّسْتَبْشِرَةٌ وَوُجُوهٌ يَوْمَئِذٍ عَلَيْهَا غَبَرَةٌ تَرْهَقُهَا قَتَرَةٌ

Some faces on that Day will be beaming, laughing, rejoicing at good news; And other faces on that Day will be covered with dust veiled in darkness.

(ʿAbasa 80:38-41)

Judgment Day is a truly fearsome event wherein Allāh ﷻ will gather all humanity and judge them according to what they have done in this life.

وَتَرَكْنَا بَعْضَهُمْ يَوْمَئِذٍ يَمُوجُ فِي بَعْضٍ وَنُفِخَ فِي الصُّورِ فَجَمَعْنَاهُمْ جَمْعًا

On that day We shall leave them to surge like waves on one another: the Trumpet will be blown, and We shall collect them all together.

(al-Kahf 18:99)

Humankind and jinn—other creations of Allāh who are possessed of intelligence and free will and are therefore held responsible for their deeds—will be left surging like waves upon one another. Allāh ﷻ is saying that He will gather everyone on the Day of Judgment. No one will be excluded, whether a king, president, or common person, whether human being or jinn. People will be stunned and worried, like fish out of water, flopping around, not knowing what to say, and afraid of Allāh ﷻ. According to the hadith of the Prophet ﷺ:

> The happiest and most tranquil people on that Day are those people who can find a place to put their toes on the ground.

Sweating

At the Final Judgment there will be no place to stand; everyone will be crowded one above the other on that horrible day. It will be a grave day, the likes of which people could never imagine. The sun will be overhead beating down on the people so intensely that it will heat their brains.

حدثنا الحكم بن موسى، أبو صالح. حدثنا يحيى بن حمزة عن عبدالرحمن بن جابر. حدثني سليم
بن عامر حدثني المقداد بن الأسود قال
سمعت رسول الله صلى الله عليه وسلم يقول تدني الشمس يوم القيامة من الخلق حتى تكون منهم
كمقدار ميل
قال سليم بن عامر فوالله! ما أدري ما يعني بالميل أمسافة الأرض أم الميل الذي تكحل به العين،
قال فيكون الناس على قدر أعمالهم في العرق (مسلم في باب القيامة)

Everyone will be sweating, as the Prophet ﷺ said:

People will be covered in sweat according to their deeds.[308]

Some people might be covered in sweat up to their knees, some up to their heads, some people to their mouth, and some people will be drowning in their sweat. Abū Hurayra ﷺ narrated another hadith of the Prophet ﷺ that the people going to Hellfire will be sweating so much that it will reach the height of seventy arm-lengths, like a river engulfing and drowning them. The sun will be burning down over their heads. There will be no shade except for Allāh's shade, which He will send over the believers.

وَعَرَضْنَا جَهَنَّمَ يَوْمَئِذٍ لِّلْكَافِرِينَ

And We shall present hell that day for unbelievers to see, all spread out.

(al-Kahf 18:100)

Allāh ﷺ will display Hell for the unbelievers to behold. Allāh ﷺ will order angels to bring Hell. The Prophet ﷺ said that *Jahannam* (Hell) has 70,000 bridles; each bridle is pulled by 70,000 angels. It will block the whole horizon, blocking the way out, the way to Paradise. Everyone will be worried because no one will be able to reach Paradise except by crossing the Bridge over Hell, the *Sirāt al-Mustaqīm*, the Straight Way. Every human being will have to cross over it, as Allāh ﷺ mentioned in the Holy Qur'ān:

وَإِن مِّنكُمْ إِلَّا وَارِدُهَا كَانَ عَلَى رَبِّكَ حَتْمًا مَّقْضِيًّا

---

[308] Narrated from al-Miqdād by *Muslim*, *Tirmidhī*, and *Āhmad*.

There is not one of you but will pass over it: this is, with thy Lord, a fixed Decree. (Maryam 19:71)

Allāh ﷻ said in the Holy Qur'ān:

وَنَحْشُرُهُمْ يَوْمَ الْقِيَامَةِ عَلَى وُجُوهِهِمْ عُمْيًا وَبُكْمًا وَصُمًّا

On Judgment Day We will take them to hellfire blind, deaf and dumb, (al-Isrā' 17:97)

and in another verse:

الَّذِينَ يُحْشَرُونَ عَلَى وُجُوهِهِمْ إِلَى جَهَنَّمَ أُوْلَئِكَ شَرٌّ مَكَانًا وَأَضَلُّ سَبِيلاً

Those who will be dragged on their faces to Hell.... (al-Furqān 25:34)

Because of their evil ways in this life the unbelievers will be ushered into Hell.

حدثنا عبد الله بن محمد حدثنا يونس بن محمد البغدادي حدثنا شيبان عن قتادة حدثنا أنس بن مالك رضي الله عنه أن رجلا قال يا نبي الله كيف يحشر الكافر على وجهه يوم القيامة؟ قال أليس الذي أمشاه على الرجلين في الدنيا قادرا على أن يمشيه على وجهه يوم القيامة (أخرجه البخاري في كتاب تفسير القرآن و مسلم في كتاب صفة القيامة و الجنة و النار)

Anas Ibn Malik ﷺ reported:

> A man asked the Prophet ﷺ, "O Prophet of Allāh! How can the unbeliever move on his face on Judgment Day?" The Prophet ﷺ answered, "Cannot the One (Allāh) Who made him to walk on his legs, also make him walk on his face on Judgment Day?"[309]

Allāh ﷻ describes the unbelievers who will be put in Hell and what they were doing in this life.

الَّذِينَ كَانَتْ أَعْيُنُهُمْ فِي غِطَاءٍ عَنْ ذِكْرِي وَكَانُوا لاَ يَسْتَطِيعُونَ سَمْعًا

Those (unbelievers) whose eyes had been under a veil from My Remembrance and who had been unable even to hear. (al-Kahf 18:101)

Unbelievers were veiled and did not want to remember Allāh ﷻ or even hear His Remembrance, *dhikr.* Allāh ﷻ is saying to always remember Him in your heart and by your tongue, as mentioned in countless verses of the Qur'ān

---

[309] *Sahīh Bukhārī* and *Sahīh Muslim.*

and authentic narrations of the Prophet ﷺ.[310] The unbelievers were veiled from remembering Allāh ﷻ, and they did not want to listen to the Prophet ﷺ remind them. He was calling them to come, remember Allāh ﷻ, but because of their enmity to Prophet Muhammad ﷺ, they refused.

The Prophet ﷺ said that when Isrāfīl ﷺ blows the Trumpet the earth will be crystal clear, and on Judgment Day Allāh's Throne will come onto crystal clear sand. This means that there will be nothing left.

$$يَوْمَ تُبَدَّلُ الْأَرْضُ غَيْرَ الْأَرْضِ وَالسَّمَاوَاتُ وَبَرَزُوا لِلَّهِ الْوَاحِدِ الْقَهَّارِ$$

That day Allah will change the earth to a different earth. (Ibrāhīm 14:48)

All the mountains, seas, winds, stars, galaxies, and technology will disintegrate with the blowing of the Trumpet, and vanish into non-existence. Allāh ﷻ orders the earth to clean itself of all that is corrupt, vile and sinful, because His Throne can never descend to a place that is awash with sins and tyranny, killing and violence. People have been killing each other since the time of the sons of Adam ﷺ, when Cain killed his brother Abel. Allāh ﷻ requires everything to be clean for His Throne to come.

The Holy Qur'ān describes that Allāh ﷻ will ask:

$$يَوْمَ هُم بَارِزُونَ لَا يَخْفَى عَلَى اللَّهِ مِنْهُمْ شَيْءٌ لِّمَنِ الْمُلْكُ الْيَوْمَ$$

To Whom belongs the Kingdom on this day? (Ghāfir 40:16)

There will be nothing left and Allāh ﷻ will say to Himself, "To Whom is the kingdom today, who is the King of kings?" No one will be able to respond out of arrogance and pride saying, "I am a president," or "I am a king." Rather Allāh ﷻ will answer Himself saying, "The Kingdom is Mine alone."

$$لِلَّهِ الْوَاحِدِ الْقَهَّارِ$$

It belongs to Allah, the Unique, the Irresistible. (Ghāfir 40:16).

Shaykh Fakhruddin an-Nūrī, a famous scholar in his time, asked Shaykh ʿAlī Ramitanī: "Allāh ﷻ mentioned in the Holy Qur'ān that on the Day of

---

[310] When one of the Companions asked the Prophet what form of worship he could perform that would be easy, the Prophet told him: Keep your tongue moist with the remembrance of Allāh. (*Tirmidhī*, Ibn Mājah, and Āhmad from ʿAbd Allāh ibn Busr.)
Dhikr may be done by reciting *Lā ilāha illa-Allāh* as mentioned in the hadith: The best dhikr is *Lā ilāha illa-Allāh*. (*Tirmidhī* , Nasāʾī, Ibn Mājah, Ibn Hibbān, Bayhaqī in *Shuʿab al-Īmān*, from Jābir ibn ʿAbd Allāh.). One may remember Allāh by saying: "Allāh, Allāh" as Allāh mentioned: "*alā bi dhikr-Illāhi tatma'inn ul-qulūb—verily in the remembrance of Allāh do hearts find peace and satisfaction*" (ar-Raʿd 13:28); Or by calling on Allāh's Attributes: Ya Rahmān, Ya Salām, Ya Latīf, etc as the Qur'ān states: "*The most beautiful names belong to Allāh, so call on Him by them ... - wa lillāh il-asma ul-husnā fadʿuhu bihā*" (al-ʿArāf 7:180).

Promises He asked, '*Am I not your Lord?*' and is answered in the affirmative, (al-'Arāf 7:172) whereas on the Judgement Day He will ask, '*To Whom belongs the Kingdom on this day?*' (Ghāfir 40:16) and no one will answer. Why is it that they answered the question, '*Am I not your Lord?*' whereas on the Judgement Day they will not answer?" In his answer, Shaykh 'Alī Ramitanī demonstrated an incredible depth of understanding of the Holy Qur'ān and hadith when he said:

> When the first question, "*Am I not your Lord?*" was put to humankind, it was the day Allāh ﷻ had placed the obligations of the Sacred Law on all human beings. To reply when asked a question is an obligation under the Law. That is why they answered the question. However on the Judgement Day, all obligations have come to an end, and at that time, awareness of the Truth and the spiritual world begins. In spirituality there is no utterance better than silence, because spirituality is a flow moving from and to the heart, unrelated to the tongue. That is why to the second question there is no need to give an answer. Allāh ﷻ Himself answers His own question, "*To Whom belongs the Kingdom this Day?*" by saying, "*It belongs to Allāh, the Unique, the Irresistible.*"

Allāh ﷻ said in the Holy Qur'ān:

يَوْمَ يَفِرُّ الْمَرْءُ مِنْ أَخِيهِ وَأُمِّهِ وَأَبِيهِ وَصَاحِبَتِهِ وَبَنِيهِ لِكُلِّ امْرِئٍ مِّنْهُمْ يَوْمَئِذٍ شَأْنٌ يُغْنِيهِ

But when the deafening cry comes, that Day shall a man flee from his own brother and from his mother and his father, and from his wife and his children. Each one of them, that Day, will have enough concern (of his own) to make him heedless of the others. (Abasa 80:34-37)

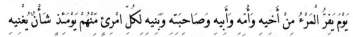

Intercession

On Judgment Day there will be no brothers, no sisters, no mothers, no fathers. Everyone will be running away from everyone else, trying to save himself. Everyone will be saying, "O myself, myself! O Allāh, forgive me! Have mercy on me."

On that Day, even those who did good in this life will realize that their deeds are insignificant before the enormous bounty and favor bestowed on them in the earthly life by Allāh. With that realization will come the fear that all of their deeds will be of little weight in the scale (al-Mīzān) when brought before the One Who administers perfect justice, al-'Adl. At that time no one will be safe from the terrors of the Judgment Day, except whom Allāh 🕮 favored with His Mercy.

حدثنا أسود بن عامر حدثنا جرير بن حازم قال سمعت محمد بن سيرين قال أخبرني أبو هريرة
قال، قال رسول الله صلى الله عليه وسلم ما منكم من أحد يدخله عمله الجنة ولا ينجيه من النار
إلا برحمة من الله وفضل قال، قالوا يا رسول الله ولا أنت قال ولا أنا إلا أن يتغمدني الله منه برحمة
قال، وقال رسول الله صلى الله عليه وسلم بيده يقبضها ويبسطها

Abū Hurayra reported Allāh's Messenger 🕮 as saying:

> None amongst you can get into Paradise by virtue of his deeds alone. They said, "Allāh's Messenger, not even you?"
> Thereupon he said, "Not even I, but that Allāh should wrap me in His Grace and Mercy."[311]

The only person who will not be saying, *Nafsī, nafsī,* "myself, myself," on the Day of dire distress is Prophet Muhammad 🕮. All other prophets' communities will run to their prophets, but they will not be able to help them. Instead, all the other prophets will ask Prophet Muhammad 🕮 to intercede for them and their communities. The Prophet 🕮 will say, "Intercession is for me" (*anā lahā*), and Allāh 🕮 will give the Prophet 🕮 permission to intercede for all the communities.

حدثنا علي بن نصر بن علي الجهضمي حدثنا عبيد الله بن عبد المجيد حدثنا زمعة بن صالح عن
سلمة بن وهرام عن عكرمة عن ابن عباس قال
جلس ناس من أصحاب رسول الله صلى الله عليه وسلم ينتظرونه، قال فخرج حتى إذا دنا منهم
سمعهم يتذاكرون فسمع حديثهم فقال بعضهم عجبا إن الله عز وجل اتخذ من خلقه خليلا اتخذ
إبراهيم خليلا وقال آخر ماذا بأعجب من كلام موسى كلمه تكليما وقال آخر فعيسى كلمة الله

---

[311] *Sahīh Muslim*, Book 39, # 6761 and many other similar narrations.

وروحه وقال آخر آدم اصطفاه الله فخرج عليهم فسلم وقال قد سمعت كلامكم وعجبكم إن
إبراهيم خليل الله وهو كذلك وموسى نجي الله وهو كذلك وعيسى روح الله وكلمته وهو كذلك
وآدم اصطفاه الله وهو كذلك ألا وأنا حبيب الله ولا فخر وأنا حامل لواء الحمد يوم القيامة ولا فخر
وأنا أول شافع وأول مشفع يوم القيامة ولا فخر وأنا أول من يحرك حلق الجنة فيفتح الله لي
فيدخلنيها ومعي فقراء المؤمنين ولا فخر وأنا أكرم الأولين والآخرين ولا فخر
قال أبو عيسى هذا حديث غرب (أخرجه الترمذي في سننه في كتاب المناقب)

Ibn 'Abbās ◈ narrated that some people close to the Prophet ﷺ came and waited for him. When he came out he approached them and heard them saying:

> What a wonder it is that Allāh Almighty and Glorious took one of His creation as His intimate Friend, Ibrāhīm ﷺ. Another one said, "What is more wonderful than His speech to Mūsā ﷺ, to whom He spoke directly!" Yet another one said, "And 'Isā ﷺ is Allāh's word and His spirit," while another one said, "Adam ﷺ was chosen by Allāh." The Prophet ﷺ said, "I heard your words, and everything you said is indeed true, and I myself am the Beloved of Allāh (habībullāh) and I say this without pride, and I carry the flag of glory on the Day of Judgment and am the first intercessor and the first whose intercession is accepted, and the first to stir the circles of Paradise so that Allāh will open it for me and I shall enter it together with the poor among my Community, and I say this without pride. I am the most honored of the First and the Last and I say this without pride."[312]

One of the keys to Allāh's Mercy is love. Love of Allāh and His Prophet Muhammad ﷺ are among the keys to Paradise. The evidence is in the following hadith:

حدثنا سليمان بن حرب حدثنا حماد بن زيد، عن ثابت، عن أنس رضي الله عنه أن رجلا سأل
النبي صلى الله عليه وسلم عن الساعة، فقال متى الساعة؟ قال وماذا أعددت لها . قال لا
شيء، إلا أني أحب الله ورسوله صلى الله عليه وسلم، فقال أنت مع من أحببت . قال أنس فما
فرحنا بشيء فرحنا بقول النبي صلى الله عليه وسلم أنت مع من أحببت، قال أنس فأنا أحب النبي
صلى الله عليه وسلم وأبا بكر وعمر وأرجو أن أكون معهم بحبي إياهم، وإن لم أعمل بمثل أعمالهم
(أخرجه البخاري في كتاب فضائل الصحابة)

Anas ◈ related:

A bedouin asked the Prophet ﷺ about when the Last Day (Hour) would come. He ﷺ said, "It will surely come to pass. What have you prepared for it?" The man said, "O Messenger of Allāh, I have not prepared much in the way of prayer and good works, but I love Allāh and His Messenger." The Prophet ﷺ said, "You will be with those whom you love." Anas ﷺ said that when they heard this the Muslims rejoiced as they never had before. Anas ﷺ said. "Therefore, I love the Prophet, Abū Bakr and 'Umar, and I hope that I will be with them because of my love for them though my deeds are not similar to theirs."[313]

God has created many means by which to free human beings from punishment—in spite of themselves—for mankind was created weak, susceptible to the influence of Satan, desire, worldly pleasures, and the evil promptings of the self. Allāh's Mercy is vast, and through it all who believe may find succor.

حدثنا قتيبة بن سعيد حدثنا يعقوب بن عبد الرحمن عن عمرو بن أبي عمرو عن سعيد بن أبي سعيد المقبري عن أبي هريرة رضي الله عنه قال سمعت رسول الله صلى الله عليه وسلم يقول إن الله خلق الرحمة يوم خلقها مائة رحمة فأمسك عنده تسعا وتسعين رحمة وأرسل في خلقه كلهم رحمة واحدة فلو يعلم الكافر بكل الذي عند الله من الرحمة لم ييئس من الجنة ولو يعلم المؤمن بكل الذي عند الله من العذاب لم يأمن من النار

Narrated Abū Hurayra ﷺ that he heard Allāh's Prophet ﷺ saying:

Verily Allāh created Mercy. The day He created it, He made it into one hundred parts. He withheld with Him ninety-nine parts, and sent its one part to all His creatures. Had the non-believer known of all the Mercy which is in the Hands of Allāh, he would not lose hope of entering Paradise, and had the believer known of all the punishment which is present with Allāh , he would not consider himself safe from the Hell-Fire.[314]

For obtaining that Mercy, Allāh made the value of a single sentence sufficient to compensate a person's evil deeds, even if they were excessive in quantity.

حدثنا معاذ بن أسد أخبرنا عبد الله أخبرنا معمر عن الزهري قال أخبرني محمود بن الربيع وزعم محمود أنه عقل رسول الله صلى الله عليه وسلم وقال وعقل مجة مجها من دلو كانت في دارهم قال

---

[313] *Sahīh Bukhārī* (5:37), Book "Companions of the Prophet."
[314] *Sahīh Bukhārī,* "Kitāb ar-Riqāq" #5988:

سمعت عتبان بن مالك الأنصاري ثم أحد بني سالم قال غدا علي رسول الله صلى الله عليه وسلم
فقال لن يوافي عبد يوم القيامة يقول لا إله إلا الله إلا الله يبتغي به وجه الله إلا حرم الله عليه النار

'Utbān bin Mālik Al-Ansārī 🕮, who was one of the men of the tribe of
Banī Sālim, narrated that Allāh's Messenger 🕮 came to him and said:

> If anybody comes on the Day of Resurrection who has said:
> *Lā ilāha ill-allāh*, sincerely, with the intention to win Allāh's
> Pleasure, Allāh will make the Hell-Fire forbidden for him.[315]

Such hadith remind us that Allāh's Mercy is beyond what we can imagine.
At the same time, they are a warning not to depend too much on His Mercy
and then fail to keep the boundaries that He has laid out in the pure *Shari'ah*.

We conclude this chapter by emphasizing an essential principle in Islam:
that in the end it is Allāh's overwhelming Mercy that will suffice for
humankind's salvation on the most dreaded day. And the embodiment of
Allāh's Mercy is the Prophet of Allāh Sayyidinā Muhammad 🕮, whom He
described in (al-Anbīyā 21:107) as:

$$ وَمَا أَرْسَلْنَاكَ إِلَّا رَحْمَةً لِّلْعَالَمِينَ $$

We sent thee not, but as a Mercy for all creatures.

It is therefore our hope in the Prophet's Intercession that is our firmest
foothold in the Hereafter, not dependence on deeds, whose sincerity and
perfection are undoubtedly lacking. It is only through the Mercy of Allāh, as
perfectly embodied in the person of His Beloved Messenger 🕮 that we can rest
assured of safety and deliverance:

$$ يَخَافُونَ يَوْمًا تَتَقَلَّبُ فِيهِ الْقُلُوبُ وَالْأَبْصَارُ $$

on the Day in which hearts and eyes will be overturned. (an-Nūr 24:37)

---

[315] *Sahīh Bukhārī*, "Kitāb ar-Riqāq" #5943.

CONCLUSION

PREPARE FOR THE AFTERLIFE

Take Charge of Yourselves

Fourteen hundred years ago Allāh ﷻ revealed the following verse in the Holy Qur'ān,

يَا أَيُّهَا الَّذِينَ آمَنُوا عَلَيْكُمْ أَنْفُسَكُمْ لَا يَضُرُّكُم مَّن ضَلَّ إِذَا اهْتَدَيْتُمْ

O ye who believe! Ye have charge of your own selves. He who erreth cannot injure you if ye are rightly guided (al-Māïda 5:105) '

حدثنا هشام بن عمار حدثنا صدقة بن خالد حدثني عتبة بن أبي حكيم حدثني عن عمه عمرو
بن جارية عن أبي أمية الشعباني قال
أتيت أبا ثعلبة الخشني قال قلت كيف تصنع في هذه الآية قال أية آية قلت
يا أيها الذين آمنوا عليكم أنفسكم لا يضركم من ضل إذا اهتديتم
قال سألت عنها خبيرا سألت عنها رسول الله صلى الله عليه وسلم فقال بل ائتمروا بالمعروف
وتناهوا عن المنكر حتى إذا رأيت شحا مطاعا وهوى متبعا ودنيا مؤثرة وإعجاب كل ذي رأي
برأيه ورأيت أمرا لا يدان لك به فعليك خويصة نفسك فإن من ورائكم أيام الصبر الصبر فيهن على
مثل قبض على الجمر للعامل فيهن مثل أجر خمسين رجلا يعملون بمثل عمله
(سنن ابن ماجه)
زاد في رواية أبي داود: قيل يا رسول الله أجر خمسين رجلا منا أو منهم؟ قال بل أجر خمسين
منكم.

Abū Ummaya Sha'banī, a Companion of the Prophet ﷺ, troubled about its meaning, asked his fellow Companion, Abū Tha'labat al-Khashnī, What should I make of this verse?" Whereupon, Abū Tha'labah visited the Prophet ﷺ to enquire of him how to interpret it. The Prophet ﷺ explained:

> Enjoin goodness and forbid evil, until you see the corrupt
> obeyed, base passions followed, and the material world (*dunyā*)
> exercising a powerful influence. [When this occurs], each
> person will cherish his own opinion and not suffer being
> commanded [by another]. At that time, you must take charge
> of yourself and abandon the popular masses and whoever

follows in their wake! For, verily, in subsequent days there will
come times that will demand untold forebearance. In that day,
whosoever perseveres with patience will be like a man who
takes hold of a blazing ember. His reward shall be that of fifty
men who do as he does.[316]

In interpreting the above verse from *Sūrat al-Mā'ida*, the Prophet ﷺ gives
us important advice for the times in which we live. He tells us to take charge of
ourselves. This is a responsibility Allāh ﷻ lays upon us. Another verse of the
Holy Qur'ān echoes the same message:

يَا أَيُّهَا الَّذِينَ آمَنُوا قُوا أَنْفُسَكُمْ وَأَهْلِيكُمْ نَارًا وَقُودُهَا النَّاسُ وَالْحِجَارَةُ

Oh believers save yourselves and your families from the fire.

(al-Taḥrīm 66:6).

This means that, as a believer, you must think first about yourself when it
comes to your behavior and not attend to the behavior of others.

Now the command to take charge of oneself does not mean refraining
from giving sincere advice to others. This would contradict the obvious
meaning of the words, "Enjoin goodness and forbid evil," an imperative
repeated many times in the Qur'ān. Nevertheless, there are factors that
condition its implementation. The hadith lists two such factors.

First, whatever advice is given must be offered in the proper spirit. It goes
without saying that sincere advice is not motivated by any effort to embarrass
the wrongdoer. That is, correction should not arise from an attitude of self-
righteousness. The reason for this is simple. If advice is motivated by self-
righteouness, it is no longer sincere. Sincere service to Allāh ﷻ is devotion to
Him for no one's sake but the sake of Allāh ﷻ Alone. The exact instant that
one feels superior to the wrongdoer, sincerity of one's admonition vanishes,
since one's advice is offered for the sake of satisfying one's feelings of moral
superiority, not for the sake of Allāh ﷻ.

When advice is sincere, whoever is receiving correction finds that advice
easy to accept and to use as a tool for self-improvement. For sincerity always
accompanies love. And love, almost naturally, brings with it obedience. This is
a profound law of the spiritual life. Accordingly, when a beloved one gives
advice, it is easily accepted and followed. Indeed, love makes people eager to
follow what they are advised to do, whether that counsel is sought or
unsought. Only in an atmosphere of love is correction ever really heeded. Only
in an environment of love is the command to enjoin good and forbid evil truly

---

[316] *Ibn Mājah* and *Tirmidhī*. In the version of *Abū Dawūd* he adds at the end of the narration: It
was said, "O Prophet of Allāh! (Do you mean) the reward of fifty of their men or fifty of our
men?" The Prophet replied, "No, the reward of fifty from among you."

effective.

But here we begin to understand the secret of how it was possible for the Companions to leave their bad habits and actions immediately upon the Prophet's command. The secret was their love of Allāh's Messenger ﷺ and belief in him. Love for the Prophet ﷺ caused this to happen and initiated their moral reform. He inspired so much love among his followers that the inspiration of his commands has lasted for many generations, even beyond the three pious generations of the Companions, the Successors, and the Successors to the Successors. These are the three generations he described as the best ones, measuring from his time to the present.

So when the Prophet ﷺ said, "Enjoin goodness and forbid evil," love and belief is the key that opens the door for people to change their character and follow the Divine commandments. Love, belief, and respect—these three features of motivation—must be present if advice is to have its intended effect. When love is absent, the entire enterprise collapses.

The Prophet ﷺ gave the second condition qualifying the command to enjoin good and forbid evil with the words, "until you see the corrupt obeyed, base passions followed, and the material world (dunyā) exercising powerful influence." "The corrupt obeyed" translates the Arabic word shahīh, an individual who is entirely corrupt (fusūq) and deviant, and, for this reason, falls into the class of individual the Qur'ān categorizes as "him who erreth." Such a person does not believe in Allāh ﷻ, nor does he or she submit to any Divine Law, not even the law revealed in Islam or Sharī'ah. When people of such low character are obeyed, society enters a deep state of corruption. When in that state, any advice to enjoin goodness and forbid evil will surely go unheeded. Thus, the hadith's command to "enjoin goodness and reject what is forbidden" receives further qualification. For the Prophet ﷺ applies the Qur'ānic verse to what the believers in times like our own must do.

According to the Prophet's explanation of the Qur'ān, Allāh ﷻ is saying, "Keep to yourself!" Do not engage in fruitless criticism, wrangling, and complaining. In times when you "see the corrupt obeyed," nothing is going to change. No one is going to listen to you. For in a time of confusion and corruption, there will be very few people in society who will be receptive to one's enjoining goodness and preventing iniquity. The people of such times will not heed admonitions and there is no hope to influence them, as it was in the days of the people of Prophet Nūh ﷺ.

Additionally, the Prophet ﷺ also qualifies the command to enjoin good and forbid evil with another condition: "until you see …the material world exercising a powerful influence (wa dunyā mu'aththira)." That is, we should command good and forbid evil until the material world exerts so powerful an influence that people grow to love it, turn their backs on Allāh ﷻ, try to hold onto this present world even as it decays and passes away, and forget about life of the world to come. These are circumstances that alter the force of the command and constitute a limiting factor regarding its implementation. To understand why this limiting factor applies today, consider the contrast between the period when the Qur'ān was revealed and our own present day.

In the time of the Prophet ﷺ, 'Umar ﷺ gave half of everything he owned to the Prophet ﷺ. Abū Bakr ﷺ gave **everything** he owned. When the Prophet ﷺ asked him what he had left for his family Abū Bakr ﷺ replied, "Allāh and His Messenger." Allāh ﷻ and the Prophet were sufficient reason to motivate their generosity because they served God for His sake alone.

The detachment of Abū Bakr ﷺ and 'Umar ﷺ from the riches of this temporary, material world stands in stark contrast to the iron-fisted grip people keep on their possessions nowadays. People are rushing to build a worldly life; a bigger house; to add more zeros to their bank account; to own more cars and so on. Today people (especially the wealthy), are not able to bring themselves to give even the smallest amount of their money in charity. They even neglect paying *zakāt*, the purifying dues obligatory on every Muslim. Everyone loves this *dunyā* so much and tries to hold onto it. Yet, at every moment in our lives the present world is vanishing and passing away.

The hadith goes on to say, "and abandon the popular masses and whoever follows in their wake!" In such times of turmoil, one must not become involved with the general confusion in society. Do not bother with organizations, both Muslim and non-Muslim, who debate and criticize each other and only succeed in creating more problems. Muslims came to this country to find their sustenance and to have shelter, not to disrupt society. This is the only way one may hope to save oneself and those one holds dear.

The text continues, "For, verily, in subsequent days there will come times that will demand untold forebearance." That is, ordinary people must exercise extreme patience. After all, nothing changes except what Allāh ﷻ wishes to change as He said in another verse:

$$ إِنَّ اللهَ لاَ يُغَيِّرُ مَا بِقَوْمٍ حَتَّى يُغَيِّرُوا مَا بِأَنْفُسِهِمْ $$

Verily Allāh does not change the condition of a people until they change their own selves. (al-Ra'd 13:11)

The Muslim leaders are not going to change the condition of the community because they do not serve Allāh ﷻ for the sake of Allāh alone. Instead, they conspire for their own benefit. They yearn for personal prestige and the prestige of the political regimes they so ardently represent. This is the situation in which we find many, if not the majority of Muslims today, not only in one country but throughout the world.

Nevertheless, the hadith offers us a cure for these present day ills. It says, "whosoever persevereth with patience will be like a man that takes hold of a blazing ember". Holding on to the burning ember of true religion and faith is the measure of spiritual health in these times. The fire will cauterize our flesh. But the metaphorical cauterization brought about by such patience is the only cure for the sickness that afflicts us in this time.

Still, you might ask how things arrived at such a state. After all, not so very long ago the highest form of learning was knowledge about Allāh, His messengers and His books. In Muslim countries the best education was education in Islam. Indeed, the main content of all education was Islamic learning. This lasted until two or three centuries ago. During those days, were not people the same as they are today? Were they not still living their lives, eating and drinking? Were they not happy and content just as people are today? They lived their lives until their term and then passed away just as people today do. Everyone dies; no one stays in this present life forever. People today still eat, drink, have families, and eventually die. Could it be that people are abandoning Allāh 🕌 simply because of the conveniences of modern life: plumbing that brings water into the house, electricity and central air conditioning? What then has changed between the sixth century and the twenty-first century?

The Prophet 🕌 explains, "and everyone will cherish his own opinion". That is, each person will be so fond of his own opinion that no one will believe that another's opinion could possibly matter or be correct. In the past when a scholar lectured, not a single student would raise an objection or question the content. They would only take notes and memorize them. One might ask a point of clarification, but argumentation was not allowed.

Contrast this traditional approach with the situation in the educational system today. In any class or lecture, one may find as many opinions as there are people present. This is true not only in institutions of learning, but generally. In forums in which people gather to put forward their opinions and engage in debate, each one says to other participants, "You are wrong!" considering only his own opinion correct. People debate, argue, and eventually quarrel, since no one is able to concede anything that appears to diminish his position. Even a child thinks he knows better than his parents, and no one is able to convince him otherwise. A husband cannot concede to his wife nor a wife to her husband. Neither one listens to the other. Everywhere we encounter a stubborn rigidity in marital relationships and in social and political life.

The clearest manifestation of the Prophet's 🕌 prediction, available to most of us, occurs on a daily basis: the television talk show. Two people at polar extremes on an issue set upon each other in a verbal brawl in which the viewer is supposed to somehow arrive at a balanced conclusion. By bringing out differences instead of focusing on commonalities, arguments only increase and fewer solutions present themselves. Add to this confusion the myriad views of the audience, all of which brings the viewer further and further from any meaningful conclusion or realization. This presentation of two extreme opinions leaves no room for a reasonable approach or discussion, resulting ultimately in a sense of despair and confusion for the viewer.

But listen again to the words of the Prophet ﷺ, no one will "suffer being commanded [by another]". That means, when a leader gives an order, it will not be followed. In fact, people will oppose him. If someone elects a leader or 'amīr and gives him allegiance (bay'a) and then disobeys him why did they elect him in the first place? Why would someone elect a leader only to oppose him? The Prophet ﷺ is telling us that rules and orders will be rejected and there will be chaos in society. There will be no regard for authority, no one's rights will be protected, and no one can object to this situation. If someone takes your money or possessions you cannot get them back. If someone attacks you, you cannot defend yourself. At that time one cannot change what is happening to the weak and the poor, the helpless, and the powerless. No one can do anything for them because the strong have overrun the weak. The law of the jungle prevails.

Lastly, the Prophet ﷺ says, "His reward shall be that of fifty men who walk in my way and do as [you have seen me] do". That is, any person who in such difficult times is able to hold fast to the Prophet's Sunnah and be patient in looking after himself and his family will have the reward equivalent to the worship of fifty pious people: praying, fasting, giving charity, pilgrimage, supplication, and working for the sake of God. Muslims who keep their families on the path of righteousness and do not engage in the tremendous societal turmoil surrounding them will enjoy such a reward.

By now the miraculous character of the Prophet's *tafsīr* of the verse from *Sūrat al-Mā'ida* should be clear. He miraculously foretold the situation of today fourteen hundred years ago, how corrupt people and ideologies would be followed. He predicted how everyone would be stubbornly opinionated, how rules and orders would be abandoned, and how chaos would threaten every human society. He foretold the way leaders in the Muslim community would forsake the pursuit of goodness and openly enjoin what Allāh ﷻ has forbidden or at the very least mix what He has allowed (*halāl*) with what he has prohibited (*harām*) and thus add to the general confusion. So when the Prophet ﷺ says that a time will come when extremely corrupt persons will be obeyed and people will run after them out of passion and base desire, we behold his words being fulfilled right now.

Allāh ﷻ put the Prophet's name with His name to show the greatness of Muhammad ﷺ when he made the following words the prerequisite for belief: *Lā ilāha illa-Allāh Muhammadun Rasūlullah—There is no god except Allāh and*

Muhammad is the Prophet of Allāh. We have to know that these verses and hadith predicting the events of the End Times are miracles, evidence of the Prophet's ﷺ perfect knowledge granted to him by God.

As the Signs of the Last Days unfold before our eyes, on television and in the news, we must pay close attention and undertake what the Prophet ﷺ advised for such times of travail. Being unmindful of clear indications would be no less foolish than someone driving the wrong way on a one-way street.

We conclude this book with some hadith which relate signs that are apparent, and whose import is that the Last Days are truly before us.

حدثنا ابن عفان قال حدثنا قاسم بن اصبغ قال حدثنا عوف عن ابى المغيرة عن عبد الله بن عمرو قال اول مصر من امصار العرب يدخله الدجال البصرة .

Ibn 'Affān related that Qāssim bin Asbagh said… that 'Awf ibn Mughīrah said, from 'Abd Allāh ibn 'Amru ﷺ who said, "The first of the Arab lands that the Anti-Christ will enter is Basra."[317]

هو موقوف؛ و اسناده صحيح؛ و ابو المغيرة القواس وثقه ابن معين . و قد تم تحقيق هذا الحديث . و قد ذكره ابي عمرو عثمان بن سعيد المقرئ الداني المتوفي سنة 444 . في كتابه الفتن وغوائلها و الساعة واشراطها . تحقيق المباركفوري . صفحة 1145 .

وقد جاء فيما رواه الامام أحمد في مسنده(216/4)

من حديث عثمان بن أبي العاص في سياق طويل . . . فأول مصر يرده (الدجال) المصر الذي يلتقى ألبحرين(يعني البصرة) .

The same hadith was narrated with slightly different wording in the *Musnad* of Imām Āhmad, as part of a long hadith of 'Uthman ibn al-'Ās ﷺ in which he said, "…the first land that the Anti-Christ will enter is the land where the two rivers meet (i.e. Basra)."[318]

و قد أورد المقريزي في الخطط(334/1) عن عبد الله بن الصامت ان أسرع الأرضين خرابا البصرة و مصر ؛ فقلت و ما يخربهما؛ وفيهما عيون الرجال والأموال؟ فقال يخربهما القتل الأحمر والجوع الأغبر؛ كأني بالبصرة كأنها نعامة جاثمة .

'Abd Allāh ibn as-Sāmit ﷺ said, "The fastest two lands to be destroyed are Basra and Egypt." I said, "What is the cause of their destruction, while in them reside the cream of the people and the [great] wealth?" He said, "The cause of

---

[317] Hadith *mawqūf*, with an authentic chain, and Abul Mughīra bin al Qawwās and Ibn Mu'īn considered it strong (*thiqa*). It is also mentioned by al-Muqri' ad-Dānī (d. 444 H.) in his book *al-Fitan wa ghawa'iluha wassa'atu wa ashrātuhā*. Verified and authenticated by al-Mubārakfūrī on page 1145 of the same book, published dār al-'asima Riyādh. Saudi Arabia.

[318] Āhmad's *Musnad* #4/216 and al-Muqri' ad-Dānī (d. 444 H.) in his book *al-Fitan wa ghawā'iluha wassa'atu wa ashrātuhā* page 1145.

their destruction is the 'red killing.' The result of that will be hunger: It is as if I am seeing Basra falling like an ostrich, from its height to the ground"[319]

The term used here is *al-qatl al-ahmar*, meaning either very intense bloodshed or killing for the sake of "that which is red." In Arab sources gold is often described as "the red." However of all red substances, the most obvious and applicable is fire, whose most prevalent source today is petroleum: oil and gas. From this one can infer that the source of fire will be the cause of the destruction of the Arab lands—oil.

وورد عن علي بن أبي طالب أنه وصف البصرة بانها أسرع الأرضين خرابا . ذكره ياقوت الحموي
في معجم البلدان (436/1) . و قد ذكر أيضا في كتاب الفتن و غوائلها صفحة 908.

It is narrated that Sayyidina 'Alī ibn Abī Tālib ؓ described al-Basra as, "the fastest land to be destroyed."[320]

From these narrations, and those in the Chapter "Fire from Hijāz," we can understand that tremendous fighting and destruction will take place for the sake of one cause—something which today is obvious for one who delves into the explanations of these hadith narrated fourteen hundred years ago. That cause is oil. As predicted by Prophet Muhammad ﷺ, the first land to be struck, in a time when oil becomes the focus of all nations, will be Basra.

Such an understanding will certainly cause people of insight to realize that what the Prophet ﷺ predicted has happened already, or may take place in the near future—and Allāh alone knows best. It behooves the thoughtful then, to heed the prophetic warnings, keeping to oneself and avoiding those who seek to draw individuals and societies into conflict.

Prophet Muhammad ﷺ was able to see all the events of the Last Days with the penetrating vision Allāh ﷻ gave him. And out of loving concern for his Community, even in its latter days, he gave advice on what the believers must do to save their souls and earn a tremendous reward. Some of these forms of spiritual shelter are given in the Appendix, "Daily Recitations for Protection from Tribulations," on page 287, in particular the first and last ten verses of *Sūrat al-Kahf*, which is an effective protection from the trial of the Anti-Christ.

❧❀❧

---

[319] Al-Maqrīzī in his book *al-Khutat* 1/334.
[320] Mentioned in *mu'jam al-buldān*,1/436 by Yāqūt al-Hamawī and also mentioned by al-Muqri' ad-Dānī (d. 444 H.) in his book *al-Fitan wa ghawā'iluhā was-sa'atu wa ashrātuhā.*, page 908.

APPENDIX

PROTECTIVE SUPPLICATIONS AND RECITATIONS

Verses of Sūrat al-Kahf

The first ten verses or the last ten verses of *Sūrat al-Kahf* should be recited for protection from the tribulation of the Anti-Christ (ad-Dajjāl).

The first ten verses are:

الْحَمْدُ لله الذي أَنْزَلَ عَلَى عَبْدِه الْكِتَابَ وَلَمْ يَجْعَل لَهُ عِوَجَا(1) قَيِّمًا لِيُنذِرَ بَأْسًا شَدِيدًا من
لَدُنْهُ وَيُبَشِّرَ الْمُؤْمنينَ الذينَ يَعْمَلُونَ الصَّالحَات أَنَّ لَهُمْ أَجْرًا حَسَنًا(2) مَاكِثِينَ فيه أَبَدا(3)
وَيُنذِرَ الذينَ قَالُوا اتخذ اللهُ وَلَدا(4) مَّا لَهُم به من علم وَلا لآبَائهمْ كَبُرَتْ كَلمَةً تَخْرُجُ من
أَفْوَاههمْ إن يَقُولُونَ إلا كَذبا(5) فَلَعَلَّكَ بَاخِعٌ نَفْسَكَ عَلَى آثَارهم إن لمْ يُؤْمنُوا بهَذا الْحَديث
أَسَفًا(6) إنا جَعَلْنَا مَا عَلَى الأَرْض زِينَة لَهَا لنَبْلُوَهُمْ أَيُّهُمْ أَحْسَنُ عَمَلًا(7) وَإنا لجَاعلُونَ مَا
عَلَيْهَا صَعِيدا جُرُزا(8) أَمْ حَسِبْتَ أَنَّ أَصْحَابَ الْكَهْف وَالرَّقِيم كَانُوا منْ آيَاتنَا عَجَبا(9) إذ
أَوَى الْفِتْيَة إلَى الْكَهْف فَقَالُوا رَبَّنَا آتنَا من لَدُنْكَ رَحْمَة وَهَيِّئْ لَنَا منْ أَمْرنَا رَشَدا

1. *Praise be to Allāh, Who hath sent to His servant the Book, and has allowed therein no crookedness:*

2. *(He hath made it) straight (and clear) in order that He may warn of a terrible punishment from Him, and that He may give glad tidings to the believers who work righteous deeds, that they shall have a goodly Reward,*

3. *Wherein they shall remain forever:*

4. *Further, that He may warn those who say, '(Allāh) has begotten a son':*

5. *No knowledge have they of such a thing, nor had their fathers. It is a grievous word that comes out of their mouths; they speak nothing but a lie.*

6. *Perhaps you are grieving and fretting youself to death, following after them, if they believe not in this message.*

7. *That which is on earth we have made but as an embellishment for it, in order that We may test them, as to which of them are best in conduct.*

8. *Verify what is on earth We shall make but as dust and dry soil (without growth or herbage).*

9. *Did you think that the Companions of the Cave and of the Inscription were wonders among Our Signs?*

10. *Behold, the youths betook themselves to the Cave for refuge: they said,
"Our Lord! bestow on us mercy from Yourself, and and provide for us a
right course in our affair."* (al-Kahf 18:1-10)

The last ten verses are:

الَّذِينَ كَانَتْ أَعْيُنُهُمْ فِي غِطَاءٍ عَن ذِكْرِي وَكَانُوا لَا يَسْتَطِيعُونَ سَمْعًا(101) أَفَحَسِبَ الَّذِينَ
كَفَرُوا أَن يَتَّخِذُوا عِبَادِي مِن دُونِي أَوْلِيَاءَ إِنَّا أَعْتَدْنَا جَهَنَّمَ لِلْكَافِرِينَ نُزُلًا(102) قُلْ هَلْ
نُنَبِّئُكُم بِالْأَخْسَرِينَ أَعْمَالًا(103) الَّذِينَ ضَلَّ سَعْيُهُمْ فِي الْحَيَاةِ الدُّنْيَا وَهُمْ يَحْسَبُونَ أَنَّهُمْ
يُحْسِنُونَ صُنْعًا(104) أُولَٰئِكَ الَّذِينَ كَفَرُوا بِآيَاتِ رَبِّهِمْ وَلِقَائِهِ فَحَبِطَتْ أَعْمَالُهُمْ فَلَا نُقِيمُ لَهُمْ
يَوْمَ الْقِيَامَةِ وَزْنًا(105) ذَٰلِكَ جَزَاؤُهُمْ جَهَنَّمُ بِمَا كَفَرُوا وَاتَّخَذُوا آيَاتِي وَرُسُلِي هُزُوًا(106)
إِنَّ الَّذِينَ آمَنُوا وَعَمِلُوا الصَّالِحَاتِ كَانَتْ لَهُمْ جَنَّاتُ الْفِرْدَوْسِ نُزُلًا(107) خَالِدِينَ فِيهَا لَا
يَبْغُونَ عَنْهَا حِوَلًا(108) قُل لَّوْ كَانَ الْبَحْرُ مِدَادًا لِّكَلِمَاتِ رَبِّي لَنَفِدَ الْبَحْرُ قَبْلَ أَن تَنفَدَ
كَلِمَاتُ رَبِّي وَلَوْ جِئْنَا بِمِثْلِهِ مَدَدًا(109) قُلْ إِنَّمَا أَنَا بَشَرٌ مِّثْلُكُمْ يُوحَى إِلَيَّ أَنَّمَا إِلَٰهُكُمْ إِلَٰهٌ
وَاحِدٌ فَمَن كَانَ يَرْجُو لِقَاءَ رَبِّهِ فَلْيَعْمَلْ عَمَلًا صَالِحًا وَلَا يُشْرِكْ بِعِبَادَةِ رَبِّهِ أَحَدًا(110)

18:101. *Those whose eyes were under a veil from remembrance of Me, and
who had been unable even to hear.*

102. *Do the disbelievers think that they can take My servants as protectors
besides Me? Verily We have prepared Hell as a welcome for the
disbelievers.*

103. *Say: 'Shall We inform you of those who will be the greatest losers in
their deeds?*

104. *'Those whose efforts have been wasted in this life, while they thought
that they were producing good by their works?'*

105. *They are those who deny the Signs of their Lord and in the meeting
with Him: vain will be their works, and, on the Day of Judgment, We shall
not give them any weight.*

106. *That is their reward, Hell, because they disbelieved, and made a jest of
My Signs and My Messengers.*

107. *Lo! those who believe and do good works, theirs are the Gardens of
Paradise for welcome,*

108. *Wherein they will abide, with no desire to be removed from thence.*

109. *Say: If the sea were ink with which to write the words of my Lord,
verily the sea would be exhausted before the words of my Lord, even if we
added another sea like it, for its aid.*

110. *Say: I am a human being like yourselves, (but) revelation is sent to me (by Allah) that your God is One (Allah). So, whoever hopes to meet his Lord, let him work righteousness, and, in his worship of his Lord, admit no one as partner.*

(al-Kahf 18:101-110)

Daily Recitations for Protection from Tribulations

To keep away from the great difficulties that will befall mankind during the last days of this world, Muslims are advised to recite the following *adhkaar* every day:

100-1000 times *Astaghfirullāh wa atūbu ilayh* (استغفر الله واتوب اليه)

100-1000 times *Lā hawla walā quwatta illa billāh il 'Alī-yil 'Azhīm*

(لا حول ولا قوة الا بالله العلي العظيم)

100-1000 times *Hasbunallāh wa ni'mal Wakīl* (حسبنالله ونعمَ الوكيل)

100-1000 times *Bismillāh ir-Rahmān ir-Rahīm* (بسم الله الرحمان الرحيم)

100-1000 times *Ya Wadūd* (يا واحد)

5000 *Allāh, Allāh* by tongue (الله الله)

5000 *Allāh, Allāh* by heart (الله الله)

2000 Salawāt on the Prophet ﷺ: *Allāhumma salli 'ala Muhammadin wa 'ala āli Muhammadin wa sallim* (اللهم صلي على محمّد وعلى آل محمّد وسلم)

100 times *Sūrat al-Ikhlās* (سورة الاخلاص)

If one is unable to perform this, then it is recommended to at least pray two *rak'ats* of *Salāt al-Hifz* (Prayer of Protection) for protection from afflictions coming from above and below, consisting of two standard *rak'ats* of prayer, reciting *Sūrat al-Ikhlās* twice in the first *rak'at* and once in the second *rak'at* following *Sūrat al-Fātihā*.

OTHER TITLES FROM THE ISLAMIC SUPREME COUNCIL OF AMERICA

Muhammad: The Messenger of Islam
His Life and Prophecy

By Hajjah Amina Adil
ISBN 1-930409-11-7

Since the 7th century, the sacred biography of Islam's Prophet Muhammad has shaped the perception of the religion and its place in world history. English biographies of Prophet Muhammad – founder of the faith that currently claims 1.5 billion followers – have characteristically presented him in the light of verifiable historical authenticity. This book skillfully etches the personal portrait of a man of incomparable moral and spiritual stature, as seen through the eyes of Muslims around the world. Compiled from classical Ottoman Turkish sources and translated into English, this comprehensive biography is deeply rooted in the life example of its prophet. Paperback. 608 pp.

The Honor of Women in Islam

Scholars in Islam Series
By Professor Yusuf da Costa
ISBN 1-930409-06-0

Relying on Islamic source texts, this concise, scholarly work elucidates the true respect and love for women inherent in the Islamic faith. It examines the pre-Islamic state of women, highlights the unprecedented rights they received under Islamic Law, and addresses the prominent beliefs and prevailing cultures throughout the Muslim world regarding the roles of women in familial, social service and community development, business, academic, religious, and even judicial circles. In addition, brief case studies of historical figures such as Mary, mother of Jesus are presented within the Islamic tradition. Paperback. 104 pp.

In the Mystic Footsteps of Saints

Sufi Wisdom Series
By Shaykh Muhammad Nazim Adil al-Haqqani
Volume 1 - ISBN 1-930409-05-2
Volume 2 – ISBN 1-930409-09-5
Volume 3 – ISBN 1-930409-13-3

Narrated in a charming, old-world storytelling style, this highly spiritual series offers several volumes of practical guidance on how to establish serenity and peace in daily life, heal emotional and spiritual scars, and discover the role we are each destined to play in the universal scheme. Written by Shaykh Nazim Adil al-Haqqani, worldwide leader of the Naqshbandi-Haqqani Sufi Order and a descendant of best-selling poet and Sufi mystic Jalaluddin Rumi. Paperback. Average length 200 pp.

Liberating the Soul: A Guide for Spiritual Growth

Sufi Wisdom Series
By Shaykh Muhammad Nazim Adil al-Haqqani
Volume 1 - ISBN 1-930409-14-1
Volume 2 – ISBN 1-930409-15-X
Volume 3 – ISBN 1-930409-16-8
Volume 4 – ISBN 1-930409-17-6

This series focuses on classical Sufi teachings, which open the heart to receive life-altering spiritual powers. *Liberating the Soul* is based on coveted lectures of Shaykh Muhammad Nazim Adil al-Haqqani, the worldwide leader of the Naqshbandi Sufi Order and descendant of best-selling poet Jalaluddin Rumi. Average length 300 pp.

COMING SOON:

Classical Islam and the Naqshbandi Sufi Order

By Shaykh Muhammad Hisham Kabbani
ISBN 1-930409-10-9

This esteemed work includes an unprecedented historical narrative of the forty saints of the renowned Naqshbandi Golden Chain, dating back to Prophet Muhammad in the early seventh century. With close personal ties to the most recent saints, the author has painstakingly compiled rare accounts of their miracles, disciplines, and how they have lent spiritual support throughout the world for fifteen centuries. In simple terms, the book outlines practical steps to develop stress, anger and time management, and to identify and prioritize what is truly important in life, all of which "awakens" the inner self to a higher dimension of spiritual consciousness. *Traditional Islam and the Naqshbandi Sufi Order* is a shining tribute to developing human relations at the highest level, and the power of spirituality to uplift humanity from its lower nature to that of spiritual triumph. Paperback. 750 pp.

Available online from www.isn1.net